SWEET ▶SOUL◀ MUSIC

Rhythm and Blues ▶and the Southern Dream of Freedom

Peter Guralnick

BOOKS

Also by Peter Guralnick

Feel Like Going Home
Lost Highway
Nighthawk Blues
Searching for Robert Johnson
Last Train to Memphis: The Rise of Elvis Presley
Careless Love: The Unmaking of Elvis Presley

First published in Great Britain in 2002 by MOJO Books, an
imprint of Canongate Books Ltd, 14 High Street,
Edinburgh EH1 1TE

First published in the US in 1986 by HarperCollins
Publishers Inc.

10 9 8 7 6 5 4 3 2 1

British Library Cataloguing-in-Publication Data
A catalogue record for this book is available on
request from the British Library

ISBN 1 84195 240 0

Designed by Susan Marsh

Printed and bound by CPD, Ebbw Vale, Wales

www.canongate.net

Praise for Peter Guralnick's

SWEET SOUL MUSIC

"The best history of '60s soul music anyone has written or is likely to write, but it is much more than that. . . . Written with rare sensitivity and understanding, *Sweet Soul Music* is as important for what it says about America, class and race issues, and the '60s, as for its outstanding musical insights. . . . A classic." — ROBERT PALMER, *New York Times*

"A stunning chronicle. . . . What Guralnick has written is . . . cultural history — a panoramic survey of a lost world. . . . That world now lives on in the pages of this heartfelt history — one of the best books ever written on American popular music." — JIM MILLER, *Newsweek*

"Guralnick teases some wonderful stories from his subjects. . . . His essays on these giants magically transform interview materials, historical scholarship, critical insight, and unabashed passion into living, breathing, and almost singing portraits." — JOE SASFY, *Washington Post Book World*

"Guralnick goes beyond the performers, writing of the storefront record labels and publishing companies that brought the music to the public, the songwriters and studio musicians, and the people behind the scenes. He ends up giving more than just history. He gives a feel for the places and circumstances that gave birth to the '60s most exciting music." — ELIJAH WALD, *Boston Globe*

"A large-scale, near-epic treatment. Few writers have ever discussed the musical partnership [between black and white], the friction . . . or the moment that gave rise to both, as movingly as it is discussed in this unusual book." — CHRIS MORRIS, *Los Angeles Reader*

"Page after page is simply filled with new revelations, ideas, and perspectives. . . . Essential for anyone with even a passing interest in rhythm and blues in the sixties. It will stand!" — ROB BOWMAN, *Memphis Star*

"Compelling. . . . Guralnick deftly orchestrates interviews, research, and his own impressions to convey the emotional impact of the music and the atmosphere in which it developed."

— MICHIKO KAKUTANI, *New York Times*

"*Sweet Soul Music* is a masterpiece, as rich and strange as the life it seeks to comprehend. . . . It should be treasured by all students of American music and culture. . . . Such a book can only encourage and inspire us."

— BOB COCHRAN, *Journal of American Folklore*

"One of the liveliest examinations of popular music ever conducted."

— KEN TUCKER, *Philadelphia Examiner*

"Certainly the most ambitious and complete examination of the subject to date. . . . [It] reads almost like a novel. . . . Required reading for lovers of the music."

— JAY TRACHTENBERG, *Austin Chronicle*

"Guralnick has written a vastly important book: it will appeal to soul triviacs, but — more centrally — it is a book that gets to the heart of the politics of race in a vital area of the music business at a time when everything was opening out and the possibilities seemed literally limitless. . . . More than anything else, it is a story of mass prejudice and individual goodwill, of trust and suspicion."   — CHARLES SHAAR MURRAY, *New Musical Express*

"A crisp and uncluttered narrative. . . . *Sweet Soul Music* is an important accomplishment in the chronicling of American musical history."

— KURT LODER, *Rolling Stone*

"A textured, complex story with a multiplicity of fascinating angles. . . . This book [is] no dusty treatise but rather flows with the exuberant detail and fine-tuned style that makes it not only informative but also scintillating to read."   — GENE SANTORO, *down beat*

*For Joe McEwen, Mr. C., without whom I wouldn't have been able
even to <u>think</u> about writing this book . . .*

*And for Solomon Burke, the undisputed King of Rock 'n' Soul,
without whom I wouldn't have wanted to.*

Acknowledgments

I N WRITING A BOOK OVER SO LONG A PERIOD, one incurs debts one can never repay. Literally hundreds of individuals have helped me with my research and my interviews, and I thank them all. The following are just some of the people who gave me a hand over the weeks, months, and years:

Dick Alen, J. W. Alexander, Hoss Allen, Estelle Axton, Homer Banks, Barry Beckett, Alexander Graham "Nero" Bell, William Bell, Bettye Berger, Scott Billington, Bill Blackburn, Julian Bond, Stanley Booth, Eddie Braddock, John Brooks, William Brown, Anne Bryant, Elek Burke, Sunday Burke, Diane Butler, James Carr, Clarence Carter, Ray Charles, Gene Chrisman, Trevor Churchill, Dave Clark, Quinton Claunch, Tommy Cogbill, Al Cooley, Tommy Couch, Don Covay, Steve Cropper, R. O. Curtis, Jim and Mary Lindsay Dickinson, Harris Dienstfrey, Don Dumont, Duck Dunn, Mickey Eichner, Bobby Emmons, David Evans, Jimmy Evans, Barry Feldman, Rob Finnis, Ted Fox, the Freeman Sisters, Joyce Frommer, Ray Funk, Gregg Geller, David Gessner, Charlie Gillett, Bill Glore, John Grahm, Al Green, Pete Grendysa, Rick and Linda Hall, Jeff Hannusch, Rowena Harris, Roger Hawkins, Isaac Hayes, Beliliah Hazziez, Terri Hinte, Eddie Hinton, David Hood, Sue Horton and Bob Smith, Sylvester Huckaby, Jimmy Hughes, Quin Ivy, George Jackson, Wayne Jackson, Johnny Jenkins, Frank Johnson, Walter Johnson, Booker T. Jones, Iris Keitel, Stan Kesler, Rich Kienzle, Buddy Killen, Allen Klein, Frederick Knight, Anne Kostick, Buddy Lee, Alan Leeds, Cynthia Leu, Eddie Lewis, Fred Lewis, Bill Lowery, Fred Mendelsohn, Willie Mitchell, Chips Moman, George Moonoogian, Melvin Moore, Michael Ochs, Spooner Oldham, Don Paulsen, Dan Penn, Knox Phillips, Doc Pomus, David Porter, Diana Price, Zelma Redding, Steve Richards, John Richbourg, Zelda Samuels, Zenas Sears, Joe Shamwell, Val Shiveley, Dick Shurman, Speedo Simms, Percy Sledge, Bobby Smith, Rick Stafford, Chuck Stewart, Jim Stewart, Hamp Swain, Tommy Tate, Queen Mother Taylor, Joe Tex, Rufus and Carla Thomas, Steve Tomashefsky, Ray Topping, Cindy Underwood, Billy Vera, Tom Vickers, Phil and Alan Walden, Cliff White, Skippy White, Val Wilmer, and Peter Wolf.

On their own initiative, and strictly in order to help me complete my musical education, my friends Joe McEwen and Bill Millar made me tape after tape of obscure soul selections that I would never otherwise have been able to track down. Bill Millar in addition read almost all of the manuscript for accuracy and supplied innumerable clippings, documents, and photographs to reinforce—or in many cases to alter—my understanding of a good many points. Kit Rachlis provided helpful editorial advice and suggestions throughout, while Alexandra Guralnick read, transcribed, and digested vast tracts of material. Susan Marsh once again proved the perfect partner in design. Cary Ryan copyedited the manuscript with a loving but unsparing eye, while my editor, Rick Kot, offered devotion (and patience) above and beyond the call of duty.

In Memphis, Michael Bane provided me with numerous telephone calls of introduction, one of which led to David Less, who freely offered up the fruits of his own extensive research as well as taking me out to Al Green's Church of the Full Gospel Tabernacle for the first time. Through a number of equally fortuitous associations I met Rose Clayton, Pat Rainer, Stanley Booth, and Jim Dickinson, each of whom took me where I needed to go in addition to supplying invaluable help, encouragement, insights, and further introductions. Roosevelt Jamison, too, took me around to meet his various friends and associates and offered help at every juncture.

In Macon, Mark Pucci introduced me to Phil and Alan Walden and Rodgers Redding, and Rodgers made it his business to see that I met key figures from all aspects of his brother's life.

Donnie Fritts was my unflagging guide and coconspirator in Muscle Shoals and, when my own knowledge or imagination failed, turned out to be an able and enthusiastic interviewer himself. It was Donnie who set up the tripartite reunion with Dan Penn and Spooner Oldham at his Nashville home from which much of the lively, thorny, and contradictory history of Muscle Shoals has been drawn. Through Donnie, too, I met Jimmy Johnson, whose memories of the era are somewhat more precise (but no less colorful), and Jimmy graciously got me to everyone in the Quad Cities area that Donnie might have missed.

Cliff White provided unstinting assistance, insight, and written documentation for my continuing investigation into the life and times of James Brown, while Jerry Wexler never ceased to encourage the project from beginning to end with his lively opinions, reminiscences, and sharing of memories and music. Solomon Burke, almost needless to say, provided laughs, love, and inspiration throughout.

Thanks to all, and to all those not named, from whom I drew encouragement, sustenance, and a continual broadening of my perspective. It's been fun!

Contents

Introduction: Soul Serenade

T HIS IS A STORY FIRST AND FOREMOST. IT IS THE story of a particular kind of music, but I hope it is more than that. I started out more than four years ago with the idea of writing a book on Southern soul music in the '60s, a companion volume to my two earlier books, *Feel Like Going Home* and *Lost Highway,* and the last installment in a trilogy covering my three great musical loves—blues, rockabilly/country, and soul. I wanted to write a different kind of book this time, though, tending more toward narrative than toward profile, and while I recognized the impossibility of telling the *whole* story (Who can ever do that—who would ever *want* to do that? As Mark Twain once wrote, a real biography is impossible because "every day would make a whole book—365 books a year."), I wanted to present as convincing a portrait of a musical movement and a social milieu as could be deduced in retrospect. In the course of researching the book I interviewed well over a hundred people and traveled from Los Angeles to Mississippi, from Georgia to New York, Alabama, Philadelphia, and Tennessee. The weight of the subtext, I hope, reinforces the narrative, because however comprehensive this book may seem, however tangled its chronology and extended its text, it represents only a minuscule portion of the time that I spent with label owners, producers, booking agents, record store operators, disc jockeys, and managers, as well as the artists themselves. And I hope it reflects my disinclination to understand things too quickly, because there is no question in my mind of the education that I got, an education in an aspect of Americana and a facet of American business that, despite my longtime exposure to the music industry, I had never really scrutinized before. I met some of the greatest characters and made some of the closest friends (often one and the same thing) that I have ever known. And I had most of the preconceptions with which I came to the writing of this book turned almost totally upside down.

WHAT IS SOUL MUSIC?

Southern soul music developed out of a time and a set of social circumstances that are unlikely to be repeated. I suppose I should make it clear from the outset that when I speak of soul music, I am not referring to Motown, a phenomenon

Off to church. (Val Wilmer)

I

Black Wall of Pride, Atlanta, 1973. (Val Wilmer)

almost exactly contemporaneous but appealing far more to a pop, white, and industry-slanted kind of audience. (Motown's achievement, said Jerry Wexler, vice-president of Atlantic Records and chief spokesman for the rival faction, was "something that you would have to say on paper was impossible. They took black music and beamed it directly to the white American teenager.") What I am referring to is the far less controlled, gospel-based, emotion-baring kind of music that grew up in the wake of the success of Ray Charles from about 1954 on and came to its full flowering, along with Motown, in the early 1960s. It was for a considerable length of time limited almost exclusively to a black audience which had grown up on the uninhibited emotionalism of the church and to a secret but growing legion of young white admirers who picked up on rhythm and blues on the radio and took it as the key to a mystery they were pledged never to reveal. In the beginning, like rock 'n' roll, it was an expression of rebellion, or at least of discontent, and Ray Charles's transformation of dignified gospel standards into cries of secular ecstasy came in for a good deal of criticism at first, mostly from the pulpit. Once it emerged from the underground, it accompanied the Civil Rights Movement almost step by step, its success directly reflecting the giant strides that integration was making, its popularity almost a mirror image of the social changes that were taking place. When Percy Sledge's "When a Man Loves a Woman," a pure example of Southern soul emotiveness if ever there was one, made the top of the pop charts in 1966, it seemed almost as if the mountain had been scaled. Here was a song uncompromised, I thought at the time (*many* thought at the time), by concessions to the marketplace, unbleached and unblemished by the endearing palliatives which Motown always brought to bear, an expression of romantic generosity and black solidarity (I thought again). I didn't even like the song all that much, but I took it as a harbinger of a new day, when a mass audience could respond to black popular culture on its own terms.

Similarly it seemed no coincidence that when the height of the Movement was past, when the certainty of forward motion and the instinctive commonality of purpose that marked that brief period were called into question by the death of Martin Luther King, the soul movement, too, should have fragmented, the good feeling clearly engendered by the music should have fled, and the charts should have been virtually resegregated, with funk and disco and then rap music rendering themselves as inaccessible, and ultimately as co-optable in turn, as rhythm and blues once had been. Soul music, then, was the product of a particular time and place that one would not *want* to see repeated, the bitter fruit of segregation, transformed (as so much else has been by the encompassing generosity of Afro-American culture) into a statement of warmth and affirmation. This was the backdrop for the evolution of soul, an exciting time, a dangerous time, a time of exhilarating self-discovery. That is the historical context.

Here is what I thought soul music was when I first started writing this book. "Soul music," in British writer Clive Anderson's orthodox and not imperceptive formulation, "is made by black Americans and elevates 'feeling' above all else. It began in the late fifties, secularized gospel embracing blues profanity, and dealt exclusively with that most important subject, the vagaries of love. The sound remains in church. More often than not soul is in ballad form and employs certain gospel and blues techniques—call and response patterns, hip argot and inflection, melismatic delivery. It is a completely vocal art. . . . Soul assumes a shared experience, a relationship with the listener, as in blues, where the singer confirms and works out the feelings of the audience. In this sense it remains sacramental."

I think that would serve as a pretty fair summary of my own more basic assumptions. Not that I was entirely without exposure to nonacademic reality. With my friend Bob Smith I saw every blues act that came to town, and when we were both sixteen, we saw Ray Charles for the first time singing his new hit "What'd I Say" at Boston's Jordan Hall. From early 1964 on, under the prodding of another friend, John Grahm, I must have gone to every major soul revue, every Summer and Winter Shower of Stars that Boston's soul station WILD put on. John and I saw Solomon Burke and Joe Tex and Garnet Mimms and James Brown and Otis Redding—we saw most of the people I am writing about in this book, in fact, many of them several times and often close up in the little clubs that John introduced me to when we were both around twenty.

The first story that I wrote for *Rolling Stone* in 1968 was an appreciation of Solomon Burke, and one of the earliest pieces I wrote for the fledgling *Boston Phoenix* was a description of the spectacular nature of James Brown's stage show in January of 1967.

I mention all this not merely to cite my credentials but also to downplay my pretensions to scholarly objectivity. I went to the shows, it is true, along with the requisite handful of white spectators, and like Mick Jagger in England, Mitch Ryder in Detroit, Peter Wolf in New York, or writer Joe McEwen in Philadelphia, I was enthralled. I would not want to say that I immediately grasped the reality. Certainly I wasn't seeing any more of the behind-the-scenes action than any other fan. But more to the point I took the shows as an opportunity for romance in which the impossible grace of the dancers was outweighed only by the exotic allure of the setting. To me soul music *was* black power. To me soul music was a kind of revolutionary statement of purpose, a bold departure from the rhythm and blues which had preceded it, and (here is where I think I got it most wrong) a kind of separatist, almost Garveyite statement of black pride, a championing of "roots" long before the formal concept became popular, whose adoption by whites only symbolized the good-will and innocent expectations that the Movement engendered. My thinking along these lines was further reinforced by such statements of social purpose as "We're a Winner" (the Impressions), "I'm Black and I'm Proud" (James Brown), "I Wish I Knew (How It Would Feel to Be Free)" (Solomon Burke), and "A Change Is Gonna Come" (Sam Cooke), and to this day I have no doubt that the rising tide of expectations and the emergence of new opportunities were a major part of the story. But it was not the whole story, any more than the whole story of rock 'n' roll was freedom and a rejection of the mood of white middle-class Eisenhower America.

I came face to face with the disparity between theory and reality almost as soon as I started my interviews for the book. Soul music, declared Jerry Wexler, who in his position as vice-president of Atlantic Records had recorded most of the great soul singers of the '60s and many of the outstanding r&b singers and groups of the '50s, was no more than "a rubric . . . a semantic fabrication. It was just a stage of the music, and it evolved to a certain point. It was rhythm and blues."

It was rhythm and blues. Right away my whole theory was blown out of the water. To me there had existed a sacred distinction between soul and rhythm and blues. Soul was honesty and truth and anguish and, as I say, soul-baring. Rhythm and blues, a genre with which I was also entranced (but for different reasons), was more of a contrivance—honking saxes and double entendres and screaming singers and pounding rhythms. Well, that's how much I knew. When I went to Macon for the first time and Otis Redding's brother, Rodgers, introduced me to Otis's widow, Zelma, he recommended me by saying, "He's a real r&b fan." Over and over again I came up against the fact that no distinction was made: all the singers that I was writing about had their roots in the '50s; the designations were in a sense the invention of critics and anthologists.

Well, all right, I could accept that. But soul was at least a clear expression of black solidarity; it expressed the "inchoate hopes of a noble people" (I might very nearly have written that), didn't it? When I earnestly sought out Julian Bond, the former SNCC leader who had written poems inspired by Ray Charles and Charlie Parker, he didn't exactly dismiss my ideological thesis, but he didn't really confirm it, either. Music may well have been important to his emerging sense of racial identity, he said, but like any other teenager, he "romanticized singers, especially Ray Charles. Rhythm and blues was looked down on. It was low-class music, it was wild music, it was sexual music, it was 'dirty' music. So far as we were concerned, it was the most glamorous life in the world. Now I know different, of course, but this was heaven to me back then." From the time that I myself first went to Memphis in the fall of 1980, the picture that I got of the Stax Record Company, and then of the recording scene in Muscle Shoals, as well as the emergence of Otis Redding from the provincial reaches of Macon, Georgia, showed not so much the white man in the woodpile, or even the white businessman capitalizing on social placement and cultural advantage to plunder the resources of a captive people, as the white *partner* contributing as significantly as his more prominent—more visible certainly—black associate. I don't mean to make too much of this, because partnership is a self-evident concept, it is the whole *point* of integration, after all; I was simply not prepared to see it happening here. Perhaps because a working union of this sort is so rare, perhaps because of my own cultural and political preconditioning, it took me a while to come to grips with the nonideological complexion of reality.

Finally, I entered into the writing of this book with what I think was the common misperception that soul music was a phenomenon that existed outside of what we generally view as "the music business." Southern soul, after all, like blues and rhythm and blues and rockabilly before it and rap and beat music after it, was a product of the independents, men and women who had circumvented the stranglehold that the major labels like Columbia, Decca, RCA, and Capitol had on the marketplace by discovering not a new music but a new market. Rhythm and blues was dismissed disparagingly in the '40s as "race music," country and western as "hillbilly," and while each music had its legitimate audience, the majors were in most instances reluctant to service it. Success in these fields was wide open, then, to the independent operator and entrepreneur, and the independent was in most cases someone who loved music, an old radio hand like Sam Phillips (the man whose Sun label gave birth to Elvis Presley, Jerry Lee Lewis, and rock 'n' roll), a collector like Ahmet Ertegun or Herb Abramson (who started Atlantic Records in partnership), a musician like Jim

Stewart (founder of Stax), a certified hipster like Jerry Wexler. Whatever their backgrounds, though—and the biographies of some of the other independents include such diverse occupations as shellac manufacturer, nightclub operator, mambo instructor, gumball machine distributor, and small-time gangster— whatever their passion for the Life and the music, their primary motive was to make money. Elementary as this lesson may sound, it took me a while to put into perspective what must have been obvious to someone like Jerry Wexler from the first: that soul music, far from taking place in a vacuum or developing an aesthetic in splendid isolation from other more corrupt and hybridized strains, was in fact developing in tandem with rock 'n' roll and country music, was competing, really, for the same dollar, could never give up the hope of tran- scending its parochial origins and breaking into the pop marketplace. Categories, it is said, are made for critics, and I have always believed this, but it took me almost two years of traveling around the country and interviewing industry figures as well as soul artists before I came to the realization that the story I was telling was as much the story of a business as it was the story of a music. Indeed, in many ways the story of soul music represents both the triumph and the tragedy of the free-enterprise system; the process of cross-fertilization by which soul music came to exist and influence in its turn the entire spectrum of American music was no more an accident than the invention of the Model T. As Jerry Wexler said in 1979 in a moment of somewhat glib self-doubt, "Just as it is with literature, where Faulkner remains on the library shelves while Jacqueline Susann hits the charts, it's the same with records. Each company must do its best to fill the pulsating needs of mediocrity in order to maximize its potential for success. We might as well be selling hubcaps."

WHAT IS SOUL MUSIC? II

This is what I mean today when I am talking about soul music. Soul music is Southern by definition if not by actual geography. Like the blues, jazz, and rock 'n' roll, both its birth and inspiration stem from the South, so that while Solomon Burke, one of the very greatest of soul singers, is a native of Philadel- phia, and Garnet Mimms, a little appreciated but nearly equally talented vocalist, made many of his recordings there, the clear inspiration for the styles of both is the Southern revivalism that fueled such diverse figures as Elvis Presley and Hank Williams on the one hand, Little Richard and Ray Charles on the other. I do believe there's a regional philosophy involved here, too, whether it's the agrarian spirit cited by Jerry Wexler ("There was always this attitude, 'Oh, man, we're gonna lose our soul if we do that. We're not gonna let machinery kill our natural Southern thing.' "), or simply the idea that Dan Penn, the renegade white hero of this book, has frequently expressed: "People down here don't let nobody tell them what to do." Unquestionably the racial turmoil of the South

Garnet Mimms, 1967. (Cliff White/Courtesy of Bill Millar)

was a factor, and the rapid social upheaval which it foreshadowed; in fact, the whole tangled racial history of the region, the intimate terms on which it lived with its passions and contradictions, played a decisive role in the forging of a new culture, one which the North's polite lip service to liberalism could never have achieved. Ultimately soul music derives, I believe, from the Southern dream of freedom.

It is not, however (contrary to most received opinion), a music of uninhibited emotional release—though at times it comes close. What it offers, rather, is something akin to the "knowledgeable apprehension," in Alfred Hitchcock's famous definition of suspense, that precedes the actual climax, that everyone knows is coming—it's just nobody is quite sure when. Soul music is a music that keeps hinting at a conclusion, keeps straining at the boundaries—of melody and convention—that it has imposed upon itself. That is where it is to be differentiated from the let-it-all-hang-out rock 'n' roll of a cheerful charismatic like Little Richard, who for all the brilliance of his singing and the subtleties of which he is capable, basically hits the ground running and accelerates from there. It is to be differentiated, too, from the cultural refinements of Motown, which, with equal claim to inspiration from the church, rarely uncorks a full-blooded scream, generally establishes the tension without ever really letting go, and only occasionally will reveal a flash of raw emotion. This is not because Motown singers were not equally talented or equally capable of revealing their true feelings; it is simply that Motown was an industry aimed specifically at reaching the white market, and every aspect of that industry was controlled, from the grooming and diction of its stars to the subtlest interpolations on its records. Southern soul music, on the other hand, was a haven for free-lancers and individualists. It was a musical mode in which the band might be out of tune, the drummer out of time, the singer off-key, and yet the message could still come across—since underlying feeling was all. Feeling dictated the rhythm, feeling dictated the pace; that is why soul music remains to this day so idiosyncratic a domain. One of the most common fallacies of a post-apocalyptic age such as ours is that there is no room for anything *but* the dramatic gesture; modulation is something as unheard-of as self-restraint. Soul music, which might in one sense be considered a herald of the new age, knew differently in the 1960s, and among the most surprising aspects of going back and listening to the music today—among its most enduring qualities—are the quiet moments at the center, the moments of stillness where action stops and "knowledgeable" anticipation takes over. Think of the great screams you've heard from everyone from James Brown to Wilson Pickett; think of the fervor of Solomon Burke's or Joe Tex's preaching on subjects as far removed in substance and seriousness as "skinny legs and all" or the price that love can exact. In gospel music, the progenitor of the style, a singer is often described as "worrying" the audience, teasing it, working the crowd until it is on the verge of exploding, until strong men faint and women start speaking in tongues. This is commonly referred to as "house wrecking." In soul music, perhaps the last of the great vocal arts, there is this same sense of dramatic structure, even if the message does not always provide the same unambiguous release. "I feel like I want to scream," James Brown announces over and over again, borrowing an age-old gospel technique. "I feel so good I want to scream," he declares, testing the limits to which the tension can be extended and in one famous recorded passage going past them as a voice from the crowd yells back, "James, you're an asshole." Over and over again the soul singer, like his gospel counterpart, begs for complicity. "Let me hear you say yeah," he implores, taking directly from the church. "There's just one more thing I want to say," he declares, just waiting to be invited to say it. "Can I get a witness?" becomes the rhetorical question—secular and ecclesiastical—of the age.

All this is merely testimony to the indisputable bond between technique and feeling, Southern soul music and the church. What is not so readily appreciated, perhaps, is the extent to which soul, once its gospel origins are gotten past, is a self-invented music—not so much in its form (which, like that of every great American folk music, is an amalgam, a hybridization of various strains that have gone before) as in its evolution on record. For soul was to a large extent a tale of three cities—Memphis, Macon, and Muscle Shoals—each of which grew up as an isolated regional outpost as far from the studio system

Jerry Wexler and Wilson Pickett. (Courtesy of Jerry Wexler)

of the majors in spirit as it was in geography and almost equally removed from any real awareness of the achievements of its fellow satellites. Southern soul music, as it evolved in the studio, was very much a homemade art (this was perhaps its one clear distinction from rhythm and blues), little dependent on direct models because direct models were not close at hand, little aware of history because history had not yet been written. The singers, it is true, had their parts down pat; they simply modeled themselves on the gospel stars. But the musicians, the writers, the producers, the managers, the engineers—the whole apparatus of the so-called recording industry—were forced to define themselves and their roles as they went along, were thrown back on their own resources. Perhaps this was to some extent a function of provincial xenophobia; if the United States was isolationist by inclination, the South remains the last bastion of true populism and regionalism triumphant.

But it was not simply the South. The recording industry itself was still in the process of self-definition, and soul music—black music in general—remained the Wild West of the music territory. "We didn't know how to make records," Jerry Wexler has said of his own celebrated start in the record business with Atlantic in 1953. "What the hell did we know then?" Jim Stewart and his sister, Estelle Axton, had scarcely listened to black music when they started recording it at Stax; the closest that Rick Hall, founder of the Fame Recording studio and label in Muscle Shoals, had come to the music industry was a little studio lined with empty egg cartons over the City Drugstore in Florence,

Alabama. Phil Walden, a recent graduate of the Sidney Lanier High School in Macon, Georgia, plotted with Otis Redding, a dropout from Lanier's black counterpart, how they were going to crack the great world of entertainment without knowing any more about it than you could pick up from agents' handbills. Dan Penn, a brash young white kid from Vernon, Alabama (population: 1500), had never seen any of his heroes (Ray Charles, Sam Cooke, Bobby "Blue" Bland) sing when he started traversing the Alabama-Mississippi countryside in a made-over hearse, putting on an act in which he imagined himself to be "Bobby 'Blue' Penn." Each region, each *studio,* developed its own distinctive approach, piecing together the hard-won lessons until a recording philosophy was evolved, improvising a system of on-the-spot, "head" arrangements (necessary in the absence of reading musicians) that, whatever its simplicity, impressed Jerry Wexler so strongly that he would say in retrospect, "We didn't really learn how to put a record together until we worked with the Stax and Muscle Shoals people." And this from the man on whom "the Stax and Muscle Shoals people" modeled their whole operation once he had sought them out, whom they revered for his track record and producing expertise!

The one other irreducible component of Southern soul music was its racial mix, and here, too, opinion remains divided about its precise significance. To some it is just one more variation on the old racist story: black workers, white owners. I have spoken earlier of my own confusion and my ultimate conviction that here was a partnership. But it was a partnership with a difference: the principals brought to it such divergent outlooks and experiences that even if they had grown up in the same little town, they were as widely separated as if there had been an ocean between them. And when they came together, it may well have been their strangeness to each other, as well as their familiarity, that caused the cultural explosion.

There are other, more prosaic ways of looking at this affiliation. Idealistically, of course, it did bear out the promise of integration, and one participant after another—black *and* white—has credited the partnership as evidence that the American dream can work, has laid the success of soul music to "blacks and whites working as a team." On a slyer level black DJ Hamp Swain (the original discoverer of Otis Redding and a prominent Macon bandleader in the mid-'50s) has cited his "secret audience": "In my early days in radio I would think that fifty percent of my audience was white—high school kids who were crazy about r&b music. At the shows they could sit upstairs and watch the black kids downstairs having a good time dancing. They just had to sit up there and watch." Soul music, Swain implies, was born when the white kids finally came down and participated. Even more circuitously Jim Dickinson, a white Memphis musician with a singularly iconoclastic point of view, saw white musicians as a necessary ingredient in the mix simply because they would take more abuse in the studio than their black counterparts. Perhaps because there was less at stake in the way of pride or place, "the white musicians would just sit there and not say anything."

Whatever the true story—if there *is* a true story—one fact is clear: blacks and whites brought very different backgrounds and offered very different contributions to the music itself. Blacks, of course, were the stars. There were no white soul singers, with the marginal exceptions of the Righteous Brothers or Wayne Cochran or a one-shot success like the Magnificent Men, and if a singer-songwriter like Dan Penn played a role similar to Fletcher Henderson's in the Benny Goodman sound, like Henderson he remained for the most part entirely in the background. The quality that other white musicians like Steve Cropper and Jimmy Johnson—primarily *rhythm* guitarists, interestingly enough —brought to the music included a country and western background, a middle-class work ethic, and a rock 'n' roll heart. By that I don't mean a musical quality so much as a sense of dissatisfaction with where they were and who they were, and a (very likely unarticulated) sense of social injustice, the kind of instinctive "white niggerism" that Norman Mailer was groping toward when he wrote of "the juvenile delinquent [coming] face to face with the Negro" and from this "wedding" arising the birth of the hipster. To the white protagonists of this book virtually without exception Ray Charles was a god for almost the very reasons that the White Citizens' Councils had warned about: sex, barbarism, and jungle rhythms. "It is to my surprise," I wrote of actually meeting Charles some twenty-five years later, "his sense of *organization,* his dedication to humdrum reality, that stands out, not the flash of inspiration, the wicked gleam of orgiastic pleasure that I first glimpsed when I was fifteen or sixteen years old and took not only for all of Ray Charles but for the essence of r&b, 1960 style."

The other side of such intense romanticization, of course, is patronization, and that is the Animal House side of the story. It was the fraternity audiences North and South—but particularly South—that nurtured the music, that held up a drunken Jimmy Reed as the prototypical "crazy nigger," that took the music and the musicians for their own as a kind of substitute for real experience, and to this day keep r&b alive in a form of institutionalized revivalism known as "beach music." To Rufus Thomas, Percy Sledge, and countless others the Southern fraternity circuit provided the best kind of gig: high-paying, dignified (you got to wear a tuxedo, and the young men and ladies were dressed to the teeth), and full of the most appreciative audiences that you could hope to encounter. For the white "cover" bands like Jimmy Johnson's Del Rays or Dan Penn's Pallbearers, the fraternities were the life's blood of the business: there was no club scene, and without records an act couldn't really travel, but with a little bit of luck (and a good reputation behind you) you could always come back to Phi Kappa Alpha year after year, sometimes several times in the same year, and find a warm welcome.

I must admit, none of this would ever have occurred to me before writing this book—and not just the fraternity side of it, either. No one knew who was actually playing on the records. "Quaint to observe white man Wayne Jackson step up to the microphone," wrote Bill Millar of the English Stax-Volt Revue in 1967. And the idea that Dan Penn and Spooner Oldham, authors of so many of the soul classics, were both white would have seemed heretical to me at the time. Far more shocking, though, was the idea that such classist and racist institutions as *fraternities,* such clear agents of wealth and privilege, could have genuinely been fostering the music that I loved. Well, that was the case, whether I liked it or not.

At the same time, in the midst of all this historical revisionism, I don't want to suggest that soul music was not socially progressive on some conscious level, or that there was not a firm substratum of idealism in its dedication to an alternative culture—for there was. Soul music was a statement of possibilities that could be taken as far as you liked, and no white participant that I know of was unaware of the implications. I think songwriter Donnie Fritts put it best when he spoke of his friendship with soul singer Arthur Alexander (like Donnie a native of the Muscle Shoals area) in those dangerous times. "How could I be prejudiced?" he said, referring to the bitter divisiveness of the era. "I'm the most prejudiced-against person there is. I'm the biggest nigger you ever met."

For the black participant, whether singer, songwriter, or record executive, the social dynamic was somewhat more straightforward. On the one hand, as Norman Mailer melodramatically pointed out in "The White Negro," there was no choice as to how you might represent yourself if you were black; race was an inescapable fact of American life, and "any Negro who wishes to live must live with danger from his first day . . . no experience can ever be casual to him. . . ." Conversely soul music represented another opportunity for upward mobility, much as sports and entertainment in general had for the previous fifty or sixty years. One of the things that surprised me most, I think, when I came to meet my heroes of soul was how middle-class they were: men and women who might have been doctors or lawyers or teachers in many instances, whose private speaking voices, articulation, and erudition were often far different, far removed from the "soul brother" bonhomie that their onstage manner would suggest. I had constructed for myself a mythology of instinctual soul, in which the Ray Charles fantasy figure would have been the archetype. This construction fit right in with my own knowledge of the blues world, or even the world of white country music, where social—if not economic—aspiration was often limited, and, particularly in country music, the rural world from which the star arose was often simply transplanted to suburban surroundings. This did not turn out to be the case in the world of soul, and perhaps that accounts for some of the problems of adaptation and identity which several of the singers I interviewed have encountered. Musically nearly everyone that I spoke to saw soul music as a step up from the blues, a clear departure from primitive chants and cotton-

Sam Cooke and Dinah Washington.
(Gordon "Doc" Anderson)

patch hollers executed on a more elevated thematic and harmonic level. "We had our type of blues gospel melody," songwriter Roosevelt Jamison explained, "but we wanted to put some poetic message and philosophy in it. The gutbucket stuff we figured wasn't really good music. We wanted to put some flavor of God in it."

Not surprisingly nearly every Southern soul singer, almost without exception, took Sam Cooke, the urbane former gospel Soul Stirrer, for a model. With his matinee-idol good looks, liltingly graceful voice, sophisticated manner, and effortless delivery (all with a subtle suggestion, or inescapable undercurrent, of gospel passion), Cooke was not only the logical stylistic choice; he provided the clear social model as well. With "You Send Me" in 1957, a #1 pop hit, he was the first "soul singer" to achieve widespread crossover success; with the creation of his own label and publishing company he became one of the few black stars to take charge of his own career; with his Ferrari, his Jaguar XKE, his appearance

The Soul Brothers Six. (From the collection of Fred Lewis)

on the *Tonight* show, and his triumphant conquest of the Copacabana Club in New York, he entered a world previously reserved For Whites Only. As urbane as Duke Ellington in the world of jazz, and no less dignified, he was revered not just for his music but for his *success,* a notion that took a while to penetrate my preconceived ideas about racial solidarity and the purity of art. Sam Cooke war looking for white acceptance, because he was looking for wider sales and a broader market. That is why he crossed over from gospel in the first place. As Ray Charles said, speaking of his own departure from the chitlin circuit, "My people made me what I am, because you have to become big in your own community first, but as far as leaving that black audience exclusively, I never even thought twice about it."

Not everyone was Ray Charles, though. Not everyone was Sam Cooke. For almost all the soul singers the chitlin circuit remained an inescapable way of life, at least to a considerable degree. What should never be lost sight of is that Southern soul music is at least as much the story of the never-weres and might-have-beens, of the one-hit artists, and the impact of their one hit, as it is a chronicle of the stars. Soul music is a message from the heart, and through the story of soul music, as I finally came to see it, runs a spiritual thread that links the Soul Brothers 6 with Sam and Dave, James Carr with Otis Redding, William Bell with Sam Cooke. Within this framework, who is to say that Oscar Toney, Jr., is not as "important" as Wilson Pickett, that George Perkins or Phil Flowers or Freddie Scott did not contribute as much to the body of the music in their own way as the more familiar names, with their instantly familiar hits?

I've tried to keep this idea in mind even as the book has settled into a more predictable pattern of social context and historical associations. I've tried to express the pulse of the music, not just its formal definition, the idea that here was a truly democratic arena open to anyone as much on the basis of desire as technique, as much on the basis of gut instinct as careful calculation. This held true for singer and businessman, songwriter and musician, from a great synthesizer like Ray Charles, who, recognizing the technical deficiencies of his voice (he had a very limited natural range), explored every nook and cranny of its emotional resources, to a compulsive performer like James Brown, who built revolutions on riffs and trusted to faith, righteousness, and determination to make a way. It is feeling in the end that we are hearing when we listen to soul music, it is feeling that gets the music rocking with that steady beat, it is feeling with which I started out the book and feeling which is the one home truth that I think will survive any tendency toward revisionism or retrospective irony.

THE STORY OF MY BOOK

I started this book in the fall of 1980. One of the first things I did was to try to get in touch with Solomon Burke. I tried his lawyer in California, called his booking agent, song publisher, manager—all without success. Then one day just as I was going out the phone rang, and my wife, Alexandra, answered it. I was already in the car when she came running out. It was someone calling on behalf of Solomon Burke, she said, or someone who said he was Solomon Burke. When I got on the phone, the voice at the other end was chipper, mild, the voice of an insurance salesman. Maybe, I thought, it was another Solomon Burke. Finally, still fearful that I was being toyed with, I explained the purpose of my earlier calls. I was writing a book; it was about soul music, Southern soul music—I didn't have to go any further. Of course, of course, interrupted the voice at the other end of the line, suddenly warming to the conversation and abandoning all pretense of polite neutrality. "And how could you do a book without speaking to the king?"

That set me off on my ride. I met Solomon shortly thereafter, and he was right: I couldn't have done the book without speaking to the king. He was everything I had ever imagined him to be through his music, and more—bigger, warmer, funnier, larger than life in every respect. Within a short time, through

Solomon and others, I had made a whole raft of contacts. One person led to another, and everywhere I went news of my quest preceded me. Everyone wanted to know how old friends were doing; Carla Thomas, a warm, gracious woman as articulate as she is talented, announced, "Next time I'm going to interview *you* and find out what all these people are saying," as soon as I closed the notebook on our interview. Some people were more interested in what others had to say about them than they were in talking about themselves; many of the insights I gained were off the record, and much of the knowledge I acquired lies buried beneath the surface of the text; some of the star interviews that I sought assiduously over a period of years never came off; but gradually I came to feel as if I were gaining entrée to, and knowledge of, a world whose dimensions I had scarcely even suspected.

I was surprised sometimes at how freely so many of the people I interviewed were willing to speak. But then I don't know if I should have been. What they were seeking, most of them, was the same directness and emotional truth that existed in their music. They were looking for their place in history. In the past I have occasionally written things that I thought might offend those I was writing about, material that involved both revelations on their part and insights that I had gained. In almost every instance I found that if the story was honest, it was accepted, no matter how painful acceptance might be, that the highest compliment that the musicians I was writing about could pay was "It's honest. It's the truth."

Well, I hope that's the case here. The truth, as I say, is not a simple thing —or perhaps it's more accurate to say that there are many truths. And when one is piecing together a retrospective account such as this, assembled from a series of interviews with more than a hundred different (and strong) personalities, it's necessary to make one's own judgments sometimes, one is forced often to create a best-case scenario. What I have tried to do is to make a coherent presentation without sacrificing individual perspectives, to sift through the sometimes bewildering maze of claims and counterclaims and arrive at a version that makes the most sense, taking into account the intended veracity of most of the parties. I am aware that some of what I have written challenges the accepted version of history, but here, too, one must remember that history has been largely written—as is the case with so much of popular culture—in promotional literature and publicity releases which, by their very nature (and whatever enthusiastic glimpse of the truth they may afford), are not always the most objective guide. At times, I must admit, I felt as if I were sinking into a bog; occasionally I lost faith and wondered what in the hell I was doing out there in a miasma of memory and allusion (or was that illusion?), set adrift in a sea of oral history without bearings or compass. But then things would start to fall into place once again; the interviews began to seem like pieces of a giant puzzle, which, even if it might never be completely assembled, was at least

Solomon Burke and me. (Scott Billington)

beginning to take shape; gradually the work suggested a narrative of its own.

My one caveat is that it should not be forgotten that this is a retrospective account, and while there are flashes of present-day description interspersed throughout the narrative, for the most part it is an attempt to recreate by documentation, first-person testimony, and portraiture *what really happened* (that is to say, the core of what really happened, whether represented by personal reminiscence with a sometimes metaphorical perspective or assembled as a third-person narrative with a presumed overview). Not to put too fine a point on it, this book lies somewhere between history and personal chronicle: I was there to interview the principals, but as to the events that we are talking about I simply was not there to be a witness, and the written documentation that exists is spotty at best. It would have been easy to introduce a lot of present-day detail, and I have done so on occasion—but only where I felt it substantiated a point that was being made about the past. The book created its own story and imposed its own limitations, limitations to which I could accede only after I had traveled back and forth from Macon to Memphis and Atlanta and Muscle Shoals a number of times interviewing and reinterviewing the principals and cast of supporting players. If I didn't accept the limitations, I realized, I would never get out of this book alive. Or I would never find a readership that could. Sometimes, my mother has always told me, you've got to be practical.

THE LEGACY OF SOUL

Soul music was a brief flowering, really. It first peered out in the mid-1950s, like rock 'n' roll, as a kind of alternative to assimilation. It came into its own no earlier than 1960, crossed over by 1965 or 1966, and, despite lingering traces of its influence throughout the culture, was spent as a controlling force by the early '70s. Certainly it can be seen as paralleling the Civil Rights Movement stylistically as well as chronologically, emerging with stealth at first, slowly gathering strength, then learning to assert itself without apology or fear, until forced to retrench in the face of a series of traumatic events and jarring disappointments. Musically, I believe, soul remains the story of how a universal sound emerged from the black church. Historically it represents another chapter in the development of black consciousness, similar to the Harlem Renaissance, say, in its championing of negritude, but more widespread in its immediate impact. At the same time it is a whole other story, too. It is the story of blacks and whites together. It is the story of the complicated intertwinings of dirt-poor roots and middle-class dreams, aesthetic ambitions and social strivings, the anarchic impulse and the business ethic. It is a story in which, indisputably, there are heroes and villains, even if, as in real life, sometimes it's difficult to tell them apart. At one point soul music appeared to represent the vanguard of the revolution, and if the revolution never arrived, I don't know that that makes soul matter any less.

Is all this too much for the music to bear? I don't think so. At the same time one doesn't want to forget that one is talking about popular culture. For Jerry Wexler it is all a little bit rhetorical anyway. "We didn't know we were at some cosmic threshold," he declares. "You never know that. I think that's all literary, all this business about decades. I think it's part of the bullshit rhetoric of rock. The only thing about it was, it's like certain movements in art, it's like that place outside of Paris where the light was so good, the Barbizon school, you know, the confluence of certain things, the myth period, the golden period, when the music was fresh, the musicians were fresh—you can't replicate it

James Brown. (Courtesy of Gregg Geller)

because there's something in the ambience, something in the atmosphere. Not that I consider rhythm and blues to be art necessarily."

What he did consider rhythm and blues to be—and the context in which Atlantic Records had to view the music in order to survive—was commerce. I've tried to view it a little bit that way, too, as a combination, at any rate, of art and commerce in which the music attained its highest level when the marriage was closest and in the absence of which the form cannot be revived today. And remember: as much as was going on within this self-contained world of Southern soul, there was that much more creating an inescapable influence (and demanding entrée somehow) from the outside. This was the age of the

Beatles, a time when Motown had twelve #1 pop hits while Southern soul music was waiting to have its first. The music itself, however, needs no apologies. To me it almost goes without saying that soul was an incomparably greater form (because it was incomparably more passionate, emotionally expressive, and individualistic) than its more celebrated contemporaries. I once quoted Murray Kempton's assertion that "one moment of Joe Turner singing that 'it's your dollar now, but it's gonna be mine some sweet day' is worth more than all [the Beatles] have ever said," and an editor took it out to save me embarrassment. "Sometimes I feel as if I grew up in a cultural vacuum," wrote Joe McEwen of his own Philadelphia origins. "The Beatles never registered with me; the hysteria and the sense of community that marked their ascendance were so foreign that when I read Greil Marcus's essay on the group in *The Rolling Stone Illustrated History of Rock & Roll,* I could only shake my head in wonder. I didn't feel left out necessarily . . . [but] when I read Greil Marcus on the Beatles ('Enormous energy—the energy of frustration, desire, repression, adolescence, sex, ambition—finds an object in pop explosion. . . .'), I [thought] of James Brown. . . . I knew exactly what he meant when he sang, achingly and somewhat bewilderingly, 'A million to one/ Ten thousand people/ Under my Father's sun/ Who need someone,' and I had an even better understanding of a song called 'Let Yourself Go.' "

That was how it was with me, perhaps not the same song but the same feeling, the sense of being clued in to something significant, of being on the edge of a Movement that was so much more than just another pop phenomenon. It was there for the audience; it was there for the protagonists. Over and over again in my talks with the people who made the music there was reference to this same kind of spiritual association, a sense of being part of a larger whole. No one has characterized it more eloquently, though, than Curtis Mayfield, lead singer of the Chicago-based Impressions ("People Get Ready," "Keep on Pushing," "We're a Winner") and later most notably composer for such film sound tracks as "Superfly." Speaking to writer Russell Gersten about the achievements of the larger world of soul, he declared, "You know, to talk about the '60s almost brings tears to my eyes. What we did. What we all did. We changed the world—me, us, Smokey Robinson, Jerry Butler, the Temptations, Aretha, Otis, Gladys Knight, James Brown. We really did. Barriers broke down for us. And for all black musicians afterwards. I mean, to have lived through that, and to have been part of that, is more than anyone can ask."

▶1▶

Prologue to Soul: Sam Cooke, Ray Charles, and the Business of Music

I, too, hear America singing
But from where I stand
I can only hear Little Richard
and Fats Domino
But sometimes,
I hear Ray Charles
Drowning in his own tears
or Bird
Relaxin' at Camarillo
or Horace Silver, Doodling
Then I don't mind standing a little longer.

—Julian Bond

SOUL STEW: A THUMBNAIL HISTORY

THE STORY OF SOUL MUSIC CAN BE SEEN LARGELY as the story of the introduction of the gospel strain into the secular world of rhythm and blues. To gospel devotees like Tony Heilbut the newcomers had no special claim on the territory and in some cases were rank imitators. "In all the great modern soul singers," writes Heilbut in his definitive work, *The Gospel Sound*, "one hears echoes of the pioneer gospel shouters. The influences are usually direct and specific. . . . " Be that as it may, soul music was never the exact equivalent of gospel music (there were simply too many outside influences) and through cross-pollination necessarily gave something back as well. Historically the change began taking place in the early '50s, long before anyone but the record buyer had picked up on it ("Beware of too much categorizing," wrote Atlantic heads Jerry Wexler and Ahmet Ertegun in a 1954 *Cashbox* article. "Record buyers don't read the charts; if a record knocks them out, they buy it and play it"); like most historic developments it may well seem more dramatic in retrospect than it did at the time. Still, it did not altogether escape notice even by contemporary observers.

The Orioles in the alley, with unidentified woman. (Gordon "Doc" Anderson)

Rhythm and blues up until this point had been pretty much what the term suggests: an uptempo, or at least rhythmically modernized (the introduction of the heavy backbeat was a direct precursor of rock 'n' roll), variation on the bedrock of the blues. Its performance was confined, of course, to black artists and reached an almost exclusively black audience. Hence its official designation as "race music," a label which was not changed until Jerry Wexler came up with the more dignified—and descriptive—term in 1949, while still a *Billboard* reporter. Just to give some idea of the breadth of the changes that took place around this time: the r&b charts between 1948 and 1950 were pretty much dominated by what we think of today as the blues and its near-relations. John Lee Hooker made his debut in 1949, with the electrifying "Boogie Chillen." Sophisticated bluesman Lonnie Johnson, who had been recording since 1925, had the #1 hit of 1948 with "Tomorrow Night." Blues shouter Wynonie Harris, one of Elvis Presley's chief models (and the source of his epochal "Good Rockin' Tonight"), had half a dozen top hits, while novelty artist Louis Jordan continued his reign as clown prince of the blues. Familiar names like Charles Brown, Amos Milburn, and Muddy Waters crop up for the first time on the charts during these years, while Sonny Thompson, Bullmoose Jackson, and Ivory Joe Hunter all contributed classic variations on blues themes. Meanwhile, the forces of modernism were grouping under a most unlikely banner: what amounted to quartet singing in a new guise. Quartet singing, of course, had a

Billy Ward and His Dominoes: Jackie Wilson far right. (Courtesy of Schomburg Center for Research in Black Culture; the New York Public Library; Astor, Lenox and Tilden Foundations)

long tradition in gospel music and in pop. In fact it was one of the few areas in which crossover sales had long been open to black artists, with groups like the Mills Brothers and the Ink Spots adopting a polite supper-club stance to achieve widespread accolades and influence. In 1947 the first of the "bird groups," the Ravens, had a smash hit with a fairly conventional arrangement of the Kern-Hammerstein standard, "Old Man River." What made the song different, and what gave the Ravens their distinctive neo-r&b flavor, was the playful emotion in bass singer Jimmy Ricks's voice, but even their most ardent supporters will concede that the Ravens never altogether crossed over into the brave new world of rhythm and blues. This was left to the second of the bird groups, the Orioles, to accomplish, along with rawer-sounding country cousins, groups like the Dominoes and the Clovers, that sprang up in their wake.

The Orioles made their first impression in 1948 with the lush ballad "It's Too Soon to Know." What made them different—and it doesn't always come through, for me anyway, on the records—is the tortured emotionalism in lead singer Sonny Til's voice. Here is what Jack Schiffman, whose father Frank owned the Apollo Theatre, had to say about Til in his book, *Uptown: The Story of Harlem's Apollo Theatre.* "Sonny affected the girls like an aphrodisiac. When he bent over the mike and leaned to one side, sensuously gyrating his shoulders and caressing the air with his hands, the girls would shriek, 'Ride my alley, Sonny! Ride my alley!' However, it was the aural as well as the visual aspects of the routine that had captured the teenagers' fancy. The Orioles had produced what we now think of as the 'group' sound—a combination of gospel and jazz, the vocals punctuated with glottal stops. . . . "

More striking still were the contributions of the Dominoes, a group founded in 1950 by singing coach and arranger Billy Ward, who built his sound around the soaring, gospel-driven vocals first of Clyde McPhatter, then of McPhatter's replacement, Jackie Wilson. Here there is little question as to the source of musical inspiration, and such songs as "Do Something for Me," "Have Mercy Baby," and "That's What You're Doing to Me" struck an undeniable blow for rhythm 'n' gospel freedom—but all these songs remained confined to the r&b charts and reached a black listening audience exclusively. There were not even any successful cover versions. To show how pervasive this back-to-the-roots movement really was (Jack Schiffman surmised that the Orioles gave a new generation "its own symbols of identification," while the success of Muddy Waters, Howlin' Wolf, and the whole school of downhome Chicago blues in urban markets could only indicate a nostalgia for familiar sounds), at the same time that rhythm and blues was undergoing this sea change, modern jazz—which had just come to terms with the bebop revolution—was putting forth its own roots sound. Hard bop, or "soul" jazz (this was probably the first time the term gained widespread currency), came into vogue in the mid-'50s and was seen by cultural critics like LeRoi Jones as the agency that " 'rescued' the music from the icebox. . . . Gospel music was the strongest and healthiest influence on jazz, and r&b, too."

It remained for two r&b songs, though, each in its own way atypical of the new genre, to establish once and for all the legitimacy of the whole process. In 1953, as if by prearrangement, both these songs shot to the top of the rhythm and blues charts and announced by their very presence that the new era had arrived.

"Shake a Hand," by Faye Adams, vocalist with the Joe Morris Orchestra (Morris had had a #1 hit with Atlantic in 1950 and tried to sell the label on his new song without success), was unlike anything that had gone before, not so much for its arrangement (conventional big-band r&b) or its goodhearted sentiment (its one-world message had been foreshadowed by Percy Mayfield's "Please Send Me Someone to Love" in 1950) as for the impassioned undercurrent of feeling that lay just beneath the surface. "Shake a Hand" might just as well have been recorded in church, so fervent was its emotional approach, so open-ended were its lyrics. Covered by country singer Red Foley at the time

Faye Adams. (Courtesy of Martin Brown and Jonas Bernholm)

and constantly revived over the years, the song has come by now to seem almost an emblem of the new secular humanism, and though it never actually entered into the pop charts, its dramatic symbolism and sound could be seen equally well as a representation of pop or of gospel. The other record that served to legitimize the new genre was "Crying in the Chapel," yet another offering from the Orioles, an "inspirational" country and western number this time which had already made the Top 10 on the country charts in two different versions. In lead singer Sonny Til's stately treatment the Orioles' interpretation of the song took on an altogether different hue and for the first time assumed explicitly many of the trappings of the church which previous Orioles' recordings had only hinted at. What linked "Shake a Hand" and "Crying in the Chapel" in particular —success apart—was their casual disdain for the commonly accepted conventions. Apparently without a great deal of prior thought, and certainly without any collusion, they muddied the distinctions—stylistic, harmonic, and lyrical— between gospel and r&b. In the past wherever a rhythm and blues number had showed a clear gospel influence, it was presented at least in an unambiguously secular setting. Here for the first time you were not sure exactly what ground

Little Willie John. (Charles Stewart)

you were on. Were these love songs or devotionals? Was the second person singular you or You? It was an intentional ambivalence that was to persist.

"It was just evolution," according to longtime observer Zenas "Daddy" Sears, a white New Englander who was first exposed to black gospel music while serving in the Army with Negro troops on the Burma Road and then went on to become Atlanta's top r&b DJ. Over the years he saw the changes that took place and was even in the studio when Ray Charles recorded his first big crossover hit, but, he says, he doesn't think "there was ever a period when it was considered a breakthrough. Jerry Wexler considered it a breakthrough, but I don't think it was by most people."

Maybe not, but the commercial possibilities were clear. Church-influenced rhythm and blues might only have appeared to be a fad in some quarters, but it was a fad that was quickly jumped on by gospel groups all over the South. The Royal Sons in 1952 abandoned their church affiliation to become the "5" Royales; the Gospel Starlighters at virtually the same time became (James Brown and) the Famous Flames. Even as white evangelicals were denouncing rock 'n' roll (the vehicle that would finally enable rhythm and blues to cross over to a white audience under a new guise and with a new imprint), black preachers and old blues singers were condemning the mixing of the two modes —ecclesiastical and secular—in equally vitriolic terms. "He's crying sanctified," reacted bluesman Big Bill Broonzy to Ray Charles's new syntheses. "He's mixing the blues with the spirituals. He should be singing in a church." Zenas Sears recalls a background singer on one of Charles's earliest soul sessions refusing to sing her part and walking out of the studio "because she was religious and she just felt it was wrong." All over the country, on all sides of the fence, firm lines were being drawn.

Once the new trend caught on, though, there was virtually no stopping it. In 1954, the same year that Elvis Presley made his first recordings, the Midnighters' "Work With Me Annie" topped the r&b charts while at the same time—without even registering in the pop Top 100—achieving the distinction of becoming the first black underground smash, as much for its salacious invitation as for its musical spark. That same year Roy Hamilton, late of the Jersey City Searchlight Gospel Singers, had his debut hit with "You'll Never Walk Alone," a soaring big-voiced inspirational number complete with wood-winds and strings, which similarly did not show up on the pop charts and similarly exerted an incalculable effect. Teen-aged Solomon Burke recorded for the first time in late 1954, modeling himself directly on the Roy Hamilton prototype. Jackie Wilson, on his own from 1957, let loose his gospel wail on near-operatic material which, with its combination of kitsch and naked passion, derived from the same grandiloquent school, while Bobby "Blue" Bland took his patented gargle from the preaching of the Reverend C. L. Franklin, Aretha's father. Little Willie John, still in his teens, was described by Jack Schiffman's brother, Bobby, who managed the Apollo for his father, as "the best male singer I ever heard. I never met a singer who had that kind of emotion and feeling in his songs." Meanwhile the hipsters over at Atlantic Records were among the first to catch on to the new trend, nudging their two most successful groups, the Clovers and the Drifters, in the direction of funkier sounds, while reinforc-ing the natural inclinations of Ray Charles, who had come to them in 1952 as a genteel Charles Brown–Nat King Cole imitator. When he finally broke out of the pack with "I Got a Woman" in late 1954, the new genre was established once and for all.

After that things took their natural commercial course. By 1955 or 1956 "race music" would have been a misnomer as well as a form of patronization: the pop charts had been busted wide open by the astonishing impact first of Bill Haley, then of Elvis Presley, then of a host of others who took the basic sound of rhythm and blues, in the words of Big Joe Turner "pepped it up," and in the process opened the door for black recording artists (like Big Joe Turner) to come pouring in. Little Richard, Chuck Berry, Fats Domino, the Coasters, the Platters, and a cast of thousands all took up the invitation without so much as a second thought, opening up the r&b field to every form of cultural cross-pollination and dangling the tantalizing promise of stardom in front of every gospel singer who had ever dreamt of worldly success.

MR. SOUL

> *He started out in church*
> *Singing in the gospel choir*
> *Every Sunday he sang a solo*
> *That made the sisters shout and cry*
> *The children danced the Holy Ghost*
> *When he sang and played his tambourine*
> *After church he'd tell the preacher*
> *All about his plans and dreams. . . .*
> *It hurt the congregation when they found out the news*
> *That he stopped singing for the Lord*
> *And started singing that rhythm and blues. . . .*
> *Now he gained the world, but he lost his soul. . . .*

—Angelo Bond, "He Gained the World (But Lost His Soul)"

SAM COOKE WAS THE FIRST OF THE BIG GOSPEL stars to cross over. He didn't do it until 1957, and then only after much hesitation, but to appreciate the magnitude of the event, it is necessary to imagine Elvis Presley abdicating his throne or the Beatles finding Jesus at the height of their popularity. For if the world of gospel was considerably smaller than that of either pop or rhythm and blues, its loyalties were all the fiercer, and the spectacle of the idolized lead singer of one of gospel's most popular groups converting, however tentatively and innocously, to "the devil's music" was enough to send shock waves through the worlds of both gospel *and* pop.

Sam Cook was born (without the *e*) on January 2, 1931, in Clarksdale, Mississippi, but grew up in Chicago, where his father, Charles, became a minister in the Church of Christ Holiness Church. At nine he joined two sisters and a brother in a gospel group called the Singing Children, and a few years later he became a member of the Highway QC's, a teenaged group that had been formed in emulation of the renowned Soul Stirrers and was coached by R. B. Robinson, baritone singer for the Stirrers. The Highway QC's (so named because their home base was the Highway Baptist Church) sang on programs with all the leading gospel groups of the day when they passed through Chicago. That was

J. W. Alexander. (Courtesy of J. W. Alexander)

where J. W. (James Woody) Alexander, tenor singer and manager of the Pilgrim Travelers, first laid eyes on Sam Cooke. "It was in 1945 or 1946," says Alexander, a well-spoken, dignified man with a shock of white hair even then (he was thirty at the time) and a diverse background, which included working for the CCC (Civilian Conservation Corps), singing popular music of the day with the Silver Moon Quartet in his native Independence, Kansas, and playing professional baseball for the Ethiopian Clowns in the barnstorming league that traveled all through the West and Midwest. "We were doing a show at 3838 South State Street, the Young Men's Christian Club, and Sam was with the QC's. He didn't really have the delivery, but he had a particular charisma. People just liked the guy; they could relate to him. I thought to myself, *This guy's a jewel.*"

Alexander ran into Sam off and on over the next few years, and in the meantime he made a connection for the Pilgrim Travelers that would have reverberations throughout the world of gospel. In 1948 the Travelers began recording for the Specialty label in Los Angeles, an independent which until then had specialized in postwar boogie woogie and jump-band rhythm and blues and would go on to even greater success and notoriety with Little Richard's rock 'n' roll. The Pilgrim Travelers were the second gospel group to be recorded

The Soul Stirrers, early '40s: E. A. Rundless, J. J. Farley, T. L. Brewster,
S. R. Crain, R. H. Harris. (Courtesy of Ray Funk)

by Specialty, and before long J. W. Alexander was the label's chief gospel scout
and sometime a&r man. In 1949 he brought in the Soul Stirrers with their
electrifying lead singer R. H. (Rebert) Harris and over the next few years would
recommend to label owner Art Rupe the Happyland Singers (soon to become
the Five Blind Boys of Alabama), the Original Gospel Harmonettes featuring
Dorothy Love Coates, and many more of gospel's most prominent names. On
the road it was the Pilgrim Travelers, the Soul Stirrers, and the Peacock label's
Five Blind Boys of Mississippi who toured together and made up what Alexander calls the Big Three of Gospel. Then in December 1950 Rebert Harris quit
the Stirrers for reasons of conscience ("The moral aspects of the thing just fell
out of the water," he told Tony Heilbut), and one of gospel's most prominent
groups was left without a lead singer. R. B. Robinson spoke up for the young
lead singer of the Highway QC's, whom he was working with back in Chicago.
Sam Cooke, just barely twenty, joined the group in Pine Bluff, Arkansas.

A word should be said here about the origin of the Soul Stirrers. Founded
in 1934 in Trinity, Texas, the Stirrers from the beginning made their mark in
the a capella world of pure harmonies. A quartet that chose to sing the newer
"gospel" songs (contemporary compositions on age-old themes, rather than the

The Pilgrim Travelers. Clockwise from top:
George McCurn, Jesse Whittaker, Ernest Booker, Louis
Rawls, with J. W. Alexander center. (Courtesy of
Schomburg Center for Research in Black Culture; the New
York Public Library; Astor, Lenox and Tilden Foundations)

traditional spirituals or jubilees), they pioneered in the use of a strong lead singer alternating with a second lead. Many of their songs have entered into the common language of contemporary gospel, but their strongest suit without question was the lead singing of Rebert Harris. "In every way," writes Tony Heilbut in *The Gospel Sound*, "Harris reformed quartet. Lyrically, he introduced the technique of ad-libbing. . . . Melodically, he introduced the chanting background repetition of key words. As for rhythm, 'I was the first to sing *delayed time*. I'd be singing half the time the group sang, not quite out of meter,' but enough askew to create irresistible syncopations." He was, in short, says Heilbut, a giant whose voice came through "with all the timeless urgency of a Robert Johnson or a Billie Holiday," a singer who never resorted to cheap tricks or melodramatics but relied on the thrilling interpretive powers of his voice. At the same time, Harris told Heilbut, "I never did appeal to the real young folk, because I was always a very conservative type." That must have been in part the image that Sam Cooke was meant to offset.

Cooke's first appearance with the Soul Stirrers was predictably unsettling. To begin with, the young singer was understandably shaken to be appearing in the company of his idols and in place of his chief inspiration (according to bass singer and original member Jesse Farley, "Sam started as a bad imitation of Harris"). There was a certain amount of resentment, too, says J. W. Alexander, of "a young fellow who has come in to push the old guy out." But mostly it was a matter of finding his own voice. "The very first night that we were together, you see, my group had a screamer, Keith Barber, and the Five Blind Boys they had a guy named Reverend Purcell Perkins, and he was a screamer, and of course Archie Brownlee was for them, too. So after the show Purcell said to Sam, 'Boy, don't you try to holler with us.' And Crain [Stirrers' second tenor and manager S. Roy Crain] says to me, 'Alex, what do you think about the kid?' And I said, 'Crain, I like the kid. And if you don't mind, I'd like to talk to him.' I said to Sam, 'Don't you try to holler with these guys. You don't have to. You just be sure you're singing loud enough for people to understand what you're saying. You just be sure they understand you. And if you do that, you can come up behind the screamers and always get the house.' And, you know, that holds true to this day."

Despite the fact that they were now in rival groups, J. W. Alexander soon took on Sam Cooke as a kind of protégé; from the beginning they enjoyed a special kind of relationship, and Sam, J.W. says, soaked up instruction like a sponge—from him, from Crain, from anyone who had something to offer. The Soul Stirrers recorded with Sam Cooke for the first time in early 1951. Art Rupe, owner of the Specialty label, had his misgivings, according to Alexander. "He didn't believe in Sam. He said, 'Well, he's a kid.' I liked the kid, though, so I went to bat for him. I said 'Art, you haven't even heard him.' He told me, 'All right, Alex. Because I've always had faith in your judgment. But this is going to turn out to be your first mistake.' "

From the first session came the story song "Jesus Gave Me Water." Like nearly all of Sam Cooke's notable later recordings, this one suggested the effect of swinging without effort, passion without strain, an indefinable depth of feeling overlaid with a veneer of sophistication that could convey all by a flick of the eyebrow, the tiniest modulation of tone. Although "Jesus Gave Me Water" betrays the youth and inexperience of its twenty-year-old interpreter, it stands as testimony to the potential that J. W. Alexander and Soul Stirrer S. R. Crain saw in him and the gospel audience seized on immediately. Like R. H. Harris's, Cooke's voice in a sense defied analysis, it appeared to flow so naturally, fit so effortlessly into a groove. When he employed melisma (the stretching of a single syllable over the course of several notes or measures), unlike many singers he never appeared merely to be showing off technique.

The Soul Stirrers: Sam Cooke, R. B. Robinson, Paul Foster, S. R. Crain, J. J. Farley. (Michael Ochs Archives)

When he wanted to suggest heightened feeling, he simply intensified his vocal tone and bore down a little harder, without resorting to shouting or false histrionics.

Even more striking was the unmistakable sense of individuation coming from a singer who had spent scarcely two months in the big time. You know virtually from the first notes of his first song that this is Sam Cooke. His warm velvety tone is just as distinctive as Harris's more bitingly astringent one, a hint of his characteristically lilting yodel ("Whoaa-oho-oh-oh-oh") is already present the first time out, and the emphasis on clarity and articulation, what Harris called the focus on the "*e*-ssential word or phrase in the song," is clearly in place.

Sam Cooke's gospel career proceeded as J. W. Alexander had predicted it would; his recordings quickly took on the confidence and the poise that "Jesus Gave Me Water" lacked, and he soon began writing numbers that had the same accessibility, the same clarity of narrative structure and simplicity of approach that would later give his pop songs such currency. Disarmingly handsome, almost breathtakingly at ease with himself and his charm, he projected an image that could perhaps best be compared to the golden-boy attraction of a William Holden or a Robert Redford, in which boy-next-door insouciance combined with dazzling good looks to appeal to men and women equally, young and old alike. Cooke's audience worshiped him, J.W. says, "not for any sexual connotation, they just *liked* the guy, they could warm to him." On the other hand, according to Jesse Farley, "in the old days young people took seats six rows from the back, the old folks stayed up front. When Sam came on the scene, it reversed itself. The young people took over."

He and J. W. Alexander stayed close over the years as their recording and performing careers continued to intersect, and J.W. was in a position to observe that something heretofore unimaginable in the realm of gospel was happening: the world was beginning to beat a path to Sam Cooke's door. Certainly it had occurred that gospel singers had forsaken the church before (Dinah Washington is a good case in point), and certainly the glittering rewards of the material world had always beckoned. But there were two reasons why the gospel stars were generally impervious to temptation. One was, of course, faith; man, it was generally believed, could not serve two masters, and forsaking the church represented the gravest profanation of trust. Reinforcing faith was the popularity of gospel music itself. In the late '40s and early '50s, gospel, if not quite as popular as rhythm and blues, could certainly invite comparison and in fact played many of the same arenas, filled most of the same halls that jazz and r&b stars of the day were playing. With the coming of rock 'n' roll all of this changed. The r&b explosion of 1953 and 1954 *proved* that black artists could reach a white audience; the success of groups like the Dominoes and the Orioles in taking a strictly gospel approach, and then of Ray Charles, who actually translated church standards into secular hits, created a new reality in which it was clear that while white teenagers might very well buy "I Got a Woman" in great numbers, they would *never* buy the spiritual on which "I Got a Woman" was based.

In 1956, as J. W. Alexander tells it, Sam Cooke wanted a new car, and "some girl was trying to turn him, you know, trying to make a pimp out of him." Meanwhile Roy Hamilton's manager, Bill Cook, was hot on his trail, and Atlantic Records was trying to sign him to a pop contract. A less cosmopolitan individual than J. W. Alexander might have been affronted (and indeed many were), but to J.W. this was the break he had been looking for all along. "Well, you see, I had sung pop myself. And to me it seemed like there was a void that existed at that particular time. There was one boy, Sonny Til with the Orioles, that had been very big with the young black girls. In Sam Cooke, though, I saw even more of a potential, because he had a certain thing going that Sonny didn't have, you know, he was more handsome, I thought, and even in the churches the young girls would scream, the old women would scream as if he was singing about love. So I went to Art [Rupe] and I said, 'Art, this kid wants

Rick Hall, Bumps Blackwell, Little Richard, early '70s.
(Courtesy of Rick Hall)

to sing pop. He's ready, and I've been working with him, and he's damn good.'
Well, Art didn't seem too interested, and I said, 'If you don't do it, someone
else will.' Art says, 'But I'm selling records on the Soul Stirrers.' Then Bumps
Blackwell [an r&b veteran from Seattle who had recently taken over a&r duties
at Specialty] chimes in and says, 'Well, I'll record him.' So that's how it
happened."

Rupe remained dubious, but Bumps went ahead and recorded him anyway. The first record, "Lovable," came out under the name of Dale Cook in
1957 and was an almost literal transcription of one of Sam's latest Soul Stirrers
recordings, a low-key revision of the gospel number (it might almost have been
the same instrumental track) with lightweight pop lyrics substituted. It sold
about 25,000 copies, enough for Rupe to let the experiment continue. The next
session, though, was the one that finished Sam's career at Specialty.

Art Rupe, according to J.W., was having personal problems at the time
and wasn't thinking too clearly. "It wasn't that he didn't believe in Sam. It was
just that he thought Sam should have been screaming like Little Richard. That
was all he knew about rock 'n' roll."

"Art would never let us make that crossover from gospel to pop. [He] was always worried about the reaction from the religious people," Bumps Blackwell explained to writer Charlie Gillett. "I wanted to record Sam Cooke doing pop. I was sure he could be as big as the Platters, [so] I arranged a [second] session. . . . Art came into the studio in the middle of the session, saw the white girl backup group I had in there, and he wanted to break it up." "He just exploded," says arranger René Hall. "Bumps and myself were running an arrangement through on 'Summertime.' [He said], 'Who the hell is going to buy Gershwin and opera and all that stuff?!'"

The upshot was that he let both Bumps *and* Sam go. Just two weeks after he had signed Sam to a solo contract, in June of 1957, Art Rupe assigned the contract and the entire session (eight songs) to Bumps in exchange for back royalties. Bumps took the tapes to Keen, a little label that was just being started as a kind of hobby by airplane parts manufacturer John Siamas. In an unusual package deal Bumps became a&r director for the new label and manager of its only star, while J. W. Alexander, too, left Specialty, briefly recast his group as the Travelers, and went pop himself (though without much success) on Keen's Andex subsidiary.

The decision for Sam had not been an easy one. The release of "Lovable" under a transparent pseudonym in the early part of 1957 had fooled no one, and the reaction of the gospel audience had reached a crescendo of bitterness and outrage. He continued to sing with the Soul Stirrers until May, but "he was being ostracized, really," says J.W. "I remember one night we met in Tuscaloosa, and the whispering campaign was really going on, and I told him, 'Hold your goddam head up and go out there and sing.'" Another time, just after the initial appearance of the Dale Cook single, J.W. had emphatically declared, "'Sam, I don't see how you can miss. But you can't stick your head in the sand like an ostrich. You've just got to be Sam Cooke as you are.' I went on to tell him about the little white girls, who had their heroes, and the little black girls, who really didn't have anyone they could relate to. I told him it was important for him to make a decision to be Sam Cooke and not worry about whether he would be able to rejoin the Soul Stirrers."

In the end the decision was made for him. After his first release on Keen there could no longer be any question of Sam Cooke's direction. The first release (from that fateful Specialty session) was "You Send Me."

It came out in the fall of 1957 and quickly went to #1—not just on the rhythm and blues charts but on the pop charts, too. This was an achievement that Ray Charles, for example, would not even come close to matching for another three years (with "Georgia on My Mind"), and it established Sam Cooke both as a commercial artist and as an original pop stylist as well. Credited to Sam's brother, L.C. (Sam was still contracted as a writer to Specialty's publishing company), "You Send Me" showcased the qualities of an undeniably great singer, albeit a great singer holding himself in check. The phrasing was distinctively Sam's own, the ululating "Whoa-oh-oh" established an immediate identity, there was the same ethereal beauty (if more of the crooner's romantic impersonality) that showed up on all the gospel sides. The lyric was focused on the simple but believable colloquialism of the title ("A song should have a lilting melody," said Sam several years later in a rare interview with journalist-photographer Don Paulsen, "and be easily remembered. I use phrases people say every day. A repetitious phrase helps put the story across."). What really put the story across, though, was the singer's delivery, the same lilting, swinging, soulful (if restrained) manner that had imparted such a unique quality to the gospel sides. It was this "sweet approach," says Jerry Wexler, who had sought in vain to sign Cooke to the Atlantic label, that made Sam "the best singer who ever lived, no contest. When I listen to him, I still can't believe the things that he did. It's always fresh and amazing to me; he has control, he could play with his voice like an instrument, his melisma, which was his personal brand—I mean, nobody else could do it—everything about him was perfection. A perfect case."

J.W. had sensed it all along. From the time that "You Send Me" hit the charts there was no looking back for Sam Cooke. In the wake of its success Art Rupe overdubbed a demo that Sam had left at Specialty, "I'll Come Running Back to You," and it went to #7 r&b, Top 30 pop. Keen quickly put out two more singles, and *they* made the charts. Over the next couple of years Sam put out in succession such lightweight but durable pop material as "Everybody Likes to Cha Cha Cha," "Only Sixteen," and "Wonderful World," all written or cowritten by Sam Cooke, the last two of which continue to be recorded with some regularity to this day. The story of Sam Cooke might very well have continued in this fashion, a show business success story typical in its way, had it not been for two factors: the magnitude of the talent involved, which simply could not be contained by such material, and the business acumen, or ambition, of J.W. Alexander.

J.W. had seen the future. Sam's success, and that of Ray Charles and all the others, indicated that a new day was not just coming, it was already here. What better way to take part in it than to participate in the profits? Not long after "You Send Me" hit, J.W. made a move in this direction by setting up his own publishing company, Kags Music, named after the stepfather of the Pilgrim Travelers' new lead singer Lou Rawls. Just how radical a step this was (it amounted to taking the first step toward seizing the means of production) is evidenced by the response of Fats Domino and Little Willie John, two of the biggest stars of the day, when J.W. tried to explain to them what he was up to. "I'll never forget their reaction. I was in the barbershop of the Watkins Hotel on Adams near Western, and I was trying to tell Fats about publishing, and he looked at me like, 'Who is this stupid nigger?,' like I was something with a tail on it. They were laughing at me. They were doing all right without knowing anything about publishing. They didn't want to know anything about it – so

Sam Cooke at work. (Courtesy of Bill Millar)

naturally I clammed up. But Sam, he always had a lot of confidence in me. He knew I had this publishing company, and one day he says to me, 'Alex, let's have breakfast.' He said, 'Tell me about this publishing, you know.' I said, 'Man, I ain't got nothing going, but I got this company.' He said, 'Who's in your company?' 'Nobody. Just me.' He said, 'What about us being partners?' We shook hands, and I said, 'I'll build us the biggest fucking publishing company in the world.' Just like that. On a handshake."

That was the final forging of the Sam Cooke-J. W. Alexander relationship ("I wasn't his manager, I was his *partner*"), and it carried with it additional reverberations. J.W. was now not only Sam's champion and friend ("For a long time I was just trying to help him because I liked the guy"); he was pitching Sam's songs and his own at every available opportunity, pulling Jackie Wilson into the nearest men's room to try out a new song on him, making contacts and gaining a knowledge of the industry that he had never had before. In 1959, when Sam had been on Keen for not quite two years, he and J.W. became concerned that he was not being given an accurate royalty accounting, a suspicion which, if it had turned out to be untrue, would have put Keen in a class by itself among record companies. On behalf of Kags, J.W. challenged the statement and demanded an audit. When all parties involved met at the lawyer's office (there was only one lawyer, because the same man was handling not only the business of both Kags and Keen but J.W.'s divorce as well), J.W. turned back the check which was offered, folded the statement, put it in his pocket, and declared that it was evidence. "I told the lawyer, 'You keep the fucking check.' He must have tried for an hour to get me to take it."

The upshot was that Sam split with his manager, Bumps Blackwell, Keen was actually put out of business (the various lawsuits brought about a judgment that eventually forced a sheriff's sale), and Sam Cooke ended up on RCA through his new manager, Jess Rand.

The new label was an odd choice in one respect. In 1960 the company had virtually no black artists and little credibility in the r&b market, but there was no question in J. W. Alexander's mind that Sam should hook up with a major label ("The majors were so strong, so predominant in the business; the independents could have a hit, but they couldn't sustain an artist's career"), and Sam and J.W., it should be obvious by now, were not taking the short view. From the outset Sam was assigned to staff producers Hugo Peretti and Luigi Creatore. Their first record, "Teenage Sonata," was as insipid as its title would suggest, and their first album, *Cooke's Tour,* a collection of "travel songs," was just as grave a misreading of their artist's talents. They cut *Hits of the '50s* next, then an album that included "Twilight on the Trail," but after that their role seemed to diminish to something like an advisory capacity with a permanent home-grown production team in place: René Hall (the arranger for "You Send Me," who had been bandleader for Billy Ward and the Dominoes for years) did all the arranging and contracted the musicians; Mills Brothers alumnus Cliff White played guitar on virtually every side that Sam Cooke ever cut; Sam and J.W. contributed songs and ideas, collaborating on a number of efforts, drawing on the Kags roster for others; RCA engineers Al Schmitt and Dave Hassinger more often than not were at the controls. The material was not really all that different from the Keen sides—the same mix of sentimental standards and teenage soul, catchy originals and light classics. This was what was perceived as the market, this was the strategy of diversification that everyone around Sam Cooke, from Hugo and Luigi to J. W. Alexander, embraced, and if it did not necessarily create great art ("I'm not even interested in his pop records," declares Jerry Wexler today), it created a climate in which Sam Cooke could become not only the black teenaged girl's idol but quite possibly the white teenager's as well. With his third RCA single release, the graceful soft-focus social commentary of "Chain Gang," Sam finally clicked, both artistically and commercially, reaching the #2 spot on the pop charts in August 1960.

J.W. meanwhile was pursuing his own strategy of diversification. In 1959 Art Rupe, who had lost much of his interest in the record business with Little

J. W. Alexander, Lou Adler, Sam Cooke, Zelda Samuels, 1962.
(Courtesy of J. W. Alexander)

Richard's first retirement from the world to study for the ministry, gave the
Soul Stirrers their release, and J.W. suggested that he and Sam should record
them independently. "So Sam and I went over and talked to the Soul Stirrers
at the Dunbar Hotel. And I said, 'Look, fellows, we don't have any money—
we got just enough money to record you and get your record played.' Then
Sam and I sat down and wrote 'Stand By Me Father' for them—you know the
Ben E. King song? This was the original—and we made a demo and took a
plane to Chicago, did it at Universal, the top studio, got the best musicians,
really topflight musicians, and did it with Johnnie Taylor singing lead. Only
thing was, Johnnie kept saying 'Jesus,' and I kept trying to get him not to
(because I was thinking about having some kind of crossover record, you know),
and finally I got kind of vexed, and Sam said, "Oh, let him go,' and we put
the record out, and it did pretty good."

   To a lot of people's astonishment the label continued to thrive, or at least to
put out strong, good-quality releases. Not everyone was prepared to see a black
entrepreneur and a popular singing idol show some expertise in the business,
and the fact that Alexander was able to get credit from hard-boiled distributors
on the strength of his word alone shocked not a few. But this success only
whetted J.W.'s appetite for expansion. In addition to the record label (dubbed
SAR for Sam and Alex Records), Kags Music, and a production company, J.W.
now set up an ASCAP publishing company named Malloy ("It sounded like
an establishment name"), plus a second label, Derby, and artists' management
concern, and—just to be ready for all eventualities—SAR Pictures, too. This

was still a "hole-in-the-wall" operation; it was still pretty much a one-man show, and more of a dream in many ways than a reality. But it was a dream, like Motown, a virtual contemporary, ahead of its time, and one that fueled a vision. J.W. was just hitting his stride.

"I was really fired up. I'd go to the club at night and get home at four or five in the morning. Then the distributor would call early next morning, and I'd wake up: 'SAR Records!' Then I'd call the record in to the pressing plant, and they'd make the shipment. I had ready-forms that I'd do my billing on; I didn't have any kind of calculator, just sit on the floor, man, with pencil and paper and ready-forms, and that was our accounting! And we were in business for about a year before we could really get the books set up, and when we did, Sam's accountant was so astonished because he could only find two mistakes—and I had thirty-five distributors! I think I had something I wanted to prove, and, you know, I had so much confidence in Sam."

SAR put out releases on the Soul Stirrers, Johnnie "Two-Voice" Morisette, Johnnie Taylor, the Sims Twins (the clear precursors of Sam and Dave), and the Valentinos, signed as the gospel group the Womack Brothers, whose 1964 release, "It's All Over Now," became a big hit for the Rolling Stones and whose lead singer, Bobby Womack, went on to become a star in his own right. All these artists without exception were gospel singers, or former gospel singers persuaded in every case (except the Soul Stirrers) to try the same route as Sam Cooke. Even more to the point, these recordings seemed to serve as an outlet for a side of Sam which, whether because of RCA's sense of propriety or his own, did not find expression in Cooke's work on the major label. The Sims Twins, for example, recorded the Cooke-Alexander composition "That's Where It's At" over a year before Sam did, and—J.W. admits—their version beat Cooke's. Johnnie Morisette did the same thing with Sam's "Meet Me at Mary's Place" (it became "Meet Me at the Twistin' Place"), and Johnnie Taylor cut a beautiful early version of "Rome Wasn't Built in a Day." In general the SAR versions were grittier, more down-to-earth, less "pale" than the more pop-oriented RCA arrangements, despite the presence of much the same personnel. Perhaps it was the producer. "My future lies more in creating music and records than in being a nightclub performer," announced Sam in a 1963 publicity release which in many ways may have mirrored his true feelings ("He loved producing. He wanted to give young artists a chance," says J.W., "and we felt like we could do things ourselves that were taboo to a company like RCA."). "Cooke," continued the story, "like Bobby Darin, who recently stated he was through with the nitery business, said he would rather be the creative producer in the control room than be the worn-out singer in the bistro spotlight. . . ."

What it all added up to, I think, was not that Sam Cooke missed his true vocation and wanted to be a businessman but that he and J.W. were tickled and intrigued by the idea that they could do something that everyone told them was beyond their reach, that they could play a much more far-reaching role than the one that was laid out for them. Sales never mirrored artistic worth, and Kags, the publishing company, probably financed SAR, which may have been more of a hobby in a way than a business. They kept SAR going, though, first class all the way ("We used the top arrangers, top musicians, our first album cover was four-color!"); they teased their distributors with the idea that Sam Cooke might eventually wind up on the label and in fact in 1961 briefly put out one of his recordings before selling the entire Keen lot to RCA. In early 1963 Sam engaged music business accountant Allen Klein on the basis of his self-proclaimed reputation for finding money for the artist in undeclared record royalties that "you never even knew you had" (he had begun with an audit of Atlantic for Bobby Darin, which eventually led to Darin's leaving the label). The upshot was a new contract with RCA, including $119,000 in back royalties and $450,000 more over a period of five years, control of his entire catalogue, and a new manager (Klein). This only reinforced the direction in which he was already heading, as earlier in 1963 he released a beautiful album of blues, *Night Beat*, which, while still nominally a Hugo and Luigi production, was for the first time a fully conceived work, not just a random collection of tunes. Then in January 1964 *Ain't That Good News* came out as the first production of Tracey Limited (Allen Klein's production company) under the new contract; it was Sam's most ambitious work to date, like *Night Beat* a masterpiece of vocal nuance and inflection.

Everything seemed to be looking up for Sam Cooke. In July 1964, on the strength of Klein's influence, and as part of his plan to break Sam into a wider market (this was certainly part of Sam and J.W.'s plan all along, too), Sam played the Copa for the second time. He had originally played there six years earlier on a disastrous date headlined by Jewish dialect comedian Myron Cohen. To J.W. the earlier date had been symptomatic: Sam was "just another little colored boy," patronized by Cohen's "schwartzeh" jokes and rejected by an audience that was attuned to Sammy Davis Jr. and Nat King Cole. He had worked up an act for the occasion and even took tap lessons. "He looks like a little doll, doesn't he?" said his tap coach approvingly to J.W. "Yeah, that's just what he looks like," J.W. had responded, "like a fucking doll. He sure don't look like Sam Cooke."

This time he went on his own terms. Klein rented a 20-by-100 foot billboard above Times Square proclaiming "Sam's the biggest Cooke in town," partly, Klein says, to announce his client's arrival in a big way but also to ensure simply that he would show up. The earlier Copa date had been traumatic in Klein's view and led to a withdrawal from anything even resembling the supper-club circuit. Klein needn't have worried, J.W. says. Sam Cooke at this point was a fully confident performer. J.W. dates his newfound confidence to

Chain Gang, with Hugo and Luigi. (Courtesy of Gregg Geller)

a 1962 tour of Europe, when Sam for the first time applied his gospel training to the pop arena.

"You see, just before we went over there, I went to see him in New York, and there was something about the show that I thought lacked something. Sam was standing around a little too much. I thought he wasn't generating enough energy, and I told him that. He said, 'You're right, you ought to stay on the road with me.' So I kept after him to keep moving, create some excitement. And one thing that helped him to see how it worked was Little Richard was on the same bill with him in England, and he could see what was happening, how no matter how Sam killed the house, Richard would always come back with that energizing approach. Then we came back home, put together a new act, and [when we] went on tour with Jackie Wilson in 1964, Henry Wynn, the promoter, says to me, 'Last time Sam and Jackie worked together, Jackie kind of cut Sam up. Will Sam want to work with Jackie?' I said, 'Oh, yes.' Man, we cut Jackie up just night after night. Before him, behind him, whatever. Jackie said, 'Man, you guys are killing me, what the fuck did you do?' But it was really because Sam had finally gotten into doing his gospel thing, you know, that real fervent approach. Before that I felt he was too sterile—is that a good word?—but after having gone to Europe, where we could talk night after night and he could try things and not be afraid and see if they worked, *then* he could really see the advantage of energy, he could really get confidence in just doing his thing."

Both Allen Klein and J.W. tell the story of Sam going to the Copa shortly before his own booking to see Nat King Cole play. "We walked into the lounge upstairs," recalls J.W., "and them chicks was doing the twist and shaking their butts in the lounge upstairs, and I said, 'Sam, these same people are going to be downstairs. Nat might not give it to them, but they like it just the same.' So we went downstairs and heard Nat, and Nat was good, and Sam said, 'Book me in here. I'll stand this Copa on its ears.' And when he finally played there, man, those chicks were popping, it was almost like a sex act, man, like he was beating up on them to get an orgasm, and when he came back upstairs after the first show, I told him, 'Lighten up, buddy. You got 'em,' like it was really fun."

The music on the album that was recorded that week bears out both J.W.'s description and the dilemma that Sam Cooke still found himself in. "Cooke dressed impeccably," wrote British correspondent Ray Coleman of an interview just before the time of the Copa engagement. "He also spoke every word as if he was delivering the presidential address. He had an infectious smile, enormous charm, and a highly developed sense of humor." "In interviews he didn't give very much of himself," says Allen Klein, "because he didn't know what he wanted to say." You can hear this duality on the record. It was supper-club soul in the best sense of the word, achieving a level of savoir faire and uptown class that other soul singers like Joe Tex, Solomon Burke, and Otis Redding could only aspire to. There was a musicality to Sam's laugh, a good-humored, slightly sardonic element to his hipness, an impossible ease to the way he could toss off the lyrics to even the corniest of songs (just as with Elvis Presley, another prisoner of RCA and high commercial expectations, after a while it didn't even seem to matter what song he was singing), and an apparent delight with both himself and his surroundings that allowed him to give twist demonstrations and, winking at his audience, toss off such bon mots as "Observation, baby" with knowing sophistication. But even in the face of his apparent confidence, there is also evident a real ambivalence, a discomfort with his assigned role, an embarrassment perhaps at what "a little colored boy" had to go through to gain the attention of a Copa audience, and an edge to his hip hauteur that borders on self-contempt running through the performance of such songs as "Bill Bailey (Won't You Please Come Home)" and "Frankie and Johnny."

One has only to listen to the live album that was recorded with saxophonist King Curtis at the black Harlem Square Club in Miami in January 1963 to sense the difference between the two Sam Cookes. For one thing the repertoire scarcely even overlaps, despite the fact that the dates are only eighteen months apart, and none of the hits from the intervening time are included on the Copa album. Of the fifteen- or twenty-minute sequence that concludes the Harlem Square Club show (the staple of Sam Cooke's live performance when he went up against Jackie Wilson or played one-nighters on the chitlin circuit), only "You Send Me" is included on the Copa set, and then in a version so eviscerated, so pale compared with the Florida performance that it seems almost like a different song. The audience participation in Miami, the way in which Sam not only teases the crowd but actually orchestrates its response, is largely absent at the Copa, though the end result ("the little girls getting hots in their pants," as J.W. says) may well be the same. And Sam Cooke's voice, which on record took on such a polite, well-bred tone all through the Keen and RCA years, here suggests an older, wiser version of the Sam Cooke of the Soul Stirrers, a little more worn, a litle more frayed around the edges perhaps when the singer really bears down on a note—but he bears down on the note nonetheless; like the twenty-year-old true believer, this performer prizes emotional substance above mere beauty. Here is the harsher, grittier Sam Cooke of the SAR sound; in the words of a number of people I know who saw him playing the clubs or r&b revues, this is "the real Sam Cooke." To these dyed-in-the-wool Sam Cooke fans there is nothing surprising about what is revealed in this live set; it was the studio recordings that never sounded right. To RCA there must have been much the same perception in reverse. The record was never released.

Perhaps too much should not be made of this. *Live at the Copa* was not only commercially successful, it was one of the most influential soul albums of all time. It was the other side of James Brown's apocalyptic 1963 *Live at the Apollo,* the album that inspired Otis Redding as much as anything he ever heard, a tribute to J.W.'s long-preached virtues of civility, perseverance, and good diction (articulation, according to J.W., was the most important distinction between gospel—which could succeed on the basis of feeling alone—and pop). And it established Sam Cooke once and for all in the forefront of the new soul scene.

From Allen Klein's and J.W.'s point of view, too, the Copa date marked a watershed in Sam Cooke's career. In early 1964 he appeared on the *Tonight* show, debuting two songs from his new album and exchanging polite banter with his host; at the conclusion of the first Liston-Clay fight in Miami he was introduced by his young admirer, the brand-new heavyweight champion of the world, as "the World's Greatest Rock 'n' Roll Singer." Just after the Copa he did the pilot for *Shindig,* network television's first real attempt to capture the youth music market since *The Dick Clark Show.* Klein had prestigious Las Vegas, Miami, and Atlantic City bookings lined up for early 1965. Musically, both J.W. and Allen Klein agree, Sam was taking an increasingly serious view of his recording, because now that he was finally established, "we

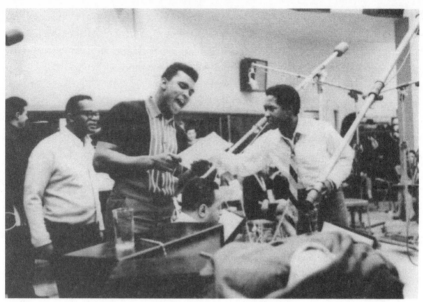

In the studio with Muhammad Ali. (Michael Ochs Archives)

felt that he needed more weight," says J.W. "We felt that light shit wouldn't sustain him."

Sam continued to write all the time; his very prolificness (he left over 120 songs in the Kags catalog) may well have guaranteed that a certain percentage of his output was bound to hit. Sometimes he would take another song for inspiration or ride on a developing trend. "Shake," for example, played off the success of Bobby Freeman's "C'mon and Swim." He wrote while watching TV, he wrote in cars, on planes, and at parties. "We'd be creating," says J.W., laughing, "while we were partying." But he wrote his greatest song, "A Change Is Gonna Come," only after hearing Bob Dylan's "Blowing in the Wind" for the first time. Never much of a militant, not even political himself (though he was interested in the Muslims around Cassius Clay and did spend a good deal of time with Malcolm X), Sam was taken aback by the message of the song. "He said, 'Alex, I got to write something. Here's a white boy writing a song like this. . . .' That was what motivated him to write 'A Change Is Gonna Come.' Which, you know, really was a civil rights song. 'Cause in the album version there's a verse that's edited out of the single, 'I go to the movies and I go downtown/But someone's always telling me/Don't hang around. . . . ' And everything in that song really had a meaning that you could refer to."

"A Change Is Gonna Come" was included initially on the *Good News* album in early 1964; Sam sang the song on the *Tonight* show, but it is not surprising that it was left off of the Copa album. Message aside, it is, along with the equally gospel-influenced "Bring It On Home to Me," the most direct of

Sam Cooke's pop compositions, certainly the most elevated, with a soaring melody line linked to lyrics which, as J.W. says, are as heavily freighted with meaning as any of the gospel sides. What direction this would have portended for the future, whether Sam Cooke would have headed for Vegas, radically refashioned his image and his art, or, more likely, maintained the balancing act that had become his career is uncertain, for "A Change Is Gonna Come" remained a kind of cult item, buried in the album until after Sam Cooke's death, when it was finally released as the B side of a single and in time became his monument.

In October, Sam took a screen test, reading a part for a new Norman Jewison film, with, J.W. says, "impressive results." In November J.W. went off the road to take up the business again; "my office had been in my briefcase all that time, my secretary, Zelda Samuels, was in charge." J.W. was preparing to produce a new Johnnie Taylor session, which he hoped would recapitulate the success of "Rome Wasn't Built in a Day." On December 7 J.W. recorded Taylor, with Harold Battiste arranging, at the RCA studios in Hollywood. Sam met them after the session and was elated with the results. "So he said, 'Let's take Johnnie out and get him drunk,' and we went down to the California Club. Soon as we begin to relax, he says, 'Well, okay, Alex, I'll see you at the office tomorrow afternoon.'

"Well, he didn't come in the next day, and he didn't come in the day after because he had a cold, but then he called that afternoon [of the tenth] and I said, 'Why don't you meet me down at the club?' It got to be around twelve-thirty that night and he still hadn't shown, and there was a guy outside selling Christmas trees, and I said to the guy that owned the club, Mambo Maxie, I said, 'If Sam comes, you tell him I bought my baby (my daughter, Adrian, was just two months old) a Christmas tree.' I said, 'I'll see him at the office,' just like that, and I went on home.

"Next day my wife woke me up and said her mother had just called her and said Sam Cooke had been shot. I said, 'Get the baby, and let's go out to the house.' I was really in shock."

The details were so sordid that many refused to believe the story as it was reported. Sam had evidently picked up a young Eurasian model named Elisa Boyer at a restaurant where he was dining with friends. After a few drinks he took her to the Hacienda, a three-dollar-a-night motel on Figueroa, where, according to the woman's testimony, he registered, then dragged her to a room. After pulling her sweater off and ripping her dress, the courtly entertainer went into the bathroom, whereupon Miss Boyer exited with his pants. Next Cooke showed up at the night manager's door clad only in an overcoat and demanding to know where his companion was. When the night manager, Bertha Lee Franklin, denied any knowledge of her whereabouts, Cooke went off to the parking lot and started up his Ferrari, then evidently thought better of it and returned to the night manager's door, where he kept shouting, "Where's the girl?" and banging on the door. Eventually he knocked in the door and angrily attacked Mrs. Franklin until she was so frightened she grabbed a pistol and started shooting. "He said, 'Lady, you shot me,'" Mrs. Franklin testified. "He ran into me again. I started fighting again with a stick. The first time I hit him, it broke."

He died with a single bullet in his body. "Shots Kill Pop Idol!" headlines screamed the next day. The funeral drew over 200,000 fans to view his body, first in Chicago, then in Los Angeles, where Lou Rawls and Bobby "Blue" Bland sang at the service; when gospel singer Bessie Griffin could not go on, *Ebony* reported, "blues singer Ray Charles stepped in from the audience to sing and play 'Angels Keep Watching Over Me.'" There was an orgy of grief, a great deal of feeling among church people that Sam's death had come as a judgment, and, in a time of assassinations and assassination conspiracy theories, considerable speculation that centered mainly on the idea that Sam Cooke had been cut down for his very pride and overweening ambition, that the Man was not going to let a nigger, any nigger, get too uppitty. Allen Klein hired a private detective but reluctantly concluded that the official story was most likely true. In the immediate aftermath of his death Sam's widow, Barbara, married Bobby Womack, lead singer of the Valentinos, and after unsuccessfully challenging J.W.'s control of Kags and SAR ("Sam and I were so fucking close," suggests J.W. regretfully, "there was bound to be a certain resentment"), sold out her share in the corporation to Hugo and Luigi. For his part J.W. was heartbroken. "It was just a waste of life, is how I looked at it. The fact that he died in a $3 hotel in a $14,000 car didn't mean shit to me, man. This was my partner, this was my friend, a kid brother, you know—and I think that I represented something to him that he could look up to as a man. Sam's untimely death kind of blew away my dreams." J.W. shut down SAR, gave all the artists their releases, and after Allen Klein bought out Hugo and Luigi eventually sold Klein his half of the catalog for $375,000. He achieved intermittent success in similar mentoring roles over the years, groomed Lou Rawls for stardom, attempted to revive Little Richard's and Solomon Burke's careers, and took on Willie Hutch as a protégé, but always the point of reference was Sam Cooke and the unique alliance they had forged.

"Rhythm and blues," pronounced Sam Cooke to journalist-photographer Don Paulsen on the eve of the Copa engagement, "is the most fervent sound in pop music. It appeals to kids when they're young and they expect a lot out of life. When a person gets older, he understands there's only so much to be gotten out of life. He doesn't have to have excitement all the time. He can take things with less intensity, hence his appreciation of jazz."

In the end there was almost no one in the world of soul music who was not affected by Sam Cooke's sound. Solomon Burke, Wilson Pickett, Joe Tex,

With XKE. (Courtesy of Joe McEwen)

Bobby "Blue" Bland, Smokey Robinson, Aretha Franklin, Al Green, Teddy Pendergrass—in each you can hear echoes of Sam Cooke, sometimes very loud ones. In the wake of his death a host of imitators sprang up, singers like Louis Williams of the Ovations, letter-perfect in the style, or Willie Hightower, who paid tribute to Sam with an unforced medley of his hits. Almost from the day of his death there has been talk of a movie, and various casting ideas have been floated, but in the twenty years that have passed no movie has gone into production, and most of the proposed leads are now too old to play the part. Perhaps the general sentiment was best expressed by soul DJ the Magnificent Montague, at the conclusion of a bantering radio interview with Sam. After trading verses and definitions of soul with the bemused singer, Montague, frequently given to poetics himself, soothingly recited to his audience: "And when the humming's over/ And time finds its soul/ All I can say to you, darlings/ Sam Cooke's yours/ He'll never grow old."

The Bishop seduces the world with his voice
Sweat strangles mute eyes
As insinuations gush out through a hydrant of sorrow
Dreams, a world never seen
Moulded on Africa's anvil, tempered down home
Documented in cries and wails
Screaming to be ignored, crooning to be heard
Throbbing from the gutter
On Saturday night
Silver offering only
The Right Reverend's back in town
Don't it make you feel all right?

—Julian Bond, "The Bishop of Atlanta: Ray Charles"

Hey, y'all, tell everybody Ray Charles is in town
I got a dollar and a quarter, and I'm just rarin' to clown. . . .

—"Let the Good Times Roll"

SAM COOKE WAS THE FIRST GOSPEL STAR TO cross over, certainly, but it was Ray Charles, as we know, who started it all. Not only did he precede Sam Cooke chronologically (although he was born in 1930, only a year before Cooke, he started recording in 1948 at the age of eighteen), it was Charles who gave Cooke and an entire generation the courage to make the leap into the temporal world. If you listen to the clunkety rhythms of "I Got a Woman" today, it's hard to imagine the impact that it had in 1954 and 1955 for blacks *and* whites, for a young Elvis Presley and an only slightly older Sam Cooke, and for nearly every singer, writer, and producer that I have interviewed for this book. The very stratagem of adapting a traditional gospel song, putting secular lyrics to it, and then delivering it with all the attendant fanfare of a pentecostal service was, simply, staggering; it was like a blinding flash of light in which the millennium, all of a sudden and unannounced, had arrived. "I couldn't get over it," recalled Bumps Blackwell (not yet Sam Cooke's producer at the time of the record's release) to rock historian Charlie Gillett. "He'd taken a gospel song that Alex Bradford had recorded for Specialty and made it into an r&b number!" That, said Blackwell in a story that differs from J. W. Alexander's version only in emphasis, is what gave him the inspiration to cut Cooke pop. It was from that point on that Ray Charles acquired his near-iconic status in the black community, and for the next ten years his success was without artistic or commercial parallel in

R. C. Robinson, Seattle, circa 1950. (Courtesy of Dave "Daddy Cool" Booth)

the business. "Recording Ray Charles," said Jerry Wexler after the fact, "is like putting a meter on fresh air—ain't nothing to it, just open up the pots." To Frank Sinatra he was "the only genius in the business." To Ray Charles: "Art Tatum—he was a genius. And Einstein. Not me."

Ray Charles. The Legend. Black. Blind. A heroin addict for nearly two decades. A man who would always reject labels and could declare with some asperity in his autobiography, *Brother Ray,* "I never considered myself part of rock 'n' roll. I didn't believe that I was among the forerunners of the music, and I've never given myself a lick of credit for either inventing it or having anything to do with its birth. Cats like Chuck Berry and Little Richard and Bo Diddley . . . did some spirited music, and it broke through some thick barriers . . . [but] my stuff was more adult, filled with more despair than anything you'd associate with rock 'n' roll." A man who insists, "Every experience I've had—good and bad—has taught me something. I was born a poor boy in the South, I once fooled around with drugs, but all of it was like going to school—and I've tried to be a good student. I don't regret a damn thing."

Nearly everyone knows the rough outlines of his life. He was born Ray Charles Robinson in Albany, Georgia, in 1930, grew up in Greenville, Florida, where at six he started to lose his sight from glaucoma after traumatically watching his brother drown in the washtub their mother used for take-in laundry. At seven his parents enrolled him in the St. Augustine School for the Deaf and the Blind, where he learned to read and write music in Braille, score for big bands, and play piano, alto, organ, clarinet, and trumpet. His earliest musical influences were Chopin, Sibelius, Art Tatum, Artie Shaw, and Wylie Pitman, operator of Greenville's Red Wing Café, who encouraged the young "R.C." on piano. When he was fifteen, his mother died, leaving him alone in the world. He quit school, moved to Jacksonville, and began his professional career in music.

It must have been an unimaginably isolated childhood. Cut off from family and friends, increasingly distanced from the very images—of sunsets, of colors, of his mother's features—which linked him to the world of sight, Ray has often come across as aloof to others, but he characterizes himself as "sort of a shy person. I don't want to go bothering nobody. I keep to myself not

The Original Nat King Cole Trio, 1939. (Frank Driggs Collection)

because I don't like people, it's just my nature. See, I grew up as a kid, and I played a lot by myself, because the other kids—I'm not saying this is the case, and I'm not trying to psychoanalyze or nothing, I'm just trying to tell you the facts—the other kids, naturally, could see and play a lot of games by themselves that I couldn't participate in. So I learned to play and enjoy myself a lot, and I got used to it. You can get used to anything." World War II, which ended just about the time of his mother's death, was little more than a distant echo. "I can remember all the fuss about the Japanese bombing Pearl Harbor, and I said, What the fuck is that? I knew there was a war in Europe, but there wasn't nobody around to explain it."

What was real was the music. When he left school to go out on his own, he played first in a Count Basie-styled big band, then in a smaller Louis Jordan-type combo. In Tampa he joined a hillbilly group called the Florida Playboys and learned to yodel. Then, as now, he was open to *sounds*—classical, jazz, rocking, romantic, he refused to discriminate. At seventeen he took his savings of $600 and moved as far away as he could get—to Seattle, Washington. According to Quincy Jones, a fifteen-year-old prodigy on the local scene who met Charles shortly after his arrival (Quincy played in Bumps Blackwell's junior orchestra, for which Ray occasionally did the arranging), he was "like forty years old. He knew everything. He knew about ladies and music and life, because he was so independent."

In Seattle he quickly picked up the life he had led in Florida, gigging at places like the Elks Club, the Rocking Chair, the Black and Tan, forming a trio with a Florida friend, Gosady McGee, that was explicitly modeled on Nat King Cole's. It was at this time that he started using junk, not because anyone "did it to me," he has written. "I did it to myself. It wasn't society . . . it wasn't a pusher, it wasn't being blind or being black or being poor. It was all my doing." It was in Seattle, too, that he became Ray Charles, to avoid confusion with Sugar Ray Robinson, the great middleweight champ. In 1948 he made his first record, "Confession Blues," for Jack Lauderdale's Down Beat (later Swing Time) label. He was fined $600 by the Musician's Union for breaking a record-ing ban.

He went on to make more than forty sides for Lauderdale during the next four years, including a couple of fair-sized r&b hits, but there was no recogniz-able sound, there was no musical identity. Each one of the records evinces a precise enunciation, a cool, rather brittle presence, a precocious sophistication that is virtually indistinguishable from that of a Nat Cole or Charles Brown hit of the period. Ray admired Cole extravagantly for his "soft, sentimental, silky kind of a touch—and, of course, he could play the hell out of a piano," but there was no sense of direction to his own music, Ray insists. How could there be?

"I wasn't seeking nothing. I wasn't headed for nothing. All I wanted to do was to play music. Good music—I didn't give a shit what vein it was. All I knew was the music I liked was the music I felt, and how the shit can you explain a feeling? I mean, come on. I didn't know nothing about publishing, royalties, none of that. And I didn't care. It's like when I made my first record. I just wanted to make a record, because to me that was the epitome of success. I didn't care about nothing else. That's why I got into trouble with the union. I just knew what I liked and what I felt. Way before I became, pardon the expression, *the* Ray Charles, anywhere I could find good music being played, I just wanted to be a part of it."

That is what he did. The records that he made reflected popular taste. The music that he made reflected Ray Charles's insatiable appetite for sounds. When Atlantic Records bought up his contract for $2500 in 1952, he had proved his facility in a number of styles, acquired professional seasoning on the road with his labelmate, blues singer Lowell Fulson, shown his technical versatility by doing the charts for Fulson's eight-piece band—but by his own admission he still wasn't Ray Charles. By his own admission, too, he was not really knocked out about any aspect of his career. He had played the Apollo with Fulson, enjoyed a couple of Top 10 r&b hits, and signed with a record label that was obviously going places.

"But if you ask me, was I thrilled, was I ecstatic about any of it, the answer to that is no. I don't know how to put this to you," he will say, whether with accurate recall or with the benefit of hindsight it is impossible to determine. "I don't want to seem egotistical or immodest, but my career has been like a ladder to me—I know you think I'm trying to act like, trying to be some kind of a smartass, but I'm just trying to tell you the true me, man. I was always happy —don't misunderstand me. I don't mean to say that I wasn't thrilled, satisfied, and pleased. But I was never into that, 'Wow, this is the Apollo Theatre, this is New York!' That just was never it."

So far as thrills go, if there was anything outside the thrill of just playing the music, it would appear to have been the time he met Art Tatum at the Club Alabam. "He just happened to come in one night, and I was there, and somebody introduced me. You knew somebody had come in the place, 'cause the place hushed. That's something you don't see nowadays. Everybody talking and then —boom! You say, 'What the fuck—' and then everybody turn their heads, and then they know. You don't see that now. People don't give a fuck about nobody. When I met Art Tatum, I was in such awe I didn't know what to say. What do you say to God?"

The Atlantic Brain Trust, circa 1953: Ahmet Ertegun, Waxie Maxie Silverman,
Miriam Abramson, Nesuhi Ertegun, Jerry Wexler. (Courtesy of Jerry Wexler)

ATLANTIC RECORDS: A BRIEF INTERLUDE

Ray Charles and Atlantic Records—in history the two will be forever linked,
seen as part of the same inevitable progression in which each was needed to
complete the other's destiny. Ray Charles was the stylistic progenitor of soul
music, Atlantic the colossus that bestrode its little world. There is only one catch
to this neat formulation, as Ray Charles himself is at pains to point out: he was
not *the* Ray Charles at the time. Nor did the name of the label itself carry any
sort of mythic connotation.

Atlantic Records in 1952 was scarcely the power that it would one day
become, but it *was* a well-respected name in the parochial world of rhythm and
blues. Started in 1947 by Ahmet Ertegun (the twenty-four-year-old younger son
of the wartime Turkish ambassador to the United States) in partnership with
Herb Abramson, a New York jazz collector who was going to dental school
on the GI bill, Atlantic—like most of the independent labels—arose out of an
enthusiasm, a passion, really, for the music. Unlike many of its contemporaries,
though, Atlantic was nurtured by a combination of creative enterprise, cultural
sophistication, business acumen, and good taste that would have been rare in any
field but that has been practically unheard of in the music industry. Rather than

simply following whatever trend happened to pop up or flooding the market with an undifferentiated flow of "product," hoping that something would stick, Atlantic went its own idiosyncratic way, drawing on the jazz inclinations of both its owners, the gospel and r&b practical experience that Herb Abramson brought to the company (Abramson was one of the founders of both the National label, which had rejuvenated the careers of Big Joe Turner and Billy Eckstine, and Jubilee, which eventually signed the Orioles), and the persuasive powers and charm of Ahmet Ertegun, one of the wittiest and canniest men in the business.

A measure of both qualities can be seen in a story Phil Spector told *Rolling Stone* editor Jann Wenner of Ertegun's being confronted by a nameless r&b group about to sign with another label for more money. "One of them said, 'Shit, man, your contract ain't worth shit.' We were in a restaurant, and Ahmet looks around to make sure nobody'd hear us. The guy said, 'Mercury gonna give me seven per cent, you only give me five per cent. That's like jiveass.' Ahmet said, 'Not so loud.' . . . And I was just sitting back waiting for what Ahmet was going to say to this cat. The guy has the Mercury contract with him, and Ahmet knows he's trapped, and we're all sittin' around, and Ahmet hit him with a line: Ahmet said, "Man, listen, man, you know what? I gonna give you fifteen per cent, but I ain't gonna pay you.' The guy said, 'What?' Ahmet said, 'That's what they gonna do. They gonna give you seven per cent, but they not gonna pay you, and I gonna give you five per cent and pay you. Now that's a big difference, isn't it?' The guy said, 'That's right—never thought of it that way. That makes a lot of sense. I'm gonna sign with you, Ahmet, I gonna sign with you, Ahmet.' "

Thus was business conducted, when there was business to conduct. It was an off-the-cuff, seat-of-the-pants operation in the early days: musicians were scouted on the spot; sessions were called when there was money available; the Atlantic offices were situated in the same sixty-dollar-a-month apartment at the Jefferson Hotel on Fifty-sixth Street in New York where Ahmet Ertegun made his home. The earliest sessions were more notable for the learning experience than for the results; perhaps the most significant event to occur in the first year came when Ahmet and Herb Abramson happened to meet twenty-two-year-old Tommy Dowd at their second session at the Apex recording studio, where Dowd had just gone to work as an engineer. Dowd, a classically trained musician/physicist whose father was a concertmaster and mother was an opera singer, would engineer nearly every one of the important Atlantic dates for the next twenty–five years and earn the ultimate accolade from Jerry Wexler, who often declared, "Nobody's indispensable except Dowd—and he can be replaced."

In 1949, after a spate of jazz and jump band releases that went nowhere, Atlantic had its first national hit with a typically oddball offering, a rerecording

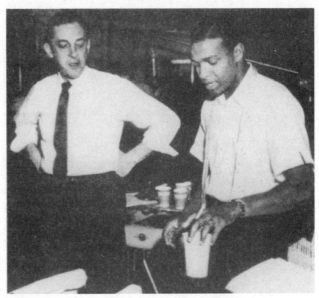

Herb Abramson and Clyde McPhatter. (Courtesy of Charlie Gillett)

of a novelty blues by Brownie McGhee's brother, Stick, called "Drinkin' Wine Spo-Dee-O-Dee," which established the kind of downhome sound with a sophisticated twist that subsequently became the Atlantic trademark. Also in 1949 Atlantic signed Ruth Brown, a band and nightclub singer whose preference was for Billie Holiday and Sarah Vaughan material, and transformed her into a national mania as "Miss Rhythm." This was a process that would often be repeated over the years, the trick of turning an uptown singer funky or doing just the reverse, of providing what Jerry Wexler later termed "the aesthetic rub." In the words of George Trow, Ahmet's biographer, Ahmet "did not seek to reproduce an older music exactly; rather he sought to introduce black musicians of the day to black musical modes older and more powerful than the ones they knew."

The details of this process were further refined when on their second Southern field trip Ahmet and Herb Abramson took Jesse Stone, Atlantic's chief arranger, along with them. Stone, a longtime black bandleader, songwriter, and sometime artist who had first recorded in 1927 and had long since left the gutbucket blues behind, came back from the trip with instructions to figure out, in Charlie Gillett's formulation, how to "take advantage of Southern music. . . . Jesse Stone managed to find a way of writing down and reconstructing music that had previously been spontaneous and unpremeditated."

"It wasn't something that I could do easily at first," he told Gillett in 1971. "I considered it backward, musically, and I didn't like it, until I started to learn

*Jesse Stone and the Cookies, soon to become the Raeletts: first edition.
(Courtesy of Nick Tosches)*

that the rhythm content was the important thing." He wrote and arranged hit sessions for the Clovers and the Cardinals, the Drifters and numerous other groups, but the biggest payoff came after Atlantic signed one of its original heroes, Big Joe Turner, and Jesse Stone wrote a song that not only reestablished Big Joe's career but marked one of the turning points in rock 'n' roll. "Shake, Rattle and Roll" became the first standard of the new music as well as establishing Bill Haley as the first white artist to truly cross over the line in 1954. "Jesse Stone," Ahmet has said, "did more to develop the basic rock 'n' roll sound than anybody else, although you hear a lot [more] about Bill Haley and Elvis Presley." Maybe so—although Ahmet will also say, in moments of more pecksniffian detachment, that the early records don't "hold up that well. The singing holds up pretty well, but the background sounds dated to me. . . . The *inventions*—the inventions of arrangers—give it leaden feet. . . . There's too much chrome on all of those records, you know what I mean? And when I listen to those old records, the things that make them of their time also make them ugly."

Regardless of the truth of this heavily irony-laden statement things were changing at Atlantic by 1954. In 1953 Herb Abramson was called into the Army, leaving his wife, Miriam, behind to protect his interests. While he was in the service, his marriage broke up, and he was never able to get fully back into the business, eventually selling out several years later. In the meantime a new face had entered the picture in the person of Jerry Wexler. Wexler, a more direct, earthy, but no less canny sort of man than Ahmet, was thirty-five when he came in as executive vice-president of Atlantic in 1953. A native New Yorker, he had a background in writing and promotion and a voracious need to prove himself. Between the time Wexler joined the company in 1953 and Abramson was discharged from the Army two years later, Atlantic had thirty Top 10 r&b hits, an extraordinary achievement for a small label and one that put it far out in front of the competition. Just as it had from the beginning, the company paid scrupulous attention to quality, authenticity, and the cultivation of good friends throughout the industry. "We were always looking for pure singers in the bel canto tradition," says Wexler, who points proudly to the weeks—sometimes

Ahmet, Jerry, and Big Joe Turner. (Courtesy of Gregg Geller)

Jerry Wexler, Ruth Brown, Private Clyde McPhatter, LaVern Baker, Ahmet Ertegun. (Courtesy of Gregg Geller)

months—of rehearsals that could go into a Drifters' session, the care and painstaking attention to detail that created so artful a sense of imperfection, that made sure that each spontaneous element was always in place. The Atlantic team was young, wise to the ways of the world, and full of energy. And the record world was very different from the conventionally claustrophobic corporate structure it would one day become: its small-town, provincial atmosphere permitted a man with curiosity, ambition, and imagination to create virtually any identity he might choose for himself.

"There was a kind of record man," Wexler has said in what might almost serve as an idealized self-portrait, "that was the *complete* record man, a Renaissance man if you will, who did the whole thing. First, he had the brass to imagine that he could do it, that he could find somebody who would spend a dollar, a good hard-earned American dollar, for his phonograph record. Then he had to find an artist, find a song, con the artist into coming into his studio, coax him into singing the song, pull the record out of him, press the record; then take that record and go to the disc jockeys and con them into putting it on the radio, then go to the distributors and beg them to take a box of twenty-five and try it out. That's the kind of experience that very few people get anymore.

"It was really what you call a biddable market. You knew everyone involved. I'd travel through the territories, see them all, be on the phone—you see, it was manageable. We didn't have any specialized knowledge. We didn't know how good it was. All we needed was to sell 6000 singles in a month to cover everything. Our release schedule was three singles every two weeks. One would be by Ray Charles, one by Big Joe Turner, one by the Drifters. We couldn't miss. We were all driving Cadillacs. We didn't know shit about making records, but we were really having fun!"

THE NEW THING

Ray Charles in many ways represented the very prototype of what Atlantic had been looking for without even knowing it, the kind of preconstructed unit that the label had been trying to put together all along. An r&b stylist with reading ability, a sophisticated breadth of musical interests, and a flavor to his music that was undeniably downhome, Charles at twenty-two was open to suggestion, but it's doubtful that anyone could have anticipated the next stage. "In his first sessions he neither composed nor arranged," Jerry Wexler has written. "His avowed models were Nat Cole and the great rhythm and blues star Charles Brown, both West Coast-based singers. His first two Atlantic sessions were with studio musicians, arrangements by Jesse Stone, songs supplied by various songwriters. The resulting sides were good journeyman r&b, but Ray was still under wraps. . . . "

He remained under wraps for over a year, prodded by Atlantic to some extent to do the kind of material they sensed was commercial: up-tempo Louis Jordan-type numbers, the slow-drawling recitatif of "It Should've Been Me," the hoarsely shouted boogie woogie update of "Mess Around," which Ahmet Ertegun contributed under the nom de disque of Nugetre and then patiently taught to Ray Charles with hilariously atonal pedantry. There were sweetly sung ballads and blues by Lowell Fulson and Guitar Slim, but no hint, really, of the revolutionary breakthrough that was just about to come. To Ray Charles himself Atlantic was just another little record company, another "step on the ladder. I got to give those cats some skin," he will say. "They let me go in the studio and fool around and do any kind of thing. They would submit songs to me, and if I liked it, I would record it, but as far as actually producing the sessions, I have to be honest with you, the truth of the matter is, they never at any time told me what to sing or how to sing it. They were letting me do what I wanted to do, so I guess they must have been all right!"

His career built slowly, he gained additional exposure—if not sales—through Atlantic, but it wasn't until 1953 that Ray Charles finally put together all the various elements of his style, and then it was on someone else's session. In September of 1953 the blues singer Guitar Slim had a date set up with

Specialty Records in New Orleans. One of the tunes on the session was "The Things That I Used to Do," a blues that went on to sell a million copies and inspired almost as many covers. The pianist and arranger on the session was Ray Charles.

On paper it is almost too perfect. Crude, untutored, musically unsophisticated, possessed of a primitive, perfervid style that most resembled the gospel shouting of the Baptist church, Guitar Slim was the antithesis of all that Ray Charles had sought to become in his musical career to date. To Ray Charles, many have said, it must have been a revelation of something he had known all along. The arrangement and mode of Guitar Slim's hit—with gospel changes, horns riffing like a soulful choir, and above all the impassioned, emotionally charged tone of Slim's voice—would appear to have set the pattern for much of Ray Charles's subsequent success.

Ray Charles denies it. He was in New Orleans by accident, not by design. He got the gig with Guitar Slim through a friend, because he was hard up for work and money. "I spent some time in New Orleans. To be honest, I got stranded there, and the people took me in. Somebody introduced me to Guitar Slim because they knew I could write arrangements. I wrote some music for him, and it just turned out that the music I wrote was successful. I liked Guitar Slim, he was a nice man, but he was not a cat I socialized with. We worked our ass off for that session. We worked all day and well into the night. Once we got through with it, everyone was happy—the record company was happy, the guy was happy, and I liked it. But that was it, man. I said, 'Okay, I'm glad to be part of it.' But my music had absolutely nothing to do with what we did with Guitar Slim."

In December Jerry Wexler and Ahmet Ertegun were in New Orleans to cut Big Joe Turner. "We ran into Ray," wrote Wexler, "at Cosimo's famous small studio, and Ray asked us please (!) to do a session with him and a pick-up band he was gigging with in and around New Orleans. . . . This was a landmark session in the growth pattern because it had: Ray Charles originals, Ray Charles arrangements, a Ray Charles band." Again Ray Charles would beg to differ. To him the New Orleans session was just another session, because he still did not have his own permanent group, just one assembled for a recording date.

"I was going crazy, man. I was losing my fucking head. I couldn't take it. Because, you see, you would go into town, and the guy would say he's got the musicians to back you, and the musicians weren't *shit!* And if you're a very fussy person like I am—I mean, I'm even fussy about good musicians! . . . " The upshot was that in early 1954 he formed his own band.

"Billy Shaw, who was booking me, recommended against it. He said, 'You ain't strong enough by yourself.' Which he was right, but I had to do it. So he said, 'We gonna put your band with Ruth Brown,' who was really hot at the time. We did about four or five dates. The second one we missed—see, I had bought two cars, one was a station wagon, DeSoto, and I had a Ford for my car. I got the band in Dallas, where I was living. The first gig we drove from Dallas to El Paso, which was close to nine hundred miles; we drove all day doing a hundred and some odd miles an hour. The next job, you won't believe this, was in Louisiana. Now, that's all the way back where you just came from and then some. It was absolutely crazy booking, and we were late and missed it. I never will forget that. Drove our ass off and got there at eleven o'clock at night, and the people had canceled the job on us. Now you talk about sick. *Sick!* We was sick! But then we worked the next three days, and that was it. Ruth Brown left and went in one direction, and we went in another."

The direction in which Ray Charles went was to make records with his band. In November he called Ahmet and Jerry to come to Atlanta to hear the group. "We met him at his hotel," recalls Wexler. "He took us across the street to a nightclub called the Royal Peacock—this was in the afternoon, and his band was sitting there, all ready to play, just sitting there in their chairs, and he went to the piano and counted off and they hit into 'I've Got a Woman,' and that was it."

MOVIN' ON

That *was* it. It was the fusion of all the elements that up till then had simply failed to coalesce. It was the uninhibited, altogether abandoned sound of the church. It was the keening, ecstatic voicings by which the world has come to know Ray Charles best. Amazingly enough the record of "I Got a Woman" never even made the pop charts, but it probably exerted as profound an influence on the course of American popular music as any single record before or since. To Jerry Wexler it was the quintessence of Ray Charles and r&b, "the archetype tune." For a generation of black listeners it served as an unabashed celebration of negritude without the covering mask of religion. To a generation of white listeners weaned on Perry Como and Teresa Brewer it opened up doors that had always been shut. Ray Charles was probably less affected by its impact than anyone—at least in retrospect. He appreciated the timing, because it allowed him to keep his band. He took the accolades and idolatry in stride—but denied any great artistic leap. "Now I'd been singing spirituals since I was three," he wrote in his autobiography, "and I'd been hearing the blues for just as long. So what could be more natural than to combine them? It didn't take any thinking, didn't take any calculating. All the sounds were there, right at the top of my head. . . . Imitating Nat Cole had required a certain calculation on my part. I had to gird myself; I had to fix my voice into position. I loved doing it, but it certainly wasn't effortless. This new combination of blues and gospel was. It required nothing of me but being true to my very first music."

And the condemnations? "I got a lot of flak because some people felt it was like an abomination of the church," he says, "but then people began to realize, 'No, that ain't it at all, the man is just singing what he feels. He's got to sing what's in him. He's got to sing it the way he feel it.' That was when I gave up trying to sound like anyone else. I said, 'Okay, sound like Ray, be yourself.' The minute I started being me, that was all I knew, I couldn't be nothing else but that."

He was Ray. He became a hero to the black community in a mythic sense that no other popular entertainer, with the possible exception of Louis Armstrong, has ever approached. He was the Bishop, the Right Reverend, the High Priest of Soul, in Julian Bond's terminology he "seduce[d] the world with his voice." Atlantic proclaimed him "the Genius." He declared himself to be a *musician*. In an interview at the time he said, "About the only records I buy myself are good gospel records. I love a good gospel song if it is really soulful. But even in that field, just because they are singing gospel songs doesn't automatically make them good. Whether blues and gospel or whether it's classical music, there is good and bad. It has to be a fine song and the artist has to feel it, or it's no good."

He retained the basic septet form (two reeds, two trumpets, piano, and rhythm); he continued to base his hits on direct transpositions of gospel numbers ("This Little Light of Mine," for example, became "This Little Girl of Mine"); he even added a female chorus, the Raeletts, as a kind of lascivious church choir. The next five years were years of unparalleled triumph—the rocking rhythms of "Yes Indeed!" and "Hallelujah, I Love Her So," the emotional catharsis of "Drown in My Own Tears," the sheer drive of "Night Time Is the Right Time," a couple of dozen more titles, both originals and strikingly original interpretations, that Ray Charles made irretrievably his own—but for all the accolades, for all the sense of aesthetic excitement that attended his every move, Ray Charles was still an r&b artist suffering the indignities of the chitlin circuit, playing almost exclusively for his own people. "We left playing to the white folks to Pat Boone. We did dances. Strictly dances. Play nine to one, go from nine to eleven-thirty, take a half-hour break, come back and work twelve to one. Big hall, somebody be frying some chicken over in the corner, some fish maybe—yeah, some of those dances were rough. Some dances were very rough. Somebody would step on somebody's toes and forget to say Excuse me, and the other guy would call the first guy a motherfucker, and then you got it. Or somebody's dancing with somebody else's old lady, and the guy happens to show up. These places were very warm, man, I don't have to tell you. You take country music, you take black music, you got the same goddam thing exactly. The same thing, man."

Of course he played segregated audiences. There was really no other kind in the South in the '50s. This he could deal with reluctantly, but at a certain point he felt it necessary to draw the line. "My thing was, if I have to go into

Ray Charles with musical director Wallace Davenport, London, 1962. (Val Wilmer)

the black community and do this and only use their facilities and I can only use the toilet in the back, I can only go in the back door of the restaurant, fine, fuck it—if that's the way you want it, it's your restaurant . . . *but you cannot tell me if I play my music for you, I got to make my people sit in the back.* I won't do that. And for that reason I got sued a few times. That had nothing to do with Mr. Martin Luther King, although I was definitely into him when he came out. My attitude was: my people made me, and I cannot deal with the fact that they cannot sit anywhere they want to sit. I just cannot deal with that."

The music itself kept evolving. In keeping with his status as a genius of both taste and experimentation, he made jazz albums with vibraphonist Milt Jackson *(Soul Brothers),* band members Hank Crawford and Fathead Newman, and other hard boppers—in fact, nearly half the album material that he recorded while he was on the Atlantic label consisted of jazz instrumentals. He would not be bound by categories, he insisted. "In my life," he declares today, "everything I did, I did what I thought was right at the time. In my music I've always sung music I've liked, and I've always sung it the way I feel *tonight,* tomorrow it may be something else altogether. The bottom line is that I must enjoy me —as egotistical as it sounds, it must knock me out first, because if I don't feel it, I can't expect you to feel it." Feelings aside, he was always a perfectionist. One time, Jerry Wexler recalls, he was cutting a session with an all-star group that included members of Count Basie's and Duke Ellington's bands and he heard a wrong note in the trumpet section. Far from being overawed by the company in which he found himself, he pursued the matter until he had isolated the problem, then overcame the musician's protest by saying, "Baby, I *wouldn't* tell you wrong, baby."

Between 1955 and 1959 he took advantage of every musical opportunity to create a body of work that remains unrivaled for its variety, originality, energy, and influence. Still, little changed in terms of his career until 1959, when "What'd I Say" came out. Born at a dance in Brownsville outside of Pittsburgh with fifteen minutes left to fill, the song was little more than a riff that Ray embroidered on and the Raeletts brought to orgasm in a panting, cooing climax that was definitely a first for the white airwaves. In many ways it was a culmination of the gospel blues style that Ray Charles had virtually created, an altogether secular evocation of an actual church service, complete with moaning, groaning, and speaking in tongues, a joyous celebration of an utterly profane love. The record went gold, Ray's first million seller. Ray Charles started playing concerts instead of dances. And "What'd I Say" marked another period in his life, too. Six months after the record became a hit, Ray Charles left Atlantic, the company that had nurtured him, for a multi-year, multi-dollar contract with ABC. He was just twenty-nine.

It was a deal that was much misunderstood at the time. To this day Jerry Wexler publicly professes bewilderment, and Ray himself admits that ABC did not provide the personal attentiveness that Atlantic had, but, he says, he no longer had any need for that. What he was after, perhaps without even knowing it, was control, and ABC, with a very weak r&b roster and the sense to recognize the burgeoning market for black music, offered him a deal that Ray says he could not refuse. In addition to a far better royalty rate than Atlantic was paying, ABC held out a production deal, profit-sharing, and eventual ownership of his own masters, a contractual point virtually unheard of at the time and a notable rarity even today. Eventually he got his own record company, Tangerine, which was distributed through ABC.

So in a real sense Ray Charles ended up with much the same thing that Sam Cooke was fighting for at RCA (and what James Brown would later proclaim to be the new Black Capitalism): a measure of independence that was not just artistic but financial as well, enough economic clout to buy into the business. "I really hadn't thought the whole thing out; I wish I could say I was that clever, but I ain't gonna tell you that kind of lie. I just thought—you know, you hear stories, and what I wanted the masters for was in my own mind I felt like if you can own your own thing, that would be like having, you know, your own publishing company. I mean, shit, you couldn't *beat* that kind of offer. I think they gave it to me because they really—well, obviously they wanted me—but I think they thought I was a lot more powerful at Atlantic than I was. But, you know, that ain't the point. Whether they was right or wrong, the point is, as long as the other person thinks you got something—you may not have shit, but as long as he thinks you have, that's all that counts."

AFTER THE REVOLUTION

Ray Charles's subsequent career was as remarkable in its way as anything he had done to date. Although dismissed in many quarters as a kind of artistic compromise, and unquestionably less cataclysmic than the classic Atlantic sides, his work for ABC allowed him to indulge his taste for the sentimental ("I'm a sentimentalist at heart. I really am, man.") as he recorded string-drenched albums like *Genius Hits the Road* and *Dedicated to You,* out of which came such hits as "Ruby" and "Georgia on My Mind," his signature tune to this day. He was also able to pursue his penchant for jazz on Impulse, ABC's affiliate jazz label *(Genius Plus Soul Equals Jazz)* while continuing to turn out a series of tough small-group r&b singles ("Sticks and Stones," "Hit the Road Jack," "Let's Go Get Stoned") as dynamic as anything he had done for Atlantic.

But if his creativity never lapsed, it certainly changed direction. In yet another surprising twist this man who was known for having written nearly all his own hits phased out of writing almost completely ("There's absolutely no difference between writing and interpreting," he insists today. "Whatever you do, you can only be yourself"), left the arrangements to Ralph Burns or Sid Feller or Quincy Jones, and put together an eighteen-piece band for his live performances. *Modern Sounds in Country and Western Music,* Volumes 1 and 2, were probably the high point of his thirteen-year ABC period. Released in 1962 and 1963, just as the gospel-based soul that he had spawned was really beginning to take off in the pop marketplace, the two albums yielded four Top 10 pop hits, several more that were in the Top 30, and one ("I Can't Stop Loving You") that sold over three million copies. It was a typically contrary Ray Charles move, one in which he challenged record company, fans, trends, and musical conventions only to come up with a new racially mixed audience of hitherto undreamt-of proportions. When he first proposed to do a country album, Sam Clark, the president of ABC Records, suggested that he might lose some of his longtime fans. "Which I thought was very legitimate, very nice. I said, 'Well, Mr. Clark, I feel that you are totally right about that. And I've thought about that.' Which I had. 'But the reason I want to do this is that I think I can gain more than I can lose.' And the rest is history. I had never heard 'I Can't Stop Loving You,' never heard 'Born to Lose,' [a&r man] Sid Feller must have sent me about 150 songs, and I picked out the ones I wanted to do, and it worked out pretty good."

His success might very well have continued uninterrupted had it not been for the increasing attention his heroin habit was attracting from the law. In 1958 there had been a bust in Philadelphia, in 1961 in Indianapolis, where a reporter for the *Indianapolis Times* saw him in jail and recalled to writer Arnold Shaw, contrary to all Ray Charles's defiant recollections, "He appeared very disturbed and lonely. He sat down on the bench in city jail and began to cry softly and then lost all control of himself. 'I don't know what to do about my wife and kids. I've got a month's work to do, and I have to do it. I really need help. . . .'" In this case he got it from the legal system, but when he was busted at the airport in Boston in 1964, there were headlines all over the world, and for the first time in over fifteen years Ray quit the road. He took all of 1965 off to kick his habit ("I had lots on my mind, and I couldn't see myself running around. I needed to stop and think."), and when he came up before the judge almost a year after the original bust, sentencing was delayed for another year in order to determine that he had really kicked. When he finally left the courtroom for the last time, as he writes in *Brother Ray,* "I walked out . . . just as I had walked in—my own man. . . . After all this I wish I could tell you that my body felt different, that I had a new lease on life. In truth I felt pretty much the same. The only difference was that I didn't need a fix every morning."

Many in the black community and elsewhere saw the whole process as a repeat of the Sam Cooke story: the stilling of a bold black voice, the tearing down of another nigger who had gotten too big for his britches in a bust that seemed as much of a setup as Sam Cooke's killing. There was one essential difference, of course: Ray Charles survived, and Ray Charles's voice could not be stilled. He remains unrepentant and proud today, as determined to go after what he wants—*and get it*—as young R. C. Robinson ever was in the early days in Seattle. Since returning to performing he has had hits right into the '80s, and if they have not been as big as the seminal sides from the '50s or the crossover hits of the '60s, he has remained a stubborn, thorny kind of institution. After his split with ABC in 1973 he formed a second label of his own, Crossover, and for the last ten or twelve years he has not only produced but engineered most of his own sessions. His mania for perfection has in some ways taken away from the music but always borne out his dignity and spiky pride. In retrospect, I think, he will be seen to have possessed a genius not so much for originality as for assimilation, but he has always, as he says, gone his own way, he has always resisted categorization. "Music, you see, is an art, and it has to always be treated that way. I'm talking about creativity, you can't talk about no fucking numbers —I'm sorry. The trouble with the record industry is that people are always saying, 'What did he do last? What's his sales?' Well, shit! The big record companies, between you and I, put the little companies out of business. But the little companies developed people like me. The little companies could take an artist and grow with the artist and let him experiment—if it weren't for experiment, Ray Charles as we know him today wouldn't exist! I'm very disturbed about this, man, not so much for me as for the kids coming up. I mean, they talk about the new computer games, how they gonna put the record companies out of business. Bullshit! What's that got to do with listening to music? There ain't never been a time in history when people didn't appreciate

Portrait. (Jim Marshall)

good music. You give them good music, and they'll listen to it—ain't no fucking computer games gonna take the place of music. I guess you gonna say, 'Ray, you kind of an embittered cat,' but some things just bug me, I just don't believe everybody got to be an idiot—that's what pisses me off about the 'family hour' on TV, man, it ain't a goddam thing but a bunch of people acting the goddam fool all the time, and I'm sorry, honey, I just don't believe the world is like that."

ATLANTIC WAVES

RAY CHARLES'S DEPARTURE FROM ATLANTIC caused severe shock waves throughout the company. It was at just about this time that Herb Abramson, relegated to the Atlantic subsidiary label, Atco, since his Army release, was finally bought out for $300,000, raised by Wexler, Ahmet, and Ahmet's brother, Nesuhi. Atlantic certainly remained successful enough both commercially and artistically. In 1960, the year of Charles's defection, the label enjoyed a #1 hit, pop *and* r&b, with the Drifters' "Save the Last Dance for Me"; Bobby Darin continued his run of chart success with updated standards and synthetic rock; the Coasters, under the watchful guidance of songwriters-producers Jerry Leiber and Mike Stoller ("Hound Dog," "On Broadway," as well as the entire Coasters' oeuvre), continued to straddle the rock 'n' roll–r&b fence; the jazz department, under the direction of Nesuhi Ertegun, maintained its reputation as one of the most progressive and adventurous labels around with fresh work from Coltrane, Ornette Coleman, and Charles Mingus, among others. From the standpoint of the revolution in r&b, though, the exciting new rhythm 'n' gospel movement which Atlantic (and Ray Charles) had done so much to bring about, according to Jerry Wexler, "We had nothing, really, we were running out of steam, the music was getting tired, our sound was gone."

For someone as ambitious as Wexler, as committed not just to the music but to the liberal ethic and the idea of putting his own stamp on history (he had started out as a writer, after all, even published fiction in Whit and Hallie Burnett's *Story Magazine*), it was a thoroughly distressing situation, to be abandoned without warning by your major star and to have no real sense of how to get where you wanted to go. Ahmet's response was to withdraw from the active recording of black music. He lay low for a while, remaining involved only with Bobby Darin, then concentrating more and more on pop sessions with artists like Nino Tempo and April Stevens, Sonny and Cher, and eventually Cream, Led Zeppelin, Buffalo Springfield, and Iron Butterfly, who represented the significant change in direction that led Atlantic into the immensely profitable and multinational '70s. Why Ahmet abandoned rhythm and blues continues to baffle Jerry Wexler, but Ahmet's biographer, George Trow, has a theory that archly mirrors Ahmet's manner, and perhaps his thinking.

"Both men [Wexler and Ahmet] had an appreciation of black musical and social forms which significantly outran the knowledge and instinct of other white men in the business, but although the two men could react as one man when they were confronted by any strong, incontrovertible excellence [e.g. Ray Charles], it turned out that in the absence of any such excellence what Ahmet most enjoyed in black music was paradox and anomaly and incongruity and excess of style, while Wexler sought instead evidence of that unspoiled energy which, taken together with eccentricity of expression, can be perceived as *honesty*.

"The separate aesthetics of Ahmet Ertegun and Jerry Wexler had difficulties that perfectly shadowed their outlines in the world. To the extent that their aesthetics converged they shared a difficulty—the difficulty experienced by all white men who seriously interest themselves in black music: that at times they felt excluded from the deepest secrets of the enterprise, and at other times they were deeply, deeply bored, and afraid that there were no secrets to learn and nothing to be included in. To the extent that their aesthetics diverged, they experienced separate difficulties. Ahmet's interest in paradox and anomaly and incongruity had led him very far into artifice and contrived juxtaposition, until there was serious doubt whether there was raw material enough left in the music to satisfy his interest. Jerry Wexler's interest in unspoiled energy and eccentricity of expression led him to actively seek what cannot be actively sought but only welcomed."

The very incarnation of this "unspoiled energy" and endearing eccentricity walked in the door of Wexler's office in the portly person of Solomon Burke in the fall of 1960.

Solomon Burke was a singer Wexler knew by reputation: a native Philadelphian who from the age of nine had been known as "the Wonder Boy Preacher." The records he had made in the '50s for Apollo, a New York independent label which used many of the same studio musicians and arrangers as Atlantic, were a peculiar blend of the sacred and the profane, employing titles like "To Thee," "No Man Walks Alone," and "You Can Run But You Can't Hide" to create a confusion between heavenly love and the real thing, and with the young singer (fifteen by his own account when he started out) employing a variety of vocal tones and shadings to suggest everyone from Roy Hamilton to Little Richard to Ivory Joe Hunter, Nat King Cole, and Elvis Presley.

Burke was a talent, then—and one to whom Jerry Wexler, with his admiration for smooth, controlled singers like Sam Cooke, would naturally have been drawn—but Wexler might well have missed signing him had it not been for the importuning of *Billboard* editor Paul Ackerman, whom Jerry had worked for in his own journalistic days, and who tirelessly, and perceptively,

Paul Ackerman and Jerry Wexler. (Courtesy of Jerry Wexler)

championed the work of Atlantic, Chess Records, and Sam Phillips's Sun label. "Paul Ackerman always used to say to me, 'Get Solomon Burke, you've got to get Solomon Burke,' and I said, 'I will, Paul, I will, as soon as he gets free of his contract.' Paul had also given me this record, this country and western record called 'Just Out of Reach' that he thought would be good for one of our artists. So one day Solomon Burke just shows up in my outer office. I just went out, I took him into the office, and I said, 'Okay, you're on Atlantic, let's go,' you know—it was as simple as that. And I gave him that song, 'Just Out of Reach,' at the first session [December 1960], so Paul Ackerman was responsible for our getting both Solomon Burke and the song that made him."

The first song to be recorded at the session, and the first one actually released as a single by Solomon Burke on Atlantic, "Keep the Magic Working," was a flop. Wexler put out the second record, the c&w ballad, without any real expectations, doubting that there would be much of a market for a straightforward country song by an r&b singer (although Ivory Joe Hunter, often cited

Joe Galkin. (Courtesy of Jerry Wexler)

by Solomon as a key influence on his style, had had a number of hits in a country vein, and Ray Charles's upbeat version of "I'm Movin' On," recorded at one of his last Atlantic sessions in 1959, only served to presage his upcoming c&w success). Wexler wasn't thinking of Ray Charles or Ivory Joe Hunter, though, and by his own admission did little more than dump Solomon's single on the market.

Some time after it was released he got a telephone call from Joe Galkin, an oldtime song plugger who had quit the business, bought a bar in Queens, gone broke, and headed South to promote records. "I told him at the time," says Wexler, " 'You're crazy. That's all they need down there is an obnoxious Jew like you coming into the radio stations'—but he went and did it, and nobody had ever promoted records the way he did it, and he called me from someplace in Alabama and says, 'I got a hit, I'm going to make a hit record for you,' and he made me guess which one, and I didn't have any idea, because I wasn't pushing the record myself. So finally he says, ' "Just Out of Reach," Solomon Burke,' and I thought he was nuts, but I gave him fifty dollars a week for his first few weeks to work the record just to see what would happen. You see, a guy like Joe had built up a very big network in the South, in his heyday he'd be in his car, and whenever he saw a radio tower transmitter, he'd stop, get out, and go hustle his records. And the way it would usually work, he wouldn't just pick a record, he'd be traveling and come into a radio station and some PD or some disc jockey would say, 'Hey, listen, I got a record up here, and I'm telling you, I like that record,' and Joe would call up and he would take it from there. 'Hey, listen, I got a record I think I can get on the radio down here'—but, you see, he'd be in cahoots with the disc jockey. They were *objets trouvés,* these records, they were found in the radio stations by these disc jockeys. And that's what probably happened with Solomon's record."

Regardless of what happened, the record took off. First it was selling 300 copies a week, then 1000, by the end of its run 30,000. It reached the #7 spot on the rhythm and blues charts and even went Top 30 pop. More important it reestablished Atlantic's direction and its leadership in the brave new world (still unnamed and largely uncharted) of soul. Listened to today, the record sounds curiously stilted, with a typically sweetened Atlantic arrangement, a sterile choir, and a country lyric that must have seemed ridiculous even at the time to such knife-edge sophisticates as Ahmet Ertegun, Jerry Leiber, and Mike Stoller. It is Solomon Burke's voice that redeems the whole enterprise, rising above the gooey concoction and suggesting an emotional depth and range that is out of the territory of most singers, certainly of this song.

That is what makes the record. Jerry Wexler has said over and over again, "We were going for great singers," and certainly Solomon fit the bill, a combination of Sam Cooke at his mellifluous best and Ray Charles at his deep-down and funkiest, an improbable mix of sincerity, dramatic artifice, bubbling good humor, and multitextured vocal artistry. "Just Out of Reach" served almost as a benchmark. Ray Charles's "Unchain My Heart" on ABC, the first taste of *his* new country-flavored soul, followed Solomon's hit by just three months. Sam Cooke was finally putting out sides that reflected his gospel upbringing. Motown enjoyed its first Top 10 success in 1961, while Stax (snatched up for distribution by Atlantic almost from its moment of inception) made its first major imprint on the charts with Carla Thomas's "Gee Whiz" in that same year. It seemed as if the new soul stew was finally bubbling up from underground, and here was Atlantic once again in the vanguard.

"We were away to the races, cutting hits," Wexler has said. There was no longer time for self-doubt. For a period of about two years Solomon Burke was Atlantic's premier artist both artistically and commercially ("He really carried the label," Wexler has stated on more than one occasion). Then, ironically enough, a song by Wilson Pickett, who had just left Detroit and the Falcons, a seminal gospel-based group ("I Found a Love" on Lu Pine, also distributed by Atlantic), brought together Wexler, Burke, and much of the focus of the whole soul movement.

"One day a tape came in from Detroit," Wexler told Atlantic historian Charlie Gillett, "with eight songs on it. One of the songs was 'If You Need Me,' which was the only one that impressed me. The singer on the demo was Wilson Pickett."

What followed points up both the fast-moving enterprise and the relative disorganization of the music business circa 1963. "If You Need Me" is a classic of the soul genre, with a fervent message, a sincere spoken passage, and strict gospel changes. Atlantic bought the publishing rights immediately but somehow neglected to purchase rights to the demo. Wexler got Solomon's impassioned interpretation down on wax right away, put it in the can, and then, before it had even been released, discovered that Pickett's original master was being marketed by Lloyd Price and Harold Logan on their Double L label. Jerry Wexler tried frantically to block the release—"I would say Pickett's record had the edge over ours"—and when the effort failed, "I went to work on that record. That record put me back into promotion, got me back into the studio, into the excitement of the record business, everything." It also got Solomon Burke a big hit, and it even brought Wilson Pickett to Atlantic eventually. Just about a year later, in the spring of 1964, "Pickett himself comes into the office with a tape under his arm. I said, 'Man, aren't you sore?' And he said, 'That's in the past.'"

By that time, though, Atlantic was fully established as the home base for soul—Southern soul, that is—the new label of Joe Tex, whose Top 10 hit "Hold What You've Got" was released at the end of that year, the nurturing ground for Otis Redding and the whole Memphis sound, which was taking the recording industry by storm. Between 1962 and 1967 Atlantic increased its sales by 500 percent, primarily on the basis of its ever-increasing share of the soul market; two-thirds of the label's singles were geared to black sales, 50 percent of its albums. By June of 1967 eighteen of the Top 100 soul songs were on the Atlantic label. Like Sun Records in rockabilly or Chess Records with postwar downhome blues, Atlantic truly dominated the world of Southern soul, and Jerry Wexler was perceived in many quarters as the hip philanthropist responsible for it all. To Wexler, never reluctant to deliver a candid opinion (but whose candor will generally serve a useful purpose), Motown defied the laws of sociology, while Atlantic "was interested in making music for black adults—that was our emphasis, that was the closest to what we liked. We didn't care about doo-wops, we didn't care about surfing, we didn't care about the Beatles—that was just not compatible with what we were into. We wanted to make records that were in tune and in time, rhythm and blues played without slop but nevertheless with a lot of strength and a lot of soul. I don't believe in being meretricious on purpose. Bad is bad, no matter what the intention is. Even in the beginning, when we didn't know how to make records, we went for a solid beat, good licks, and good intonation. Our records sounded good, they sold, and they're still around."

King Solomon:
The Throne in Exile

W HEN I WAS ON ATLANTIC, IT WAS A REAL
record company, it was a family. Now I hear Jerry and Ahmet don't
even get along—that's a shame, that's a shame. Maybe it's their oil
wells. Hey, hey, hey. Maybe it's Jerry's oil wells in Iran and Ahmet's
oil wells in Saudi Arabia—that would cause you, you know, to fall out. That'll
do it every time."

Everyone has their favorite soul singer. To Phil Walden and many critics
Otis Redding was without peer; Sam Cooke and Ray Charles are cited as the
unquestionable originators, James Brown was the greatest showman of them all,
and even Wilson Pickett has his partisans. For Jerry Wexler, on the other hand,
there are different orders of choice. "I was talking with Jimmy Bishop once,
who used to be a very big DJ in the Philadelphia area, and we were sitting
around talking about who was the best soul singer of that time. People were
saying Otis Redding, Wilson Pickett, Ben E. King. Jimmy said, 'No way. The
best soul singer of all time is Solomon Burke. With a borrowed band.' Which
I agree with. Both parts."

I remember the first time I saw Solomon Burke myself, in 1964. He was
wearing a gold tuxedo with a gold cummerbund and was headlining a show
that included Joe Tex, Otis Redding, and Garnet Mimms. Solomon had no
competition. There has never been a warmer, more charismatic presence on
stage, and when he stretched out his arms to the audience, when he declared at
the outset, "There's a song that I sing, and I believe if everybody was to sing
this song, it would save the whole world," there was scarcely anyone in that
frenzied crowd who could resist either the message or the conviction that
seemingly lay behind it. When I first met him some fifteen years later, he was
just the same, only bigger. His 200-plus pounds had swelled to 300-plus pounds;
his congregation, on the other hand, had diminished from a theater full of secular
parishioners ready to testify to a small club in New York City whose sparse
audience was made up mostly of white faces and a few curious Japanese tourists.
He was no longer hailed as King of Rock 'n' Soul, or, if he was, it was evident
his kingdom was in disarray. And yet the voice was still there, as smooth as silk,
as capable of swelling to an impassioned, effortless crescendo, as likely to soar

Getting back the crown: New Orleans, 1985. (Alan Edelstein)

to a thrilling high note or drop to a confidential whisper. The talent was intact, and so was the charm. Solomon Burke remained king.

There has never been any doubt in Solomon's mind of his lineage. Everywhere that I have gone with him in the last few years, whether to the filming of a television pilot in Nashville, a revival in Bedford-Stuyvesant, his own church in Los Angeles (Solomon is an ordained minister and bishop of the faith), or a restaurant on Broadway, Solomon has remained centerstage; he has created a drama, or several—it's like a royal roadshow in which waiters, deacons, family, reporters, and always women, countless pretty women, make up his traveling court. Everywhere he goes he picks up an entourage of men and women both (though women certainly predominate) who become his supporting cast in a shifting drama which can turn in an instant from moments of high comedy to passages of the utmost depth and profundity without so much as the blinking of an eye. Throughout it all Solomon maintains the poise of the master showman, animating all, orchestrating all, a storyteller who spins tales of the past, his own and the planet's, which hold his audience spellbound until the punch line—which as often as not turns out to be a joke. He is that rare spirit, a "character" who is also a serious artist. Everyone I spoke to for this book remembers Solomon (he is so much larger than life, who could ever forget him?), some as "a big liar," one as "crazy as a damn loon," almost all with fondness and something close to awe for his outsized spirit and outsized talent.

You can't spend time with Solomon Burke and not begin to wonder, not so much because of the improbability of the stories he tells but because so many of them are confirmed as the characters he is speaking about walk right in the door.

Father of twenty-one, grandfather of fourteen ("I got lost on one of the Bible verses that said, 'Be fruitful and multiply.' I didn't read no further."), spiritual head of a church that Solomon says has 40,000 parishioners across the country (there are 168 allied churches in all, with outposts in Jamaica and Canada), Solomon has survived a career that saw him begin preaching at the age of seven, reach worldly heights in his twenties, survive what he describes as at least two descents into "the pits of hell," only to emerge with a best-selling gospel album and a gospel Grammy nomination in the early '80s. The two elements that have sustained him throughout this heady rise and fall and rise again are his resourcefulness and his talent: a quick-wittedness that very likely would have made him a success in any field that he chose to enter and might very well have brought him down again (because Solomon has always found it next to impossible to resist a laugh); and a talent that sets him apart from almost any other performer that I have ever known, both because it is so inspired and because he can turn it on and off so easily, seemingly at will, rouse a whole hall or congregation and then come back to earth again, without missing a beat, after the performance is over. Solomon Burke—the Bishop, the King of Rock 'n' Soul, the man who would once again be king ("Here's to the throne," he declared one time, raising a jar of honey. "We in exile trying to get it back."), with a biography as singular as anything else about him.

He was born in Philadelphia in either 1936 (the commonly cited date) or 1940, the confusion arising, Solomon says, because he came to his grandmother in a dream twelve years before his actual birth. It was on the basis of that dream that the grandmother, Eleanora A. Moore, founded a church, Solomon's Temple: The House of God for All People, in anticipation of the arrival of its spiritual head. His father, Vince, a native of Kingston, Jamaica, was a chicken plucker in a kosher market and (again according to Solomon) a black Jew. Solomon was the oldest of seven children and obviously the cynosure of every eye. "It was such a big deal when he was born," says his mother, Josephine, herself an ordained preacher. To his grandmother he was the confirmation of a long-held faith, and with his uncle, Harry R. Moore, who was seven years older, he undertook spiritual leadership of the church at a very early age. At seven he delivered his first sermon; at nine he was widely known as the Wonder Boy Preacher; at twelve he was conducting a radio ministry and traveling on weekends, with a truck and tent, to Maryland, Virginia, and the Carolinas to carry on the spiritual crusade.

According to Solomon none of this was anything to turn a young boy's

The young Solomon Burke. (Michael Ochs Archives)

head, and in a sense, looking at Solomon conduct affairs of church and state today with nearly imperturbable good humor, you can almost believe it. Solomon has described his House of God for All People in a less serious vein as the church of Let It All Hang Out, and he points to basic differences with his uncle, who died in 1982 and did not believe, as Solomon does, in miracle healing, liberal interpretation of the Bible, or informal dress. "My ministry was totally different than his, still is. We still stand under the same things, teach basically the same philosophy, but mine is a little more open and a little more flamboyant than my uncle's. God, money, and women, hey, hey, hey; truth, love, peace, and get it on. It never bothered me, because I was in the world but not of it. Part of my belief is to be able to serve God anywhere at any time and still come out saved, so I could be around people with cocaine, pot, booze, and it wouldn't mean a thing to me, even as a kid. My leadership was beyond question."

In 1954 his life took a turn. "I wrote a song for my grandmother for a Christmas present. God gave me the song on December 10, I finished the song on December 17, and on the eighteenth she said that she wanted to speak to me. She said, 'I want you to see your Christmas present.' And I said, 'Now?' She

Roy Hamilton. (Michael Ochs Archives)

said, 'Yes, look under my bed.' And I looked under her bed, and there was a guitar wrapped in a pillow case. And then I sang my little song that I had written for her, called 'Christmas Presents From Heaven,' not knowing that it was a prophecy for me, to alert me to the future. Then on the morning of the nineteenth my grandmother passed in her sleep, so she only heard the song one day—but that whole day she was briefing me and telling me the different things that were going to happen and all the children that I would have, the loves in my life, just laying it out: 'You'll have big homes, fancy cars'—but I'll never forget the most exciting thing she said to me, and then the most depressing thing, too. The most exciting thing was that I would be able to reach out and touch people and help them spiritually, thousands of people, millions of people, and then she said to me that I would go down to the pits of hell and submerge at will, and I've been there a couple of times, Pete, I've been there, you know."

Just months after his grandmother died there was a gospel talent show down at the Liberty Baptist Church, and Solomon tried to get his group, the Gospel Cavaliers, to enter. One of them had just gotten a TV, though, and another had tickets to a football game, so Solomon went down alone in his uncle's pants and father's too-small pepperpot jacket, borrowed a guitar from one of the other groups, entered, and sang "The Old Ship of Zion." He must have been a big success, because Viola Williams, wife of Kae Williams, a prominent Philadelphia DJ, spotted him there and introduced him to Bess Berman, the owner of the New York independent label Apollo. It was for Apollo that he made his first records in early 1955.

Like so many of his contemporaries who came out of the church, Solomon was clearly in the process of change. These early sides are very much based on the big-voiced gospel-laden style that Roy Hamilton had recently pioneered (ambiguous words, inspirational setting). The genre, and indeed many of the songs, are clearly modeled on Hamilton's 1954 best-seller, the improbably authored Rodgers and Hammerstein collaboration "You'll Never Walk Alone," and there are definite bows to other popular artists of the day (including one of Roy Hamilton's most devoted admirers, Elvis Presley). What stood out most clearly, though, even in these tentative stylistic ventures, was the protean Solomon Burke voice, distinguished, whether at the age of fifteen or nineteen, by its control, range, and astonishing variety of textures and hues. Surprisingly, for a singer who was to become so strongly identified with the foundation of soul, there was almost no racial inflection, none of the broader accents of the church. Nor did there appear to be any interest on Apollo's part in recording him strictly as a gospel artist. But then, by all appearances Solomon wasn't much interested in that route either, having discovered, as he says, "a new avenue, a new dimension to spread the gospel." He appeared frequently at the Apollo Theatre, where he met rising stars like Joe Tex and Little Willie John, and he traveled all over the country in the next couple of years with a piano player named Slim Howard as his accompanist. He played shows with Wynonie Harris and Amos Milburn and recalls singing "One Scotch, One Bourbon, One Beer" without realizing it was Milburn's hit. "The people all went wild, and I thought, I'm gonna kill him, I'm gonna kill him—I didn't know he'd made the record, I was into my church thing, man. I'll never forget, I finally ran into Lottie the Body's dressing room, because I didn't know if he was going to murder me or not. She was just standing there with her body, and I says, 'Lady, oh, lady, I'm so sorry.' And she says, 'Stay, honey.' I say, 'Right!' "

His biggest success came with a song called "You Can Run (But You Can't Hide)," for which cowriting credit was assigned to ex-heavyweight champion Joe Louis, who had used the saying as his boxing slogan. Louis helped promote the song in exchange for the credit, even appearing on *The Steve Allen Show* with his young protégé but unfortunately forgetting Solomon's name. "Steve says, 'You know. Solomon Burke.' And Joe says, 'Oh, yeah. And Dick Haymes has the same song out on Decca Records.' My poor little record company must have had a heart attack. Here we are on national television, and the guy's plugging a record by somebody else. Those were funny days, man."

They were funny days and ended as oddly as they had begun, as Solomon came to the conclusion around 1957 that neither his manager nor the Apollo label had been paying him all the money that he felt was his due. His reaction was to withdraw not just from the record business but from the world as well. It was his first descent into the pits of hell. "My manager told me that I could not record for anyone, that I would be blackballed all over the world. So I became a bum, because I was just really terrified, I thought my whole little world had crumbled. Well, it had. And I'll never forget, I asked a guy standing on the corner of Sixteenth and Ridge in Philadelphia in the summertime to loan me fifty cents, and he took fifty cents out of his pocket and kind of tossed it to me. Well, in Philadelphia we have grates on the sewers, and the fifty cents landed right on one of those grates, and you had to be very careful how you picked it up, 'cause otherwise it would fall down the sewer. So I got down on my knees and very gently tried to get that fifty cents from the sewer grate, and all of a sudden something came over me spiritually that said, 'If you pick up that fifty cents now, you'll be picking up change for the rest of your life.' I made the decision, and I kicked the fifty cents in the sewer. And the guy said, 'You gotta be crazy. You crazy nut.' Well, he went to run after me, and I run out in the street, and a lady hit me with her car, and when she hit me with her car, she got out and offered to take me to the hospital and come to find out she knew me (her name was Lathella Thompson), because I had been dating her niece. Well, she took me home with her, and that whole cycle of my life was over. That's when I went back to school and became a mortician."

An unlikely twist, perhaps—but then, that's the way things always seem to have happened for Solomon. With the encouragement of his aunt, Anna, who owned and operated the A. V. Berkley Funeral Home in Philadelphia, Solomon went off to Eccles Mortuary College, where he became a Doctor of Mortuary Science and then rejoined the family firm. Very successfully, too, by all accounts, as Solomon's funeral homes became a significant pillar of his burgeoning financial edifice, which in later years would include a limousine service, a chain of drugstores, an unsuccessful restaurant or two, and a whole string of "nonprofit" ventures ("they're nonprofit as far as I'm concerned") that have gotten him involved in feeding programs, academies for the performing arts, and other enterprises of varying degrees of improbability. As Solomon has said, "You know, the beauty of America is that you can try anything, and if people go for it, you can keep on doing it."

The funeral business led him, indirectly as always, back into the record business. "I was very content to become a successful mortician and build an empire of funeral homes," he declares, but then a man named Babe Shivian came along and said, " 'You got to be out there singing. Baby, can I manage you?' Well, I wasn't into singing at all at this point—I had the churches, I had the funeral home—but he convinced me by giving me this red Lincoln limousine; he kept it sitting in front of the funeral home, and there was no way we could let this red Lincoln convertible sit in front of the funeral home—it was just the wrong place for it. So the family talked to him, and he said, 'Man, you need to make a record.' Well, we went back in and made a few records for him and Artie Singer, Singular Records, and the next thing you know we had a deal with Atlantic."

Almost from the beginning it was a very different situation with Atlantic. Whether by happenstance or because of Jerry Wexler's perception of the enormous potential that Solomon possessed, Atlantic from the beginning seemed to

With Jerry Wexler: "Just Out of Reach." (Courtesy of Jerry Wexler)

have much more grandiose plans for its artist than either Singular or Apollo. After a lushly orchestrated first outing that didn't go anywhere, in the summer of 1961 Atlantic finally put out the c&w number that *Billboard* editor Paul Ackerman had presented to Wexler for the first session, a bathetic ballad that had been a recent country release for Billy Brown on Republic and did as little for Brown as it had previously done for Faron Young, Patsy Cline, and T. Texas Tyler. Solomon doesn't claim any more credit than Wexler for the song choice. "I liked country music," he says, "but I don't think it was deliberate. I think it was something we just accidentally happened onto. By my being versatile. By my being able to sing different songs—being able to change my tone quality, having the different octaves. You must remember, I was capable of singing anything."

Indeed he was, as he proved during his Atlantic stay, covering everything from the smoothest of ballads to the roughest of soul imprecations, often in the course of the same song. He turned out to have a real predilection for country, too, whether because of his diction or because of his feeling for the more exalted emotions or because of the ability, which he shared in part with Elvis Presley, to descend from the purest of tenors to the most thrilling of bass notes, and then rise back up again. None of it seemed like such a big deal at the time, though. According to Jerry Wexler, "When the session was over and we started to listen to it, Solomon cut out; he wasn't going to listen. I said, 'Where are you going?' He said, 'I'm going back to Philadelphia. I'm on a snow-removal gig at $3.50 an hour.' He had eight children to support!" According to Solomon, who remembers the incident vividly, "I had to split because they were telling me, 'Well, uh, hey, man, let's do one more song.' So I say, 'Well, man, this is hurting my income.' Hey, hey, those were the days. And I got a lot of assistance from Jerry. Being there, he gave me a lot of freedom—to do whatever I wanted to do. He would sit there and say, 'That's great, that's great, do that again.' Or just the encouragement of 'Do you want a sandwich? Let's send out for some sandwiches.' Or 'What are we going to do about the publishing? What about the writers?' Hey, he's a genius!"

"Just Out of Reach" was an r&b and pop smash. So was the follow-up, "Cry to Me," which was written and coproduced by Bert Berns, a vastly underrated composer and producer (he shared writing credits for "Twist and Shout," "Piece of My Heart," "Cry Baby," and "Hang On Sloopy," as well as producing such diverse artists as the Drifters, Neil Diamond, Van Morrison, and Aretha Franklin's sister Erma), who more or less took over Solomon's recording career at this point. Under Berns (with Wexler's executive supervision) he recorded transcendent versions of "Down in the Valley," the Eddy Arnold ballad "I Really Don't Want to Know," Jim Reeves's classic "He'll Have to Go," as well as the Wilson Pickett-composed "If You Need Me." Even more compelling were his own "Everybody Needs Somebody to Love" with its inspired and inspirational message and "The Price" with its no less extraordinary sermon, improvised one night at the Apollo Theatre, which declares: "You cost me my mother / The love of my father / Sister / My brother, too. . . ."

It was a remarkable run and a remarkable four-year string of hits. According to Jerry Wexler, Solomon practically kept Atlantic alive between 1961 and 1964, and even allowing for some degree of poetic license, one still feels that there was an undeniable spirit of creative involvement, a sense of high drama that couldn't have failed to capture the imagination of anyone caught up in the life and work of Solomon Burke at this stage of his development. Each of the songs achieved a climax of feeling, each of the songs was a masterpiece of

Jerry Wexler, Nesuhi Ertegun,   *Success. (Michael Ochs Archives)*
Bert Berns, and friend. (Courtesy of
Jerry Wexler)

emotional orchestration. The country-oriented numbers showed off the breath-taking range of Solomon's voice, the ballads throbbed with a seething undercur-rent, and when Solomon shifted to a blacker emphasis, the barely latent accents of the church—the broader diction, the impassioned preaching, the abandoned transport—all emerged. The force of his voice in songs like "The Price" is almost frightening. It sounds sometimes as if he is addressing a congregation right there in the studio, and indeed singer Don Covay, who wrote or cowrote some of Solomon's biggest hits and has been close to him over the years, has said, "Solomon wouldn't record without his pulpit in the studio. We'd dim the lights. Solomon would stand up there in front of that pulpit, and we'd have church." Not surprisingly Solomon reinterprets the story, saying, "All I had to do was be there. Just show up. There was no need for any special atmosphere. All these songs were part of my life, things I lived."

Recording was probably only a very incidental part of his life in any case. Recording was the straw that stirred the drink, the promotional device that supported his touring. The road was where you made your money and met the public that could sustain your career. Sometimes, though, the public could surprise you, and sometimes you could surprise the public. When he first went out behind "Just Out of Reach," says Solomon, there was considerable confu-sion about the racial identity of the singer; in those days, before mass television exposure—particularly for an r&b or country singer—people just flocked to see the person who had made the hit, without much idea of who it might be.

Solomon has lots of stories of that innocent era when "I was just about the most popular singer in the South," but perhaps the funniest has to do with a Friday night booking down in Mississippi.

"This was in some little place in Mississippi, between Tupelo and Philadelphia, and we had everything we could ask for. They had those big flatbed trucks with the loudspeakers hooked up, and the black people was just bringing us fried chicken and ribs. Oh, my God, they got corn on the cob, they making cakes and pies, they got hot bread, barbecued ribs, they barbecuing the whole hog— oh, man, they got ten whole hogs over there, sides of beef, looked like they were going to feed about 20,000. Oh, man, I can't even begin to tell you— it looked like the festival of the year!

"My band come up to me, they say, 'Man, this is the greatest job we ever played.' I said, 'See? Don't it pay to get here early? These guys got tents set up for us, they got sleeping cots, they got a portable toilet, what more can we ask for?' Well, round about seven o'clock this man says, 'You boys got enough to eat?' Then they had some girls come over and entertain us. Then a little later this guy comes and says [nasal peckerwood accent], 'I'm Sheriff Stanleyhoop, and my name's on the contract, and I want you to know I'm forced to give you seventy-five hundred dollars, and here's your money.' I say, 'Great! This is a fantastic gig we got. Seventy-five hundred dollars for the one show, and we got another gig on the same night for the same amount. In other words, black people paying fifteen thousand dollars for me to perform on a Friday night —in Mississippi. This is heavy!'

"So he paid us, and he said, 'Now I want you boys to hit the bandstand at eight-fifteen sharp. It's going to start to get dark, and they hooking up the lights, and I don't want you boys to worry about a thing. When you get ready to leave tonight, we going to escort you all the way to the main highway. Y'all going to Jackson, right?' 'That's right.' 'Well, don't y'all worry about a thing. You got police protection. In fact I'm going to make you an honorary deputy sheriff tonight. Would you like that?' I said, 'Yes, sir, that'd be great! Yes, sir. Right!'

"Five of eight, I told the band, 'Come on, you guys, we got our money, get ready, I want you to hit the stand at eight-fifteen, just like the man said. Don't forget, we got two shows tonight.'

"Man, ten after eight came, the drummer, he's out there, testing, testing. It's really getting dark now, right? Man, about eight-fifteen they start playing. I'm just relaxing, enjoying myself—the chicken legs and chicken wings, homemade sausages and stuff. I said, 'Lord, this is ridiculous.' Big old jug of lemonade, just push the button and it come out. It was great.

"Well, it come time for me to go on at about quarter of nine, I walked out there and noticed—man, I was singing and trying to see what was going on—all the way as far as your eye could see was lights, like people holding a blowtorch, coming, they was just coming slowly, they was coming towards the stage. And I started singing, 'I'm so happy to be here tonight, I'm so glad-glad-glad . . .' They got closer and closer. Man, they was 30,000 Ku Klux Klanners in their sheets—it was their annual rally. The whole time we played that show those people kept coming. With their sheets on. Little kids with little sheets, ladies, man, everybody just coming up, just moving under the lights, everyone dancing and having a good time. I'll tell you, we did a forty-five-minute show like this. Frozen. Man, my band was so scared that when I told them to pack up, the drummer just picked up his drums, didn't break down the set, just picked up the whole kit, man; the guitarist picked up his Fender amp, no problem, no problem. They escorted us right out onto the main highway, and we played our other show."

Another time, Solomon insists, a local promoter hired him, not knowing he was black, and then, when he showed up, he was made to go on with his face all covered with bandages so that the audience didn't get out of hand. Obviously taken with the idea, Solomon feels his face for tape and pokes a hole for his mouth and nose through the imagined mask.

You wonder how fanciful the story might be, but then you come up against someone else's depiction of the same scene, you run into other participants who instantly recall many of the same tableaux, if not all of the little fillips, that Solomon has so vividly conjured up. They may not remember the details as colorfully, they may not tell the tale as well (no one tells a story like Solomon), but there is no story that Solomon has told me that does not appear to have a basis in fact. The musicians at Muscle Shoals remember him interrupting a session to confer with a parishioner come to seek spiritual solace. "He said, 'Wait a minute, guys, I got to go make a witness.' And there was a sister out in the hall, and he went out there and prayed for her. She gave him $500, and he walked back in and fanned himself with it, said, 'Okay, let's go.' " Everyone remembers him selling concessions on the crowded tour bus, offering orange juice, tomato juice, sandwiches, and ice water at prices that started out low and, by the end of a long, hot bus ride, had appreciated considerably. "Solomon," says Rodgers Redding, Otis's brother, "always carried stuff like ice water, cookies, candy, gum; even though he didn't drink at all, you'd go into his room at the hotel and see all this Courvoisier, different kinds of wine, the whole room would be full of booze. He'd have a hot plate, frying pan, flowers, roses, everything, just for his guests, whoever would come by. I remember one tour, I think it was Dionne Warwick who was the headliner, and Solomon was selling his ice water for ten cents, sandwiches for a dollar—everybody just laughed at him. By the time they got about halfway there, he was selling that water for a dollar, sandwiches for $7.50!"

"Solomon had so many side gigs," recalls Jerry Wexler, not without asperity. "The game between me and Solomon was how much jive he could

England, 1965. (Courtesy of Bill Millar)

lay on me before I would set him down. He had his mortician's license, which I think he got by mail order. Also at one time he was an herbal doctor, he had a beautiful fitted case of herbal extracts, you know, root medicines—every kind of mojo juice and conjure, peppermint and all of those kinds of things. He had a drugstore, too, but it was a jive drugstore because it didn't have a prescription department. You'd have someone in a white coat take the prescriptions, and then at the end of the day he'd get on his bike and go down to a real drugstore and have them all filled. I once had this idea to have a sign made for the drugstore: Dr. Solomon Burke, Notions, Lotions, and Potions, Roots, Fruits, and Snoots."

And, of course, no one will ever forget the time he played the Apollo Theatre at the height of his popularity and demanded the right to sell concessions. Which was fine with owner Frank Schiffman, since it was not unusual for singers to sell their pictures and records, and Solomon was known for marching up and down the aisles during intermission to sell souvenirs. This time, however, Solomon had something else in mind. Somewhere or other he had gotten hold of a truckload of popcorn. When he started selling it, Frank Schiffman was outraged. Here's the official story.

"Who'd want to sell popcorn when he's pulling down four grand for a week's engagement?" declared Bobby Schiffman, in his brother Jack's *Uptown: The Story of Harlem's Apollo Theatre.* "But Solomon arrived . . . with a cooker on which he fried pork chops to sell the gang backstage, and a carton of candy. . . . I decided to humor him—until the truck pulled up. The truck was loaded with popcorn. I put my foot down, but Solomon said, 'It's in the contract. Read your contract.' . . . I finally made a deal with him. I bought all that goddamned popcorn from him for fifty bucks."

Signing autographs: England, 1965. (Courtesy of Bill Millar)

Here's Solomon's story, abbreviated, and unpunctuated by the guffaws and imitations, the takeoffs of uncanny accuracy and comic diversity that will simply have to be imagined.

"The truth of the whole story was that I was in Miami Beach at the Holland House Hotel on vacation with my family, and Bob Schiffman calls me from the Apollo and says, 'Man, I really need you.' Well, I'd just gotten involved with my drugstores (Notions, lotions, and potions, roots, fruits, and snoots), and I'd just bought the popcorn business, and I was supplying popcorn for all the theaters in Philadelphia, and I had the Mountain Dew franchise for Philadelphia, too, first one. But I had bought too much popcorn, and I had like a whole house stacked with popcorn that was already popped. Would you go for 15,000 twenty-five-pound bags? And I had deals going on with my popcorn, jack, any of my stores you get free popcorn, just bring the box back for a refill! So I had to do something, and I agreed to play the Apollo under one condition: that I have the concessions. Bob Schiffman thought about it for about a minute and said, 'Okay. You got it.' And I said, 'Send me a telegram to that effect, I must have a telegram today that I have *all* the concessions, because I must get everything ready.'

"Now back in those days a black man who had the concessions meant that you would come in and sell your pictures, your records, and those felt hats that you take some glue and write your name over it with sprinkles. But *my* idea of concessions was the hot dogs, the hamburgers, the candy (I had three drugstores, right?). *And* the popcorn. I didn't really care about the candy, the hot dogs, the hamburgs, not even the sodas, but I want to unload that popcorn, jack. I even brought a trailer along with me to Florida, man, and I was giving popcorn to the people along the highway. Bags of it. Anything to get rid of that popcorn.

"Well, anyway, I had about 10,000 stickers printed up to go on the boxes of popcorn saying, 'Thank you for coming to the Apollo Theatre from Solomon Burke, Atlantic Records Recording Artist. Your Box of Soul Popcorn.' I ordered a tractor-trailer truck with union personnel to roll in immediately. I had my people stack that tractor-trailer with candy, sodas, pretzels, potato chips, and I had my people loading up 10,000 boxes already packed—with popcorn. Well, everything was cool, I got to the Apollo, I said, 'Hey, what's happening? The concessions are set up, my people are here to go to work.' They said, 'What are you talking about? You can set up out on the sidewalk.' I said, 'No. No, man, ain't setting up on no sidewalk, brother, *we* got the concessions.' Said, 'I have a contract here. What it say? Man, I can't read it. I'm dumb, I went to Catholic school. It say concessions? It say *all* concessions? The word *all* is very important. That means I *can* put a meter on the toilets, but we're not gonna do that, y'understand, we gonna be a nice guy.' The regular concession people from ABC say, 'Do you believe this? Man, I gotta sell my stuff.' I said, 'Well, jack, you gonna sell it across the street. It's in my contract.'

"Then Bobby Schiffman came down and said, 'What are you doing to my father? Do you want to give him a heart attack?' I said, 'What's the problem, man? You gave me the concessions.' He says, 'What's wrong with you, fool, don't you know what concessions mean?' I said, 'No, you tell me.' He said, 'You know, you sell your pictures and your hats and your feathers.' I said, 'No, let me tell you what concessions mean. It means anything that you sell here. Food, beverages, *all,* the word *all* means programs, books, magazines, hot dogs, popcorn. *Popcorn*—very important.'

"Then Mr. Schiffman comes down, and he was a little upset, he's screaming, 'Who does he think he is, Nat King Cole, Ray Charles? Let him take the damn theater.' I said, 'No, just the concessions, man.'

"Well, we finally bargained down to a figure because ABC did have a legitimate contract on the concessions, but I agreed to the deal on one condition only: that I give the popcorn away. I said, 'I won't sell it. I'll take a loss on the candy, the Baby Ruths, the Snickers bars, Oh Henrys, Hersheys, and the Mounds. I'll take a loss on the peanuts. I'll even take a loss on the pretzels and the Mountain Dews. But the popcorn must go.'

"By the end of that week everybody in New York had popcorn. Bob Schiffman, Honi Coles, everybody was out there in the street handing it out. The next week, when I came up to Atlantic Records, there was boxes of popcorn on everybody's desk. Everybody was telling me the story of the popcorn.

"To this day they never let me back in the Apollo Theatre. I wanted to buy it and make a church out of it, but they wouldn't even sell it to me. That's been my problem my whole life in entertainment: I utilize my educational background, and maybe that makes me a little too smart for my britches. They assumed that my intelligence was limited, that my ability to supply a demand was limited. I wasn't even thinking about singing that week. My biggest shot was: *get rid of that popcorn.* But it was the greatest publicity thing that I ever did."

Everywhere that he went Solomon employed his ingenuity to challenge the ways of the world, and maybe even to test its love for him a little, too. To Solomon it was all a trip, and when he says that he thrived on it, delighted in it all, you can believe that he did, the con as much as the material rewards, the contact with people as much as the stardom, the transcendent, almost religious experience of his art as much as the accumulation of transitory riches and temporal wealth.

"We played places no one else could, because we had the hits, and we had the manners, and we had the reputation. We had our own security, we moved in and out like that. I paid top dollar, and we had twenty-six people on our payroll. I loved those little country towns down South, I wouldn't take nothing for 'em. They brought out them old beat-up albums, you know what I mean, them old ladies bring food around to you, say, 'Son, you looking a little peak-ed. Son, you got to eat.' After a while I told my band, 'Don't eat nothing. Don't you be going to no restaurants.' 'Cause I couldn't eat everything them old ladies would be bringing me. I couldn't handle it. We'd get to the next town sometime in the morning after the night of a show, and I'd start looking for dogs. We'd be cruising back alleys, looking for dogs. Well-fed dogs, 'cause they're always a sure sign. Then them old ladies would come out with their biscuits and fresh-baked pies, they'd say, 'Here's some fresh milk for you, son, just be sure and bring back my thermos.' Fried chicken, barbecued ribs, ham hocks, collard greens, man, it was great. Then one of them old ladies would say, 'Son, would you drive my granddaughter out to the main highway? Don't you worry none, she can find her own way back.' No sooner do we get in the car and pull away from her grandmother than up come the dress—she isn't wearing no underwear—and she say, 'I'm sorry, I can't go back to the hotel with you, but I can give you something right here.' 'Okay, great!' 'What can I do for you?' 'Are you kidding? What have you got in mind?' Half the time they were so quick, man, I wasn't even ready."

"The first time he played Chicago," says Jerry Wexler, "he ordered a chicken dinner, and the chef, it was a black chef, heard it was Solomon Burke and brought the dinner out himself. He said, 'Is there anything I can do for you?' Solomon said, 'Just one thing. Can I get fifteen of these dinners and wrap them in wax paper and put them on the bus?' Sometimes when they were traveling in the South and they'd come to a crossroads, Solomon would turn his collar around and walk into a crossroads store and say, 'Man, I've got some hungry boys out there,' and con the guy out of Swiss cheese and ham, you know. You've got to remember, this was the South."

It all sounds like a lot of fun, and Solomon relished every minute of it. The food. The women. The games. Today, in his more meditative moments, he will say, "I'm a homebody. It's no life living in hotels. I like TV and home and fireplaces—and lawns, you must not forget the lawns," but in his heyday I doubt that he would even have been capable of so disingenuous a statement. He loved the crowd, he loved the adulation—there was no singer who responded more generously to the outstretched arms of his audience, and Solomon would typically conclude his act by turning over the microphone to a frenzied fan or get so deep into the message of a song like "The Price" or "Cry to Me" that it would become an extended sermonette, a small show in itself.

But music, as should be evident by now, took up only a small portion of the day. On the package shows each singer was allotted no more than fifteen minutes to a half hour of time, and even if there were two shows a day—or, at a sit-down gig like the Apollo, as many as five or six, in a continuous loop —more time was spent making contacts than making music. There was more dead time than live, and for many artists this was the real dark night of the soul, when the question arose and re-arose: What am I doing out here? This was the time when so many artists, major and otherwise, got themselves into trouble. For Solomon Burke, who is nothing if not creative in his use of everything, from spiritual resources to the telephone, there was scarcely enough time even to begin to fulfill all the roles in which he had cast himself.

"I'd go to the radio station and see the disc jockeys, go to the church and, of course, have prayer, go to the homes and bless the homes and babies, and then maybe baptize a few people. My schedule, you see, has always been a three-way personality. There's the artist, the religious leader, and just plain old Solomon Burke, who had his problems, who had his love life problems. Sometimes that's another movie, you know, God help us, Jesus."

Through the church he had contacts in every town. Even his peripheral interests exposed him to out-of-the-way places and experiences. One time as he was driving through Little Rock he was speaking to the members of the band about his background in mortuary science, and they disbelieved his estimate of the price of caskets. Piqued, he stopped the bus in front of a funeral home. "They're saying, 'Doc, there's no way that a casket can cost $2000.' I say, 'Are you kidding?' So we walk into this funeral home, and the guy's in there struggling with this body, he's using too much formaldehyde, he doesn't know what to do with it, you know. He says, 'Oh, God, it's too dark.' I'm saying, 'Wait a minute. Hold it.' And I wind up forgetting what we come in there for, I'm in there embalming. The cats are saying, 'What are you doing, man? We got a gig.' I say, 'I'm working on a gig right now.' " If it wasn't one thing, says Solomon uncomplainingly, it was another. There were always the old ladies to charm, and their young daughters, granddaughters, or perhaps even the ladies themselves to satisfy. And satisfy them he undoubtedly did—because Solomon is nothing if not considerate in his apportionment of attention and energies, and he never likes to let an audience go away calling for more.

And then, of course, there were his fellow artists, whom Solomon appreciated to the same degree that he appreciates anyone else of striking or eccentric individuality. He tended to gravitate, he says, toward the more "serious" members of the tour, singers for the most part who lacked a drug or alcohol problem and took a somewhat disciplined approach to their careers. He idolized Sam Cooke, as well he might, not only for Cooke's contributions to his musical style but also as someone who was canny enough to beat the man at his own game. Don Covay, whose songs Solomon admired and who in turn admires "Big Sol" extravagantly himself, was a particular friend, and so were Otis Redding—only then emerging from the shadow of singers like Solomon and Cooke—and Joe Tex, whom he had met at an amateur show at the Apollo (Solomon won, they both agree) soon after they both arrived in New York. "We'd always hang out together, ride in each other's limousines, stay in the same hotels—we interlocked ourselves, so to speak. You got to remember that the Otis Reddings, Joe Texes were never alcoholics or dope addicts; we never had a problem with booze or drugs, we just had fun. Real fun."

To other singers like Little Willie John, less disciplined in their personal conduct, Solomon was something of a father figure. "I think they had respect for me. For example, if the guys were all drinking and gambling, and I'd be coming into the room, they'd say, 'Oh, Doc's coming, Bishop's coming.' And everybody'd stop gambling and say, 'Hey, yeah, how's it going? Yeah, hey.' And I'd begin to catch on, you know, and one time Bobby 'Blue' Bland walked in and said, 'Hey, you're holding up the game, baby.' Which is cute—but to me it made me feel good, because it said, 'Hey, they're giving you the respect.' Or they'd come to me and say, 'Hey, I've got a bet on so and so, I'm betting $500, you hold the money.'

"Okay. I remember one night when Sam Cooke was playing with Jerry Butler, Little Willie John, Dee Clark, and a guy named Lotsa Poppa. Lotsa was a big guy, two times as big as me. You've probably seen him on the show with me—he sings all my songs. I found him in Atlanta, and I'm crazy about the guy. Every time I'd see him, I'd call him up on stage 'cause he was bigger than me and he made me look small. And when he got up there, he could barely move around, and I could just dance all around him, it really made me look good. I *loved* to have the guy around.

"Okay, Lotsa was the smallest act on the show, he didn't even have a record, you know what I mean, and this particular night he took $5000 off of Sam, he walked away with a ring of Jerry's, he had a diamond stickpin of Dee Clark's, maybe about $6000 more he won from that crap game. I said, 'Lotsa, you had a successful night.' He said, 'What should I do with it, Doc?' I said, 'What you should do now is send some money home, buy yourself a house.'

Coronation in Baltimore, 1964: Rockin' Robin crowns the King of Rock 'n' Soul. (Courtesy of Bill Millar)

He says, 'I'm gonna get me a Cadillac.' I say, 'Get you a nice house. Call your wife. Let *her* buy the house.' You could get a nice house down in Georgia for three or four thousand dollars then.

"Lotsa wouldn't listen. Lotsa went out the next day and bought this and that. That night we were some other place, some other city, and he wanted to start the crap game again, and I said, 'Lotsa, don't get into that crap game, you can't never win again.' Lotsa says, 'Thousand dollars a roll.' They wiped out poor Lotsa that night. Sam was throwing, he got like a streak, I want to say he made eleven straight passes with the craps, sevens and elevens eleven times straight. He must have gotten those guys for twelve grand, and he come to me and says, 'Doc, you hold it.' And I said, 'Where's J.W.? Where's your manager?' Hey, hey, hey, poor Lotsa Poppa."

In 1964, after a dozen straight hits, Solomon was crowned King of Rock 'n' Soul by Rockin' Robin of radio station WEBB in Baltimore. Needless to say, he took the title seriously. From this point on, it seems, at least for the next decade, he never performed without a robe and a crown and all the trappings (which occasionally included midgets strewing flowers) of royalty. In England, he claims, perhaps a little fancifully, he was almost deported for practicing religion without a license, and his shows at their peak did take on all the air of a religious revival. "People fainted, people would break out into fights on certain songs, whenever I'd sing, 'I'm throwing away my little black book' in the song 'I'm Hanging Up My Heart for You,' some lady would scream out, 'How come you didn't throw it away already?' 'Tonight's the Night' always created problems in certain cities. Yeah, people took it seriously. One time in Atlanta this lady committed suicide. A very weird and troubling experience."

There were sour notes, to be sure, and there were disappointments along the way, but Solomon was unquestioned king in his day, his popularity rivaling that even of the legendary James Brown, who was known not so much for his royal aspirations as for his reputation as "the hardest-working man in show business." Brown is virtually the only one of his former colleagues about whom Solomon has less than kind words to say, but even James is dismissed with relative equanimity, as Solomon makes it clear that their differences were one-sided only and Brown is more to be pitied (for his monomania and humorlessness) than scorned.

"Well, there was no rivalry," Solomon declares. "The only problem we ever had, and it wasn't really a problem—I thought it was very amusing—you see, being the King of Rock 'n' Soul was not a situation where I had to fight for it, but a James Brown, who was the only other person with a cape out there, felt at one point after he had 'Papa's Got a Brand New Bag' and a few other songs that *he* should be the King of Soul. Now he hired me to perform with him one time in Chicago. And he paid me $10,000 for the one night, great date, because it was an early Wednesday show, we were off anyway, and when we got there, we come to find out he didn't even want the band to work, his band was going to play. So I said, 'Great!' 'Cause he had a bigger band. I was only carrying seven or eight pieces at the time, and he had a big sixteen-piece orchestra. So I said, 'Fantastic. No problem.'

"Well, we got out there, and his man comes up and says, 'Mr. Brown would like to know if you have your robe and your crown.' I say, 'Yes, I do.' And he says, 'Mr. Brown would like for you to wear it.' I say, 'No problem.' The other guy comes and says, 'Mr. Brown would like to know if you have your carpet.' I say, 'Yes, I do.' He says, 'Fine. Mr. Brown would like for you to use it.' Fine. The other guy comes out and says, 'Mr. Brown requires that you be ready to go on in five minutes.' I say, 'Okay, no problem, great.' I say, 'Could you do me one favor, though? Could you tell Mr. Brown I'd like to take care of the contract.' So another little guy comes over with a briefcase and says, 'Mr. Brown never pays the artist till after the artist performs.' I say, 'My contract requires that Mr. Brown, Mr. Blue, Mr. Black, Mr. White pays before I perform.' So it goes back and forth, it was not for real. Next thing I know

James come over with all the money and threw it on the table and says, 'I got your money, I got your money, you just be out there.' He says, 'I'm gonna show you something tonight.' So this guy says, 'Mr. Brown is going to show you something tonight.' Okay, great.

"It came time for me to go on, and they had my carpet brought up to the stage and everything, and the guy says, 'Ladies and gentlemens'—a big fat guy—'the man you've all been waiting for'—and they rolled my carpet out. And I say, 'Sounds like they gonna introduce me just like they do James.' And I'm standing in the wings, you know, with my robe and my crown on. 'The man that had million sellers,' and so on and so forth. ' "You Can Make It If You Try" '—and I say, 'What is this?'—' "Please, Please, Please" '—I say, 'What?'—' "Papa's Got a Brand New Bag," James,'—dadedadeda—'Brown, the new King of Soul!' And James came on with his cape, dancing on the carpet. That was funny, man. He says, 'Your job, just watch me. Watch the real king.' And they kept trying to tell me, 'Mr. Brown wants you to go out now and take your crown off and put it on him.' I say, 'Man, you're crazy! Y'all are crazy.' They *would* not let me go on. He did the whole show, and the people holler, 'Solomon, Solomon, Solomon,' and he says, 'Solomon Burke cannot perform because he's been decrowned.' I never did find out what 'decrowned' meant. But it was, as I say, very amusing, and the one thing I said to James after that, I said, 'James, I want to tell you something. I enjoyed watching you perform. Really great. If you got another little job for us to do tomorrow night, we'll do it. And for only $8000. Providing we do the same thing we did tonight.'

"Oh, there were so many great times," says Solomon, who has just as many great times today and who, as we flip through a book on the Harlem Renaissance, lights up as he spies a picture of one of his idols, Father Divine. "Now that's a great image," he says. "Don't you think that would make a great image for me, Peter? Just get rid of some of the jokes."

▶3▶

Beginnings: Stax

There's an old saying
That goes like so
Keep trying
And you'll get where you want to go
When things get rough
Buckle down
Don't give up
You can conquer the world with your original sound.
They knocked at the front door
And couldn't get in
They heard a sound and went to the back door
Thus the sound let them in.

—Unattributed poem in a Stax publicity release

I'm a soul man
Got what I got the hard way

—"Soul Man," Isaac Hayes and David Porter

STAX RECORDS. THE NAME TODAY IS STILL rich in associations. Otis Redding, Carla and Rufus Thomas, Sam and Dave, Booker T. and the MG's—the roll call could go on and on. A tiny label that started out in 1960 renting a disused movie theater in a shabby neighborhood that was going from white to black. On the theater marquee would soon appear in giant letters of red plastic, SOULSVILLE U.S.A. (for a while, in more socially conscious times, STAY IN SCHOOL). In later years the theater would be pointed to as The Cause: it was the configuration of the sloping floor, it was the giant, bass-heavy U-8 movie speakers that made everything sound that much better on the playback. It was the retail record outlet, the Satellite Record Shop, which occupied the former candy and popcorn stand and served as a kind of on-the-spot barometer of taste for the fledgling operators of the label. It was the neighborhood: local kids dropping in after school, future songwriter David Porter bagging groceries at the Jones Big Star across the street, Booker T. and William Bell attending the same church nearby. Actually the anonymous poem printed above (it was originally pub-

Soulsville U.S.A.

lished at the front of Stax's first proud publicity booklet) probably comes as close to the truth as any of the other explanations. Stax, in its own estimation, and to some extent in the eyes of the world, was the Little Engine That Could, the little record company that kept trying. The amazing thing is that when it began, neither of its founders even knew what a record company was, let alone what a rhythm and blues record was supposed to sound like. The austere classicism of the Stax sound did not come about by aesthetic choice but by necessity.

Stax Records in the beginning was the creation of two people, brother and sister, Jim Stewart (the "St") and Estelle Axton ("ax"). Brought up in the country in Middleton, Tennessee (population: 230), Estelle came to Memphis in 1934 at the age of sixteen to get her teaching certificate and then returned one year later to Middleton, where she was her brother's first-grade teacher. By the time she was married and had school-age children of her own, Jim, twelve years younger, had joined her back in Memphis, where he studied business at Memphis State in preparation for a banking career. He graduated in 1956 at the age of twenty-six after a stint in the Special Services, where he indulged his penchant for playing the fiddle ("I used to tease him," says Estelle. "I told him he played the fiddle when he was a young man and went to college and got educated to play the violin."). Actually, even during his attendance at Memphis State he continued to play the fiddle in several Western swing bands that became well known in the Memphis area, and he appeared frequently on the radio with Don Powell and the Canyon Cowboys on WDIA and Clyde Leoppard and the Snearly Ranch Boys on West Memphis's KWEM.

Occasionally during those years he played out at the Clearpool, where the manager, local DJ Sleepy Eyed John Lepley, would sometimes hire a young unknown singer named Elvis Presley to perform solo during the breaks between the sets. After graduation Stewart started law school at night, still moonlighting in music, and he went to work in the bonds department at the First National Bank. Estelle meanwhile had been working for three years as a teller at the Union Planter's Bank. It was not exactly a classic background for a rhythm and blues man or woman. As Jim says, "I had scarcely seen a black till I was grown. I didn't know when I started, I didn't know there was such a thing as an Atlantic Records. I didn't know there was a Chess Records or Imperial. I had no desire to start Stax Records, I had no dream of anything like that. I just wanted music. Just anything to be involved with music—one way or the other."

He started fooling around with recording in his wife's uncle's garage on Orchi Street around 1957. A barber friend named M. E. (Marshall Erwin) Ellis had some equipment and some knowledge of the business (Ellis had his own Erwin label for a while). So with Ellis's help, and in partnership with a disc jockey at KWEM named Fred Byler, who had sung in one of his bands, Jim Stewart brought out his first record, a c&w song called "Blue Roses" that he had written and Byler sang. The record label was called Satellite because "satellites were big at that time." Stewart's theory was that with Byler's radio connections they would get a lot of airplay, but it didn't work out that way, and his attempts to record Donna Rae Jackson, a hostess on the WHBQ *Dance Party,* and Nadine Easton (for whom Stewart's East Publishing was named) were equally unsuccessful, despite the presence in the studio of a young guitar player from LaGrange, Georgia, just bursting with attitudes and ideas. Chips Moman had recently drifted into town at age twenty-one after a brief stay in

Jim Stewart and Estelle Axton, circa 1963. (Courtesy of Charlie Gillett)

California, where he had established his credentials as a sometime session guitarist at the Gold Star Studio in Los Angeles. He had also put in considerable time on the road with Gene Vincent and Johnny and Dorsey Burnette among others, and, not altogether surprisingly, gave off the flinty-eyed look of a professional gambler (gambling competed with music as his chief passion). He quickly took over Jim's sessions, as he would one day take over much of the Memphis music industry, producing the Box Tops, B. J. Thomas, the Gentrys, even Elvis Presley, along with countless out-of-town acts in his American studio.

It wasn't until 1958 that Estelle became involved. "My brother brought that first record by the house, and I didn't have anything to play it on but a little-bitty record player that somebody had given the kids, but he wanted to know what I thought about it. And I said, 'Well, it's all right, the sound seems a little thin,' and all that. And he said, 'The only way we can make it better is to have better equipment to record it on.' So that's when he asked me if I would be interested in investing any money."

In a well-known story Estelle took out a second mortgage on her house for $2500—not an inconsiderable amount of money in 1958 for people who "liked music but held down laboring jobs"—and they bought an Ampex monaural recorder. They moved out of the garage, too, and into the country, to Brunswick, thirty miles east of Memphis, where another friend of Jim's, another barber, named Mr. Mitchell, had an old storehouse that was sitting idle. Mr. Mitchell had a daughter, too, whom he was anxious to see make records.

"He said we could use the warehouse if we wanted to go out there and clean all the old shelves and stuff out of it. So we did that, went out there, fixed it up, and nailed up our acoustics. My brother had been around recording equipment a fair amount by this time. Of course it doesn't take much engineering for a one-track machine. Even I learned to run it. But we had a little group. Steve Cropper was in that group. My son, Packy, was playing tenor sax. Charlie Freeman on guitar, Terry Johnson was the drummer, Duck Dunn—they all went to Messick High School, they were just a little rock group that called themselves the Royal Spades. When Packy was introduced to the band, they had enough guitar players, so they said, 'Well, why don't you learn horn?' Well, he traded in his guitar and got the horn, and that's how he became a tenor player. But I put all of these guys in my car every Saturday—because I worked five days a week at the bank—but on Saturdays they'd load up all their equipment, instruments, and such, and we'd go out to Brunswick. They'd set up, and they'd jam and practice and everything, and that's when I learned to put something on tape."

It became something like a consuming passion—every weekend out in Brunswick, woodshedding mostly, with perhaps one or two "professional" sessions behind Charlie Heinz or Nick Charles, another local DJ, thrown in for good measure. Estelle set up an ice cream stand to bring in a little money (Satellite Dairy) and began carrying out records from the city to sell. Jim tried out different sounds. The "little high school rock group" practiced endlessly. Whenever there was a real session, it seemed, the train would go by and rattle the windows. To Jim, who discovered rhythm and blues at just about this time, through Ray Charles's "What'd I Say," the whole prospect of making records was something like a dream. "I was like the addict, that was about my second fix and I was gone. Hooked. That was it." For Estelle the experience was no less all-consuming. "I never thought of it till I got in it, and then I lived it, twenty-four hours a day. When I wasn't working, I was dreaming about it."

They put out three or four records—country, rockabilly, and rhythm and blues—but none of them did anything, least of all the r&b record, which was picked up for distribution by Mercury but went nowhere in the late fall of 1959. In 1960 the opportunity arose to move back into town. Chips Moman spotted an old movie theater on East McLemore, the Capitol, which had been used for country and western shows, then converted into a church, and was currently vacant. For a hundred dollars a month rent Jim and Estelle snapped it up. They went through the whole process of setting up once again. They ripped out the theater's seats, built a control room in the stage area, laid down carpeting, padded the walls, and for acoustics hung drapes from the ceiling that Estelle had made at home. Because the theater was far too big for their little Ampex tape recorder, they divided it down the middle with a makeshift partition, and converted the popcorn and candy stand out in the lobby into the record shop from which they

The Mar-Keys: Packy Axton, Duck Dunn, Wayne Jackson, Terry Johnson, Don Nix, Steve Cropper, Smoochy Smith. (Phillip Rauls)

would derive much of their early income. Almost all the work was done at night or on weekends, in whatever time Jim and Estelle, Packy and his friends, and Chips Moman could grab from their regular jobs. Then, just as they were finishing up, Rufus Thomas walked in the door.

Rufus Thomas was something of a local legend. MC of the Amateur Night talent competitions at the Palace and Handy theaters (where both B. B. King and Bobby "Blue" Bland had gotten their start), Thomas had made blues and novelty records himself for several labels, including Sam Phillips's Sun Records, for whose success he has always claimed to be the foundation. He did, in fact, have Sun's first hit with "Bear Cat," the answer to Big Mama Thornton's "Hound Dog," in 1953, and he might have continued with Sam Phillips for some time had Elvis Presley not materialized at this point and changed the whole direction of Sun and American music. Rufus continued to seek recording sessions for smaller Memphis labels like Meteor and was a well-known disc jockey on the same radio station, WDIA, on which Jim Stewart had played the fiddle in various country swing bands (WDIA was known throughout the South as "The Mother Station of the Negroes" but featured hillbilly bands and music through the early fifties); he held on to his job tending boilers at the same textile mill where he had worked since 1940, though, because show business remained an uncertain venture for a man with a wife and three kids that he wanted to see get a decent education. When he stopped by the one-time Capitol

Rufus Thomas, July 1968. (Don Paulsen/Michael Ochs Archives)

Theater, forty-three years old, dapper in dress and up to the minute in his genial jive ("I'm young and loose and full of juice," he proclaimed in his radio theme, "I got the goose, so what's the use?"), Jim Stewart was working on yet another pop number with Charlie Heinz. Nothing much was happening.

Rufus, who is nothing if not enterprising, had stopped by at the suggestion of a friend, blues pianist Robert Talley, who felt that something might be going on at the new studio. He didn't remember Jim, though Jim knew Rufus from pitching "Someday" by the Veltones, Satellite's one r&b record, down at the WDIA studio. Since it was by a local group, Rufus had been helpful, but the record still hadn't gone anywhere, even in Memphis, and the Veltones remained strictly a club attraction.

Rufus, as always, had an idea. If there is anyone in the business who fits the much-abused description of a survivor, it is Rufus Thomas, self-described as "the world's oldest teenager," who started out in the minstrel shows and ended up in his mid-forties showing the Rolling Stones how to walk the dog. His idea this time was that he and his seventeen-year-old daughter, Carla—then a senior at Hamilton High School, but a veteran of almost ten years of show business through her performing with the Teen Town Singers—should cut a jaunty up-tempo song he had written, "Cause I Love You," as a duet. By the time they finally cut the song and released it in August of 1960, Carla was already on her way to college at Tennessee State in Nashville. Carla's brother, Marvell, played piano on the record; Robert Talley played trumpet, Steve Cropper, who was present at the session, was inaudible on guitar; and a very young Booker T. Jones, who was brought into the studio by David Porter (the Jones Big Star delivery boy and would-be songwriter and artist), played baritone sax.

With some astuteness Satellite Records assigned part of the publishing credit on the tune to John R. (Richbourg), the deep-voiced r&b hit-maker on WLAC in Nashville whose strong late-night signal was heard all through the South. Through John R.'s influence (he now had a vested interest in the record), through Rufus, and through Rufus's colleague Dick "Cane" Cole at WLOK, Memphis's other rhythm and blues station, "Cause I Love You" turned out to get a surprising amount of local airplay and was something of a hit throughout the South (Rufus even got it played in San Francisco through the Sonderling chain, which owned WDIA). When it had sold fifteen or twenty thousand copies, it even came to the attention of Jerry Wexler in New York, through Leon McLemore, the manager of Music Sales, Atlantic's (and Satellite's) Memphis distributor. Wexler leased the record for $1000 and took a five-year option on what Jim and Estelle interpreted to be all other duets by Rufus and Carla. "They offered us $1000 for that master," says Estelle (Jim thinks $2000). "Well, that was the biggest $1000 we had ever seen, because that was the first money we had ever made in the three years that we had been in the business." "I didn't know what label distribution was or a production deal or anything," says Jim. "We got a percentage rate so small it was unreal. But it was a start. I was really bitten, and this was the big time for me."

All the money they got from Atlantic they put right back into the company. There was another song that Carla had been playing around with on piano at the first session, and everyone was convinced that it could really be a hit. No one at Satellite was about to give up at this point. Jim and Estelle had finally seen the light at the end of the tunnel, and if it was rhythm and blues, then so be it. "It wasn't any conscious decision, I don't think," says Jim. "We didn't just sit down and say, 'We're going on with the black music.' It just happened from a combination of things, I guess: the record store, the people who started dropping in at the studio. Once we had the success with Rufus and Carla, it was as though we cut off a whole part of our lives that had existed previously. We never looked back from there."

"GEE WHIZ"

"Gee Whiz," Carla Thomas's first solo outing, cut in the fall of 1960, was the first record that Stax could call a national hit. After the success of "Cause I Love You," recalls Carla, "Daddy said, 'Well, you got another song, you know.' I said, 'What song?' And he said, ' "Gee Whiz." ' Well, this is just to give you an idea—I mean, I'm trying to tell you it was just a hobby and a love; I had

Carla Thomas with WDIA baseball team, circa 1956.
(Courtesy of Jonas Bernholm)

actually written this song and stuck it in my notebook more than two years before. Because who says, you know, 'Gee whiz, look at his eyes,' when they're eighteen? You say that kind of thing at fourteen or fifteen maybe. When I wrote it, I had no idea I would want to cut this. To me it was just a God-given song. But I said, 'Do you think "Gee Whiz" will sound good on a record?' 'Cause I used to just sit there and pick it out, and it was so simple. He said, 'Well, I like it.' And it's been twenty years now, but people still relate to it. That's why I say it was just a God-given song, just out of the heart."

"I knew 'Gee Whiz' was a good song," says Rufus. "I had already taken it to Chicago, a little home recording of it—this was before I ever even heard of Stax, and I took it to Vee Jay on my vacation and let them listen. They said, 'Well, you know, this is all right,' but it stayed up there a whole year, and so when I went back on vacation the following year, I picked it up and brought it back. And that's when it was recorded here, in November of 1960, and it was sort of a sleeper, went on past Christmas, past the New Year, and all of a sudden it hit like a ton of bricks."

Hit it did. It hit so hard, in fact, that Atlantic, which had already more or less passed on distribution (at least that's what Jim and Estelle assumed when they brought it out on their own label), protested loudly and vehemently that they had a contract to distribute *all* Satellite product. Jim and Estelle countered that the contract was strictly for duets by Rufus and Carla, but the upshot was that Carla Thomas, while remaining signed to Satellite, ended up on the Atlantic label; Jerry Wexler paid a first, memorable visit to the McLemore Avenue offices; and Satellite extended its distribution agreement with Atlantic to encompass all product. "I thought at the time of going independent," says Jim, "and Wexler said, 'Man, you'd be making a big mistake, you don't know how bad collections are, etc., etc.' I finally decided to sign with him for five years and then see. Looking back on it, it was a mistake; I could have made it at that time because the industry was still healthy, but in the long run, you know, it served its purpose and allowed us to concentrate on production and the creative aspects."

Whether Satellite really could have made it on its own at this point is open to question, but with "Gee Whiz" the studio's creative element, and somewhat haphazard methodology, had more or less fallen into place. The record itself was produced by Chips Moman, engineered by Jim. Strings were arranged on the spot by Jim and Memphis Symphony conductor Noel Gilbert after the arranger who had been hired failed to show up. The initial session was held at another studio (Hi) because, says Jim, "I was a dumb asshole. I didn't know what I had and figured maybe they were better equipped." Even Jerry Wexler's involvement in the project was not altogether clear-cut and in fact set a tone for his ambiguous relationship with Memphis over the years. By his own account Wexler invited Rufus and Carla, Mrs. Thomas, and Jim Stewart to his hotel suite to celebrate the new association. They met at the hotel, says Wexler, because of Memphis's continued public segregation and because, says Wexler, Jim was not yet ready to invite Negroes into his home. Wexler and Stewart picked up Thomas at the radio station and then, at Jim's suggestion, went in the back entrance of the hotel, picking their way among the garbage cans. "Same old shit," commented Rufus wearily.

"After everybody left, I went to sleep," recounts Wexler, "and there was a knock on the door. 'Vice squad,' says this voice. 'Open up. You got a girl in there.' I said, 'Just a minute. Get the manager.' While they sent for the manager, I wrote a letter to my partner, and when the manager came up, I dashed by them and stuck it in the mailbox. I didn't know who they were. I didn't know what they were going to do to me. No idea—in Memphis, nineteen-sixty-whatever. Maybe I overreacted. I thought maybe I was going to wind up in Mississippi in the trunk of a car."

Carla Thomas's "little poem" was a Top 10 hit, pop *and* r&b, in early 1961, but the company was still somewhat lacking in direction. The song, with its soft, ethereal, gauzelike tone, augmented by candy-cane strings, was not exactly hard r&b, and the artist, as fresh and talented as she was, was no more typically slated for success. In fact it took visits from both Jerry Wexler and her parents to convince the college dean that she should be given a weekend or two off to tour, once she had established her grades. Satellite had no follow-up in mind and, aside from Rufus and Carla, no artist roster to speak of at all. It was still a fly-by-night operation that had yet to prove itself as more than a one-shot success; it was still a mom-and-pop (sister-and-brother) outfit that was geared to whatever was the opposite of banker's hours.

And yet it was rapidly taking on a cast and a character all its own, unorthodox even for Memphis, which has always been known for its unorthodox operations. Every morning Estelle's son, Packy, would open up the studio, prompted by a reminder call from his mother at the bank. Packy and his friends had been out of high school since June of 1959 (Steve Cropper was currently an engineering student at Memphis State), but for Packy—as for his mother and uncle—there was nothing but the music business by this point. Any night he wasn't playing with the Royal Spades (the high school band which had rehearsed such long and enthusiastic hours out at the studio in Brunswick), he was club-hopping with some of the characters he had met at Satellite, soaking up the atmosphere at various r&b joints around town, showing up, according to William Brown (one of the neighborhood kids who gained a job in the record store and went on to become both an artist, with the Mad Lads, and the company's first black recording engineer), in places where few other whites would dare to venture. He was, says fellow musician Jim Dickinson, "one of the most transracial individuals I've ever met."

Once Packy had opened up, generally Chips Moman would float in sometime during the afternoon, having played a gig somewhere the night before. Not long afterward the whole gang from Booker T. (Booker T. Washington High School, which boasted among its recent graduates and undergraduates singer/songwriters David Porter and Homer Banks, as well as multi-instrumentalist Booker T. Jones, whose father taught science and math at the school) was likely to come bursting in the door to see what, if anything, was going on. Packy's friends and fellow bandmembers—guitarist Charlie Freeman, Steve Cropper, Duck Dunn, and sax player Don Nix—might stop by at any hour of the day or night to join Packy in a jam, or just sit around and listen to the latest records, study them with the idea of being the first white band in Memphis to be able to reproduce the Midnighters' or the "5" Royales' latest hits note for note.

At four-thirty every afternoon "Miz Axton," as she was universally called, would fly in, freed from the drudgery of her work at the bank, ready to take on a whole other identity in a world in which she pictured herself an inspired housemother or, perhaps, a curator of dreams. Jim, mild-mannered in appearance ("He was a bank teller," more than one of his former colleagues has said), less

Jim Dickinson and Ace proprietor Johnny Vincent, Jackson, Mississippi.
(Pat Rainer)

personable than his sister, unemotional-seeming but of a nervous and somewhat
authoritarian disposition, was not always able to get away so early, but he was
there every night. He had given up playing by now; all his musical interests were
focused on the recording studio. Every night they would experiment, try out
different sounds—inexperienced black and white kids, with the occasional seasoned black horn player thrown in (Fred Ford or Gilbert Caples, from the
Plantation Inn, bandleader Willie Mitchell's brother James), all under the direction of a timid bank officer and a hard-edged guitar player who might have
preferred to be a professional gambler. Over and over they sought to repeat the
formula that they had stumbled across with Rufus and Carla's hit songs; they
sought to recapitulate their success and go beyond it.

Not surprisingly the record store was a central part of this experimentation.
For one thing it gave them access to every new sound coming out at just about
the moment that it first appeared. More important, it gave them a finger on the
pulse of the community. William Brown recalls: "Poplar Tunes [Joe Cuoghi's
retail operation, out of which the Hi label had grown] was the biggest, but we
were the best. You could just hum a line, and we could tell you the name of
the song—it was just so good." Booker T. recalls Miz Axton playing any record
that a customer wanted to hear; he remembers the atmosphere of the record store
as being "magical." To Estelle it was an opportunity to talk shop with all the

Estelle Axton: Going to work. (Jonas Bernholm)

promo men who came through to push their product—old-time record men like Joe Galkin, who might come in hustling Solomon Burke's new record on Atlantic but didn't mind having his brain picked on the side.

"I used to have a ball with Joe, because he'd come in and we'd talk about records—just because I had the shop. That shop turned out to be one of the best tools that Stax had, because musicians would come up to listen to records that were hits and pretty well analyze *why* they were hits, because they had the facility to actually come in and listen to it. Chips Moman was one of the world's worst about coming up there and figuring out what was the hit part of a song, pulling that hit part out and developing a whole new sound from it. Jim used to like to come up there, too, when I was real busy and just stand around and see what records were selling. And he did give me credit for one thing: he said I was the damnedest record salesman he had ever seen. He said he had seen people come there so poor, but if they had twenty bucks, I'd get nineteen before they left, because I'd find something to sell them. You see, if I didn't believe in the record, I wouldn't push it, but when I believed in something, I believed in it wholeheartedly."

"I used to spend Friday and Saturday nights in the record shop if we weren't cutting," Jim recalls, "because those were the great times. At first it was necessary, because we couldn't hire help. Then, later on, I still hung around. It was a great experience for me, probably one of the happiest times of my life. Just to work behind the counter and really deal with the consumer—I think a lot of these ivory tower executives, if they spent a few weeks behind the counter, might put out some better records. I know when I got away from that, I really missed it."

The other factor that contributed to the magic in the air was that "transracial," almost bebop atmosphere which has been variously ascribed to Packy, to Chips, and to the McLemore location, and which would have been remarkable for anywhere in 1960, let alone Memphis and the South. Memphis in 1960— and not just on the testimony of Jerry Wexler, either—was a strictly segregated town. Despite the social revolution struggling to take place, despite Memphis's reputation as the home of the blues, despite WDIA and the birth of rock 'n' roll at the Sun studio at 706 Union, there were not a lot of places for black and white to mingle easily. White teenagers who wanted to be "daring" went over to the Plantation Inn in West Memphis (rhythm and blues the fare, clientele strictly white), where Phineas Newborn, Sr., Ben Branch, and trumpet player Willie Mitchell led jumping little bands, where Gilbert Caple's sax and Larry Brown's bass playing continued to inspire Packy Axton and Duck Dunn, where the Largoes provided near-perfect renditions of the latest hits (and steps), and where a singing waiter named Tennessee Turner, also known as "Sissy Charles," performed "Danny Boy" and "He's Got the Whole World in His Hands" at least twice nightly. Stories about the PI abound—myth and reality intertwined—and no one who grew up in that era and frequented the club fails to recall the illuminated sign that announced "Having Fun With Morris" (this was Morris Berger, the owner, manager Louis Jack's father), or the fights that accompanied the fun, or sitting in the parking lot with a date just feeling the music pulsate through the long low building, or Big Bell the drummer, or Blind Oscar the keyboard player, or Raymond Vega the bouncer.

For the more dedicated followers of r&b the "5" Royales—at this point recording locally for Reuben Cherry's Home of the Blues label, with Willie Mitchell producing—were not infrequent visitors to Memphis and occasionally played the Beverly Room at the Clearpool, one of the very places where Jim Stewart had started out, with a location (on Lamar Avenue) easily accessible to the Messick High crowd. Black kids meanwhile were hanging out at Clifford Miller's Flamingo Room on Hernando Street downtown, where a fourteen-year-old Booker T. Jones was snuck in to play bass or baritone sax with Willie Mitchell's band and thereby met Willie's drummer, Al Jackson, Jr. (Al Jackson, Sr., was an accomplished bass player himself and leader of one of the three big society bands in town). The old Club Handy was still operating on Beale Street under the stewardship of Sunbeam Mitchell. Johnny and Susie Curry's Club Tropicana featured topflight entertainment, and Little David (Porter) and Barbara Griffin (Al Jackson, Jr.'s future wife) were performing regularly at the Tiki

Club. William Bell and the Del Rios, Isaac Hayes and the Do-Dads, Ben Branch's big band, and Bowlegs Miller's all appeared with some degree of frequency all over town—and this is not even to mention the talent shows at the Palace and Handy theaters. It was a flourishing entertainment scene, in other words, one that could readily encompass big-band jazz, r&b, and the blues— but it was for black audiences exclusively, plus the occasional white kid with the do-rag on his head, like Packy and his friend Don Nix if they happened to wander in.

The only truly integrating factor was radio. Who knew, as various White Citizens' Councils have suggested, what evil lurked in the hearts of adolescents, or what music they were listening to as they tooled around town in their open-top cars? Who knew, in Memphis, how many white kids were being turned on by the savage jungle beat that was retailed on the airwaves by such radio personalities as Rufus "Bear Cat" Thomas, Al "Moohah" Williams, Robert "Honeyboy" Thomas, or Dick "Caine" Cole? And who would ever have suspected that all these various strands, all these barely discernible connections would somehow come into focus under the banner of Stax (Satellite) Records, that all this raw energy would somehow translate into the bubbling beehive of activity that was rapidly gathering force under the marquee of the old Capitol Theater at 926 East McLemore?

Because that is where it all came together. That is where the whole unlikely cast of characters, plus or minus one or two, gathered and met on nearly equal ground—at least for a while. Where else could neophyte Packy Axton have gotten the benefit of Gilbert Caples's longtime experience? Where else would an ambitious young guitar player like Steve Cropper have had the chance to play with a bass player like Lewis Steinberg (of the musically prominent black Steinberg family) or drummer Curtis Green from the PI? Where else would a wet-behind-the-ears Booker T. Jones ever have gotten the chance to escape both the ghetto *and* the black bourgeoisie, to interact with such a lively and different musical intelligence as Chips Moman's? Where else could a partnership like the Memphis Horns, uniting a white West Memphis dirt farmer's son like Wayne Jackson with black counterparts like Andrew Love and Floyd Newman (Newman was studying to be a teacher when they met), ever have come about? Estelle Axton calls it "a school, really. It was a learning process for all of us. We had an open-door policy at that time. If you wanted to be heard, if you had something unique or different for us to listen to, well then, bring it in, and we'd take the time to listen. Our kids just picked up so much technique and soul— up until then it had been mainly rock 'n' roll, just twang-twanging the guitars and the drummer going wild, but when it really got down to feeling, they were just taken with the black musicians. They learned how to write. They picked up the feel. And they became great at it."

Rufus Thomas, somewhat more acerbic in point of view, and feeling, characteristically, that his own contributions were not properly appreciated, says: "Jim didn't know nothing about that kind of music—at that time."

Even Jim, though, would not hesitate to agree, at least in general terms, with Rufus's assessment. "I didn't think it was so much a sound we were trying to accomplish; I don't think we really set out to do it. It was just the people involved, the way they came together—it was just a natural, it was a natural form of musical expression. It was the combination of white and black musicians and their ideas. It just happened."

"LAST NIGHT"

The next quantum leap forward—into a new name and a new sound—was equally accidental, or perhaps, in Jim's formulation, equally inevitable. "Last Night," by the hitherto unheard-of Mar-Keys (actually they were a studio group who were eventually incarnated by Packy's old band, the Royal Spades), came out in the summer of 1961 without much fanfare—one more in a long line of Memphis instrumentals—and quickly shot to Top 10 pop. A simple blues riff based on a crude hook that today sounds almost atavistic in its repetitiveness, the record went through so many changes in direction and personnel over several months of recording that no one is quite sure who played on the tape that was eventually released. Packy got one-fifth of the credit on the writing and, his mother fiercely insists, provided much of the inspiration for the song. Charlie Freeman, who at the very least had been equally responsible for the musical and spiritual direction of the Royal Spades, left the group just before the record hit to join the Joe Lee Orchestra, a "real" band with uniforms and big-band scores. Chips Moman has always felt that his own contribution, here and everywhere else at Stax, has been overlooked. He produced. Steve Cropper claims that he had to go to Jim Stewart to get his share of the credits recognized in the form of a small financial settlement. None of which would be particularly significant one way or another if the record had simply been a hit, but "Last Night" established not only the sound but the nucleus of the group that would become one of the twin foundations for the Stax label.

The Royal Spades had come a long way from the high school pickup band that piled into Estelle's car every Saturday afternoon and drove out to Brunswick to rehearse. Originally strictly a rhythm section with rock 'n' roll and blues ambitions (guitarist Steve Cropper played harmonica with a rack, imitating everyone's favorite blues hero, Jimmy Reed), the group had metamorphosed very early, with the simultaneous introduction of horns and Packy's anarchic spirit, becoming over the last three years *the* white r&b band in Memphis. They prided themselves not only on knowing the originals (referring back to the Gladiolas, not the Diamonds; unearthing the Spiders' version of "Witchcraft" as well as some of the Midnighters' and the "5" Royales' most obscure sides)

Hank Ballard and the Midnighters. (Michael Ochs Archives)

but also on being able to deliver their own versions earlier and better than anyone else in town. They were lower-middle-class kids (their parents were teachers, bank tellers, respectable blue-collar workers) who were totally serious about music. Steve Cropper, for example, was elated when he got a cut by Bill Justis on a song he wrote senior year in high school, and he still recalls the moment that he decided to become a rock 'n' roll guitarist, when he saw upperclassman Ed Bruce perform at the Friday morning chapel program his sophomore year at Messick. For Duck Dunn going to work for his brother Bobby at the King Records distributorship was not like work at all, and Packy and Charlie Freeman, who both died young, knew no other life but music.

It probably should be stated at this point that the political dynamics of the Royal Spades as a group are somewhat subject to interpretation. If you listen to Estelle, it would seem that Packy was the leader, though in fact Packy was something of a johnny-come-lately (he didn't join till the band was already under way, and some say his presence was due more to his mother's studio than to his own ability at the start). Many place Charlie Freeman clearly at the center, and certainly Charlie was the most sophisticated musically (when they were all still in high school, Charlie's parents paid for him to take lessons from jazz guitarist Lynn Vernon, and Charlie in turn gave pointers to Steve) as well as providing the James Dean role model. According to Steve, though, "I was the leader. I started the whole thing. I made most of the decisions on where we played and when we played and how we played." And by everyone else's account—depending on how mad they are at Steve at the moment (Steve is like certain gifted athletes in this respect; like Rick Barry or Jim Palmer, for example, he can appear so serenely self-confident, so wholly self-absorbed that

The Mar-Keys in the studio: Packy Axton, Wayne Jackson, Duck Dunn, Don Nix, Terry Johnson, Steve Cropper, Smoochy Smith. (Phillip Rauls)

he will often provide a convenient lightning rod for others' resentment)—it was something of a combination.

That is how I would guess that it was. Very likely there were two kinds of leadership at work in the Royal Spades: the visionary kind that Packy and Charlie offered (they might not always show up, they might not be altogether coherent, but they were always out there, ahead of the pack) and the practical sort that Steve provided in making sure that the gigs were properly booked and the band arrived more or less sober and ready to play. Any clearer perspective is complicated by the fact that Packy was to become very much a bone of contention between Jim and Estelle, and that Steve was even further resented by everyone else for his assiduous courtship of the two. Obviously a thumbnail sketch like this can only suggest the complexity of relationships that intertwine over twenty years, but it seems important at least to suggest that all was not harmonious from the start, that as romantic as the story may seem, it, too, is tied to the usual bedrock of ambivalent reality.

The Royal Spades' first real gig outside of high school dances and teenage canteens was at a rough club ("rough as a fucking cob") called Neal's Hideaway in Millington out by the Tipton County naval base. It was a three- to six-night-a-week gig that lasted for six months, and this was where, according to Steve and Duck, "we really cut our teeth and learned to perform." Jerry Lee "Smoochy" Smith was playing piano; Ronnie Stoots, otherwise known as Ronnie Angel and later the designer of many of the rather basic-looking Stax record jackets, joined up as vocalist; Packy, Wayne Jackson, and Don Nix made up the three-piece horn section; and, of course, the original unit—Charlie Freeman and Steve Cropper on guitars, Duck Dunn on bass, and Terry Johnson, the sole remaining high schooler, on drums—remained intact. Many nights the entire band would make the forty-minute drive out in Steve's '49 green turtleback Chevrolet. They all wore jackets with black felt spades embroidered on them; Don Nix customarily wore a turban like that of recently deceased r&b star Chuck Willis; and they endlessly practiced the precision turns, steps, and unison horn swings that would make them even more like the bands they admired out at the Plantation Inn.

In the fall Steve started college at Memphis State, attended classes from eight to three, worked at a grocery store from four till nine, and raced out to Millington to join the band for the second set. "It took forty minutes to get out there, and I'd literally change clothes in the car. We wouldn't get off stage until two in the morning, and I would leave and drop some of the guys off and I guess get a hamburger or something, and then I'd go home and either study or go to bed. Back up the next morning at seven, and in class at eight. I was living by myself, because when I came out of high school, my dad got trans-ferred by the railroad to Tulsa, Oklahoma. I was an only child, and my mom and dad all but told me I was going, but I told them, 'I got the band. I've got my friends. I just can't leave Memphis, because we've got something happening.' So my dad and I found a duplex, we went around and looked for a refrigerator; I guess I convinced them because I hadn't really done anything wrong, and I wasn't a problem child. With the money the band made and the money I made at the grocery store and the money Dad sent for me to go to college, I sort of maintained everything. It was a hard time, but it was fun."

That was the way it was for everyone, it seemed, to one degree or another: for Duck Dunn, married already and working for his brother at the King distributorship; for Packy, running the record shop for his mother—when he could get up in the morning; for Charlie Freeman, always working on his scales and on getting high. It was a hard time, but it was fun. There were probably half a dozen bands like the Royal Spades in every halfway-decent-sized city and rural area throughout the South, kids dreaming of some kind of transcendence, partly slumming, partly looking for an edge, but mostly looking for a nameless kind of beatitude, a future they couldn't quite envision but that was different from anything they knew. Maybe Packy and Charlie Freeman could have identified it, but for Duck Dunn, an easygoing sort with a cherubic face and curly red hair, heaven would have been "to become the best bass player in Memphis and to play with Ben Branch," the prominent black bandleader from the PI whom Duck eventually did join in one of the rare instances of racial mixing on a Memphis bandstand. Steve, far more reserved and always described as the most diffident of the group so far as racial matters were concerned, still

Charlie Freeman. (Sid Selvidge)

vividly recalls the one time he saw the "5" Royales *live,* recounting the evening with a passion that belies his reputation. Lowman Pauling, the group's leader and guitarist, "was my total inspiration," says Steve. "You listen to me play, and you listen to him play, and you know that a lot of my licks come from him." "We stayed after," says Duck, "and Steve *made* him show us how to play that stomp thing of his." It was almost as if they had gotten in too far to get out, and though for Packy and Charlie Freeman the result was not the glory that came to some of the others, with "Last Night" the former Royal Spades (they became the Mar-Keys at this point because Estelle, casting about for a more suitable appellation, happened to look up at the theater marquee, thought it was a "cute connection," and changed the spelling "so that it would connect up someway with the music") realized an ambition that every white garage band in the world, including the Rolling Stones, has always dreamed of: an authentic r&b hit.

The history of "Last Night," though, was not a smooth one, and the story that Estelle tells of its evolution is instructive on the developing dynamic of the company. Basically the song was no more than a riff that was worked out in the studio and recorded probably over a period of more than six months, which explains why there is so much debate over who was actually present on the record. Duck Dunn, for example, is sure he played on the take before the final version but did not participate in the master session because he had some chores to do at home. Instead, Bob McGee, the bass player on "Gee Whiz" and a number of the other early sessions, participated. Charlie Freeman had already more or less left the group for greener pastures. The drummer was the drummer from the PI, Curtis Green, not high school student Terry Johnson. In fact the only Royal Spades to participate fully were Smoochy Smith on keyboards (Steve Cropper recalls adding a chord or two on piano or organ, whichever Smoochy wasn't playing at the time) and Packy Axton, relegated to a section role in an all-star horn lineup that featured Gilbert Caple, the veteran black tenor player, taking the solo, and Floyd Newman, the black baritone player, repeating the vocal hook ("Ohhh, last night") with comic suggestiveness. It all came pretty much under the direction of Chips Moman, who at this point was probably the only one who knew what he was doing in the studio, and getting an acceptable final take was the product of months of experimentation, fooling around, and painstaking work. What happened next, though, was symptomatic of the whole history of Stax.

"Jerry Wexler came down," says Estelle, who had finally been able to leave her job at the bank (this was in the spring of 1961, nearly a year after the first hit), "and we were working on the album of *Gee Whiz,* some of which we did over at Stax studios and some of which we took to Nashville, because their equipment was so much better. Well, they had already made a tape of 'Last Night' at this point, and then they cut a dub. And, of course, having the record shop, and with our music beginning to happen in the r&b market, I had become very close to WLOK and WDIA, talking to the disc jockeys from these various stations. When the program director from LOK heard that instrumental, he said, 'That's a hit record. Let me just take a dub down there and see if we can get any response on it.' So sure enough, he took that thing down, and the first day he put it on the air, people began to stop by at the shop asking for that instrumental. So I told Mr. Wexler, 'We got a new instrumental that the radio stations tell us is a hit.' And I went to play it for him. You see, Jim wasn't pushing this instrumental bit—he was so involved with Carla and the other vocalists. But because my son was in there, I was pushing that instrumental. And because I knew it was a hit.

"Well, Mr. Wexler said, 'Oh, well, it's all right, we need to put some more horns on it,' this, that, and the other thing. In other words, he was stalling for time, and here I am biting the bit, you know, to get this record out. So I had had it up to my neck with people coming in asking for the record, because I knew we needed the money and, hey, I knew we had a product that would sell. So one night I was in the record shop, it didn't close till nine o'clock, and Chips and my brother came up front, and my husband was standing there wanting to go home because he had just come from work at Kimberly Paper Products, and I said, 'Nope, I'm not leaving here tonight until I settle something, and that is that either we're going to pull this dub off the air or we're going to put that record out.' Well, they began to hem and haw, and, you know, I started out asking them in a nice way, and then I started crying, trying to get their sympathy, and when that didn't work, finally I started cussing. Well, my brother had never heard me cuss before, I don't think, and that kind of blew his mind, so finally he said, 'All right, in the morning have Packy go back there and get the tape and take it to the plant.'

"Well, you can imagine how I felt. I couldn't wait to get to the studio in the morning, and when we did, Packy goes back there to get the tape and starts to playing it, and would you believe that about sixteen bars off the front end of that tape had been erased! My son come running up front, saying, 'Mother, what in the world are we going to do?' I said, 'Well, Packy, we won't let that stop us.' I said, 'With all the times that you all have done that tune, there's got to be another take that's about the same tempo. We'll splice it on.' And to this day I know exactly where that splice is on that record.

"Anyway, when we put it out, it exploded like nothing had ever exploded before. I'm telling you, I sold over two thousand of it one by one over the counter. They certified a million on it eventually; it got to number two in the nation, pop and r&b. And I was so proud of it. I've never been so proud of a record in my life. And right in the middle of that record [in the summer of 1961] a company out in California says, 'We gonna sue you. 'Cause you got a Satellite label, and we have, too, and we had ours first.' Well, we had already started plans to have Stax as a subsidiary of Satellite, so what we did was just drop the name (we never much liked it anyway) right in the middle of 'Last Night'—so half of it is on Satellite, half of it is on Stax. And that's how it happened. From there we just began to build our label."

Not everyone's recollection is as dramatic as Estelle's. Jim claims that he does not remember any tape erasure, and Chips recalls it only as a simple splice. The result was the same, in any case. It gave to a reborn Stax Records the first national hit that could actually be followed up and promoted. All that was needed was a band to go out as the Mar-Keys, and obviously the Royal Spades fit the bill. They went out on the road right away, nine in a rear-engined, four-cylinder Chevrolet Greenbrier, with Carla Thomas crammed in, too, since she was on summer vacation, and a somewhat flustered Miz Axton acting as chaperone. Carla and Miz Axton left the tour after playing *The Dick Clark Show* ("Those boys were real cutups," says Estelle). Steve soon quit college; Duck quit his regular job. At first it was an adventure of the sort that could not even have been dreamt of.

"We had a hit record," recalls trumpet player Wayne Jackson, seventeen at the time and never having imagined that he would do anything more glamorous than crop-dusting. "Somebody bought us some clothes, gave us a little money, and we just thought we were going to be stars forever, we were just having the biggest time in the world. We worked the chitlin circuit—black —that's why there weren't any publicity pictures of the group. One place in Texas I remember in particular, we rolled up and they were barbecuing a goat, and you could stand on one side of this club and look through the cracks in the wall to the cotton patch on the other side, and they didn't believe we were the Mar-Keys. 'You can't be the Mar-Keys!' 'Well, we are,' we said. 'Here's our agent's number; you can call him.' Well, at first they were a little hostile (this was before integration, you know, before a lot of things), but then, when we started playing, they loved us. We were young and full of enthusiasm, and we played pretty good, and the music was what they wanted to hear. We were seventeen, eighteen, nineteen, we liked to drink and chase tail and have a good time. Jim was a very serious man, I don't think he was ever ready for the things that went on around him. I remember one time we were going to Birmingham in our Greenbrier; we were doing a promotional gig, and Jim was coming along. Well, we couldn't wait to get there and play and meet the disc jockeys who had been playing our records, but Jim just kept sucking on peppermints and drinking his nerve elixir, very nervous type, we like to drove him crazy. And Miz Axton just trying to corral all of our energy, and not really knowing what she was doing, and it was running out of her hands like quicksilver."

It all came to a head in Bossier City, Louisiana, where the tension that had been building between Steve and Packy finally snapped, and Steve left the

Steve Cropper at the board. (Jere Cunningham)

touring band. Here's Steve's account: "It was definitely because of Packy. It was always, 'Well, my mama owns the company, so I should be the leader of the band.' I said, 'But Packy, it was my band to start with. I hired you; you didn't hire me. It's my band. I run it.' Well, I guess he had gone around to other people, and I guess I didn't feel that I was getting total support from the others. So I finally said, 'Hey, if it means this much to you, you got it.' I remember the night I quit. In Bossier City. We finished a set. I pulled him in the bathroom and said, 'You been wanting it, here it is.' I left the next day, and when I came back, I went to work in the record store."

That was the way the Stax operating hierarchy was established. Chips and Jim were cutting records, while Steve was running the record store for Estelle and spending as much time as he could in the studio to discover for himself how records were made. The band for the time being was out on the road (they came in every few weeks for a break or to contribute to a horn part). As for the black musicians who had inspired the Royal Spades to begin with and then actually played on their hit record ("We couldn't play anywhere near as good as they could," says Wayne. "I'd stand up there with Ben Branch or Gilbert Caple and do my best just to play the melody, and every so often I'd take a solo, and I was in heaven.")—they kept on playing in the local clubs and in the studio. They were pretty much left behind. Many are understandably bitter today. As Wayne Jackson says, "I don't think they were exactly tickled. The fact was, we had a hit record, and they didn't. They were making local records and trying to do something, and we had tripped and fell down in it and came up with a hit." For some, though, the opportunity *was* going to come through Stax. Booker T., now entering his senior year in high school, was spending more and more time in the studio and even working after hours on occasion in Chips Moman's band ("Some of them good old boys didn't like it much, I guess," says Chips). David Porter had by now been hired as a full-time artist/songwriter, Stax's first black employee, at the munificent sum of fifty dollars a week. Then in November Chips brought in another friend of his, William Bell, formerly lead singer with the Del Rios, another group that had sung at the Plantation Inn. William, who had been out on the road with Phineas Newborn, Sr. (Newborn is a Memphis legend who not only led one of Memphis's foremost jazz and society orchestras but also fathered jazz pianist Phineas, Jr., and guitarist Calvin Newborn), came into the studio with an original song: a gospel-flavored blues in waltz time.

"YOU DON'T MISS YOUR WATER"

William Bell shared a number of attributes with many of his fellow Stax artists. One was a middle-class background: his parents were horrified by the idea of his going into music, and William himself originally wanted to be a doctor.

William Bell. (Don Paulsen/Michael Ochs Archives)

Like almost everyone else at Stax—like most of the other black musicians, anyway—Bell, whose real name was Yarborough and who took his last name from his grandmother, had at least a semester of college. (Even Rufus Thomas, a full generation older than any of his labelmates, had put in some time at Tennessee A&I.) Later Stax publicity handouts would always portray him as a conspicuous pipe smoker, a voracious reader, a paragon of manners, and the cultivator of an intellectual image that seemed at odds sometimes with the pursuit of popular success. He was also, like so many of his colleagues, the possessor, at age twenty-two, of an extensive professional background in music.

He had been discovered while still in high school (his age at the time has always been given as fourteen, but he was more like seventeen) when his group, the Del Rios, won second prize at the annual Mid-South Talent Contest in 1956. Their prize was a week's trip to Chicago, where they played at the Club DeLisa with the Red Saunders band, and a one-shot record contract on Memphis's Meteor label, for which they cut a Midnighters sound-alike, "Alone on a Rainy Night," backed by Rufus Thomas's band, the Bearcats. During the rest of their time in high school the group worked the Plantation Inn and then at Clifford

Miller's Flamingo Room in town (where Elvis was rumored to have once hung out) as featured vocalists with Phineas Newborn's band. They probably cut a few unreleased sides for Satellite, but then various members of the group were drafted, and after one term at college William had the chance to go out on the road with Phineas to play New York resorts and Long Island clubs. He took it as an opportunity that wasn't likely to come his way again and dropped out of school with the idea of returning the following semester. The Newborn band lingered in New York for more than a year, and William eventually went back to Memphis only because he had gotten his draft notice. When he returned, he completed his education at Stax.

"During that time Stax was just, I guess you'd call it a mama and papa operation with Estelle and Jim and Chips, and a few of us hanging around as writers. Frankly I didn't know if I wanted to make a career of it, because I was still thinking about becoming a doctor. When I got home, I went to the draft board, and they said, 'We'll call you within two weeks.' They never did, though, so I kind of sat around home. Then I ran into Chips Moman again, and he asked me a couple of times about recording as a single. So I thought about it for a while, figured what have I got to lose, and went down one day and played this song I had written while I was in New York that he and Jim had both liked. We just went in to do a demo, but they liked it so well, they said, 'Let's finish it up.' We had just a three-piece rhythm section on it, bass, drums, and organ, I believe, plus the horns."

The song, "You Don't Miss Your Water (Till Your Well Runs Dry)," was definitely a trend-setter for Stax. If Rufus and Carla's duet was something of a fluke and "Gee Whiz" was, as Carla says, a magical song whose musical formula and winning innocence could never be repeated, if "Last Night" was little more than a novelty instrumental, William Bell's record finally set a pattern for future success. Light, restrained, but with an unmistakable gospel feel and an almost lilting stateliness, "You Don't Miss Your Water," like most of Bell's hits for himself and others ("Share What You Got," "Everybody Loves a Winner," "Every Day Will Be Like a Holiday," "Born Under a Bad Sign") retailed a familiar folk saying and expanded upon it with a simplicity and craft that rendered it quietly eloquent. The writing probably most resembled that of William's hero, Sam Cooke, while the voice, neither a powerhouse instrument like Solomon Burke's or Wilson Pickett's, nor a soul-wrenching cry like Otis Redding's, was perfectly suited to the spare elegance of the message, unselfconsciously complementary to the compositional technique.

William Bell became Stax's first real solo star, a somewhat surprising turn of events given Bell's disarming modesty and genuine inclination toward self-deprecation. By the time the record hit (it was a regional smash in the South and made the top pop 100 in the spring of 1962), he was already back on the road with Phineas Newborn's band. When he finally got his draft call-up just about a year later, he had played nearly 300 one-nighters all over the country, joining Henry Wynn package shows that headlined Solomon Burke, James Brown, Jerry Butler, and in the process acquiring a professional polish and education that no one else at Stax had achieved. He developed a practiced attitude toward performing, and a philosophy about fame and stardom that would carry him, relatively unscarred, through the vicissitudes of a lifetime career in the entertainment business. It was probably this same philosophy that permitted him in later years to undertake such unlikely tasks as the role of Stanley Kowalski in an Atlanta production of *A Streetcar Named Desire*, the formation of his own record and production company (which, like Sam Cooke's SAR label, unearthed promising artists and introduced them in appropriate settings, as well as occasionally serving as an outlet for Bell's own work), and a term as vice-president of the Atlanta branch of NARAS (the National Academy of Recording Arts and Sciences).

"Entertainment," says Bell today, "is my job, my work. I'm fortunate enough to love my work, but when I go home, I leave my work. I believe it takes a lot of sorting out, a lot of soul-searching to keep your head screwed on right in this business. All that yelling, screaming, pushing, pulling—when you get back to your hotel, get back in your room, you're just an ordinary person. So you just have to accept the admiration for what it's worth. They like you for what you do, but maybe the real you they wouldn't like at all. A lot of people get caught up in being a star all the time, but if you get caught up in that, you miss out on so much of the enjoyment of life and you're no longer just a common person. I always tried to do that, to keep a low profile, to remain a common person, because I think that in order to be creative, to be effectively creative, you've got to keep a pulse on the everyday person, because that's who's got to relate to whatever you're writing about. Maybe that's just a form of insecurity on my part. Maybe if you analyzed it psychologically, you'd find that I don't want to get used to it—to the limousines, to the red carpet treatment —because I'm afraid next time it just might not be there. Then again I've had the gold records; I just don't want to get to the point where I lose my privacy. I suppose it's like being caught between a rock and a hard place in a sense, because you make records to get the recognition, but you realize very early that with recognition comes loss of privacy. You just have to learn adaptability in this business."

When William Bell was finally drafted in the spring of 1963, he was trained in jungle fighting and stationed in Hawaii for two years. When he got out, Stax was thriving, and after taking some time off to study the new market, he soon resumed his career where it had left off, but he had in a sense lost his special place in the organization, replaced to a large degree by the more charismatic Otis Redding. He remained a key figure at Stax, though, both as a writer and as a performer, and after the Stax collapse even had his own brief fling with genuine stardom with the 1977 million-seller on Mercury, "Trying to Love Two." Everyone was glad for William when it came; everyone from the Stax days speaks highly of William, refers to him as a "gentleman." "I was so proud of him," Estelle says, "when he had his big hit. It was almost like he was still on Stax."

"GREEN ONIONS"

For all the success enjoyed by the Stax "stars" (by Carla, by Rufus and Carla, and now by William Bell), the Stax sound really coalesced around the loose studio group that had grown up to provide the backing for each of the solo artists' efforts. While the Mar-Keys were still out on the road under the nominal direction of Packy (though they were never able to come up with a follow-up hit, and as a result Packy, too, eventually quit the group, leaving Charlie Freeman, who had replaced Steve sometime after Bossier City, with the name and the occasional booking), things were solidifying in the studio in a way that

The Original Booker T. and the MG's, circa 1963: Booker T. Jones, Steve Cropper, Al Jackson, Lewis Steinberg. (Courtesy of Bill Millar)

would soon make even the Mar-Keys' limited role obsolete. The horn section, it is true, remained a somewhat amorphous mix, though trumpeter Wayne Jackson and tenor player Andrew Love were appearing with increasing frequency on many of the sessions and would one day strike up an integrated partnership called the Memphis Horns. The rhythm section, however, was rapidly falling into place. Booker T. Jones, who had been present almost from the beginning ("I would just hang around pretending to look at the records, but I was really just listening to what was going on behind the curtain separating the record store from the studio"), was the keyboard—or baritone sax/trombone/bass—player on most of the early sessions and played organ on nearly all William Bell's hits. Steve Cropper was becoming more and more the person on whom both Jim and Estelle depended ("Steve was my right-hand man," says Jim. "He would come to the studio and sit there and keep the doors open and take care of business; he was disciplined and responsible. Steve was the key.") as well as adding his lean, slashing rhythm guitar to just about every record. Lewis Steinberg, the well-known black bass player, had taken over most of the bass chores, with Duck Dunn (off the road now that the Mar-Keys were no longer in demand) sitting in occasionally when Steinberg was tied up. And Al Jackson, who had played with Booker at the Flamingo Room in Willie Mitchell's band, was brought in by Booker to play drums on a date and never left. There was no place for Packy in this newly streamlined operation. "Packy was not an organizational type man," says Jim with characteristic understatement. "He would show up one week, and the next week he was gone." "Packy was a playboy," says Steve more dismissively. "He was a mama's boy. He wasn't a total goof-off, but Packy was allowed to do what Packy wanted to do." The rhythm section, three black, one white, was the nucleus.

One Sunday afternoon in the summer of 1962 this group was in the studio for a jingle date booked by Dale Bowman, which Billy Lee Riley, the rockabilly singer from Sun Records days, was supposed to be cutting. Riley never showed up, and the group started fooling around, just playing. "We started playing some blues," says Booker. "We just started jamming. There was no tape on or anything, but Jim liked the blues, so he put it on tape. He was really happy about it, you know. He said, 'While you're here, why don't you make something for the B side?' That's when we made 'Green Onions.' It was an idea Steve and I had worked on, and we just cut it."

"They did a little blues number," says Estelle. "And I told them, 'It sounds like somebody acting up, and somebody says, "Behave yourself." ' And Jim was so impressed with that blues number—I was up in the record shop that day, working on my books, and he comes running up front, saying, 'Come on, I want you to hear something. These boys have really got an instrumental that'll knock you out.' Well, I agreed with him that it was fantastic. So as soon as they finish this tune, everyone says, 'Well, we gotta have a double side.' So they started

Booker T. and the MG's, post-1964: Booker, Steve, Duck, Al.

fooling around and cut the record within the hour that we had allotted for the commercial. And put it out and started promoting 'Behave Yourself,' which was the blues side, but the disc jockeys flipped it over and 'Green Onions' was a million seller. That's just the way things happen sometimes."

That's pretty much how everyone tells the story. The origin of the recording group's name is somewhat more in dispute. Once Stax had become famous and "the Memphis sound" served as a kind of eponym for the label, all the company publicity releases declared that Booker T. and the MG's had come up with the initials to stand for Memphis Group. Booker says that it was Al Jackson, a little older than the others and something of a big brother to Booker, who named the group after its youngest member, and that may well be so. But Chips Moman, who did not happen to be in the studio when "Green Onions" was cut but was in on just about every other Stax session of that period, insists that the MG's were the MG's because of his sports car, which happened to be a Triumph ("I remember the year by the car I was driving"). In fact he had actually named an earlier studio version of the group, in which he and Booker played, the Triumphs, and, he says, it was only when he left the company that they started giving out the other explanation—"which was bullshit."

Chips left Stax with some abruptness shortly after the success of "Green Onions." It was, as Wayne Jackson puts it delicately, "just a matter of the placing of a decimal point. I was sitting there in the hall the day it broke up.

(Don Paulsen/Michael Ochs Archives)

I still had pimples, and I couldn't believe it. I thought, 'People don't talk to each other this way. This is big time.' " Jim today attributes the breakup primarily to Estelle's differences with Chips, and by extension to Chips's dismissal of Packy (actually Chips and Packy seem to have been closer than Jim and Packy). Jim in fact professes to feel nothing but the highest regard for Chips and his work and regret over the fissure. Chips is a little more blunt. "Jim Stewart stood there and just said to my face, 'I'm fucking you out of it.' We had made over a million dollars at that point; I'm supposed to have a 25 percent share. And I got nothing. I lost my house, my car, everything. I left a part of my life there at Stax. I spent just about a year not knowing what I was doing, staying drunk all the time, just about going crazy. Boy, I was a down sonofabitch. I know the true story of Stax, and I could tell it, but it wouldn't do me any good, and nobody wants to know anyway."

Whatever version of the story Chips would tell, Estelle would just as hotly dispute it. As bitter as his feelings are toward Jim and her, what Estelle has to say about him is no less rancorous and no less blunt about the misappropriation of certain funds and credits. It was indeed a misunderstanding over "the placing of a decimal point," and after a while Chips got together with Seymour Rosenberg, a ubiquitous Memphis music lawyer who also represented Stax on occasion, and won a $3000 settlement, with which he started up his own American Studio in partnership with Seymour, an arrangement that eventually turned out some of Memphis's biggest hits of the late '60s. Meanwhile Stax continued on just as strong or stronger than ever. Without so much as a blink Steve took Chips's place in the studio. (Steve and Chips were not involved in any mutual admiration society, either. "There's an old saying about Chips," says Steve. "You can put it on tape if you want to: Chips would bet his grandmama in a poker game.") Jim, who had been doing more and more of the engineering, was giving increasing thought to quitting his position at the bank. ("I was always rather conservative; I thought, I'd better hold on to my job—well, you know, we might not make it. In the end it was costing me money to work for the bank, so I finally quit in 1964.") Booker T. and the MG's were now firmly ensconced both as a recording unit and as recording stars (the crack horn section that had developed out of the Mar-Keys' sides filled out the studio band with shifting personnel). With the substitution of former Royal Spade Duck Dunn on bass sometime in 1964, they had the lineup that would carry them through the next five glory years with no further changes and an undiminished creativity of approach. The "Stax sound" was set, then, solid, not flashy, sparse, eloquent, competently engineered. "Nineteen sixty-two was the year that started the Stax sound," says Jim. "That started the continuous flow of product and the studio musician concept. Music was our common denominator, and through that we learned about each other as human beings." And that was the year that Otis Redding first came in to the Stax studio.

"THESE ARMS OF MINE"

Like almost everything else that happened at Stax, the arrival of Otis Redding was both unforeseen and unplanned for. He was only there in the first place because he had driven his friend, guitarist Johnny Jenkins, up from Macon, where Redding and Jenkins had a group, the Pinetoppers, for whom Redding was featured vocalist. Jenkins had just had a regional hit with "Love Twist," an instrumental that was initially put out by a local label, then picked up by Joe Galkin and in turn sold to Atlantic for distribution (Jerry Wexler claims he didn't want to see Galkin lose money on the deal). Through the success of the single Galkin had come into contact not only with Jenkins but with his twenty-two-year-old manager, Phil Walden, a recent graduate of Macon's Mercer University. He pushed for a follow-up session and arranged for it to take place at Stax. Legend has frequently suggested that Redding was strictly along for the ride, that he generally served as Johnny Jenkins's driver and valet —but in fact it was as much his group as it was Jenkins's, and he had already had a couple of other records out himself both on another local label (Bobby Smith's unfortunately named Confederate) and as Otis and the Shooters on a California label called Finer Arts. Another legend has long held that it was Galkin who spotted Redding's talent and intended to bring him centerstage all along (Jim Stewart firmly believes this), but Galkin told British writer Charlie

Gillett that it was Phil Walden alone who insisted on Otis's going up with Johnny.

"I told Phil, 'He's a lousy singer.' Otis had just made a record called 'Shout Bamalama' down there in Athens, Georgia, that was the worst record I ever heard. It had got play on WLAC with John R., but nobody ever bought a copy."

Walden wasn't at the recording session, however, which turned out to be something of a disaster, and it was Galkin, for all his misgivings, who finally insisted that the vocalist be given a chance.

"After about two and a half hours," Galkin told Gillett, "Jim Stewart said, 'Joe, I cannot make a record with this group,' so I didn't want to waste the last half hour of studio time and I said, 'Okay, then, let's do something with this guy.' Steve Cropper and Al Jackson were going to walk out, and Jim and I argued back and forth. He says, 'What'll you give me?' And I said, 'Fifty percent of the publishing rights.'"

"I said," recalls Stewart, " 'We got no keyboard man.' Because Booker had *already* walked out. So Steve can play a little, just triplets, you know. So Johnny played guitar, and Steve played piano, and Lewis Steinberg was still there, and of course, Al. So we ran in there and didn't spend any time and got Otis at the microphone, and he did this thing, 'Hey Hey Baby,' or something like that, Little Richard, you know. And I say, 'Shucks, the world doesn't need another Little Richard.' 'Well, look, I know, I know, he's got another song he's written,' Joe says. 'It's a ballad.' Well, in those days it's up-tempo on one side and a ballad on the other, that was the procedure. So we did the ballad, 'These Arms of Mine,' and I don't remember, I probably wasn't impressed, I was too tired or whatever, too bummed out—I was just, you know, who cares? At the time. I mean, it would be just as easy for me to say now I knew we had a monster. Joe Galkin knew he had a monster—or thought he did. But we just took the record and put it out locally, tried a few markets. I gave over my share of the publishing to John Richbourg—John R. at WLAC in Nashville—and he must have played that record for six months literally, every night over and over, and finally broke it. Six months, and it still wasn't that big-selling a record, completely in the r&b market, and we couldn't even get all of that because it was just a black, country-sounding record, and in Chicago, for example, they were getting out of that sound."

If everyone who claims to have been present in the Stax studio on that momentous day had actually been there, the studio would have been packed to overflowing. There was in reality probably only a handful of people, and for most of them the session would have been no more memorable than it was for Jim Stewart had it not been for Otis Redding's subsequent history. He was at that point very much of a Little Richard imitator and Sam Cooke admirer, though on the second side, the ballad, there is evidence of that patented quaver

Otis Redding, early publicity shot. (Michael Ochs Archives)

in his voice, the strained sincerity that was Otis Redding's mark. Jim Stewart thought it was nervousness at first. "His voice was quavering, he didn't really have good control over it, and you couldn't really tell whether he was just nervous or that's just him. Like I say, you didn't even know he was in the studio that day. 'Cause he was very shy at first. Later on, when he got confidence, he was a different person." "He was a very humble type person," says Estelle, who was working in the record shop as usual but probably caught snatches of the session. "I don't think he even had any inkling at all that we would pay any attention to what he did, but as I say, we were always analyzing people for their uniqueness—and he was definitely different than anyone else we had."

Duck Dunn, who has sometimes been credited with playing bass on the session and played on just about every other Otis Redding record, has vivid memories of that day. "I was trying to get out of there to go to work. I was leading a band down at Hernando's Hideaway, and if it hadn't been, 'Well, you won't be back tomorrow if you don't do this,' I'd have just jumped up and left right then. Otis had on overalls, and I said, 'This guy sounds like Little Richard. Who wants another Little Richard?'"

"The cat sang about two lines," says Steve Cropper, "and everybody's eyes just went like this—Jesus Christ, this guy's incredible!"

"He was just like Leonard Bernstein," says Booker T. dreamily of the myth that Otis Redding would soon become. "He was the same type person. He was a leader. He'd just lead with his arms and his body and his fingers." Booker didn't happen to be around when Otis's sides were cut, but he remembers Otis's impact, and the impact of the session, as clearly as if he were. "That place had a mind and soul of its own. It was like the music took over—or the spirit of the music took over. By him just singing. I'm sure there was some discussion about the notes and who was doing what and all that, but it was more like a happening, a natural thing."

William Bell, who was just hanging around the studio, has memories colored by layers of legend. "Otis was an original. It was an unusual thing— everybody from the secretaries to the shipping clerks [even these functions are probably the inventions of memory] started peeking in to find out: who is this singing?"

The object of all this scrutiny, both real and retrospective, was a blocky-looking twenty-one-year-old from Macon, Georgia, whose solidity gave him the appearance of someone older than his years. With his arrival Stax entered a whole new phase, and though he did not return to the studio for another nine months, it was his subsequent success that brought Jerry Wexler back to Memphis to record, that made Stax a byword in soul circles, that would eventually open up the world of Southern soul to a large-scale white audience. Otis Redding in many ways exemplified the Stax Philosophy, a vague rubric that Jim Stewart kept coming back to over the years without ever achieving much success at definition. "The Stax Philosophy is a flaunted statement in the Organization," one publicity release declared and went on to identify it as "the basis of the Stax sound presentation" without ever really getting any more precise than that. What it all boiled down to, obviously, was a commitment to hard work, honest effort, and a team philosophy. Unlike Motown, which attempted to provide a totally controlled environment, Stax encouraged individual initiative within the context of corporate development, and Jim Stewart's first organizing principle of business seems to have been the same as the Boston Celtics' in basketball: to surround himself with people not simply of talent but of character, people on whom he could rely, individuals who were capable of growth. In Otis Redding he found the exemplar of these qualities. For Otis Redding was the heart and soul of Stax.

Backstage at Hunter College, January 1967. (Don Paulsen/Michael Ochs Archives)

▶ 4 ▶

Otis Redding

OMING INTO MACON TODAY OFF THE INTER-
state, you're likely to cross the Otis Redding Bridge, which was once just
known as the Fifth Street Bridge and looks as if it should be going by
its more prosaic name still. Otherwise it's almost as if nothing out of the
ordinary had ever happened in this once-thriving marketplace of 120,000—not
Otis, not the Allman Brothers, nor the remarkable rise and fall of Phil Walden,
the local entrepreneur who was responsible for both. Macon is just another
graceful Southern city gone to seed, its pretty brick buildings spared by Sher-
man's march to the sea but looking slightly ramshackle more than a century
later, its downtown decaying with urban renewal stalled, and the old black men
sitting on the curb in front of the boarded-up railroad station. It's a picture you
could take in Almost Anywhere, Smalltown, USA. But only a few years ago
things were jumping: Broadway was jammed with clubs; the House of Kings
Barbershop was crowded with customers; and Cotton Avenue, where Phil
Walden's offices remain to this day (though his business was brought to a halt
by the 1980 record recession), was still "the street of dreams." It's almost as if
Macon had set aside what must at times have seemed to its predominant white
and middle-class population like somebody else's bad dream and then gone back
to sleep.

Otis Redding was born on September 9, 1941, not in Macon but in
Dawson, about a hundred miles south. He came to Macon in 1944 at the age
of three, when his parents moved into the Tindall Heights Housing Project. His
father, Otis senior, worked out at the Robins Air Force Base, one of the
principal local sources of employment for blacks, and preached occasionally on
weekends. Throughout much of Otis's childhood his father was sick, and the
rest of the family—a younger brother, Rodgers (né Roger), four sisters, and
Otis's mother, Fannie—learned to cope as best they could. For a while they had
a little shotgun house of their own in a West Macon section known officially
as Bellevue but to its residents as Hellview; when it burned down, they moved
back into the project. When Otis was in the tenth grade, he dropped out of
Ballard-Hudson Senior High School. "Everyone was just flat broke," says
Rodgers, a compact, upbeat version of his older brother and a well-known
Southern booking agent today. "My father was ill, he had TB, and he was in
the hospital more than he was at home; my mother was working, and it was
just a burden. I can remember when Otis quit school he went out on the road

with Little Richard's old band, the Upsetters, and he would send home twenty-five dollars a week. That was a lot of money in those days."

Otis worked other jobs, too. For a while he worked for a well-digger, for an even briefer period he was a filling station attendant, but always his mind was on music. The city already had a rich musical tradition. James Brown had started out in Macon after getting out of the Alto Reform School and finding a patron in Clint Brantley, a local black entrepreneur who had his finger in every musical pie and was managing Little Richard, a Macon native, at the time. Brantley also owned the Two Spot, one of the numerous clubs thriving on Broadway, above which Brown and his group lived for some time, and he set up the demo session at which Brown cut his signature tune, "Please, Please, Please," then arranged to have it played on the air by local DJ Hamp Swain, whose jump band was yet another act in Brantley's stable. That was how the record companies first heard of James Brown and how Ralph Bass of King Records came to sign him when he was still driving around town in a beat-up old station wagon with a poster that announced: "James Brown and the Famous Flames Tonight at 8:30, $.50 at the Door." Brantley was also the man who booked all the big shows into the City Auditorium, shows that featured the Clovers, the Drifters, Louis Jordan and the Tympany Five, Otis Williams and the Charms, while at the same time concentrating his promotional energies on building Little Richard's reputation throughout the South. Locally Richard played Miss Ann's Tick Tock, was a familiar act at the Douglass Theater and as an add-on at the City Auditorium shows, and, of course, with his capes, spectacularly upswept pomaded hair, and heavy makeup was not the sort of person you were likely to overlook. His sensational success within the next few years only fueled the fire of Otis's ambition. "I remember Otis saying," Rodgers recalls, "he'd say over and over again: 'One of these days I'm going to be like them.' He was just determined, there was nothing that could have stopped him."

His commitment to music went back further than any professional ambition, however. "From the time he was a little kid," says Rodgers, "he was singing in a gospel group in church, and he was a drummer in the school band. Every night the guys in the neighborhood would get together, him and another guy, Little Willie Jones—he used to do *all* of Little Willie John's songs—and a guy by the name of Eddie Ross sang the bass, and every night they used to sing just when the sun was getting ready to set on the sidewalk. In elementary school he was crazy about drums, every time you see him he was beating on something, a spoon, pencils, just riding in the car and beating out a rhythm. I remember when he had his tonsils taken out—oh, boy, he was pitiful. And I remember him saying, 'Will I be able to sing again?' And my father said, 'Sure. Probably you be able to sing better.' Then he started getting into piano and trying to write—oh, around the eighth grade. There was a nightclub in the area where we were staying at the time called Hillview Springs Social Club. They didn't let kids in, but they had a piano there, and there was a lady by the name of Gladys Williams who had a band at that time. She was good on piano, and Otis just loved to get on her piano and do a Little Richard song and steal the show."

Gladys Williams was a prominent local musician who had a number of bands out on the road under her name. She ran a Sunday night talent show at the Hillview Springs that Otis and his friends always managed to sneak into. Otis would do a Midnighters' tune or an Elvis Presley number occasionally; "One Night" and "Money" were firm favorites; but it was with Little Richard's "Heebie Jeebies" that he really made a hit. "I remember it went, 'My bad luck baby put the jinx on me,'" Otis told writer Stanley Booth. "That song really inspired me to start singing. I won the talent show for fifteen straight nights with that song, and then they wouldn't let me sing no more, wouldn't let me win that five dollars any more." With the five dollars that he won Otis and his friends would go out and get hot dogs and a bottle of wine. He had a little coterie around him even then, but they were as confident that Little Willie Jones or Oscar Mack (who eventually did cut a couple of records for Stax and today works on an assembly line in Detroit) would be the one to make it.

Otis stayed with the music. He went out with the Upsetters and got stranded in Florida; he sang with one or another of Gladys Williams's bands. He played all the little clubs around Belleview and wherever he could get a gig for five or ten dollars a night. But he didn't really start getting known until he played *The Teenage Party* at the Douglass Theater.

TEENAGE PARTY

The Teenage Party was started by Hamp Swain, the same DJ who with Clint Brantley had helped give James Brown his start, around 1958. For Hamp, a smooth-spoken Maconite with a little bit of college who had started out selling insurance and switched to radio for an Atlanta Life-sponsored broadcast only at the insurance company's request ("They thought I could talk jive, as they called it then, and they were aware that I knew something about music"), it was just another opportunity to get ahead. He had already had experience doing live broadcasts from the clubs, sock hops for the teenagers, and midweek gigs with his own band (Little Richard was at one time his featured vocalist). So that when the program director at WIBB, where Hamp had just taken his popular *Night Ride* program, suggested the idea of doing a live broadcast talent show from the Roxy and then from the Douglass Theater, Hamp was receptive. He hired some musicians, publicized the show at his regular gigs, and every Saturday morning MC'd and played the sax, told jokes and offered up toasts. Almost from the beginning—certainly from the time the show moved to the Douglass—Otis Redding was the consistent winner, week after week. "At the

Teenage Party, 1958. (From the Macon Telegraph and News *Negative Collection, Middle Georgia Archives, Macon, Georgia)*

time, though," says Hamp, a car salesman today, "I thought Oscar Mack was *the* talent over Otis. Both of them were influenced by Little Richard initially. It was a modified Little Richard style."

Johnny Jenkins, however, took a different view. Jenkins, a flashy guitarist and one of Macon's biggest local stars, was a light-skinned black man described as "Hollywood-handsome" by all who knew him, and renowned for both the acrobatics and pyrotechnics of a style that would one day have considerable influence on Jimi Hendrix (once again via the ubiquitous Little Richard, for whom Hendrix started out on guitar). With the drummer Pat T. Cake and Little Willie Jones on vocals, Jenkins played all around the area, for white fraternities as well as black clubs, and because of his local celebrity he was probably considered a little too slick for the amateur contests. Jenkins was in the audience when he first saw Otis.

"I heard Otis at the Douglass, and the group behind him just wasn't making it. So I went up to him, and I said, 'Do you mind if I play behind you?' And he looked at me like 'Who are you?' 'Cause he didn't know me. And I say, 'I can make you sound good.' And I played behind him. And you know how the guitar can make a singer sound good by covering up his weaknesses? Well, he sounded *great* with me playing behind him—and he knowed it. The first gig we played, we play at this little lounge. I say, 'How much you pay me?' He say, 'Twenty-five cents.' I say, 'Well, that be all right, maybe you better pay me fifteen cents now, ten cents at the gig."

The Douglass proved even more significant to Otis, for that was not only where he met his first musical mentor, it was also where he encountered the two other people who would be most influential in his life: his wife, Zelma (who was fifteen when she first met her future husband after a broadcast); and Phil Walden, a brash, fast-talking white kid just one year older than Otis who would soon become his partner and manager. In fact Phil heard, but never actually saw, Otis for quite some time. *The Teenage Party* was broadcast on Saturday mornings, and Walden, still in high school but head-over-heels in love with r&b, was managing a little group called the Heartbreakers who competed regularly on the show. Because Macon was still strictly segregated, Walden never got to see his group perform. Instead he listened to them on the radio every week while sitting outside the theater in his car, and every week he heard them lose—to Otis Redding. He had gotten into rhythm and blues himself a few years earlier when his older brother, Clark, brought home records by the Clovers, the "5" Royales, and the Midnighters, classic Atlantic and King sides. From there Phil started listening to the radio, and of course he picked up on Little Richard.

The Pinetoppers: Johnny Jenkins in foreground, Pat T. Cake on drums, Otis Redding with mike. (Courtesy of Mark Pucci)

"He was just outrageous. I remember the first show I ever went to, I finally got it together and went down to the City Auditorium in the ninth grade. Amos Milburn and the Chickenshackers were headlining a two-billed show, and the opening act was Little Richard. Strictly a local act. And I can remember Amos Milburn kind of disappointed me, just a fat guy sitting at a piano. But Little Richard just destroyed me. He was doing a lot of the songs that he later recorded, but off-color, like 'Tutti Frutti.' 'Tutti frutti / Good booty / Miss Lucy is juicy / Miss Tight is all right / It ain't the ocean, it's the motion'—oh, all kinds of things. And he would wave to all the gay guys, all his 'sisters' in the audience. Man, I can remember when 'Tutti Frutti' came out, the first night I heard it on the radio. We were sitting at the dinner table, matter of fact I was listening to King Bee, Hamp Swain—he had an early evening show called the *Night Ride* program—and he said, 'I got a new single by Little Richard. He's got a hit . . . "A wop bop a loo bop a lop bam boom." ' I turned it up real loud, and my daddy says, 'Turn that goddam thing down.' I saw him downtown not too long after that, it was hot as hell and I saw Little Richard on the other side of the street twirling a *parasol,* and I said to my friend, 'That's Little Richard,' and he crossed the street and walked right by me, and I was scared to even address him, I was in awe of him, but I said, 'Tutti frutti.' And he said, 'Oh, rooty.' God!"

Walden, whose father continued to be disapproving until he joined Phil and Phil's younger brother, Alan, as part of Otis's management team in the mid-'60s, never looked back after that first shock of recognition. He started listening to Hamp Swain religiously and, late at night, to John R., whose 1–3 A.M. show ("This is John R. way down South in Dixie," announced the melodious voice) on 50,000-watt Nashville station WLAC traveled as far as Detroit, Chicago, Iceland occasionally, Greenland, and even Australia on some nights. He started dropping by WIBB to deliver requests to the King Bee and reading the colored edition of the local paper (marked by a star), whose social pages detailed who was playing where and who was coming to town. He became a regular at the City Auditorium shows, dragging his little brother, Alan, along and taking his place in the balcony with the scattering of white kids who would peer down enviously at the blacks on the floor dancing to the music of the Midnighters or the "5" Royales. And as president of his fraternity at Sidney Lanier High School he carried his devotion one step further: he started booking r&b shows.

"Well, you see, we had themes back in high school, and our theme the year I was president, in 1958, was Rock 'n' Roll Party—we imitated, we would lip-sync to Midnighters' records. And I remember the first guy I ever booked was an old local guy named Percy Welch, he had a couple of records out, kind of a local hit called 'Back Door Man,' and I booked him to play a big rush party. I can remember I went over to his house, and he gave me an autographed record, and I thought I had met a star. It was at that rush party that I realized there would have to be a market for somebody who could take a black band that if nothing else would have the same personnel for at least three or four weeks in a row and equipment that was not borrowed and that had all the tubes in their amps and was guaranteed at least to be able to perform, with uniforms and a PA system and everything (the night we hired Percy, he forgot his PA system, so you can imagine how that turned out), I realized there was some potential there. So I got me a band, Pat T. Cake and the Mighty Panthers, and I started booking them. Johnny Jenkins was the guitar player, Little Willie Jones was doing the singing. Well, then Johnny left the band and formed another one, and I went out to Lakeside Amusement Park (which I now own) to hear the new band [this was the Pinetoppers], and when they took a break, he introduced me to Rockhouse Redding, as they then called him, whom I knew, of course, from the old talent contests down at the Douglass."

That was the beginning of a lifelong friendship and a business partnership that would carry Phil, his brother Alan—the whole Walden family, in fact— along with Otis, Rodgers, and Zelma Redding to heights and places previously unimagined. At the beginning it was an unlikely enough association. Otis's

Jimmy Hughes, Alan Walden, Phil Walden, Johnnie Taylor, with Otis Redding seated. (Courtesy of Alan Walden)

father never liked Phil, and Phil's father wouldn't hear of his son, now a student at Mercer University in Macon, hanging around with niggers. At first Walden was booking the Pinetoppers on the college fraternity circuit exclusively, mostly within a few hours' drive of Macon. "To get around detection I used to say I was going out on a date, go out and pick up the band, drive 200 miles to a college date, then come back and clean up the car of cigarette butts and all that shit." Otis was doing songs like "Endlessly," "There Goes My Baby," and, of course, his Little Richard material, but he was overshadowed most of the time by Johnny Jenkins's theatrics. He wasn't satisfied, obviously, with the progress he was making, so he went out to California briefly, stayed with his sisters, got work in a car wash, and cut a session in July of 1960 out of which a couple of records were eventually released on Trans World and Alshire. When he came home, he hooked right up again with Johnny Jenkins, reclaiming his place in the Macon firmament. Bobby Smith, a local car salesman who was managing Wayne Cochran, another Georgian who would soon enjoy a good deal of success as the white James Brown, describes a concert that he booked with Wayne and Otis and Johnny and Wayne's guitar player, Joe Carpenter, that was billed as the Battle of the Bands.

"It was out at the Lakeside Park, and that night you couldn't get within a mile of the place. I remember they were doing 'Shout,' some damn song like that, and they would drop their microphones all the way to the floor, lay down, and come up singing 'Shout' together. All-white audience, but, man, they was going crazy." It was the only concert Bobby ever booked (he later got hooked up with Shelby Singleton and became the manager of the born-again Elvis clone, Orion), but he did cut a record on Otis a few months later on his own Confederate label. The record, whose A side was a Little Richard imitation called "Shout Bamalama" (it was a hit years later on Shelby Singleton's SSS label for Mickey Murray), enjoyed some local success, but not before Bobby was forced to change the name of the label to get airplay on r&b stations. John R. in Nashville stayed on the record all through the summer of 1961, and it seemed as if Otis was beginning to get somewhere professionally, but sales died out and he appeared to have reached another dead end. When he and Zelma got married in August 1961, they were broke with no prospects, but Otis never thought of anything but music.

"I was determined to take a job and work," says Zelma, "and he was determined to just go out and mess around with musicians every day and say, 'I'm gonna get a hit record, I'm gonna be a star.' And everything he told me, I just believed him, because he believed in himself to the fullest. I've never seen his weakness; I guess that's what made me strong. He was very positive about himself and his music. Even if what he told you wasn't definite positive, he was so sweet you just say, 'Okay.' That's how much I loved him, and how much confidence I had in him. Otis didn't want to be nothing but himself. His philosophy was: 'I eat and sleep music, because this is me, you know? And to be successful at it, you gotta concentrate on this stuff twenty-four hours a day.' "

TAKING CARE OF BUSINESS

Phil, meanwhile, had set up an office downtown on Mulberry Street in the old Professional Building, now known as the Robert E. Lee, after its principal occupant, an insurance firm. It was also the home of WIBB, Hamp Swain's radio station, and Bobby Smith had offices upstairs. Phil was an upperclassman at Mercer by now and had expanded his booking activities somewhat. His agency was known as Phil Walden and Associates, though there were as yet no associates, and he and Otis painted the ten-by-fourteen-foot room just inside the building door and fixed up the office together. They had two Army desks "painted flat black" and publicity shots of everyone from Solomon Burke and Little Willie John to Joe Tex and Bobby Marchan, which Walden had obtained from various New York booking agencies and to which he had attached logos reading "Another Fine Attraction Available From Phil Walden and Associates." When the phone rang, Walden answered in a falsetto voice, he swears, then announced, "Mr. Walden will speak to you now." Most of the acts he was actually booking centered around the Johnny Jenkins-Otis Redding-Pat T. Cake-Little Willie Jones axis, and Sylvester Huckaby, one of Otis's friends from the Hillview Springs days, who had just come back to town from a sojourn in Florida, remembers Otis and Johnny playing one gig at Mercer as a duo, with Otis on drums. Almost all the jobs were still within easy driving range, and it seemed doubtful for a while that things were ever going to pick up. To Phil and Otis, though, it was the playing out of a dream. Though Phil downplays it now, he undoubtedly felt himself to be in the position of a cultural pioneer.

"I don't think many people knew what I was doing. I wasn't really under a lot of peer pressure. I'll tell you, in college to be going out to a lot of black nightclubs and all that stuff was very hip—*until* someone started shooting. Then it wasn't so hip. Some people felt, What's he doing hanging around with all them niggers? But then there are always going to be people like that, I don't care whether it's North or South. Later my parents started getting phone calls: 'Your son's gonna marry a nigger.' I disappointed them, though. Unfortunately."

For Otis there was no question of direction: this was it. There was no question of loyalty, either. When Phil overspent one semester and it didn't look as if he was going to get the money to go back to college, Otis saw to it that he continued his education. "I was pretty free-spending with my money," admits Phil, who seems to have retained that characteristic over the years with correspondingly precipitate rises and falls in his fortune. "I bought expensive clothes, paid my own way through school, all that stuff. But going into the winter quarter, I had slightly overspent during the holiday season. I went down to my father to borrow money to pay for tuition, and he said, 'You made the money, you spent it.' Oh, I was just all depressed; I was president of my fraternity, and this was just a tremendous blow to my social status. Otis came in and asked me what was wrong. I told him what was happening. He said, 'I'll be back in a little while.' He came back about three, four hours later, he had a brown sack filled with change, dollar bills, whatnot. He went out and borrowed rent money from people, utility bills, everything else, all crumpled up in a paper sack. He said, 'You do the learning, I got to do the singing.' "

Then Johnny Jenkins had a hit with "Love Twist." It came out originally on the Tifco label on a deal Phil set up with a local banker. When it started getting some regional play, Joe Galkin, Atlantic's southeastern rep and an admirer of Phil's gumptious spirit, brought it to Jerry Wexler, and Atlantic took an option on Jenkins's next record. It was Galkin who set up the Stax session, and Galkin who insisted, however reluctantly, that Jim Stewart record Otis Redding, and Galkin who shared in one third of the publishing throughout Otis Redding's career.

"These Arms of Mine," the "hit" from that first Stax session, was released on Stax's new r&b subsidiary, Volt, in October 1962 but didn't make the charts until the following March—and then only after assiduous play by John R., who had been cut in for Stewart's share of the royalties on this record alone. Jim obviously had no more faith in his artist than the public, for he didn't call Otis back into the studio until the following June when he recorded a beautifully realized "That's What My Heart Needs" and a ridiculous "Mary's Little Lamb," which combined to make the worst-selling Otis Redding record on Stax ever. Then in September 1963, nearly a full year after his first session, Otis went back into the studio and recorded a self-composed song called "Pain in My Heart," which turned out to be patterned so closely on Irma Thomas's "Ruler of My Heart" that it occasioned a lawsuit and a reassignment of rights. The song reached the top of the r&b charts, regardless of who wrote it, and Otis was finally off and running. In November, when he went up to the Apollo Theatre in New York to take part in the recording of a live album for Stax's distributor, Atlantic (Ben E. King, the Coasters, the Falcons, and Rufus Thomas can also be heard on the record), he was something of a one-hit star.

The Apollo trip was hardly glamorous. Otis and Huckaby and Otis's brother, Rodgers, drove up "in a '63 Ford, XL convertible," says Huckaby, a burly ex-boxer who has been in and out of trouble all his life and looks it. "I didn't even have no driver's license. We went up to Bluefield, West Virginia, then Virginia, Maryland, and on to New York—my first trip out. They paid us $400 a week, and of course they had a house band, so we thought it was lots of money. But then we had to get the music arranged—Otis used to just go up and tell people, but this was the King Curtis band, and they wanted sheet

On the Town. Seated from left to right: Rufus Thomas, Alan Walden, Lucy Bell, Otis Redding, Al Jackson, Barbara Jackson, Jim Stewart, and Joe Galkin (foreground). Standing: Sylvester Huckaby. (Courtesy of Alan Walden)

music—so that cost us $450, and we had to wire back home to Phil to send us some more money. We were staying in a big old raggedy hotel called the Theresa. It was famous 'cause you had all these African diplomats and stuff, and Muhammad Ali had the whole seventh floor. All of us ran together, Rufus Thomas and Muhammad Ali and all the singers, and I thought the Apollo was going to be a great big huge theater, but it's not so big as hometown, it's just so famous. Ben E. King was the star of the show, and after we had played there and Otis had explained to him what had happened with the money, he gave him an extra hundred dollars. He said, 'Man, you're really good.' "

Jerry Wexler remembers Otis as being awkward in performance, picking up tips from Rufus Thomas on stage presence. "He didn't know how to *move* in those days," Wexler recalls. "He just stood still, and he'd bend from the waist. He wasn't even singing 'Shout Bamalama' anymore then." Nonetheless he came across, as Wexler says, because "you could feel this plea coming from him." More and more, in fact, that was the source of Otis's appeal: an aching vulnerability seemingly at odds with the self-confidence he exuded to friends and associates. You can hear it on the live recording that was made at the Apollo. I remember the same quality in the singer I saw in the Hot Summer Revue of

Otis Redding and band, including Jai Johanny Johanson on drums. (Courtesy of Mark Pucci)

1964, where Otis appeared down on a bill that headlined Solomon Burke and Garnet Mimms. In their company Otis Redding appeared stiff and blocky, considerably older than his twenty-two or twenty-three years, but it was obvious, too, that he touched the hearts of the crowd, that his thin quavery voice, emanating more from the throat than the chest, received the understanding it pleaded for. "These Arms of Mine," "Pain in My Heart," "Mr. Pitiful"—these were yearning songs by their titles alone; Otis delivered them with a sincerity that reached out to an audience that was mostly female and seemed unable to resist responding to his plea.

"SECURITY"

The Apollo date marked a watershed. From then on it all started happening: the tours were more extensive, the sessions were more frequent, the hits got bigger, and Otis and the band he put together were out on the road almost constantly. They traveled at first in a station wagon with a U-Haul hitched behind. Soon they would graduate to an Econoline, then to one of the old Flexibuses that a country star had abandoned, and finally to a real tour bus. Phil went into the Army just about this time, and his younger brother, Alan, blond, innocent-looking, no more than 120 pounds—Alan is the original self-invented "baby-faced assassin"—went on the road with Otis. It was quite an awakening for him.

"In those days we would go out thirty-five to seventy days straight. I was still young—I was just twenty years old!—and I wanted to see as much of the world as I could. Sometimes it was like going to war. I carried a gun. All of us carried guns. You had to in those days. If some fucker was gonna mess with you, you had to be prepared to blow him away. I wasn't going to get written off like some of them civil rights workers by the side of the road. I'll tell you, with Otis it was never dull. There was always something going on. He had tremendous sex appeal to the ladies, there were always flocks of ladies backstage waiting just to touch his hand or whatever. Being single and all that, I thoroughly enjoyed traveling with a guy who had such an appeal. I stayed in his room one time and had more sexual conquests in one week than I had had maybe in a year before—and all I was doing was answering the phone. It was outrageous. He was just an overpowering figure. Wherever you went, people would wonder, *Who is that?*"

To everyone around Otis success brought a substantial change. Phil and Otis, of course, had grown up in the business together (Phil always recalls going out with Otis and sharing a bed with him in the colored hotels when they couldn't afford a second room; as Zelma says somewhat acerbically, "They ate together, slept together—and fortunately they made money together."). Speedo Simms, who had joined Otis's troupe as an opening act, would soon take Rodgers's place as road manager when Rodgers, too, went into the Army. Huckaby for the first time got out of his bad-boy role for a while. Hamp Swain was becoming known all over the South as the DJ from Otis Redding's hometown ("It was one of the reasons I think I stayed in Macon; when I went to conventions, everyone quickly identified me with Otis. If it hadn't been for Otis, I would have been just another little disc jockey from a secondary market."). Even Otis's hairdresser, Walter Johnson, who located his barbershop and cosmetology salon, the House of Johnson, on Broadway in the midst of all the clubs ("That was the location. That was what was happening."), became known throughout the rhythm and blues world for creating the Otis Redding look; as a result he got to do the Percy Sledge weave (with its characteristic flip) and to style Sam's and Dave's hair, too. Phil Walden and Associates, meanwhile, had grown as a result of *its* association with Otis to the point where it was one of the top r&b booking agencies in the country (no more phony pictures); at its height, in 1967, it was booking forty-six of the top soul acts, including Percy Sledge, Sam and Dave, Joe Tex, and nearly every other r&b headliner that you could think of.

For Rodgers perhaps, growing up in the shadow of his brother, it was the greatest education of all. "Well, you've got to be strong to handle success, especially someone who had nothing to begin with. People will take you and lead you wherever, and that's where you got to learn to say no sometimes; regardless of who you are or what you are, you got to learn to deal with the leeches that surround you. The strong ones survive, the others just get washed away. My brother was always strong—I don't think there was anything that could have stopped him. He knew exactly who he was, and he knew he had nothing to prove. Sometimes it was rough out on the road. We used to carry guns just for protection only. Sometimes we used to run into little small problems. If you're intelligent enough, you can deal with them. You just have to know how to handle yourself out there."

Otis seemed to know almost instinctively how to handle himself. He was the center of everyone's life, family and friends, and listening to them all talk about it today, you get the impression that there wasn't anything they wouldn't have done for Otis, there was nothing of which they would not have believed him capable. There were fights, naturally, and fallings out, brief disaffiliations and temporary defections from the ranks. At one time or another every member of the entourage left in a huff—over salary, over a domestic situation, out of a feeling of being insufficiently appreciated—only to join up again just two or three months later, with all forgiven or forgiving all. As Zelma says, it was a heady time, and there were moments when she herself—a canny woman and a fast learner, but one who had had little preparation for the roller coaster ride—worried that she was being left out. "I just felt like I wasn't going to fit with him 'cause he was outgrowing me, but it turned out just the opposite, really. In the end I think it pulled us together. Oh, he was still a little wild, but after 1965 he changed completely. Well, see, Otis would come home and just talk about things that had happened out on the road, just things that was funny. And he would always get into town to see his friends on Broadway and Poplar, all the people he had grown up with and used to hang out with and who was really on the streets. Come about two o'clock, he would say, 'Time to get to work,' and he would go over to Phil's office, but he just had to go see all his friends first. That stop had to be made."

"Otis," says Phil, something of a street person himself, "had a great street quality about him. That's what people loved about him. He never did get too big for his britches. He did not act like a star. At the same time he didn't want a lot of strangers hanging around his house. If he wanted to see those people, he would go hang out in the clubs. But home was home."

There were times when the division was not so clear. Solomon Burke remembers the first Otis Redding Homecoming—it must have been 1964, and the show subsequently became an annual event at Macon's City Auditorium—when Otis was caught in the middle of a family feud and was reluctant to go out on stage for fear of getting shot. There were shoot-outs even after recording success, there were high-speed chases on the highway. "He loved to drive fast," says Huckaby. "He was daring. The sheriff see us sometimes, he just throw his hands up." Huckaby admits quite frankly to being the muscle, although he also wrote some of Otis's early songs, including one of his best-known, "Security" ("I didn't really write that one. A girl gave it to him, a girl who lived in Tindall Heights. It didn't rhyme, so he gave it to me to make it rhyme, and he recorded it."). Huckaby "went away" for a while, but when he came back, his place was right there beside Otis, at the center of the little group that had remained largely intact from the start. In fact, of all the old gang only Johnny Jenkins was left out in the cold.

The original idea, when "These Arms of Mine" had become a hit, had been for Johnny and Otis to go out as a duo—with Otis doing the singing and Johnny providing the spectacular effects. "That would have been the perfect shot," says Rodgers, "but Johnny wouldn't travel." Johnny instead retreated into a private world, withdrawing more and more into the shadows of bitterness and paranoia, focusing his resentment not so much on Otis as on the Waldens and Joe Galkin and Steve Cropper, whom he accused of stealing his style on the basis of their one meeting in the studio. To Johnny the failure of that single Stax session loomed larger and larger, grew to assume the proportions of cultural theft. As Johnny remembers it, Jim Stewart got him to play for hours ("They had me in the motherfucking studio, and I played the best I knowed how"), then sat down and analyzed his style and passed it on to Cropper. According to many of his friends Johnny Jenkins's life stopped in 1962, although he remained an attraction for Phil Walden and Associates on the fraternity circuit for a good number of years after that.

Otis's world, on the other hand, just kept on expanding. The tours (eight or ten acts to a bus, plus an eight-piece band) put him in contact with singers who had been his idols just one or two short years before. Otis wrote "I've Been Loving You Too Long" with Jerry Butler in a Buffalo hotel room. He learned from Solomon Burke the spirit of the independent entrepreneur. Joe Tex was even then leaning toward the Muslim religion. Little Willie John conned Sam Cooke out of $5000 with the story that his mother died ("Boy, did that nigger go for it," recalls one of the entourage. "And nobody was supposed to hustle Sam."). Every town was an adventure. In every town there were contacts to be made, people to see, DJs to meet, parties to be set up. Otis took it all in. Among all the people I've talked to there is no one who has a bad word to say about Otis. Sam Cooke was too independent for some; Solomon Burke was too much of a wise guy; Little Willie John was definitely untogether; and Joe Tex's conscious distancing of himself from some of his white associates seemed like a bad move—if only from the standpoint of commerce—to many. But Otis is described admiringly by black and white alike as a man who "took care of business," a businessman, a straight shooter. Otis was so universally respected, according to Phil and Alan, that even the local KKK appreciated him.

Otis Redding, Jim Stewart, Rufus Thomas, Booker T.,
Carla Thomas seated. (Courtesy of Gregg Geller)

Not all of the tours were glamorous, by any means. One time, according to Huckaby, they "almost starved to death" in Florida. They were still playing the fraternity circuit extensively (about half and half with the black clubs and revues), and though things were changing in the South, the new tolerance itself was fraught with its own brand of danger. "They really admired you," says Speedo of Otis's young white audience, "but you still always had to keep that eye out, just, you know, watch yourself, because you could get in some situations that were uncomfortable. I remember one time we played this place, and the guitarist, the way he did his act, he fell on the floor just playing his guitar and looking up, and this white girl just literally walked over and stood over him with her legs apart, and we're all going, 'Whoaaa. Wait a minute!' Well, they were all just clapping and carrying on, and she's going, you know, doing all that stuff, and when it was all over, we just go, 'Wheww,' and when we go out, I notice up on the top of the bulletin board there were these three K's on these key racks up there, because that's where they met. But, see, every now and then it would just get real loose."

Whatever the vicissitudes that he encountered, Otis carried himself with a natural dignity and a sense of direction almost unprecedented in the world of rhythm and blues (Jerry Wexler called him a "natural prince"). His mind, as Rodgers and Zelma are quick to point out, was always on his career, always on the music. And his music continued to develop. He soaked up influences like a sponge. He listened to the Beatles, he listened to Bob Dylan ("Too many words," commented Otis, speaking of "Just Like a Woman"), just as earlier he had "studied" Sam Cooke, taking Phil's copy of *Live at the Copa* and wearing that record out, not only adapting his trademark chant "Gotta, gotta" from Sam's more smoothly lilting imprecation but also taking such cuts as "A Change Is Gonna Come," "Shake," "You Send Me," and "Try a Little Tenderness" directly from Sam's repertoire. His early compositions had been somewhat self-pitying, though a far cry themselves from the Little Richard imitations with which he had started out his career. As he grew more confident of his own identity as a performer, his vocals became more assertive, too; the horn lines that he dictated to the Stax session musicians came to dominate the Stax sound; his music took on a voice and coloration of its own.

And he wrote. He wrote on buses. He wrote in motel rooms. He wrote in the back seats of cars. His cheap little red guitar was never far from his side, and he almost always carried a tape recorder with him. He would bounce ideas off whoever happened to be around—off Speedo or Rodgers, or Huckaby or Alan or Steve Cropper, who coauthored some of his best songs in the Stax studio. One time Cropper played him the Rolling Stones' record of "Satisfaction"; Otis didn't know the group, and he didn't know the song, but he wanted to record it, so he did a new version, and when his "Satisfaction" came out in 1966, it was so convincingly his own many people thought that the Rolling Stones had gotten the song from him. His music had its own structure, defined by the beat, transformed by the sense that Otis was zeroing in on something with the full force of his personality, set off by the lean muscularity of the Stax sound.

Everyone describes the Stax sessions as an event, an occasion that Otis almost willed to happen, stripping off his shirt, furiously directing the horns, his body glistening in the sweltering studio. "It was never a routine session with Otis," says bassist Duck Dunn. "You'd go along six weeks, say, eight hours a day, and all you'd ever see was a man with a hand on his chin [this was Jim Stewart], and then Otis would come in, and, boy, he'd just bring everybody up. 'Cause you knew something was gonna be different. When Otis was there, it was just a revitalization of the whole thing. You wanted to play with Otis. He brought out the best in you. If there was a best, he brought it out. That was his secret."

The Premiers—"The Singing Demons," with Speedo Simms far left. (Courtesy of Earl "Speedo" Simms)

He got his inspiration sometimes from the oddest sources: "Fa-Fa-Fa-Fa-Fa (Sad Song)," for example, was suggested by the theme from *The $64,000 Question;* "Mr. Pitiful" came from the nickname a DJ in Memphis, Moohah Williams, had given him. There is no question that his success was the result of a team effort: not simply the Stax team or the Atlantic team but the Otis Redding team as well. Everyone in Otis's entourage contributed in one way or another. There has never been any mystery about the origin of many of the songs attributed to Otis, save for the copyright line (and that was business). "Respect," for example, is one of the songs most identified with Otis, and perhaps his most covered composition, but it stemmed in fact—according to everyone's unembarrassed recollection—from a session that he had originally scheduled for Speedo.

" 'Respect' was a song that came from a group that I was singing with at one time, and we were going to record it, but we never did. Otis rewrote the song in order for me to sing it—it had been more of a ballad type, but a lot of the lyric was still there and the title line—and he took me into the studio at Muscle Shoals to give me a chance to record. Well, that's when I found out that singing on stage live, I have no problem, but in the studio I just couldn't hold the tune. So finally he said, 'Why don't I do the song?' And I said, 'Sure. I fought with it long enough.' He told me I would get credit, but I never did, but I just consider that water under the bridge and move on. A lot of people have said I should sue, and I can listen to what they're saying, but I make up my own mind. And I believe that to learn I guess you have to pay for your own learning."

In 1965 alone Otis Redding had three Top 10 soul hits and a fourth and fifth that went to #11 and #15 respectively. Phil was just getting out of the Army; the booking agency was thriving; when Otis called up Atlantic and asked for "Omelet," he was put through immediately to president Ahmet Ertegun; the world was beating a path to Macon's door. It was a comfortable kind of stardom. All the public relations were taken care of by Phil (to the point that Phil actually wrote most of Otis's interviews himself, questions and answers both). All the singing was done by Otis. Phil and Otis and Alan were inseparable. Each had a new Cadillac El Dorado, "so we'd go out in our El Dorados clubbing it," says Phil. "We'd go down Broadway, it's all torn down now, and Cotton Avenue—they were just *full* of nightclubs. You couldn't make up a story like ours. It was too good to be true. To take all these people from diverse backgrounds, different cultures, different races, mix them all together in a small little Georgia town, it's a helluva story. But I think the real uniqueness of it, what gave us that special edge was that we *had* to be better than anyone else, because if we weren't, we couldn't compete."

"With Otis," says Alan, "it was just family. It was, Hey, we're gonna conquer the world! We're gonna let 'em know who you are all over the world. It worked in a triangle. If Otis was wrong, Phil and I would go to Otis and tell him. If I was wrong and Phil couldn't get it across to me, he'd go get Otis to straighten me out. I can safely say we sat down at several meetings and figured out how to conquer the music industry. After those meetings we could all walk out of that room and say, 'You know, if we decided to do anything, we could do it.' Because there was that much love between the three of us."

▶5▶

Stax: The Golden Years

IT WAS THE SUCCESS OF OTIS REDDING THAT brought Jerry Wexler to Memphis. In early 1965 he signed a duo out of Miami who had recorded for Roulette a couple of years earlier without anything much happening. He signed them to an Atlantic contract, but because of the sound, and the hits, that Stax was getting on Otis, he assigned them to the Memphis label. Sam and Dave (Sam Moore and Dave Prater) had their first, fairly uneventful Stax session in March. Then in June forty-year-old Tom Dowd, Atlantic's chief engineer from the beginning and the man who had set industry standards in multi-track recording, came down for the Otis Redding album session that produced "I've Been Loving You Too Long" to "straighten out" the Stax technology. Stax had up till now been relying on the same mono Ampex for which Estelle Axton had mortgaged her home. Jim Stewart had engineered most of the sessions, and though the sound he got out of the old Capitol movie theater studio was undeniably unique, and undeniably Stax's own, it was obvious that if Atlantic was going to use Stax as a serious outlet for its artists and label, the recording facilities would have to be upgraded and modernized.

Dowd installed a two-track recorder—soon to be replaced by a four-track—and showed Jim Stewart how to use the equipment. Everyone acknowledges his beneficial influence. "He opened our eyes to what goes on in recording," says William Brown, then a member of the Mad Lads singing group and soon to become one of Stax's chief engineers. "He's a walking genius in electronics. He took some medieval equipment and made it function like it was modern." "Tom had been in and out of the studio since '61," says Jim Stewart. "Usually you'll find someone whose expertise is either in electronics or they'll be creative in the studio, but he's amazing. I can't find words to describe how much we learned from him, although I think he learned some things from us, too, 'cause he had been cutting in a different way from the way we were recording up till then."

Indeed he had. Atlantic was renowned everywhere for the quality of its recordings. Even DJs like WLAC's John R. and Zenas Sears in Atlanta picked up on the sound that Atlantic Records got in addition to the music that was being presented. So far as clarity of recording, trueness of pitch, and engineering balance were concerned, there was little comparison with other independent labels, and that was mostly attributable to Tom Dowd. But it was also attributable to the way that sessions continued to be conducted. All were meticulously rehearsed and arranged; for the most part Jerry Wexler and Ahmet Ertegun still took advantage of the same core group of New York studio musicians and arrangers who had given them their early hits. Atlantic's approach to soul, in other words, was pretty much the same as its approach to rhythm and blues had been since Big Joe Turner and the Clovers had first entered the studio: take a vocalist or vocal group capable of real sophistication, hook them up with musicians with at least a working knowledge of jazz, employ an experienced arranger, and then put the entire ensemble to work reproducing "musical modes older and more powerful" than the ones they were accustomed to. That was the way the Ray Charles band had operated, more or less, though it was a self-contained entity, and the ideas and inspiration were almost exclusively Charles's own. That was the way Solomon Burke's seminal sessions for Atlantic had been approached. In Memphis Jerry Wexler saw an altogether different way of making records.

"Memphis was a real departure," Wexler has said, "because Memphis was a return to head arrangements, to the set rhythm section, away from the arranger. It was a reversion to the symbiosis between the producer and the rhythm section, and it was really something new." To Jim Dickinson, a hip, somewhat cynical observer of the scene who grew up with Packy Axton and recorded as a sideman on many of the non-Stax rock and rhythm and blues sessions coming out of Memphis, the doppelganger effect was even more startling. "The people at Atlantic came here and were amazed by what they saw the people from Stax doing. The people from Stax were exactly the same way. They saw these people from Atlantic, and they said, 'Damn, that's it, we'll do it that way.' And they started copying each other without even knowing it. It used to be a joke, when they redecorated Stax a couple of years later, just how garish it was. There was this bright green carpet everywhere. It was like the yellow brick road, only it was green. Everyone made fun of it for years; then I went to Atlantic in New York, and I saw this green carpet, and I said, 'Well, there it is.' I've heard Wexler and Dowd both say, 'We didn't know you could cut sessions that way.' It never really dawned on them to put the session together one step at a time—rhythm section, horns, the whole thing—and then they saw Jim Stewart in this tremendously racially aggressive situation pushing these people around and doing this thing that was working like a charm. Hell, if you interview Wexler at all, you know that this could be very appealing to him."

It was into this climate, "racially aggressive" or not, that Jerry Wexler brought Wilson Pickett in May of 1965. Pickett, who had signed with Atlantic in 1964 after providing the label with the song and the demo for one of its greatest Solomon Burke hits ("If You Need Me"), had been making records with Bert Berns in New York City for about a year, expensive, elaborately produced, magnificently sung records but ones that didn't sell. "His manager, Jimmy Evans, finally called me," Wexler relates, "and he said, 'Look, I need

The Wicked Pickett. (Courtesy of Bill Millar)

a record or else let him go.' I didn't want to let him go, so I got the bright idea of taking him to Memphis." According to Wilson Pickett, "I told Jerry Wexler that I didn't want to be recorded this way anymore. He asked me how I wanted it, so I said I heard a song by Otis Redding out of Memphis, and that's the direction I wanted to take, so that's where they sent me." The session, on May 12, 1965, was an epochal one which produced Pickett's signature tune, "In the Midnight Hour," along with three other classic recordings.

Pickett, who was referred to customarily by Evans not by name but by epithet and who is the possessor of a notoriously volatile personality (a later gun battle with the Isley Brothers that made headlines was not atypical), would go back to Memphis two more times in the next seven months, cutting "634–5789," his second #1 hit, in the final session in December. The first session in May, however, is revealing, not only for the way the session was put together but for its effect on Stax as well. As usual nothing was fully prepared when Pickett arrived. Steve Cropper, who by now exercised de facto control in the studio, had been listening to the few Pickett records he could get hold of, which included an appearance on Atlantic's live-recorded *Saturday Night at the Uptown* album. On one of the songs, "I'm Gonna Cry," Pickett kept making reference to "late in the midnight hour" at the fade.

"I thought that would be a heckuvan idea for a tune," Cropper told *Rolling Stone* editor Jann Wenner in 1968, "and when he came in I presented it to him, and he said 'That's a good idea, I've got this little rhythm thing I've been working on for a good while.' It was really nothing to it, it was just a couple of changes and we just started working with this. When I wrote the tune I had it going in a completely different way. Basically the changes were the same, basic feel was the same, but there was a different color about it. During the session Jerry said, 'Why don't you pick up on this thing here?' He said this was the way the kids were dancing, they were putting the accent on two."

"Well, the bass thing," said Duck Dunn to Wenner, "was really Jerry Wexler's idea. Like Steve said, we had it going another way. Jerry came out and did the Jerk."

"We had the funk," said Cropper, "but he knew what the kids were dancing to."

That, in a nutshell, tells the story of Jerry Wexler's relationship with Memphis. Like the great prestidigitator that he is, Wexler recognized right away the opportunity that he was being presented with. Neither an arranger nor an engineer (Steve Cropper takes great pains to point out that it was Tom Dowd who provided the *musical* tips and inspiration), Wexler must have known that here was a combination of elements that no session "producer," no matter how gifted, could ever hope to put together by design, and he didn't hesitate to take advantage of it. From Stax's point of view Wexler's very presence in the studio was a dramatic revelation. Not simply because of the high-gloss production that was applied to the Pickett session (this was Dowd's contribution) but for the very reason that the Stax studio was important enough to warrant this visit. Almost to a person everyone connected with Stax at this time speaks of his or her own provinciality. Not only were they from Memphis; because of the way that the studio operated, they couldn't get *out* of Memphis. At a time when Stax Records was acquiring an aura, and a legend, all its own, no one at Stax—including Jim Stewart—had the slightest idea what was going on in the outside world. To them it was not Wilson Pickett who was the star; Wilson Pickett was just another rhythm and blues singer. It was Jerry Wexler and the Atlantic label, after which they had patterned their whole sound, who were the stars. Jerry Wexler was an exotic presence; his very speech (a "Jewish brogue") was like a foreign tongue to Memphians who had never even seen New York City. This was the ultimate validation.

Stax Records at this point was a real anomaly, to say the least. Though held up in many ways as the Motown alternative and themselves looking upon Motown as the competition ("The records they do are made from the switchboard," said Al Jackson), Stax could scarcely compete on any basis but the ideological, for Motown had had a dozen #1 hits when Stax had no more than a dozen acts on its roster. Of those dozen the majority (Rufus and Carla Thomas, the Mar-Keys, the MG's, the Mad Lads, Otis Redding, and William Bell) had been with them virtually from the beginning. Sam and Dave were new, and Eddie Floyd and Johnnie Taylor were just about to enter the picture, but for a company with a worldwide reputation as the source of downhome soul, the game was still being played surprisingly close to the vest. Over and over Stax has been described in retrospect as a family, and indeed it was—a close, tight-knit family in which Jim Stewart played the role of the stern but proud father, Estelle was the doting mother, and Steve and Packy were the good and bad sons (*East of Eden* was undoubtedly as formative for the Stax crowd as it was for Elvis Presley). As in any tight-knit family, there was warmth and sharing, but also, as in any such intimate group, there was jealousy and a suspicion of outsiders, too.

To Homer Banks, working during this period in the record store and struggling desperately to get his songs heard (in 1968 his "Who's Making Love?" would be the breakthrough song for Johnnie Taylor, and a breakthrough song for Stax as well, when it made the Top 10 pop as well as the top of the r&b charts), Stax was "a kind of closed shop. It was great if you were a member of the family, but if you were on the outside, it was a little difficult getting in. It really wasn't as open as a lot of people believed." In truth, for those who were on the inside the opportunities were distinctly more limited than anyone on the outside had reason to suspect. Booker T. and the MG's, for example, were one of the most popular groups on the roster, but they were virtually unable to go out and capitalize on their popularity for two reasons. One was that Booker T. was still in college, earning his degree from Indiana University, which he had entered at almost the same time as "Green Onions" hit the charts. The other, perhaps even more compelling argument against touring (after all, someone could easily have replaced Booker, as Isaac Hayes occasionally did, with or without billing), was that Stax needed the group in the studio. They were the stable rhythm section that Jerry Wexler talked about, they were the core of the Stax sound and worth a lot more, obviously, to Stax in the studio than on the road. The limitations—financial and otherwise—that this kind of thinking imposed upon the various members of the group are sometimes difficult to fully grasp.

For Duck Dunn, for example, the onetime Mar-Key who had replaced Lewis Steinberg in the MG's sometime in 1964, playing at Stax had to be sandwiched in between all the other jobs that were necessary just to make a living. Dunn, an easygoing sort who would get the "best-friend" role if a Hollywood movie were ever based on this story, was flattered, certainly, to be included in the MG's but to this day professes bewilderment as to why he was selected. ("Come on," his wife, June, will interpose irreverently, "they just

Homer Banks, summer 1968. (Jonas Bernholm)

wanted a young white player. It makes sense.") During the day he continued
to work at the King Records distributorship which his brother Bobby managed.
"Sometimes when they'd call me for a session, I'd have to put a note on the
door that I'd be back in five minutes. Then I started playing with Ben Branch
—I mean, that was really an honor. I think I was the first white guy to play
in a black band in Memphis, and that was where I really started to learn
something. But I had my daytime gig five and a half days a week, Ben was
working Tuesday through Sunday at the Penthouse Club, we had Mondays off,
but on Monday we had to rehearse. And if I did have a few hours off, we went
over to Stax to make a demo. I used to do a lot to make $150 a week—$60
at King, $60 with the band, and I think Stax used to pay maybe $15 per session
in those days. Of course it got better. By 1965 we were all working on staff,
but I still never thought it would last. I always wondered if I was doing good
enough. I kept waiting for them to get someone else."

Even the songwriting, often pointed to as the cornerstone of Stax success,
was pretty much catch-as-catch-can up until 1964–1965. Steve Cropper, of
course, joined in as cowriter in the studio on a great many songs; Otis generated
most of his own material; and William Bell contributed a number of songs to
other artists. But as for the vaunted stable of Stax writers, Deanie Parker, a high
school student hired as a secretary by Estelle who went on to become national
director of publicity, recalls that when she started working at Stax, "you had

to do everything. . . . I even wrote songs, though I had never written a song before in my life!" Even Isaac Hayes and David Porter, the team that came to define Stax songwriting, were scarcely on the staff at all, though David had been hanging around since Stax first opened its doors, and Isaac had been playing keyboards on MG dates since the winter of 1963–1964. In fact Hayes and Porter were so far removed from any hope of success that they took a leave from Stax just before Sam and Dave were signed to go in on a new deal with Chips Moman, cutting Satellite Record Shop clerk Homer Banks on a song called "Lady of Stone" on the Genie label.

"HOLD ON, I'M COMIN'"

Hayes and Porter are a story in themselves, and in their way they both epitomize Stax success and were undone by it. David Porter, an affable go-getter who would probably make a good Rotarian, grew up not too far from McLemore on East Virginia Street, four doors down from Maurice White (founder and moving spirit of Earth, Wind and Fire), with whom as a child he formed a gospel quartet. In high school he recorded for a local label, Golden Eagle, then for New Jersey-based Savoy as Little David (with the Stax rhythm section backing him) and for Hi across town under the name of Kenny Cain. He played around town with a group called the Marquettes, sang at Clifford Miller's Flamingo Room with Barbara Griffin, and with Barbara (who married Al Jackson) even entertained at one or two of Elvis Presley's New Year's Eve parties. Porter remembers the early Satellite sessions with singer Charles Heinz, and he remembers the day Estelle opened the record store. Just out of high school, and with a semester at LeMoyne College behind him, he got a job at the Jones Big Star Grocery across the street, sang background on a couple of the earliest McLemore sessions, cut his own version of "The Old Gray Mare" (Jim Stewart calls it "The Rockin' Ole Gray Mare"), which, he says, thankfully was never released, and pestered Jim and Estelle long enough so that he became the first black on staff, however marginal.

Isaac Hayes, born nine months after Porter in August 1942, moved to Memphis from Covington, Tennessee, at seven, was forced to repeat a grade, and didn't graduate high school till 1962. Like Porter, who was trying to sell him life insurance when they first met (Hayes was a packer at a meat plant), he came out of a succession of groups, almost all of which he brought down to the Stax studio to audition at one time or another. "I made three different attempts to get into Stax. One with a rock 'n' roll band, Sir Isaac and the Do-Dads, one with a rock 'n' roll vocal group, the Teen Tones, one with a blues band, Sir Calvin Valentine and His Swinging Cats. Each time we were turned down by Jim. When I failed at that, I started working with Floyd Newman, playing keyboards in his band—Floyd played baritone sax on a lot of sessions;

he was also one of the Mar-Keys, and we were playing over at the Plantation Inn in West Memphis. Well, Floyd was up for a record himself, and Howard Grimes, Floyd's drummer, and I wrote a tune called 'Frog Stomp.' We went in the studio, and Jim Stewart heard my keyboard work and offered me a job as a side musician, because Booker T. was off at school then. My first session was an Otis Redding session."

This was in early 1964. At this point Hayes started playing keyboards on quite a few sessions, including a number of Booker T.'s own gigs. It was at this point, too, that Hayes and Porter, one-time rivals in high school (not only did they attend competing schools, their singing groups were in competition at the Wednesday Night Amateur Night contests at the Palace which Rufus Thomas MC'd), first hooked up as a team. They seemed like a natural combination— Porter, a born salesman with a smooth-spoken gift for gab, and Hayes, a somewhat more introspective and eccentric sort (with his shaven head and dedicated weight-training program he looked like Mr. Clean) but an equally gifted and ambitious artist. Their first composition together was a song that Porter recorded called "Can't See You When I Want To," and then they wrote a number for Carla Thomas, but it was when Jerry Wexler signed Sam and Dave in early 1965 that they finally got their chance.

"Jim said, 'We got some guys coming in, I want y'all to get some material to show them.' And out of all the writers they liked our stuff; they wanted David and me to write for them. So we worked the tunes up, got a rhythm section, got the horns and everything together—at first we didn't even have an office. We'd go to David's house or my house or either in the studio at the piano. We slept on the floor at night. Get an idea and start playing something, and he'd say, 'Yeah, man, okay,' and he start coming out with the lyrics. And then we'd teach them to Sam and Dave."

The first couple of sessions with Sam and Dave didn't yield any real hits, but then in October they went back in the studio and cut "You Don't Know Like I Know," which shot to the Top 10 r&b but only foreshadowed the success of their next song, "Hold On, I'm Comin'." "Hold On, I'm Comin'" was Stax's first #1 r&b hit since "Green Onions"; in fact it was the first time Stax's vocal sound had made a significant impact on the pop charts since Carla Thomas's "Gee Whiz" (with a couple of exceptions Otis was to be found almost exclusively on the r&b lists). "Hold On, I'm Comin'" was no fluke. With its call-and-response vocal, the gospel overtones of Sam's soaring lead and Dave's rougher-edged response, the deliberately "coarse" lyrics and strong church-centered accompaniment featuring Hayes's choppily chorded piano and Steve Cropper's vibrato-laden rhythm guitar, in many ways it epitomized the very formula that Jim Stewart had been groping for ever since he had first heard Ray Charles and started recording rhythm and blues. Otis was too country, William Bell too restrained ever to achieve real pop success, but Sam and Dave established

Sam and Dave. (Jean-Pierre Leloir)

Stax once and for all as pop contenders—and as worlds apart from Motown, in intent as well as effect. They established themselves also as Stax's hottest act. And their success set a pattern for a wealth of hits, by a variety of different acts, which Hayes and Porter turned out for nearly four years without interruption.

"Hold On, I'm Comin'," like many of their song ideas, arose from a purely accidental association (some lyrics came from comic books, others from head-lines; "When Something Is Wrong With My Baby" grew out of the lead in a *Teenage Confidential*-type story). In this case it was nothing more glamorous than Porter going to the bathroom, Hayes growing impatient, and Porter calling back, " 'Hold on, man, I'm coming.' I swear, right then I broke out of the rest room shouting, 'I got it!' When I told Hayes the title, he had the perfect thing for it on the piano. We had the whole song in five minutes."

Nearly all their writing seems as casual, and as inspired. In short order they had an office and a small baby grand on whose surface every Stax artist would eventually carve his or her name and initials. Every song session would start off with Ike and David (and maybe Sam and Dave, too) shooting craps on the green carpeting of their office. Or they might shoot a little miniature golf to loosen up before getting down to business. If Johnnie Taylor was coming in, they concentrated on a blues; for Carla Thomas it had to be "something soft; for Sam and Dave it would be something coarse in attitude. We were always writing with the styling in mind, and the artist's personality," says David Porter. "We would try to make it like a tailored suit."

Isaac Hayes and David Porter.

A typical day at Stax undoubtedly involved a lot of hanging around. Stanley Booth, a Memphis writer who was there on assignment from the *Saturday Evening Post,* paints a characteristic moment in 1967—at the very height of Stax success—with deft strokes.

> Nearly every man at Stax dresses in a kind of uniform: narrow cuffless pants, Italian sweaters, shiny black slip-on shoes. But now, standing in the lobby is a tall young Negro man with a shaved head and full beard. He is wearing a Russian-style cap, a white pullover with green stripes, bright green pants, black nylon see-through socks with green ribs, and shiny green lizard shoes. In a paper sack he is carrying a few yards of imitation zebra material, which he intends to have made into a suit, to be worn with a white mohair overcoat. His name is Isaac Hayes. With his partner, David Porter, Hayes has written such hit songs as "Soul Man" and "Hold On, I'm Comin'" for Stax singers Sam and Dave. Porter, dressed less spectacularly in a beige sweater and corduroy Levis, is sitting at a desk in the foyer, not making a phone call.
>
> "Come on," says Hayes. "Let's go next door and write. I'm hot."
>
> "I can't go nowhere till I take care of this chick."
>
> "Which chick is this?"

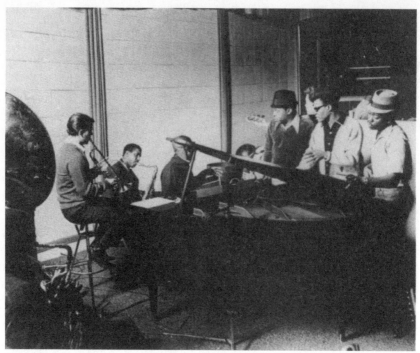

"Soul Man" session at Stax: Booker T. (tuba), Wayne Jackson, Andrew Love, Isaac Hayes, Joe Arnold (hidden), David Porter in hat, Duck Dunn with back to camera, Sam and Dave. (Courtesy of Wayne Jackson and Dave Booth)

"You know which chick. You think I ought to call her?"

"What the hell do *I* care? I want to go write."

"Well, she's occupying my mind."

"Let's go, man, let's go. I'm hot."

Porter shrugs and follows Hayes to an office next door where there are three folding chairs, a table littered with old issues of *Billboard* and *Hit Parader,* and a baby grand piano. Hayes sits down at the piano and immediately begins to play church chords, slow and earnest. As he plays he hums, whistles, sings. Porter hums along. He has brought with him a black attaché case, and now he opens it, takes out a ball point pen and several sheets of white typing paper, and begins writing rapidly. After about three minutes he stops, takes a pair of shades from his pocket, puts them on, throws back his head, and sings: "You were raised from your cradle to be loved by only me—"

He begins the next line, then stops. "Don't fit, I'm sorry." He rewrites quickly and starts to sing again. Then Hayes stops playing, turns to Porter, and says, "You know what? That ain't exactly killing me right there. Couldn't we get something going like: You can run for so long, then you're tired, you can do so and so—' "

"Yeah," Porter says. "Got to get the message in."

The door opens, and a small man wearing a black suit, black hat, and black mustache comes in, leading a very thin girl in an orange wig. "You got to hear this," the man says, nodding toward the girl, who is visibly shaking.

"Are you nervous?" Hayes asks her. "Just relax and enjoy yourself. Don't worry about us. We just two cats off the street." The girl smiles weakly and sits down.

Porter is writing "Forever Wouldn't Be Too Long" across the top of the page. Then,

> *My love will last for you*
> *Till the morning finds no dew*
> *'Cause I'm not tired of loving you—*

He stops, puts down the pen, and yawns: "Naw, I had something flowin' in my mind."

"How long you be working?" the man in the black suit asks.

"How do I know?" Hayes says. "We don't observe no time limits."

"Yes," says Porter, "Hayes will probably be here all night. He don't observe no time limits."

Hayes laughs, Porter stomps his right foot once, twice, Hayes strikes a chord, Porter closes his eyes and shouts: "Cross yo' fingers." He sings, bouncing, the chair squeaking, getting louder and faster, as if he were singing a song he had heard many times, and not one which he was making up, in an incredibly fluent improvisation. The girl smiles, then breaks into a giggle. When Porter stops, he groans. "Man, we should've had a tape recorder, I'll never get that feeling again. Damn! That's a hit! 'Cross Yo' Fingers!' That's a hit title!" He turns back to his writing paper and begins to reconstruct the lyrics.

Hayes looks at the girl. "So you're a singer?" She gulps and nods. The wig, high heels, a tightly belted raincoat, only make her seem thinner and more frightened. "Would you like to sing something for us?"

She swallows and nods again. They pick a song, a key (Hayes asks, "Can you sing that high?"), and she begins to sing. At first her voice trembles, but as she sings it grows stronger. She shuts her eyes and moves softly back and forth, as her voice fills the room. Porter stops writing to watch her. She is so frail-looking that one expects

Isaac Hayes, Eddie Floyd, Al Jackson, Bettye Crutcher: Stax 1968.
(Don Paulsen/Michael Ochs Archives)

her to miss the high notes, but she hits them perfectly each time, as her voice swells, blossoms. Finally she stops, on a long, mellow, vibrating note, opens her eyes, and gulps.

Porter applauds. "Wasn't-that-beautiful," he says.

"Where did you go to high school?" Hayes asks the girl.

"Manassas."

"Man— I went to Manassas. How'd you escape the clutches— When did you graduate?"

She looks away and does not answer.

"Haven't you graduated? How old are you?"

The girl mumbles something.

"What?"

"Seventeen," she whispers.

"Seventeen? A voice like that at seventeen? Old Manassas. Damn, you can't beat it." Hayes begins singing the Manassas Alma Mater song. Porter joins in. They get up and start to dance. Porter takes the girl's hands, and she joins him, singing and dancing. They all whirl around the room, as the man with the mustache closes his eyes and smiles.

(© 1969 Stanley Booth. Used by permission.)

Both Hayes and Porter maintained their own performing ambitions. Hayes continued to appear as vocalist and keyboard player with Ben Branch and

Sam and Dave in England, 1967. (From the collection of Fred Lewis)

Bowlegs Miller, and as Booker T.'s replacement on the MGs' few live gigs, well into the huge success of Hayes and Porter as a writing team. David Porter, who had originally modeled himself on Clyde McPhatter as a singer, also continued to play places like Johnny Curry's Club and the Tiki Lounge. David and Isaac together became a kind of underground legend, with their shows known to session players and club-goers around town for being just as hot as Sam and Dave's. "Sam and Dave were actually the extension of Isaac and David," says Jimmy Johnson, the Muscle Shoals guitarist who played on many of Stax's later hits. "If you had ever seen Ike and David work out and write, it was just like going to church. They'd walk in that room, it was so hot, man, they'd walk in that room with their sharp suits on and sit down at the piano, and David would be jumping up in the air, just screaming out the words. I mean, Isaac and David should have been the artists."

Jim Stewart was not interested in seeing either one of them as a featured performer, though. Perhaps, understandably, he did not want to break up a winning combination; perhaps he foresaw the strain that the success of one could put on the team, or that the demands of live performing could impose on a perfectly happy marriage. But most of all, Isaac Hayes says, he was not interested in Isaac Hayes or David Porter as artists because he had his own decided ideas about r&b. "He would say, 'Isaac, your voice is too pretty for you to sing.' 'Cause his concept of blacks in r&b is that they got to have those rough voices. I was Nat King Cole-influenced. I wanted to sing jazz. I remember, Carla Thomas's brother, Marvell, played keyboards, and he and I used to argue with

Jim Stewart on the floor about certain chords. Sometimes Booker would, too. Because we wanted to put some pretty progressive things in there. Jim'd say, 'Don't put no jazz chords in there.' We'd say, 'But, Jim—' 'No, no, I don't want that.' Naturally he won. He was the boss."

Sam and Dave, meanwhile, were becoming the hottest stage act in the country. Booked, like nearly all of Stax's acts, by Phil Walden's newly named Walden Artists and Promotions, they combined the frenzied activity of James Brown and the vocal dynamism of Wilson Pickett with the rough gospel harmonies of Sam Cooke's SAR label discovery, the Sims Twins, whose 1961 hit, "Soothe Me," they revived some six years later. "The Sam and Dave Revue was an awesome, well-oiled machine that virtually defined the '60s staging concept of soul," wrote critic Joe McEwen. Jon Landau declared in *Rolling Stone* that "as live performers, there is little doubt that Sam and Dave are the finest soul performers working today," and I don't think anyone who saw them at their peak soon forgot the impact of their performance. Certainly not Otis Redding. The first time Otis Redding went out with them, it just about killed him to come out on top.

"The name of the game was upsetting the show," says Alan Walden, who was now booking both acts. "Otis did thirty-seven days with them that first tour, the first seven days at the Apollo. I arrived at the Apollo to find him sucking lemon and eating honey backstage; he was as hoarse as he could be and more nervous than I'd ever seen him in my life. 'These motherfuckers are killing me,' he said. 'They're killing me. I'm going as fast as I can, but they're still killing me. Goddam!'

"Well, I took him over to Atlantic to get his mind off of it, and we went to lunch with Jerry Wexler. In the middle of lunch it came to me. 'Goddammit,' I said, 'you're going too fast. You've got to slow down your show. You're just pushing too hard.' He said, 'No, no, Red, I gotta keep the groove going.' Then Jerry said, 'I been noticing the same thing. Man, you could bring it down a little and still keep the same groove. You know, you almost look like you're nervous, like you're in a hurry to get off the stage.'

"Well, Otis thought about it, and when he got to the Apollo, Sam and Dave had just left the stage, burning as usual, they had it hotter 'n hell. Well, Phil walked up to him and looked him in the eye and said, 'Otis, go out there —you *are* the star, now go out there and star the motherfucker like you should.' And he did. And Sam and Dave were history that time.

"Well, after seven days of this Otis says, 'Goddam, we got thirty-seven days of this, I ain't gonna put up with them right in front of me for another thirty days. Let them close the first half of the show, and then let it build back up to another climax when I close the second.' After the third day he told Phil, 'Put those motherfuckers right in front of me. They're making me work harder than I ever did in my life.' And they did the whole tour right in front of him,

Otis with Sam and Dave. (Jean-Pierre Leloir)

but when he finished, he came into the office, and he looked beat, and he said, 'Okay, while I got the both of you here, don't you *ever* book me with Sam and Dave again. I don't never want to work the same bill with them again.' And we said okay, and then Phil said, 'Oh, my God!' And Otis said, 'What?' And Phil said, 'I just signed a contract for thirty days in Europe with them with the Stax-Volt tour.' [Actually this took place in the spring of 1967.] And Otis said, 'Okay, I'll do that one. But after that I don't ever want to see those two motherfuckers again.' "

MR. INSIDE AND MR. OUTSIDE

So it went, life on the road. Back on the homefront the success of Sam and Dave was mirrored by the growth and growing ambition of the company. All of a sudden things were happening. Sales were jumping. Otis had had a #2 r&b hit in May 1965 with "I've Been Loving You Too Long" (this went to #21 pop and was his top seller till the posthumous "Dock of the Bay"). Wilson Pickett had recorded one #1 r&b hit with "In the Midnight Hour," and at the beginning of 1966 "634-5789" would become another, while Don Covay, too, made the Top 10 of the soul charts with the Memphis-recorded "See-Saw." Not surprisingly, Jerry Wexler was talking about sending down more and more of Atlantic's most popular artists, and Jim Stewart was beginning to think that Stax's

Al Bell and Jim Stewart, circa 1967. (Gérard Pestre/Courtesy of Dave "Daddy Cool" Booth)

success might last. Then, in the fall of 1965, at the prompting of his sister, and with the active encouragement of Jerry Wexler (who sprang for half of the new man's salary), Stewart hired Al Bell as national sales director, with special responsibility for promotion. Bell (born Alvertis Isbell in Little Rock) was a big (six feet four), bluff, outgoing man of twenty-five, who had put himself through two years of Arkansas's all-black Philander Smith College as a gospel DJ. From there he had moved on to become one of the most popular jocks at Memphis's powerful WLOK, finally settling at WUST in Washington, D.C., where he started his own label, Safice (distributed by Stax) and promoted Stax product in the area. Bell was ready for the move. Almost from the day he arrived he took over leadership of the company in a way that no one could have foreseen, filling a vacuum that no one had fully perceived to exist.

There is some dispute about how Al Bell got there in the first place. Jerry Wexler has taken credit for his hiring, pointing to the money that Atlantic contributed to his salary and Wexler's own strongly expressed feeling that Stax needed a black executive. Jim Stewart says that it was all his idea and that it was only proper that Atlantic should pay a man who was, after all, hustling Atlantic product. Steve Cropper says that he and Estelle brought Al into the company. "I felt like when he left Memphis for Washington I had lost a friend. Al Bell was one of the sharpest guys in black radio that I ever met in my life, and I knew that Al was the force that could put Stax on the map."

That was exactly what he did. Whatever the precise truth about his hiring, there is no question about its effect. For one thing he brought with him Eddie Floyd, formerly a member of the Falcons (Wilson Pickett's old group in Detroit) and a partner in, as well as an artist for, Bell's own little label (he was the *e* and the *f* of Safice, Bell the *a* and the *i*, while Chester Simmons was the third partner). Floyd went on to become one of Stax's most dependable songwriters (with Steve Cropper alone he composed "634-5789" for Pickett, "Don't Mess With Cupid" for Otis, and his own "Knock on Wood") as well as a very popular recording artist in his own right. More significantly Bell—young, upwardly mobile, black, in a very visible position of real power—must have struck a responsive chord not only among the radio jocks and promotion men that he was hired to impress but also within the Stax family itself. ("Although his gift of gab accounts for the greater portion of our phone bills," announced an early publicity release, "he takes care of the business.")

Al Bell's most immediate effect, however, was to offset Jim Stewart's somewhat pallid personality. Stewart certainly recognized his own deficiencies in this area and the positive contributions that Bell would be able to make to the company's image. As Stewart has characterized himself, "I was a conservative bastard. I wasn't running any popularity contests. Whatever I did, I did what I thought was best for the company." Bell, on the other hand, was flamboyant, a glad-hander, a jaunty, self-confident, expansive presence who, "whatever he believed in, was going to try to make it happen." "I was Mr. Inside," Stewart proclaimed in *Stax Fax,* the ambitious company magazine that Deanie Parker started up in late 1968, "and he was Mr. Outside." "Al Bell gave me my social conscience," declared Stewart in another issue of the promo sheet. "Al was a very aggressive individual," Stewart declares in summation today, "and, of course, being so aggressive, he barely tolerated my conservatism, but he needed that balancing factor, and up to a point we were a very good team."

Duck Dunn, however, saw it another way.

"Jim could be a pain in the ass a lot of the time, most of the time, in fact. It was never a pat on the back, always a kick in the ass. I guess that was the way he had to be, and about seventy-five percent of the time probably he was right. But then Al Bell would come along and be buddying up with you and patting you on the back, and you'd believe anything he said. And I'll tell you what, if he was lying, then he was a good liar, because I believed him. At one point in the late '60s we were all telling Al, 'You go ahead and start your own company, we're ready to go with you.' This was later, but he had us all that way."

To most of the blacks in the company, Al Bell was a kind of secret hero, the "Jesse Jackson" of in-house politics. To Isaac Hayes, Bell represented a wedge in the all-white executive hegemony in which Steve Cropper was little more than a "Jim's boy." Even William Bell, more moderate and readier by far to take the long view than Hayes, declares without hesitation: "I think Al was good for the label. Jim was more or less business oriented, and Al was a wheeler-dealer. Go-getter. The deal-maker. I think the combination of the two of them was really good for the label, because our record sales just about a year after Al had been there really exploded. Al was the one who loved to meet people and rub elbows and talk deals, and that was good for the company because we were growing both in terms of the caliber of the artists we were acquiring and also the number of records we were selling. And we had to come from a mama and papa record label into a million-dollar conglomerate."

Bell saw the change for what it was, the inevitable linking of growth and progress, but it brought with it its own problems, problems of business and art which could never be fully resolved. By the end of the decade the Stax roster would have grown from a dozen acts to nearly a hundred, with sales mirroring this expansion. Content from the beginning to be another loyal soldier in the Atlantic fiefdom, with the coming of Al Bell Stax all of a sudden sought to establish its own publicity department (Deanie Parker), its own sales force and promotion team (initially Al Bell), its own independent mystique. As national sales director—soon to be executive vice-president—Al Bell was constantly on the move, achieving a rapport with the black radio stations ("To them he was God," says Duck Dunn) that had never previously occurred to Stax as a possibility and that depended far more on Bell's liberal personality than on an equally liberal dispensation of favors. Before too long Bell was spending more time in the home office, concentrating on expanding both production and Stax's own vision of itself, while dispatching legendary promotion men like Chester Simmons, his old Safice partner, and Eddie Braddock, a fast-talking white Memphian known as "the Arranger," who had grown up with Duck and Steve and Packy and who boasted that there was no black radio station that he could not enter with his line of talk. Braddock recalls working three cities a day in the late '60s and '70s, breakfasting in Cincinnati, lunching in Saginaw, having dinner in Salem, Oregon, with DJs anxious to receive the Stax word and the Stax largesse. Back home in his office there was a giant picture of Al Bell hanging behind his desk and a slogan that demanded: "How many radio stations can you service today?" In 1965 this was still some years in the future, but it was all part of Al Bell's plan, all part evidently of his grandiose conception of himself and of the company.

It was all happening, but whether it was happening too fast or not was somewhat a matter of personal conjecture. Jim seemingly welcomed the change and even sought to take on some of the characteristics of his new employee. When he quit work at the bank in 1964, he says, "I really didn't fit into the banking atmosphere anymore—they were looking at me a little funny. My hair was starting to grow long, and my suits were a little too continental, and the bank just didn't appreciate it." To Estelle the various alterations, both in style

Al Bell: Charting It Out. (Don Paulsen/Michael Ochs Archives)

and substance, were profoundly disturbing, and it was during this period that the first signs of serious friction between brother and sister began to emerge. For one thing Estelle was not happy with the musical direction the company was taking. Up till now she had played a prominent part in the decision-making process, or at least had made her opinions known ("She was very opinionated," says Isaac Hayes admiringly. "She was open to new ideas."). In 1966 the decision was made by Al Bell to cut Carla Thomas doing some country tunes. "I think," recalls Estelle, "it was just before 'B-A-B-Y,' one of her biggest tunes, and I told them it just wouldn't work. Well, they went up to Detroit and spent about $40,000 producing a country number and brought it back, and we were all invited back to the control room to listen to it. Well, all the musicians agreed, naturally, for fear of losing their job or getting some controversy going; they all said, 'Oh, it's great.' When it came my turn, I said, 'I don't think Carla Thomas is right for country. I don't believe it will sell. It's the wrong direction.' And consequently that was the last time that I was invited back."

In the view of Jim Dickinson, admittedly a dedicated iconoclast, this kind of thinking (cutting Carla Thomas country) was symptomatic of the deepening embarrassment, almost crippling class consciousness that Stax was beginning to feel about the music and milieu in which it saw itself mired. "They never really understood what they were," Dickinson says, referring not just to Jim and Estelle but to Al Bell's "new Stax" as well, "and they got to be ashamed of what they had been. I remember when they had the lock changed on the new control room door, and they jokingly wouldn't give the key to Stewart because they didn't want him to break the new console. That was the kind of mentality that killed Stax. If they could have just gone back to using basically broken equipment and rednecks and stupid people, they would have stood a better chance."

There was more to it than that, of course. Estelle was feeling increasingly pained over her son Packy's growing exclusion from the company, though in retrospect everyone agrees that it was inevitable. Packy has been variously described by his friends, over the years, as a "playboy," a "very carefree-type person," and a free spirit, "hipper than anybody else," who at one point turned the record store into a "center for vice" in south Memphis. Nonetheless, he had been present from the creation, he was the reason Steve and Duck and black musicians like Gilbert Caple had originally gained entrée to the Satellite studio, and now he was getting less and less session work as it became obvious that his uncle, Jim Stewart, had little faith in him. "Packy loved to party," says Isaac Hayes, an admirer, "and Jim couldn't tell Packy what to do. Jim just didn't want to deal with it." "There were better horn players," says Duck Dunn, another close friend, "and, you know, I suppose there were more reliable people. I guess that's just the way Jim looked at it. I'd feel guilty sometimes when I'd get called on a session and Packy wouldn't. It hurt. But you have to do what you have to do. You have a wife and two kids, you got to make a living."

Estelle, the fiercest of loyalists and the most tenacious of enemies, was both more explicit and more resourceful in her defense of her only son. "Jim and I had quite a few words over Packy. I felt like he had been taken advantage of, but there wasn't a thing I could do about it at the time."

In July 1965 Packy and his friend, "Congo" Johnny Keyes, set out for California to start a new life. In August Estelle shepherded a whirlwind Stax package tour of the West Coast, which ended up at a club in LA next door to the very liquor store which the next night, according to Steve Cropper, would be the first building to burn in the Watts riots. That particular gig was set up by the Magnificent Montague, the flamboyant DJ who had come up with the slogan "Burn, baby, burn," which was taken over, ironically enough, at this very juncture to incite not just musical but political mayhem. With Estelle's encouragement Montague signed Packy to his Pure Soul Music label, and with Estelle's explicit permission the entire Stax rhythm section, Booker T. and the MG's, entered the studio to back up Packy and "Congo" Johnny. The result was a #5 hit record ("Hole in the Wall"), credited to the Packers but instantly recognizable as by the MG's. The further result was a deepening estrangement between Jim and Estelle. "It was like giving away a hit record," Jim says accurately enough. "It was a real thorn in my side at the time, but I couldn't do anything about it, because my partner had done this." As for Estelle, who was increasingly removed from the business, hurt by what she saw as her brother's indifference, and wounded by his treatment of her son, she was only getting a little bit of her own back. In the next couple of years Al Bell would more and more usurp the position she had once held, not just politically but financially as well; she would watch her brother defer to the younger man to a greater and greater degree and find less and less in the direction that the company was taking that she liked.

These underlying tensions couldn't be altogether masked, but they were not altogether apparent, either, when Stax was riding high in 1965 and 1966. In 1966 Al Bell managed to sell an astonishing eight million singles. In 1966 Otis Redding went to Europe for the first time. In 1965 and 1966 the Stax studio produced four of the top thirty soul hits.

The overall feeling was one of sheer exhilaration, a growing and irrepressible sense that Stax was on the move, the Stax family ready to take on any challenge, ready to take on the world if necessary—together. William Brown, the engineer, remembers getting snowed in one night on a session and spending the whole night huddled around the heater, after the lights went out. "That was a wild night. There was just that one heater on the far wall. You play a session, get cold, huddle around, then go back to playing. You could call Isaac Hayes down the hall and say, 'Hey, I need you to play piano on this session.' He wouldn't worry about no money. David Porter would be over here, and Ike'd say, 'Hey, man, what do you think about this melody?' If he liked the melody, he'd say, 'Play it again.' Then David would start writing lyrics, and a little while later they'd have something. Sam and Dave, it was magic, man, they did it right there. Start off the session shooting craps. Then they'd get broke and create."

"We were going around the clock then," Isaac Hayes recalls. "I remember one time Otis had a session at about 3 A.M., and the Bar-Kays [the young black instrumental group that had succeeded the Mar-Keys] came down to the studio after they finished at the club, and we just went in and cut all night. Carla, Al Bell, Otis, Dave, and myself were in the studio all night on more than one night just writing. I didn't have a car, but David did, and he and Otis would come by my apartment and pick me up. On the way back to the studio sometimes we'd pull over to the side of the road, and Otis would get out his guitar and say, 'Hey, man, what about this?' Me and Dave and Otis in the car, working on a song—boy!"

When Otis Redding came in one hot July day in 1965, he had no more than thirty-six hours to cut a record before getting back out on the road. The result was the album *Otis Blue,* an almost immediately recognized masterpiece, for which ten tracks were cut in a twenty-four-hour period. "We went from ten to six on a Saturday," recalls Duck Dunn, "and then we all went and played our gigs till about two—I was playing down at Hernando's Hideaway, I think, with Deanie Parker singing and Wayne Jackson, too—and then we all came back in to finish cutting, from about two till eight in the morning. Otis just had so much to do with the feeling at Stax, that was one reason it held together so long. See, you'd go along six weeks, say, cutting nothing but blues sessions —Johnnie Taylor, Albert King—and it got so bad guys wouldn't even show up, and you'd have to put the session off. We finally quit playing Mondays altogether; we never could get anything on a Monday. But nobody was ever late for Otis's sessions. With Otis you'd feel like you'd accomplished something. And that'd pick you up for a few weeks, and then you'd slump back off." "Otis made everyone *work*," Jim Dickinson recalls. "You see, they would all reach a point where nobody would say anything negative in the studio. I mean, they would reach a point of the lowest possible compromise and then cut off. Otis wouldn't go for that. He'd keep pushing, and each time Al Jackson would go with him. He would enable the rest of the musicians to reach whatever Otis was trying for. Otis would record stripped to the waist. He put bath towels under his arms. He wanted those horn players live on the floor; he'd sing their parts to them and put that whole session together. Otis got a live feel that nobody else on that label ever got."

Still, there was no way to prevent the little cracks that were beginning to form from deepening. For Rufus Thomas, always jealous of his position and the regard in which he was held, the coming of "professional songwriters" like Isaac Hayes and David Porter meant the end of the little company he saw himself as having gotten off the ground just four short years earlier. "People like David Porter had one helluvan ego," says Rufus. "I told David: 'You around here bragging all the time. Every time I turn around, I hear you bragging what a helluva songwriter you are.' I said, 'Until you write a hit song for Rufus Thomas, you ain't shit.' And he never did." Even to someone as mild-mannered as William Bell, there was a real injustice in the situation. "I really don't feel any of us, the pioneer people—myself included—got our just due. We saw money spent on new acts that was never spent on ourselves, even though in terms of sales we were consistent. That was the only source of jealousy that I found at Stax." Homer Banks, who had worked for Estelle in the record store and never got his chance as a songwriter until the advent of Al Bell, put the situation in a broader perspective. "The biggest thing was how Miss Axton felt Stax should be administrated, and how Jim felt. She wanted the company to be a little more conservative for a little longer. Al Bell came, and everything began to grow—and grow very fast—until it became a monster. I think a better balance should have stood. I think the growth was needed, and the conservativeness was needed, too. Growth just came a little too fast."

Perhaps as much as anything else the fissures that were beginning to appear in the Stax facade were evidence that the children in the family were growing up. No longer could they accept the simple authoritarian rule of Jim Stewart, and as the label grew more successful—though nowhere near as successful in its own eyes as it appeared to the outside world (this was at a time, remember, when the Beatles and the Rolling Stones had expressed their clear admiration

Rufus Thomas and David Porter. (Don Paulsen/Michael Ochs Archives)

for the Stax sound); "we were living in a cocoon," says Booker T. plaintively —the standard rationale that it was all for the sake of the company no longer carried quite so much weight. Jim Stewart tried to counter what he correctly perceived as a business problem by creating what he called the Big Six, a pooled method of production, and a form of profit-sharing, which included Steve, Booker, Al Jackson, Duck, David Porter, and Isaac Hayes, as well as an eventual seventh, the Bar-Kays' producer, Allan Jones. As Jim explains it:

"They were on a salary, plus they were all drawing an override on the records. They were involved in the publishing, and of course David and Isaac were making more money from their writing for Sam and Dave. We had the basic unit, the studio musicians, and more and more time and effort was being spent in developing writers, because we recognized, Okay, we've got the production staff. We've got the artists. Now we've got to have good songs. If we can get the right songs, there's no limit to what we can do. And David was more or less in charge of developing the writing teams. You see, back then it was just cooperation and total involvement, really, there were no limits to the input that everybody could give, it was totally open to experimentation. No one was a producer as we think of a producer today. The credits just read: 'Produced by the Stax Staff.' No one treated the music as just a piece of product. Hell, we didn't even know what product was. We were talking about a record, a hit record."

Although even this has been seen in retrospect as a cynical co-optation by Stewart of workers who never really received their due, I think Jim's words should be taken at face value, and it seems inconceivable to me that anyone could have doubted the sincerity of his gesture at the time. Despite its rapid success Stax was still a small business, and like any small business, prey to rumors, speculation, and in particular to what Jerry Wexler calls "the little refined tendrils, the impossible curlicues of Memphis intrigue, most of it imaginary and paranoid." Certainly Jim and Estelle were having problems, Packy was an outcast, and Al Bell introduced a whole new incalculable element into the equation. These were nothing more than the ordinary complications of life, though, and when Jerry Wexler, venerated by Jim and perceived by all as the benevolent godfather who had beamed approvingly on all of Stax's successes to date, left in somewhat high dudgeon after the third Wilson Pickett session in December 1965, the entire Stax family rallied round and cast Wexler in a new light, as an exploiter or "outside agitator" perhaps.

Much speculation has focused on why, exactly, Wexler left, characteristically never to return. Perhaps the most logical explanation has suggested that it was merely another difference over a decimal point, that Jim, emboldened by the success of Stax and the sale of Pickett's singles, demanded a bigger cut, or royalty, for his studio and production staff. According to Wayne Jackson, "Some of Jerry's New York thinking and New York ways didn't go down too well in Memphis. Jerry was great, but he was New York fast, get the buck, that kind of stuff. Jim was, too, but he was Southern, so he was more laid back about it." Jim's explanation has always stressed that Stax was simply too busy with its own artists, that they were working practically around the clock, and that Stax no longer had time for outside production. Undoubtedly this was part of the reason, but no less certainly Wilson Pickett's unique personality entered into it as well. "Well, the guys pretty much shut that door," Jim says today. "Wilson couldn't get along with anyone, and they just said, 'Hey, man, don't bring that asshole down here again.'"

So Wexler departed with Pickett in tow, and Atlantic broke off its incipient production deal with Stax, though the two companies remained on cordial terms and continued their highly profitable distribution arrangement without interruption. Stax itself continued to thrive, and after only a momentary delay Wexler headed straight for Muscle Shoals.

Fame and Muscle Shoals

MUSCLE SHOALS WAS THE THIRD POINT IN what might be considered the Southern soul triangle. Like Memphis and Macon, it had its own distinct musical tradition, but one that had grown up even more improbably than the other two—and certainly in greater isolation. Memphis, of course, was a kind of cultural crossroads with a rich musical heritage, and Macon remained a thriving regional marketplace into the '50s, but what we refer to today as the Muscle Shoals area didn't even exist until the 1920s, when the city was incorporated and Wilson Dam obliterated the dangerous shoals after which the region was named.

The area in fact is made up of four towns whose metropolitan population comes close to 125,000: Florence, Sheffield, Tuscumbia, and Muscle Shoals itself, the smallest of the four. They sit on either side of the Tennessee River in separate counties (Colbert and Lauderdale). Sam Phillips, founder of the legendary Sun label in Memphis, was originally from Florence. Buddy Killen, the prominent Nashville music publisher and discoverer of Joe Tex, left the area to play bass in the Grand Ole Opry. W. C. Handy was born in Florence and Helen Keller in Tuscumbia, which is currently national headquarters for one of the warring factions of the KKK. The Ford Motor Company was at one time going to construct its primary assembly plant not in Detroit but in this corner of northwest Alabama, where it purchased land for, but never built, Ford City. Reynolds Aluminum established its huge plant in Florence in 1941 and has been the biggest local employer ever since. So the world had touched Muscle Shoals, but until the mid-1960s, it was said—and not with any inaccuracy—you had to leave Muscle Shoals to become famous. In the '50s, under intense pressure from the local churches (this is the *Bible* belt, everyone will tell you approvingly or disapprovingly), both Colbert and Lauderdale counties were voted dry, and you had to drive twenty or twenty-five miles to the Tennessee line if you wanted a legal drink at one of the state-line joints. This, too, conspired to limit the local music scene, at least so far as clubs were concerned.

But then in the late 1950s a hunchback named Tom Stafford, whose family owned the City Drugstore in Florence and who was himself in his early thirties at the time, decided to establish a song publishing company. Stafford was in many ways a recognizable small-town figure: an eccentric visionary who was set apart by his deformity, a nonconformist surrounded by a family whose success was recognized throughout the area (one of his five older brothers was

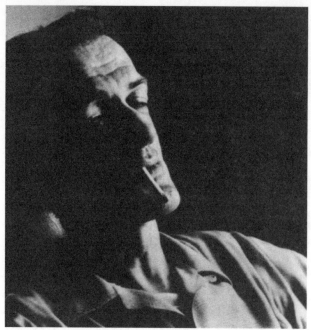

Tom Stafford. (Alvin Rosenbaum, courtesy of Donnie Fritts)

a psychiatrist, several were prominent local businessmen), a kind of hometown beatnik who refused to be bounded by the prevailing standards of the day. To Donnie Fritts and Spooner Oldham, who grew up in Florence and Center Star respectively and met Tom while they were still in high school and he was managing the Princess movie theater, he was "kind of an inspiring cat. He was the soul of that place. He had been to Nashville and knew there was such things as publishing companies when we didn't know nothing at all. Tom rubbed off on everyone. He didn't give no faulty advice." According to Dan Penn, who came to town at the age of sixteen or seventeen and immediately became the local sensation, with his knowledge of, and feel for, rhythm and blues and the free-spirited life of the road, "he could hang out with the boys, but he wasn't no boy. He was kind of a street person, like somebody in New York would be now, hanging out on the lamppost and watching the people go by, talking to shoe salesmen and aspiring photographers—he was good at that. You'd go up in that theater balcony, see all the movies for free, and everything was cool. That was the coolest place in the state that I knew of, and I knew some pretty good places. Go up and see Tom, that was the thing to do. He'd be all folded up, he could fold up just like a bat so you wouldn't see his legs or nothing, and he'd listen to all your little fears and tell you, 'Yeah, you can do it, we gonna go get us a hit record.' There wasn't nobody like him then, and there ain't nobody like that now."

Actually Tom Stafford was not the start of the Muscle Shoals music scene, strictly speaking. In December 1956 James Joiner, who owned the local bus line and was a big country music fan, had set up a publishing company and bought a little recorder to put down demos in the back of the Florence bus station. In February 1957 he cut a song called "A Fallen Star" on a singer named Bobby Denton, who later became a prominent local politician. The song was quickly covered and became a Top 100 hit that summer in separate versions by Ferlin Husky, Jimmy "C" Newman, Nick Noble, and the Hilltoppers. Despite his surprising first-time success, Joiner never seems to have approached the business with total dedication, but the widespread sales of "A Fallen Star" in each of its five versions and the very existence of Joiner's Tune Publishing Company in Florence attracted a good many aspiring songwriters to the Muscle Shoals area. Two of them were Rick Hall and Billy Sherrill, who had been playing in rival bands (Carmol Taylor and the Country Pals and Benny Cagle and the Rhythm Swingsters) and in early 1958 hooked up in a group called the Fairlanes and begun writing together. Hall and Sherrill started riding the bus up from Hamilton, a distance of sixty miles, to play Joiner their songs. In not too long they had gotten cuts by country singers as prominent as Roy Orbison, Homer and Jethro, and Brenda Lee, and they began to wonder what was the point of going to Joiner when it seemed as if they could simply take the songs to Nashville themselves. And this, according to Rick Hall, "was when Tom Stafford heard about us and sent word that he wanted to have a meeting. We had never heard of him, but people said he had money to spend, and we began to work day and night." This was the beginning of Fame Music.

The name, though it suggests all kinds of richer connotations, was easy enough to come up with, standing as an acronym for Florence Alabama Music Enterprises. The location, too, was logical enough. Tom Stafford's father had given him the space over the drugstore formerly occupied by a podiatrist. There were plaster casts of people's feet scattered all around, and everything was "really cruddy," but Billy and Rick threw themselves wholeheartedly into the new enterprise in the spring and summer of 1959. They set up Army cots among the plaster casts, "and we began to staple egg cartons on the wall. Which is the story," Rick says, "of every Southern producer in the business, but we did it anyhow for acoustic purposes, and we drug in old used carpet that they tore out of the theaters and put it on the floor. The whole place was full of dust, and I put drapes, old curtains off of the theater, on the walls and put a little paned glass window between two of the rooms, and we set up a little table with a Berlant-Concertone recorder on it, and we went to Birmingham and got three cheap mikes and a little mixer, and we began the task of putting together demos of new tunes, and everybody was writing them. I was writing. Billy was writing. Tom was trying to write. All of a sudden big time had hit Muscle Shoals."

Spar Music, Florence, Alabama, 1962. (Courtesy of Rick Hall)

The studio above the City Drugstore became the place to hang out, not just in Florence, it sometimes seemed, but in all of Alabama. Difficult as it may be to imagine today, the very idea of a recording facility in rural Alabama, *anywhere* in Alabama for that matter (there were no studios to speak of even in Atlanta or Birmingham in 1959), not to mention the fact that this recording facility was getting songs cut in Nashville by famous stars, attracted every aspiring musician for miles around—and undoubtedly created some more. Donnie Fritts, the son of a successful contractor but a self-styled outcast who referred to himself and his friends as "a bunch of bluegums," was there both day and night. Spooner Oldham, a piano player in various high school bands,

Rick Hall and Etta James, with two unidentified musicians. (Courtesy of Rick Hall)

started at the University of North Alabama in town and describes his quick dematriculation as he almost inevitably began to spend more and more time at Fame. To Dan Penn, who came up from Vernon to make a record just before high school graduation in the spring of 1960 (it was Billy Sherrill who suggested he give the big time a try), the movie theater may have been cool, but the studio was "the hottest place I ever walked into in my life, and still overall one of the hottest places I've ever seen. It was electric, and Tom Stafford was the hub of it. He could tell you things without sounding like a schoolteacher, and you just knew he wasn't going to pitch you wrong. We all met right there at that drugstore. Everyone I knew met there. It was nothing but pure-D hanging out."

No one, though, knew quite what to make of Rick. "I was so very aggressive and fired up," he declares today with little indication that anything has changed in the intervening years, "and I was the guy who was beating and banging and slinging sweat over everybody else till it got to the point where I was fighting with Billy and Tom. I think I intimidated them, you see, to the point where they thought, *This guy's crazy!* just because I was so determined. You know, they'd be watching a movie after hours, and I'd come over and say,

'Billy, we need to get a song together, I'm going to Nashville tomorrow,' and they just didn't want to be bothered; they saw me as busting up their good times. In other words, my feeling about it was that Tom and Billy was in it for fun —well, Billy was serious about it, but it wasn't life to him. It was life to me." The upshot was that Rick was pushed out in mid-1960, little more than a year after he had first hooked up with Tom Stafford in business. He kept the name and some of the publishing. Tom kept the artists and the studio. "I thought this was the worst thing that ever happened," says Rick, whose success at this point scarcely matched his boundless ambition. "It was like they'd put the roller skates under me and pushed me out the door. So I just went home to Phil Campbell [his hometown in southwest Alabama] to lick my wounds and began drinking heavy. Then after a few months I took kind of an arrogant attitude and dug in for the kill."

THE FREEDOM HILLS

This pretty much introduces all of the main characters present at the start of the Muscle Shoals story. I think in order to get a better sense of their personalities, though, and how they interacted, we should backtrack a little and take a look at some of the individuals involved, particularly Rick Hall, who went on to build a recording empire, and Dan Penn, about whom Jerry Wexler unequivocally declared: "Penn is by far the most soulful Caucasian singer I have [ever] heard."

Rick Hall was born in 1932 in Franklin County, about forty miles from Muscle Shoals, "in what we call the Freedom Hills, which is exactly what it says it is—there's nobody there. You get a little freedom. I grew up there with the whiskey makers and whiskey runners and sawmillers. My father was a sawmiller. When I was four or five years old, my mother and father divorced, and my mother left home, so my father raised me and my sister. At best we were on starvation; my father was a pauper.

"I started school when I was eight years old, out of necessity—the truant officer came around, and I started riding a bus to a little community school called Rock Creek School. It was a three-room building; I think they had two or three teachers who lived on the premises because it was so remote they couldn't travel back and forth. That's where I got my first motivation in the music business. Well, actually my father was very fond of the old Southern gospel music, Stamps-Baxter Quartet songbooks, shape note singing. To him it was like a golf game; he would sit up late at night, we had kerosene lamps, and we'd hear him fa-sol-la-sol-la, learning the melody. On Sundays we would walk—ten miles was no big walk for us to go to a community singing. He was also a singing teacher, ten-day singing school: get twenty-five people in a community, charge them so much apiece, and have a ten-day singing school in the fall when the crops were laid back. And he tried to get me and my sister interested in that, but I never was interested, it just was not intriguing to me.

"When I was six years old, my uncle, who lived in the house with us, brought home a mandolin, old-fashioned eight-string mandolin. Well, I began to get interested in that, and one day I ran into a neighbor, a guy who lived two or three miles away, that had a guitar, and he began to show me how to play. At this time—and this was in the early '40s—we didn't even have a radio, I don't think I'd heard the Opry yet. The first radio I heard was another neighbor's—we'd walk there three or four miles on a Saturday night to listen to the Opry. And I recall the battery was always worn down or almost down, and you had to pour water on the ground wire to strengthen it up, and then everybody would get real close to the radio and kind of report on what was happening. At midnight my father would wake me, shake me, and start me out the door, and we'd go back home. And the only two things I recall hearing on the radio was the Grand Ole Opry and the Joe Louis fights, that and Gabriel Heatter, who scared me to death with the news, 'Oh, there's bad news tonight.' I thought we was gonna get killed any minute by the Germans."

In 1944 Rick's father moved to Cleveland to take a job in a defense plant and shortly thereafter sent for Rick and his sister. "The idea was to get rich up there, Southern rich, and come back and buy a piece of ground, and we'd live happily ever after." Rick was immediately put back two grades, saw his first blacks ("Back in those days blacks wouldn't even pass through the Freedom Hills; if the truck they was on stopped, I don't think they would even get out"), fell in love with trolley cars and bowling alleys, and quickly sensed the necessity for a broader exposure to life. "I had much more savvy as far as doing things with my hands than the kids I went to school with, but I couldn't compete with them on the streets or in wit and things of this nature. That's why Southern people, I think, sometimes take up the roughneck style; they can't compete with the brain, so they take it up in fisticuffs, violence—you know, it's sad to say, but it's true."

When they moved back to Alabama at the end of the war, his father remarried and started sharecropping, and Rick quickly finished with school, quitting after his junior year. Before he did, though, he got involved in an FFA (Future Farmers of America) string band, which traveled to the state competition at Auburn University, gaining a first place prize one year and second the next. "That was probably the only thing I ever accomplished in school. There was fourteen of us, and we would practice one night a week at somebody's house, and I was one of the stars."

By the time he quit school, Rick was heavily involved with music for social as much as professional reasons ("Because I was a musician, I was quite gifted with the tongue, I was a good salesman, I could do a tap dance, I was believable—at least to the Southern girls"). When in 1951 he moved to Rockford, Illinois, and went to work as an apprentice tool and die maker at Rockford Clutch Division, he continued his involvement with music, playing with a band at Corey's Bluff Tavern for "tips and all the beer we could drink," plus plenty of girls and freedom for the first time from the constraints of home. In 1952 he was drafted and promptly became a conscientious objector, putting himself through a good deal of humiliation for a complex of reasons that neither started nor stopped with religious strictures ("I didn't have any more belief probably than any of the rest of them; I just didn't want to die, and I didn't want to kill anybody."). He stuck to his guns, so to speak, and he remained as abstemious from the day he entered the Army as he had been till he moved to Rockford —until he went home on leave just before he was about to be shipped off to Korea as a front line medic. At home he went to a dance, got drunk, turned his car over, and broke his back. When he got out of the hospital more than a year later, the war was over and he was no longer a conscientious objector but instead joined the honor guard of the Fourth Army, "supernumerary division," where he played in a band with country star Faron Young and fiddler Gordon Terry. Upon discharge he returned to Alabama, got married in 1955, and went to work in Florence for Reynolds Aluminum. A career in music must have been the furthest thing from his mind.

He had been married only eighteen months when his wife died in a car crash as they were on their way to hear fiddler Bennie Martin play a show. Two weeks later, on April 15, 1957, Rick's father was killed when a John Deere tractor Rick had given him overturned. This started Rick off on the chaotic swing that ended up in the Fame studio over the City Drugstore.

"After I lost my wife, I quit Reynolds. I didn't have any interest, no reason to—so I just started playing music. I was sort of a drifter, and wherever my car was found was where you found me, it didn't make any difference. I wasn't worried about storms, tornadoes, or depressions. I had no desire to be anything but a bum. I became a heavy drinker again, hauled whiskey, hauled moonshine, made whiskey, there's nothing hardly I didn't do in those days except commit murder. I mean I was the guy that wanted to try everything, you know what I'm saying? I wanted a broad life, and I wanted to know as much about every aspect of it as possible."

He traveled all around the Hamilton-Haleyville-Winfield-Fayette-Muscle Shoals area with Carmol Taylor and the Country Pals, playing nothing but country music, taking turns on guitar, mandolin, fiddle, and occasional vocals. Benny Cagle and the Rhythm Swingsters were the competition, more of a pop group who played the same circuit and had for a piano player/saxophonist the son of a circuit preacher named Billy Sherrill. At first, it seemed, Rick and Billy were brought together almost as much by their opposite backgrounds and temperaments as by their common bond.

"Billy grew up in a different world. His father was an evangelist, one of

The Fairlanes: Rick Hall, Charlie Senn, Randy Allen on drums, Billy Sherrill, Terry Thompson. (Courtesy of Rick Hall)

these hellfire-and-damnation preachers that traveled in tent revivals, and Billy was the piano player and guy that did the singing. He was the kind of guy, I never cussed around him; if I took a drink, I'd hide it from him. He never condoned it and used to sulk with me for a week if I got drunk. He was another culture is what I'm saying. I was the roughshod one, the guy who grew up in the woods, beating and banging and knocking and rough and girl-crazy, and Billy was the reversal of all those things, very conservative, very mild-mannered, sophisticated, isolated from the world, had very few friends, and didn't talk a lot."

Over the course of the next year or so they became best friends, Rick quit the Country Pals ("I just thought I was a helluva lot better than the band was"), they became roommates, started writing songs, and together they formed the Fairlanes, a straight-ahead rock 'n' roll and rhythm and blues band in which Billy Sherrill played electric sax. Describing another of those startling reversals of direction that seem to make up his life, Rick Hall, who had once "lived, breathed, eaten, and slept country," claims he never took country music seriously again. And Dan Penn, still just a junior in high school but with the evangelical fervor (and true conviction) of an r&b believer, came over from the Rhythm Swingsters with Billy Sherrill to become the Fairlanes' new vocalist.

Dan Penn. (Robert Melhorn)

"OUT OF LEFT FIELD"

Dan Penn is in many ways the secret hero of this book. A singer-songwriter-occasional guitar player from Vernon, a tiny town eighty miles south of Muscle Shoals, he arrived in Florence with a song that he had written ("Is a Bluebird Blue?") which everyone *knew* was going to be a hit and which subsequently became one for Conway Twitty in 1960. He also came as something of a fully formed personality, even at the age of sixteen or seventeen. Rick Hall, it's true, had definite ideas of his own when it came to just about anything under the sun, from the kind of peanut butter and jelly he would eat (Jif and Welch's) to the way he liked his eggs cooked. But Rick Hall's taste in music, like Jim Stewart's in Memphis at this time, was only just beginning to form. Dan Penn, on the other hand, was as definite about his musical likes and dislikes as he would

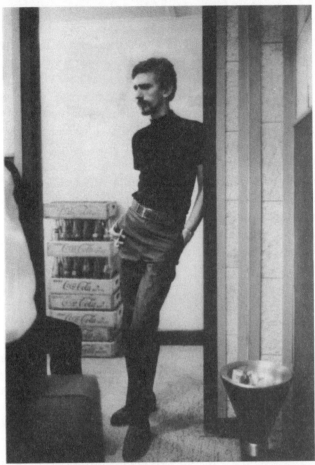

Spooner Oldham. (Sid Selvidge)

be ten or twenty years later—after he had teamed up with Chips Moman, written dozens of classic r&b hits ("Dark End of the Street," "Take Me (Just As I Am)," "Sweet Inspiration," "Out of Left Field," "Do Right Woman") with either Chips or Spooner Oldham, produced the Box Tops' #1 hit, "The Letter," and tossed off hundreds of rough demos and studio versions of his own songs which by the account of most of the participants easily surpassed the records that were actually released.

"Dan Penn came up from Vernon," says Rick Hall, "and just absolutely intrigued us all, because here was this kid, white, sixteen years old, singing like Ray Charles, just in love with black music. He was the real thing. He wasn't a rip-off or a fake. He knew more about black music than the rest of us put together. I confided in Dan. I respected his opinions—along with my own, of course. I especially was impressed with his depth of perception on songs and material. He wasn't a yes-man for nobody. If he didn't like something, he'd tell you, 'I think it stinks. Worst thing I ever heard.' Dan had a mind of his own."

That may well be the understatement of the century. Actually Dan's independent mind turned out to be Rick's temporary undoing, one of the major causes of his split with Tom Stafford, but how Dan got that way is a matter for conjecture. Born Wallace Daniel Pennington on November 16, 1941, Dan grew up next to a junkyard and claims it was two things that made him crazy, second year algebra and sniffing gasoline. It was listening to John R. on the radio that gave Dan his first exposure to black music. He didn't buy any records because there was nowhere to buy them, but from the moment he first heard Ray Charles and Bobby "Blue" Bland, he was hooked.

"I had three distinct personalities in those days—my own just got lost in the shuffle. When I wasn't Ray Charles or James Brown, I was Bobby 'Blue' Bland. There wasn't no such thing as Dan Penn then. It was, 'Here comes Bobby "Blue" Penn!'"

He never got to see his heroes, he had limited access to their music, but somehow through radio and empathy he picked up the message from the air. In the tenth grade he joined Benny Cagle and the Rhythm Swingsters, which was how he met Billy Sherrill. "We used to play these gigs, play a half hour of square dance music, half an hour of rock 'n' roll, like that. Sherrill played the electric saxophone, Benny played the drums with the fiddle bow, and I started calling the damned square dances, because a guy named Tony Couch from Winfield, Alabama, who was two years older than me was doing the singing at first. I started singing when Tony left to go with Rick Hall, and that was when I started playing Billy some of my songs, back behind stage after the gig. You know, 'Moon, Where Have You Been, Boy?,' that kind of stuff, stupid stuff. We raged from Florence, Alabama, down to Columbus, Mississippi, nothing but roller rinks and VFWs, good clean fun, wildcat whiskey and square dancing. Then Billy went to Florence, and I went on up with Tony Couch, the guy I had replaced in the band. I didn't know what to expect, but Billy had said, 'Come on up. Let's cut some records.' In school I was just Emmett the Singing Ranger, the guy with the guitar. I hadn't never seen a studio or nothing, and I walk into this room, and there's Billy and Rick Hall and Tom Stafford and Spooner and Hershel Wiggington and Donnie Fritts—we all met right there at that studio, everybody I ever knew met right there. I didn't know what to think!"

At this point Fame was little more than a stopover on the way to Nashville, with Rick taking the song demos that were cut to Chet Atkins at RCA or ex-local boy Buddy Killen at Tree Publishing with varying degrees of success. Not long after Dan first arrived, a promo man named Gary, who was a friend of MGM producer and a&r head Jim Vienneau, stopped by the studio and heard Dan's version of "Is a Bluebird Blue?," the song that everyone was convinced would be a hit. Gary (no one remembers his last name) brought it with him to Nashville, where Conway Twitty promptly recorded it, though it sat in the can for some time. Shortly afterward, on his second or third visit to Florence, Dan cut a record of his own called "Crazy Over You," which made him the first and last artist—certainly the only fully promoted one—on the Fame-owned Spar label. After the record came out, Tom and Billy took Dan over to WLAY, the Muscle Shoals area's number-one radio station, where Al West, the station's top DJ, put Dan on the air. "He said, 'Dan, tell us something about yourself.' I said, 'Well, I'm sixteen years old [actually he was eighteen], I weigh 125 pounds'—and I stopped. He said, 'Well, you got a girl friend?' I said, 'Nope. But I'm looking.' I think I was expecting everybody to run right down there to the radio station and check me out. He said, 'Dan, you got anything else to say?' I said, 'Nope, that's about all there is to tell.' I think Billy and Tom just got in the car and left."

From then on Dan was a local superstar. Not only did he have a song that was rumored to have been cut by Conway Twitty (and would shortly make its appearance on the charts), he also had a record on the radio, and he had started singing with the Fairlanes, just about the hottest local group around. It is little wonder that he got something of a swelled head, especially with his own confessed predilection for stubbornness. "Rick was all the time telling everybody what to do, he was really burning on wanting to work. He'd tell us how to write, he'd tell us how to sing, he'd tell us how to play. Nobody liked it. Billy and Tom didn't like it, because they didn't give a shit about working, really. And here I am, their only artist of the moment, and I didn't like it, either. I was a pretty forward kid, you might say, and I went up to Tom and I said, 'Tom, Rick's up there trying to tell me how to sing, and you *know* I don't need nobody telling me how to sing.' I said, 'Either he goes or I go.' Well, that was it. I remember Tom just kind of slumped off and went, 'I'll take care of it.' And the next thing I knew, Rick's out and Billy Sherrill's my producer. They give him the name, that was about it, and one day I seen Rick down there in Florence about a month or so after he left, and he had a piece of paper sticking out of his back pocket, and I said, 'Rick, what is that?' And he said, 'That's Fame Publishing Company. That's my company.' That's all it was was a piece of paper. You got to respect a guy can go from a piece of paper to where he did."

What was left of the partnership didn't go anywhere at this point, which was mid-1960. Rick went home to Phil Campbell, Tom and Billy never put out another record together, and Billy left for Nashville shortly thereafter, where he became the dominant force in commercial country music in the late '60s and '70s. Donnie Fritts, Spooner Oldham, David Briggs, Norbert Putnam, and Jerry Carrigan still hung around the studio above the City Drugstore, soaking up the street wisdom of Tom Stafford and making a formidable impression on younger musicians like David Hood and Roger Hawkins and Jimmy

Johnson, one or two years behind them in school, who would one day form the core of the Muscle Shoals sound. Dan Penn formed a band called the Mark V's with Putnam, Briggs, and Carrigan, who were doing virtually all of the demo work that came Tom Stafford's way, having just graduated from high school themselves. In person they had horns, and they had moves, and they just tore up their audiences ("I'd do anything to put a show over," says Dan, "except take my pants off"), becoming as much a part of local legend as the Royal Spades were in Memphis. Then to everyone's bewilderment (including his own) Dan moved to Dallas to work in a Cokesbury Bible store in his one youthful attempt to put the night life behind him.

"I wasn't going to do that sinful stuff anymore. I honestly don't know what got into me. Well, I worked in the bookstore for about three months, and then one night I pulled up at a hamburger joint, and there were some kids there with a little amp and a little guitar and a little microphone just trying to get it, and they couldn't play shit. So I said, 'Gimme that guitar.' (I wasn't never shy.) 'I want to show you some stuff.' Which I did. I sat down and played every damn song I knew, which wasn't too many—about twelve. So I came back and said, 'I ain't gonna spend my damn life like this, going around to these damned hot dog stands, I'm going home. And I got right back in the thick of it."

When he returned, he reclaimed leadership of the Mark V's and went to look up Rick. "I asked around, and I finally found him, and he was standing on this concrete slab he'd just poured for the studio that now stands. So anyway Rick said, 'Hey, Penn, why don't you come over here and write for me?' I said, 'What do you mean? Move here?' 'Cause I was still staying in Vernon. I said, 'Man, I got to make a living.' 'Cause I was fixing to get married at the time. He said, 'I'll give you $25 a week.' And he went to the bank and cosigned with me to borrow about $400 to get moved and all this. Of course this was after Arthur Alexander, and there was money to be made."

"RAINBOW ROAD"

Arthur Alexander was a bellhop at the old Sheffield Hotel on Montgomery Avenue. According to Rick, his mother worked as a maid occasionally for Tom Stafford's family, but Donnie Fritts just remembers him coming in to the theater that Tom Stafford managed with his singing group, a huge, gentle black man ("He looked like he could have played professional football") whom everyone called June because, of course, he was a junior. He was a songwriter as well as a singer, and this was what Tom seized on initially, adding him to the already unlikely stable of Fame writers, which included high school students, traveling salesmen, and local poets. "The group didn't sound so hot," Donnie Fritts recalls, "so Tom just took Arthur aside and got him to come back on his own and worked with him awhile—Spooner or David Briggs would sit down with him

Arthur Alexander, with Bill Millar. (Courtesy of Bill Millar)

at the piano because Arthur didn't play an instrument, and they would work with him on his songs." Tom kept Arthur as a writer after he and Billy Sherrill split with Rick, but at this point they weren't making any records and didn't really know what to do with him.

Within nine months after the split Arthur Alexander was a star. In late 1961 Tom, who had never been much for the technical end of the business, went to Rick Hall for help. With the financial backing of his brand-new father-in-law, Hansel Cross, for whom he occasionally cut radio jingles and sold cars, Rick had already set up another studio in Muscle Shoals in an old tobacco and candy warehouse on the road to Wilson Dam. "Tom told me, 'I believe Arthur has written a hit song. I want you to hear it and see what you think.' So Arthur came in and popped his fingers and sang his song. The song was 'You Better Move On,' and I said, 'I think it's a hit. I'd like to record it on you.' So we brought in Carrigan and David Briggs and Terry Thompson (Tom wasn't doing nothing in his studio at this point), and we set up three microphones, and we had the acoustic guitar playing on the same mike as the singer—Peanut Montgomery was playing the acoustic—and I would say, 'Peanut, you're a little loud,' and he'd back off, and we'd lose the guitar, so I'd move him in again. See, we didn't have the advantage of a lot of microphones. It was all a matter of distance and placement. Anyway, we dubbed some voices on afterwards, and I took it to Nashville—to Mercury, to RCA, to Capitol, to just about everybody who had offices in Nashville, and they all turned it down. Said it was too black. So finally I went to Noel Ball, who was music director at WMAK in Nashville, and Noel was representing Randy Wood, who had Dot Records and who had got big with Pat Boone and moved out to the Coast. Noel sent it to Randy, and a couple of weeks later he calls me up and he says, 'We'd like to make a deal with you. Call Tom Stafford and tell him; we'll give you three percent, give the artist three percent, just get the session unionized.' So we all got in the car and went to Birmingham and joined the union, Local 256, which began a whole other learning process right there. But anyhow, the record came out, and lo and behold, five or six weeks the record was in the Top 20 in the pop charts across the country and then in the Top 10 [actually it made #24 on *Billboard*'s Hot 100 and was successfully covered in England a couple of years later by a new young group, the Rolling Stones]. I made something like $10,000, which was phenomenal to me with my meager beginnings and the kind of money I'd been used to making. I took that $10,000 and built the first section of the building we're now in, my first real studio and the start of the whole Muscle Shoals sound."

The effect on the other principals was of nearly equal significance. For Arthur Alexander, dismissed by Nashville according to Rick because he sounded too black (ironically he possessed a gentle, somewhat uncertain voice and a flair for writing country and western melodies with crossover potential), instant stardom was something he was ill prepared to handle. In addition to "You Better Move On" he had a number of regional hits and two more national chartmakers in 1962 alone, and he became even better known through others' versions of his material (the Beatles covered both his own composition, "Anna," and two other songs that he had originally cut; "You Better Move On" became a country, pop, and r&b standard). Unlike Otis Redding, though, he didn't possess the temperament to take advantage of these opportunities; he was neither sure enough of himself nor sufficiently self-directed, and he was naturally somewhat timid. Donnie Fritts remembers taking him to a gig in Birmingham at just about the time Otis was starting out, before he had even signed with Stax. The Pinetoppers were at the bottom of the bill on the strength of the regional success of "Shout Bamalama" and "Love Twist." "Jesse Hill and Benny Spellman were the warm-up acts, and Arthur was the headliner. Me and Spooner were responsible for him, and we didn't think anything about it, but Birmingham was dangerous back then, and I mean dangerous, son. As best I can remember, the show was for some high school graduation, and it seems to me like it was at the Jewish Community Center. Which was two strikes against us right there. It wasn't long since those three little colored girls had been blown away, and we got some bomb threats that night at the Jewish Community Center. Arthur was scared to fucking death. He wouldn't get out of the car.

"I remember another time, I can't remember exactly what we were doing, but me and David [Briggs] and Spooner and Arthur and a couple of Arthur's friends drove over to Birmingham, and for some reason David wanted to go visit a friend of his who was working at Southern Bell right in the middle of town. So I said to David, 'Don't stay in there too long.' Anyways, we was waiting on him, and me and Spooner got out and went into this café, and the lady behind the counter said, 'Are you guys with those niggers out there?' I said, 'Yeah. Why?' She said, 'Look, it's none of my business, but I been watching this car that's circled the block twice with some guys in it, and if I was you, I wouldn't be here the next time they come around.' I said, "Nuff said, ma'am.' "

There was legitimate cause to be fearful certainly, but Arthur's world became increasingly circumscribed, and although he kept recording off and on for the next fifteen years, his story is not much different in certain respects from Johnny Jenkins's in Macon. Donnie and Dan Penn wrote a song called "Rainbow Road" (which Arthur later recorded), which details in fictional form some of Arthur's mental trials and tribulations, and his career never regained the momentum of its beginning.

For Rick Hall "You Better Move On" obviously pointed the direction to the future. At the very least it provided him with some financial wherewithal, and it also permitted him to begin thinking of himself as a producer, someone who could direct sessions and engineer and assemble a musical unit. For the Muscle Shoals musicians it was a tremendous shot in the arm. David Briggs, Jerry Carrigan, and Norbert Putnam had played on a hit record, and along with guitarist Terry Thompson, who had written the B side of the hit, the much-covered "A Shot of Rhythm and Blues," they were the crack recording unit that Rick called upon whenever he had a session scheduled at his new studio.

For Tom Stafford the results were a little more mixed. Evidently Tom could handle success no better than his principal artist could. There have always been jokes that Tom Stafford's father's drugstore was the real basis for Fame's success, but Spooner Oldham insists, "He wasn't no dark kind of guy trying to get young cats on pills. All he did was a few uppers, sneak into his father's drugstore and sample a few. I mean, I started taking pills, but he didn't start me, I had to ask him. You know, I just think he was so good that when the money started coming in, he fell to pieces, couldn't handle it."

"Tom didn't never make too many stupid moves," Donnie Fritts agrees, "up to that point. Then he just kind of fell apart. Me and David Briggs were involved in the publishing. I remember, when 'You Better Move On' came out, we split up the check, and everyone was smiling. But then Tom sold the publishing right out from under us; some guy from Atlanta—I don't want to say his name—bought Arthur's contract, and Tom just did some crazy moves at the end. But, you know, even then it was still all on the moon, unreachable; none of us ever dreamed you could make a living from writing songs. And in my own mind I was paid back; I got a great education from the whole thing. What better education than being involved in the making of Muscle Shoals when it was born?"

"Tom was into black voices," says Dan. "In fact he was into it enough he went and got one when no one else was interested. 'What a Difference a Day Makes' was one of his favorite songs. You know, he could handle the street, but when it got down to money coming in and everybody quarreling and stuff like that, he just ended up in the State Rehabilitation Center in Montgomery. After that he married a nurse and started giving drug speeches at the schools, which was hard to believe, because he loved that aspect so much. He died a few years ago. He was just kind of a funky guy who never really achieved anything, most of the deals he made fell through, but he told us things that finally came true, you know. He was always hopeful, even though he lived in darkness."

"TWO STEPS FROM THE BLUES"

Rick Hall meanwhile completed construction of his new Fame studio in the fall of 1962. It was built according to the specifications of the RCA studio in Nashville, "a cinderblock adobe shack" in Rick's description, approximately twenty by seventy feet long, with eighteen-foot ceilings, not because Rick had made a study of the matter but because this was the only model he knew. He had no more dealings with Arthur Alexander, because Tom had sold his contract. He was recording demos on various local artists but could find no one to take them despite his recent success. So Rick was stuck with a new studio, grandiose ambitions, and no foreseeable way to realize them, or even just to make some money. That problem was at least partially solved when, in the late summer of 1963, Bill Lowery brought some of his Atlanta-based artists to Muscle Shoals.

Lowery, a former radio announcer and station manager, had been a moving force behind the Atlanta music scene since 1953. Some of the songs that he had published were: "Be-Bop-A-Lula," "Young Love," and the country standard "Walk On By." Some of the artists that he was associated with when he first came to Rick Hall were: Tommy Roe, Joe South, Mac Davis, the r&b group the Tams, Ray Stevens, and Elvis Presley's future producer, Felton Jarvis. A large, florid man known affectionately but only semijokingly to his associates as "King William," Lowery had for years been trying to get a record industry

An early Fame session: Rick Hall, Felton Jarvis,
Tommy Roe, Ray Stevens, David Briggs, Norbert Putnam,
Jerry Carrigan at front. (Courtesy of Rick Hall)

started in Atlanta, but at the time he first contacted Rick Hall, his own National
Recording Corporation had only recently gone bankrupt and he was affiliated
in a new deal with ABC. For Rick it was the call that changed his life.

"Bill called one day and said, 'I've been hearing some things about you
and about Muscle Shoals, and I wondered if I could come up and work with
you and bring some of my acts?' And I said, 'Sure.' So he comes up, and I meet
him at the airport, and Bill can probably tell you the story better than I can,
but when he got off the plane and there's just this one little room and he walks
out and all he can hear is the birds singing—well, I think he was expecting
something a little more elaborate. Basically it scared the shit out of him.
Anyway, I picked him up, and we went back to the studio, and we began to
work together, and the first records were hits—Tommy Roe, the Tams—and
Bill thought I was really a hotshot because I had my shit together. Not only
did I engineer the sessions, I got out there and played on them, put them together
on the floor, told the musicians what to play—anyone who's ever seen a session
with me will tell you that I'm a complete dictator, that what you hear on my
records is what I want, they're the licks that I call, and every record I cut is
a hit to me—I don't care how bad the song is or anything about it, I always
tried to pull it off. So all of a sudden I found I was a producer, and Bill became

Donnie Fritts and Jimmy Johnson. (Courtesy of Jerry Wexler)

the first client, and the only client for quite some time—and Bill said to me one time, 'Hey, you know what? The world is looking for it, and we have found it. Right here in Muscle Shoals of all places!"

The records that Lowery was putting out seemed dated even at the time, with only the Tams escaping the generally antiseptic atmosphere and Tommy Roe most notable for his influence on the early Beatles. The overall effect on Muscle Shoals, however, was as incalculable as the effect of a real hit had been on Stax in Memphis. Not only did it give the musicians a new sense of themselves and their importance, it made the local songwriters, too, a visible part of the record-making process. Until Lowery started coming in, there was simply no way that any of the writers could claim to have a vocation. With virtually Lowery's first Muscle Shoals-produced record, Tommy Roe's "Everybody," Dan Penn and Donnie Fritts had a hit, not with the A side but, characteristically, with the B (Donnie will frequently refer to himself, not without irony, as "Flipside Fritts"), a forgettable item called "Sorry I'm Late, Lisa." "It was another one of those 'Oh, man, where you been tonight?' kind of songs," says Penn. "We didn't know nothing about what we were doing. But I remember when the big check came in to Florence, boy, everybody was running like squirrels. 'Oh, go get you a check. Let's cut it up. Let's cut it up.' The check was in. Money had been made."

After that everyone took themselves a little more seriously. Dan and Spooner and Donnie started writing all the time. Rick gave Dan a key to the studio, and he began hanging out there all night long, fooling around with different types of songs, imitating the Supremes, the Four Tops, the Temptations, trying different kinds of production. "Me and Fritts were a team. Me and Spooner were a pretty long-lasting team. He'd play piano. I'd sing and beat on a guitar. I was squealing like a pig. I had thirty-eight different voices in those days. I could sound like anything I wanted to, but I couldn't sound like myself. We'd stay in the studio all night long, get three songs a night, everything sound just like something else, it was all messed up. Goddam, we didn't fuck around. We'd play a Temptations record, we'd write a Temptations song. But we started getting that extra thing by being able to play it back over them big speakers and being able to check ourselves out. That was when I first found out I had a voice. That was a *big* plus. Without that I know we would never have been as good writers as we were."

Another big plus was the purely intangible sense of inspired chaos that seemed to infest Muscle Shoals—both the locale and the personalities. Maybe this is the natural ambience of any provincial ensemble; certainly it had its analogue at Stax, except that at Stax the anarchic element (in the person of Chips Moman) was quickly discarded for a "professional" prototype. Muscle Shoals, on the other hand, uneasily maintained its amateur status, despite the determination of one man—Rick Hall—to crash into the big time, perhaps because of the equal determination of another—Dan Penn—to retain the freewheeling spirit that had first inspired him. With the exception of the thirty-year-old Hall, no more tamable in his own way than his younger colleagues, what you had was half a dozen enormously talented twenty-year-olds thrust upon the world stage while stranded in the backwoods of Alabama. They were too hip for their environment but too comfortable in it ever to want to break out. Dan was still storming around the countryside with the Fame rhythm section in a hearse, now billed as Dan Penn and the Pallbearers. Donnie Fritts, who had already moved to Nashville part-time to pursue an independent career as a songwriter ("I was the only one not to sign with Rick. Rick signed everybody who could write a fucking poem."), maintained an apartment in Florence that was affectionately known as Funk City and was painted black. There were names for everyone: Guy Bingo and Gene Audit, Mr. and Mrs. Weenie, and Sky High (that was Donnie), and when squares showed up on the scene, it was Ozzie and Harriet time. Donnie and Spooner and Dan hung out together constantly, referring to themselves without blinking as "a bunch of niggers."

On weekends Donnie played drums with Hollis Dixon, the Muscle Shoals area's longest-running rock 'n' roll act, which also employed drummer Roger

Hawkins from time to time ("I let him play the damn square dances," says Donnie) and Spooner Oldham on keyboards. Rick was still playing with the Fairlanes, who boasted a vocalist named Charlie Senn, just as good as Elvis, according to Rick. The other band in town was the Del Rays, led by Rick's only salaried employee, a local guitarist named Jimmy Johnson, who had been going to the University of North Alabama in Florence since his discharge from the Army and working part time as Rick's secretary (the Army had taught him to type 105 words a minute), gofer, and apprentice engineer. All of these bands were playing the fraternity circuit; it must have seemed to them, as it seemed to the Royal Spades in Memphis or the various groups around Macon, that there was nothing out of the ordinary about what they were doing, that there were hundreds of local scenes like these, thousands of bar bands playing the same repertoire with fully as much ability and belief. Maybe it was just the driving personalities of Rick Hall and Dan Penn that made the difference; perhaps it was the generalized sense of displacement that only found its focus in the air-conditioned balcony of the Princess Theater. Tom Stafford's spirit hovered over the Muscle Shoals scene long after Tom Stafford himself was no longer a part of it.

And in the background, unavoidably, were drugs, sometimes vast quantities of drugs. For Dan and Donnie and Spooner, and not a few others back then, it was virtually impossible to separate a chemically induced exhilaration from the sheer exhilaration of the times, and the discovery of a new high could be almost as exciting as the creation of a new song. It has been said many times, "Behind every great song is a great pill," and the Muscle Shoals creative element undoubtedly tried them all. Sometimes today they look back on that period with the nostalgic perspective of forty-year-olds and bemoan the passing of a time when speckled birds, black beauties, and white crosses were commonplace and life seemed without serious risk. Everyone today is on a health food diet; everyone seems to have been rescued from the brink of death by a devoted wife or a revelation which has put them on a strict regimen of religion and early rising, but sometimes when they get together, someone will say, "I wish I could just get high like we used to, get high and stay high, find that good groove we had ten years ago, and to hell with all these fucking bean sprouts!" And well they might lament the passing of that era, because it was during that five- or six-year period that the excitement happened, it was during those years that their lives turned around, and seemingly it is on those years that their reputations will rest.

Each developed his own style during that period, in 1963, 1964, 1965. They were all young, they were all crazy, they were all mad about rhythm and blues. As Dan Penn tells it, it was almost like a crusade. "It seemed like Rick didn't believe in r&b during that time, after Arthur. I don't know why, something must have happened to him. He told me he didn't want any black people in there anymore. That's when I got him to listen to Bobby Bland, *Two Steps from the Blues*. After that we started seeing 'em pop up. Up to then I couldn't stick to no kind of music, either—it wasn't pop music, it was kind of watered-down Elvis, but it wasn't even that. We didn't know nothing until black people put us on the right road. I never would have learned nothing if I'd have stayed listening to white people all my life."

"STEAL AWAY"

The first hit to actually originate at Fame (Fame-born and Fame-bred) was, oddly enough, the very first song that had been put on tape in the new studio back in the fall of 1962. This was one of the demos that Rick had been trying to peddle for nearly a year when Bill Lowery showed up in the late summer of '63. The record was Jimmy Hughes's "Steal Away," and it was Muscle Shoals's *second* r&b success, establishing a pattern that would pretty much hold for the next decade.

Jimmy Hughes was a local gospel singer from Leighton who was working at the Robbins Rubber Company Plant when he first came in to see Rick at the old Wilson Dam studio. He had been singing lead for a number of years with the Singing Clouds, a local group that appeared on the radio and performed in the style of the Soul Stirrers and Claude Jeter and the Swan Silvertones. A friend of Hughes's, Bob Carl Bailey, today program director of a local black station, had been trying to persuade him to switch over to the secular field for some time when Arthur Alexander's record took off at the beginning of 1962. Although Jimmy lacked any burning ambition of his own, Arthur's hit convinced him that it might be worth at least giving the music business a try. He went over to the studio, sang a few songs for Rick ("Naw, he didn't know nothing about me"), and started cutting demos from time to time. One of the demos, "I'm Qualified," which was written by Rick and local DJ Quin Ivy, was eventually picked up by Jamie-Guyden, a Philadelphia label, and enjoyed some Deep South success in early 1963, but Rick was still unable to find anyone to put out "Steal Away," a strong gospel-based number that took advantage of Jimmy's soaring church tenor to tell a tale of guilty adultery. He put voices behind Hughes's lead, modeling the effect on a pop song called "Candy Apple Red" that Bonnie Guitar had had out in 1959, but there wasn't a glimmer of interest on the record companies' part, and he was just about to give up on Hughes (and vice versa) when in the early spring of 1964 Bill Lowery suggested that he put the record out on his own.

Lowery advised him to press up a few thousand copies initially and start out with the seven major distribution centers in the South (Memphis, Atlanta, New Orleans, Nashville, Miami, Washington, D.C., and Charlotte), going

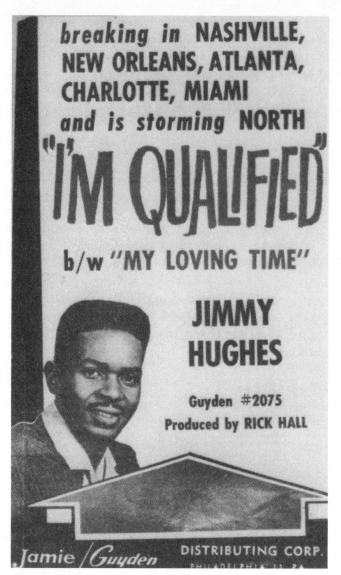

breaking in NASHVILLE,
NEW ORLEANS, ATLANTA,
CHARLOTTE, MIAMI
and is storming NORTH
"I'M QUALIFIED"
b/w "MY LOVING TIME"

JIMMY
HUGHES

Guyden #2075
Produced by RICK HALL

Jamie/Guyden DISTRIBUTING CORP.
PHILADELPHIA 21, PA.

(Courtesy of Bill Millar)

around to the black stations himself to see if he could get them to play it. The one catch was to make sure that all orders were shipped COD; otherwise success could bankrupt him, as it had so many others.

"So Dan and I took out an old Ford Fairlane station wagon from the lot —I was still working part time for my father-in-law at the used car lot to make ends meet—put the records in the back of the station wagon, got us a couple of cases of vodka, and started out from here. We went to Memphis first—LOK,

DIA. We'd sit up all night with the night man, be half drunk when we got in, half drunk when we got out, and we'd go out and get him coffee and burgers and we'd all get happy and he'd be on the air and he'd play our records, you know, while we were sitting there, interview us, do the whole thing. We spent a couple of days drunk in New Orleans, did our whole number, brought in our record, gave them a fifth of booze—we had no money, I mean, it was peanut-butter-and-crackers time to survive on the road, and we were sleeping in the back of the station wagon, but it was great. I mean, here we are, white Southern boys, young, our lives were an open book, and I would say, 'Hey, look, my name is Rick Hall. This is my second record. I produced Arthur Alexander's "You Better Move On," and I'm trying to break into this market, but I need help. I don't have any money, this is all I got—a bottle if you drink, if you don't drink, we'll take you out to dinner or whatever. But I promise you if I ever have a hit, I'll never forget you. That's all I can promise. I'll always be a friend if you ever need me. So at least give me a break.' "

They were out about two weeks, Rick says. When they got back, the orders were piled up. It was 1300 to each distributor one week, 2600 the next (300 free records were given away customarily for each thousand sold). "Now, I'm pressing and paying as I go, ten cents a record at the two pressing plants —they wouldn't deal with me on credit—so I'm saying, 'Jeez, I'm in a lot of trouble here. I've got a hit record, and I may go broke.' So I called Bill Lowery, he was my confidant, and I said, 'What the hell am I going to do?' "

Lowery eventually set Rick up in a distributing arrangement with Vee Jay Records, a black-owned company which had just moved from Chicago to Los Angeles and which at that point (mid-1964) was disputing American rights to the Beatles with Capitol (Vee Jay had issued both "Please Please Me" and "Do You Want to Know a Secret?"). Rick's record was an enormous hit, Top 20 pop, and a very influential number, too, both for its theme (it started a new string of increasingly explicit "sneaking around" songs) and for its delivery. It was an important connection for Hall as well, since he now started producing soul for Vee Jay ("Let's Do It Over," a Penn-Oldham song, was a big hit for Joe Simon in 1965, the partnership's first legitimate r&b success). Unfortunately Vee Jay went out of business a little more than a year after the initial distribution deal; Jimmy Hughes, although he had a number of other hits, never again achieved the dramatic success of "Steal Away" (he never brought in another song like that one) and went on to a somewhat lackluster career before retiring without regret in 1974; and Rick's first rhythm section, the band that was known throughout the region first as the Mark V's and then as the Pallbearers, quit shortly after the record's success and guitarist Terry Thompson's premature death and moved to Nashville.

For the band it was a simple business decision. They saw a lot of money being made, and they were getting scarcely any of it. No one will tell you that

Rick was overly generous with his cash in those days, not even Rick, and at this point he was paying hardly anything, despite his union affiliations. The beauty of Muscle Shoals for an outside producer was that he could bring in an act, bring in a Joe Simon, say, and then turn the act over to Rick, who would engineer, produce, most likely come up with the songs, while at the same time providing a tight working band that would play behind the singer and accept union minimum for a single session, no matter how long cutting the session actually took. This was the very situation that Jerry Wexler had been looking for when he went to Memphis, but Stax had its own artists to look after. Rick Hall, on the other hand, was in business strictly to satisfy the client. With the exception of Jimmy Hughes he had no label roster. With the exception of Jimmy Johnson he had no salaried employees. The most that a musician could hope for was the fifty-three-dollar session fee that the union demanded—if the session was placed. It wasn't much of a way to make a living, and gradually Rick's musicians became aware of the inequities of the situation. Bass player Norbert Putnam described the slow dawning of this realization to writer John Grissim:

"Guys like Ray Stevens and Felton Jarvis [who both came in with Bill Lowery] were saying things like 'You guys are crazy to stay down here for this amount of money. Come to Nashville, and you can get all the dates you want. Working conditions are better. You'll be respected.' And Rick was saying, 'Aw, you guys will never make it up there. You can't do it.' Well, finally David and Jerry [piano and drums] decided they were definitely gonna move. I wasn't sure I could afford the move. So Rick says, 'Look, I'll guarantee you a minimum of a hundred dollars a week and make you leader on all the sessions.' And I asked myself, 'Why should he do this? He's never been so nice before.' And that's when I definitely decided to take the chance and move up."

This first exporting of the Muscle Shoals sound proved as great a success as had been predicted (Briggs and Carrigan in particular played with Elvis often in his last years, and all three musicians operated Quadrafonic together, one of the most successful Nashville studios of the '70s). Rick's attitude was a fairly predictable mix of arrogance and hurt. "Musicians are important," he said in one interview, "but without direction they are nothing." "Most of these kids couldn't carry a tune in a bucket," he said on another occasion. "I say that musicians are like basketball players," he told Charlie Gillett, in response to an implied criticism of his methods. "They need a manager to tell them when to drop a play. My engineering ability and advice . . . contributed more than the individual musicians."

His chart record makes a point for him in any case. When his first rhythm section left him, he put together a second. When they in turn left several years later, to form a competitive studio of their own, the enormously successful Muscle Shoals Sound, Rick embarked upon his most successful commercial period yet, as pop stars like Bobbie Gentry, the Osmonds, Paul Anka, Mac Davis, and Liza Minnelli all trooped to Muscle Shoals to absorb the Rick Hall touch. Today he looks back on his professional life and times, and says he has mellowed, he has learned his lesson; if he had the opportunity to do it all over again, he would do it somewhat differently. But it's hard to imagine a younger Rick Hall doing it any differently at all.

"ANIMAL HOUSE"

The second rhythm section was the group that had been waiting in the wings practically from the beginning. Drummer Roger Hawkins had been hanging around Tom Stafford's studio ever since he was twelve years old and understudying Donnie Fritts in Hollis Dixon's band. Rhythm guitarist Jimmy Johnson (much like Stax, Fame had no flashy lead guitarist in their studio group; rhythm was the key component) knew something about recording from his work with Rick and was a longtime veteran of the fraternity circuit. Junior Lowe generally played bass, though David Hood (who would eventually join the group and was then a member of the Mystics, just a notch or two behind the Del Rays, the Mark V's, and, of course, Hollis Dixon in popularity) was clamoring to come in. And the keyboard player was Spooner Oldham, the thin wraithlike presence who rarely spoke above a whisper and who had contributed

The Del Rays at Ole Miss, 1965: Roger Hawkins, Norbert Putnam, Jimmy Ray Hunter, Jimmy Johnson. (Courtesy of Tommy Couch)

(whether as writer or accompanist, or both) to nearly every one of Fame's significant hits.

The first year or two of the new section's tenure was mostly woodshedding, getting used to playing together in the studio, probably getting used to the idea that this was their big break, that they were at last the first team. When Buddy Killen brought Joe Tex to Muscle Shoals in November 1964, he didn't even give a thought to using Rick's new band. Killen knew Rick, he knew the studio, and he felt the downhome atmosphere could give his artist's career a boost. When it came to recording, though, the band that played on Tex's breakthrough hit, "Hold What You've Got," was Joe's own, and Muscle Shoals got no more credit for the creation of "the Joe Tex Sound" than any other custom studio would have received. "We wasn't good enough to play master sessions at first," says Jimmy Johnson, heavyset, jovial, with a remarkably retentive memory for names, dates, places. "We were just demoing, really, that's all we did for just about two years. We came up under the Mark V's, you see, playing the fraternities, Jimmy Reed, Bo Diddley, really it was kind of crossover blues stuff, and we were real solid on the Southeastern fraternity circuit. I remember, we kind of patterned ourselves after Hollis Dixon at first, but then the Mark V's just appeared, and we went down there cocky, man, to see who was playing, and we walked in to hear this rival band, and they blew our shit away. At the University of North Alabama. Right here in town. I went home with my tail feathers burned that night. They was playing music, and I didn't even know what was going on. They was playing practically jazz!

"Everybody had their own little worlds. It was like the movie *Animal House,* that was exactly the parties that Hollis Dixon and the Del Rays and the Mark V's and the Mystics played for at the fraternity houses. Exactly. We used to play next door to Slim Harpo; Muddy Waters might be next door to him. There was one group, the Thirteen Screaming Niggers, then there was Doug Clark and the Hot Nuts—they were famous 'cause they'd all get naked. I remember Andy Anderson and the Dawn Breakers—they were heavy. The strongest one was from Jackson, Mississippi, the Rolling Stones—Joe Tubb and the Rolling Stones (this was back before the other Rolling Stones). They sang r&b with white gospel harmonies, and I remember the first time I ever saw them, they pulled up in a Cadillac, black '56 Cadillac, the kind that had air-conditioning tubes coming out from over the back seat, and they'd let me sit in the back seat on their break, the heater was blowing through the back seat, God, I couldn't get over it. We'd make thirty-five, forty dollars a night, pull in there with a U-Haul trailer, unload, set up, then we'd have to go change clothes in the house—we had our blue and green tuxes with bowties. Just like the movie. We didn't play any clubs, zero clubs. This is the Bible Belt. We didn't go anywhere else, we didn't know what was going on anywhere else—this was all the world we knew about. See, we could go to Athens, Alabama, and we was lost."

Muscle Shoals burst upon the consciousness of the world at large in the spring of 1966 with a single record that was homegrown, home-produced, and would forever eliminate the necessity of Jimmy Johnson finding his way to Athens or anywhere else. "When a Man Loves a Woman" established Muscle Shoals as a national recording center, brought Jerry Wexler directly from Memphis to Fame, and became the first Southern soul number actually to top the pop charts. It was also as significant an integrating factor in its way as Elvis Presley's "That's All Right," Little Richard's "Tutti Frutti," or Martin Luther King's march on Birmingham of two years before. The artist was Jimmy Hughes's cousin, Percy Sledge, from nearby Leighton; the enginer was Jimmy Johnson, who also played on the date along with the rest of the new rhythm section; the session, oddly enough, though, was neither recorded by Rick Hall nor put out on the Fame label, despite the fact that Rick played a major role in its release and reaped most of the benefits from it.

Quin Ivy, a quiet-spoken twenty-eight-year-old native of Oxford, Mississippi, who is today a college professor, was then the top local DJ at radio station WLAY, playing a mix of pop, country, and r&b that just about everyone in the area, black and white, listened to. Ivy had been in radio for seven or eight years already but had ambitions to go beyond just being a jock, and he had been writing—lyrics only—for Rick Hall's publishing company practically since Rick got started. As Rick's business picked up in the mid-'60s—not just with his own label but also with sporadic session work, of which Joe Tex's "Hold What You've Got" is the most notable example—Ivy saw a need that was not being filled. Rick, never the most diplomatic of men, was turning away most of the custom business: jingles, people who wandered up from Mississippi looking for a place to cut a gospel tune, local artists who just wanted to try their luck and pay to hear the sound of their own voice. Quin asked if Rick would mind his opening a studio to take up some of this slack. When Rick said no, he didn't mind a bit, in fact he was even willing to help get Quin set up in a new studio, Quin inquired if he might approach Dan Penn to be his chief a&r person. Here Rick seems to have been tempted—two such strong personalities as Rick Hall and Dan Penn did not escape their abrasive moments—but in the end he determined that he needed Dan more than he wanted to be rid of him, and he suggested another musician he had been working with for some time, trumpet player and guitarist Marlin Greene, who did in fact go with Quin into the new Quinvy studio.

It wasn't much of a studio. The control board was an old RCA radio station console that Quin picked up from WLAY for $150. He found a used Ampex in Nashville and some old A7 speakers, and the studio setup was such that, as it was said at the time, "it had a few bugs in it." "Those bugs," laughs

Percy Sledge. (Courtesy of Jeff Hannusch)

Jimmy Johnson today, "never left. By now they're very old bugs." In any case it was adequate for what Quin had in mind, and for musicians he was able to use Rick's rhythm section, since they were not actually under contract to Rick and were free most of the time, with Jimmy Johnson available to do the majority of the engineering.

It is with the entrance of Percy that the plot thickens, and everyone has his own version of how it actually happened that Percy Sledge wandered into the Quinvy studio in late 1965 and recorded a multimillion-selling record his first time out. Here is what seems to have happened. Sledge, a twenty-five-year-old hospital orderly at Colbert County Hospital, had been singing since he was a kid but had never really done much professionally. He says he sang with his cousin Jimmy Hughes's gospel group, the Singing Clouds, but Hughes doesn't remember it. He did sing in the chorus in high school, but in fact he was better known as a shortstop and third baseman, playing for the local Leighton team. According to Percy, in 1965 he had only just started singing with the Esquires, a local group with three alternating lead singers, who did a mix of Miracles, Temptations, Beatles, and Bobby "Blue" Bland material. Percy was drafted into the group by Sterling High School music director James Richard when one of the singers fell ill. "He remembered me from when I used to sing when I was in high school, so he asked me to substitute for his singer, and I hadn't sung in two years. I said, 'Man, you must be kidding. Man, I ain't sung in five years.' He said, 'Aw, you can do it.' So I just kind of fell in."

The Esquires were made up of four pieces: drums, sax, a man named Calvin Lewis on bass, and Andrew "Pop" Wright on Hammond B-3 organ. They played locally, played many of the same fraternities that the Del Rays were playing, were even booked into Ole Miss on the recommendation of Jimmy Johnson, who had a friend, Tuscumbia native Tommy Couch, who was entertainment chairman of Pi Kappa Alpha (Couch would soon start his own label and studio, Malaco, modeled on Muscle Shoals lines, in Jackson, Mississippi). Couch remembers the first dance the Esquires played, not long before Percy's recording session, but he remembers Percy less for his singing than for his curiosity, as the young singer hovered on the edge of the stage all night long, even when he was not performing. When asked why he didn't take a break, Percy explained that he just wanted to see the fraternity boys do that "mop dance" again. After considerable questioning it turned out that what Percy called the mop dance was more commonly referred to as "the alligator," an abandoned moment when couples got down on the floor and generally flailed around. "They ain't doing no alligator," Percy staunchly insisted. "Those people are doing the mop dance. They busy just mopping up the floor." Which might have been the beginning and the end of the legend of Percy Sledge if shortly thereafter Percy hadn't discovered his song.

"Well, it's a short story, but then again it can be a long one, too. I was standing up on stage, I'd had a few Scotches, so I guess my mind was a little blowed up, and all of a sudden I just hollered out, 'Why did you leave me, baby?' So Quin Ivy just happened to be in the club that night, and he liked the way I sounded and the way I felt, and he asked me if I'd come down to his studio. He said, 'I like the way you sound on that song. Now, if we could change the lyrics so we could get something more dynamic, then you would get some more feeling.' So we changed 'Why Did You Leave Me?' to 'When a Man Loves a Woman,' and all the musicians say, everybody in the studio say, 'I believe we might have a smash.' Now, when they hollered smash to me, I didn't even know what smash meant!"

That's the short version. One of the long versions is that Percy and the band went over to Fame to begin with and ran into Dan Penn.

"I was engineering at Rick's. I'm the hamburger man and engineer. There was nobody else around. So Rick tells me, 'I got this little group coming over. I want you to record 'em, and I'm going to listen to them later and analyze 'em.' Well, I'm just dying to cut a record at this point. I got my chops on the board by now, and I knew I could do it, and here comes Percy and his little band. When I heard Percy, it was not that I recognized all that much, it was just that I wanted to cut something. Anything. I said. 'Rick, I can cut this guy.

Listen to this tape.' He said, 'Naah. He's just another bluegum.' I said, 'Rick, this guy's great.' He said, 'Well, you can't use my studio or my money.' So I guess I had told Percy, 'Oh, hell, the sky's the limit for you. Rick's gonna love you. Why don't you just come back on Tuesday.' Well, he came back all smiles, and I had to tell him. But I knew Quin was starting a new studio. And I said, 'Percy, if I could, I would cut you, because I think you got yourself a hit. But they're starting a studio right over in Sheffield.' And I told him how to get there. 'You just go over and tell 'em Dan Penn sent you!' "

Quin Ivy remembers Percy showing up at his record store, Tune Town, where Jimmy Johnson was now working as a clerk, when a friend of Quin's, Leroy Wright, happened to be there. As Percy was leaving, Leroy turned to Quin and said, " 'By the way, did you know Percy sings?' I said, 'No, I'd like to hear you sometime.' And he said, 'Well, what are you doing this afternoon?' And he showed up with his whole group, they hauled a Hammond B-3 down there in the back of a pickup truck and brought it in the studio and hooked it up, and he sang the song that became 'When a Man Loves a Woman.' "

Whatever the means by which the various parties got together, they worked on the song all fall, changing the lyrics, reshaping the melody, leaving very little of the original version or group in place. When they finally cut it around Christmastime, it was pretty well turned around, with only Percy's deep-throated and dramatic tenor still featured. They cut the track at Quinvy with two mono machines, six inputs on the console, no EQ, and one chance for an overdub, because after one tape transfer sound quality dropped off too precipitously to risk further reproduction. Jimmy Johnson engineered; Spooner Oldham played a ghostly Farfisa organ; it was Roger Hawkins on drums, Marlin Greene on guitar, Junior Lowe on bass. Later they overdubbed voices and horns, three local players who were completely out of tune, which was okay with Jimmy because Percy was out of tune, too ("Percy was so out of tune we thought his voice might break a window. It was almost painful."). When they finished the session just before Christmas, everyone felt they had something, but no one knew exactly what to do with it.

"I had been working with Rick off and on for a long time," Quin remembers, "and at this point I respected Rick an awful lot for his opinions; still do. So the first thing I did when I cut the record was take it to Rick and play it for him. Well, after he heard the record, he asked me, he said, 'Quin, what are you going to do with it?' And I said, 'I'm going to send it to Atlantic Records.' Even though I'd never had any dealings with Atlantic or Jerry Wexler up to this time. And he said, 'Well, look, I've been dealing with Jerry for a long time, and we're pretty tight, so why don't you let me send it to him?' "

Rick remembers that Quin called him on a Sunday when Quinton Claunch, a hardware supplies salesman who had only recently left Hi Records to start his own Goldwax label in Memphis (Quinton was yet another native of the Muscle Shoals area transplanted to Tennessee), was over at the house. "We went down to Quin's studio, and on the wall he had a little bitty player and he had a cheap little acetate he'd made, and he put it on and we listened to it, and Quin said, 'What do you think?' And I said, 'Let me listen to it again.' I listened to it again, and I said, 'I'll tell you what I think. I think it's a #1 record.' He said, 'Rick, you've got to be kidding.' I said, 'I'm telling you, I feel as strong as death about it.' He said, 'You think you could get me a deal with a label?' I said, 'Yeah.' So he left me with the acetate, and I picked up the phone and I called Jerry Wexler. I'd talked to him only once on the phone when 'Steal Away' was hot (Joe Galkin was the one who made the call), and he'd said to me then, 'Rick, if you ever get anything you think is supergood, just give me a call, maybe we can do something together.' So I told him, 'You told me to call if I heard something good, and I heard something. I found a record that is a #1 record without any qualifications whatsoever, not #2, not #3, a #1 r&b record. And he said, 'Jeez, that's awful strong.' And I said, 'I know that's strong, but I'm telling you what it is.' He said, 'Well, you need to get me a copy.' Three or four days later he called me back, and he said, 'Well, I've got the record. You really think this is a #1?' I said, 'I'm positive.' He said, 'Okay, I'll tell you what, you have Quin call me, and I'm going to make a deal. I'm going to give you one percent as a finder's fee, and I'm going to ask Quin if he'll give you one percent from his end.' "

That is exactly what Wexler did. In a typical ploy he called up Quin, who knew no more about the intricacies of the record business (points, publishing, guarantees) than Jim Stewart did at a comparable stage, and asked him what he wanted. As Quin tells it, "I said, 'Well, I want a thousand dollars in front and eight percent.' And he said, 'You got it.' And he said, 'Now what about the publishing [this was probably the most valuable consideration, and something owned outright by Quin at the time]?' And I said, Well, I hadn't considered that. And he said, well, he'd give us half of the publishing on it, and I said, fine. And I agreed to the point for Rick."

It is an open secret that Wexler also urged Quin to take at least partial writer's credits for himself, but here Quin—known behind his back, but affectionately, to some of his colleagues as "Mr. White Bread"—refused because, quite simply, Quin saw it as a dishonorable act, and also because Quin was contracted to Rick as a writer. "Another thing that was humorous about it— and I don't mean to cast Jerry in a bad light—but one of the things he did was call me and say, 'This thing is great, but I think it could be better. I want you to recut it. We'll pick up all of the expenses and everything.' I said, 'Okay. Great.' We were excited that for the first time we'd been given carte blanche on a recording session. So we got everybody in, I remember it was snowing like the devil on the night we were going to cut and somebody had to put chains on their car and go way out in the country to get Junior Lowe. And so we cut

Jerry Wexler and Quin Ivy. (Courtesy of Jerry Wexler)

it, and we worked on that thing for I don't know how long, weeks, got the Memphis Horns this time from Stax, and finally I sent it out to New York, and after the record came out and it was obvious it was really a hit record, Jerry called me and said, 'Aren't you glad you recut it?' And I said, 'Jerry, you used the original, out-of-tune horns and all.'"

"When a Man Loves a Woman" completed the process of chart integration begun, really, by Joe Tex's success of the previous year (James Brown had by now enjoyed a number of big crossover hits, starting with 1965's "Papa's Got a Brand New Bag," but James Brown was as much a category unto himself as Motown). Southern soul had at last entered the mainstream of pop in the unlikely guise of the ultimate make-out song, the kind of song that affected its fans so powerfully that, as Jimmy Johnson says, "I've heard stories of people driving off the road when they heard that record come on the air."

For Percy Sledge the results were almost as unexpected. At the conclusion of his first tour, Dan Penn and Donnie Fritts recall (perhaps with some fancifulness), he checked into the same hospital in which he had worked as an orderly, ensconced himself in its most expensive room for a week, and let those for whom

Percy Sledge, Quin Ivy, Esther Phillips, Jerry Wexler, at New York party celebrating the success of "When a Man Loves a Woman." (Courtesy of Quin Ivy)

he had worked wait on him in turn while he suffered from "nervous exhaustion." Though he continued to have hits for the next few years, and ironically was for a while one of the most popular singers in the Republic of South Africa, he was never able to repeat his initial success or translate it into a solid career, primarily because, as his discoverer Quin Ivy says regretfully, "he was never really prepared for it." Ivy managed Percy for thirteen years, except for those times when Percy by his own account got "lost" (there was one period, Percy says, of three or four years that have disappeared into the recesses of time). In the end, one feels, it became more of an obligation than an opportunity for Quin, whose greatest regret was that he was never able to become more than a "one-artist producer."

Just to show how complicated things can get, Jimmy Johnson, who thought he had an ironclad understanding with Quin, got fired in between the first and second versions of the song and went back to work for Rick for another couple of years. Quin himself, who dreamt of a label of his own and did start his own South Camp label for a while, never really hooked on with the record industry and in the end went back to school and became a professor of business administration at the University of North Alabama. Meanwhile Rick Hall, the man who had overlooked Percy Sledge in the first place, made more money than anybody else connected with the record, as he collected his finder's fee and the publishing on the back side as well as reaping the benefit of the relationship with Atlantic Records. It was scarcely one month after the explosive success of "When a Man Loves a Woman" that Jerry Wexler himself arrived in Muscle Shoals with Wilson Pickett in tow.

ATLANTIC COMES TO MUSCLE SHOALS

"After Percy's record went to #1, my stock went up with Wexler, way up, a full nine on a 1–10 scale, and the next thing I know he called me and says, 'Look, I'm having these problems with Stax, and I've got this act that I'd like to bring down, that I'm very fond of and we've had a lot of success with and all, and I'd like to do some work with you.' And I said, 'Well, why don't you come down? Who are you bringing?' And he said, 'Well, I'm bringing Wilson Pickett.' And I almost shit in my pants! Wilson Pickett! We just thought he was the greatest. So Wexler says, 'Get the best musicians available. I'm sending Pickett down.' So I pick up Pickett at the airport, and he had on a black and white hound's tooth coat and black pants, and back then he wore his hair slicked down, and he reminded me—he was such a good-looking black man, muscular —he reminded me of a black leopard, you know, look but don't touch, he might bite your hand, that kind of guy. But he was from Prattville, Alabama, and he had the gift of gab, too, and we hit it off, and we rode back, and I had this old Chrysler that I picked him up in, and he looked at me, and it was like, 'I don't know about this. . . .'"

"I couldn't believe it," Pickett recalled to reporter Mark Jacobson. "I looked out the plane window, and there's these people picking cotton. I said to myself, 'I ain't getting off this plane, take me back North.' This big Southern guy was at the airport, really big guy [actually Rick is fairly average-sized], looks like a sheriff. He says he's looking for me. I said, 'I don't want to get off here, they still got black people picking cotton.' The man looked at me and said, 'Fuck that. Come on, Pickett, let's go make some fucking hit records.' I didn't know Rick Hall was white."

Jerry Wexler, at any rate, never had any doubts about the hit-making potential of Muscle Shoals. Now that he had a taste of the kind of recording that Southern studios had to offer, he was not about to give it up. He walked into the little Fame studio just four months after Pickett's last Memphis session and practically took everyone by storm. "Not so much because of his reputation," says Jimmy Johnson, "because we didn't know his reputation. It was his talk, that accent. 'Hey, baby.' The Jewish brogue. We had never heard anything like that. It blew us away. I mean, to us wine was Mogen David. We didn't know about Château Lafite, which he turned us on to. He was a very dynamic person. He scared the shit out of us. We just quaked in our shoes."

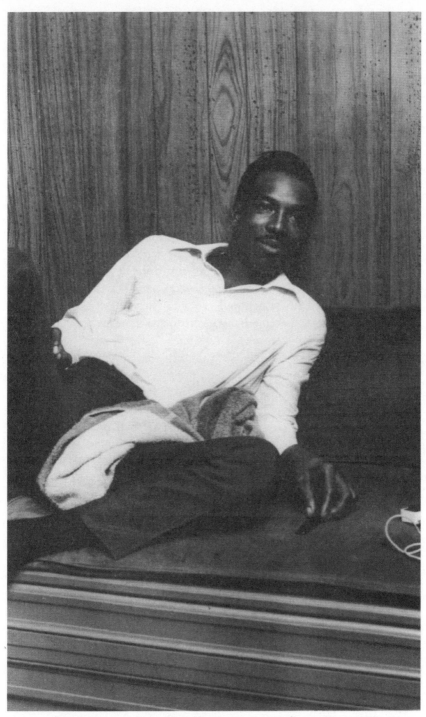

"He reminded me of a black leopard." (*Don Paulsen/Michael Ochs Archives*)

At this point the band—which consisted of Jimmy Johnson, Spooner Oldham on keyboards, Junior Lowe on bass, and Roger Hawkins on drums, with Dan Penn, of course, always hanging around the studio and throwing in ideas—had been woodshedding for almost two years. In addition Jerry Wexler had asked that guitarists Tommy Cogbill and Chips Moman (who, like Rick, had had quite a bit of contact with Wexler—particularly in the pioneering days at Stax—without ever actually having met him) be brought in from Memphis. Everyone on the session had played on hit records, but Jerry Wexler was the man who had made them. To all of the musicians, and to Rick, too, who had patterned the Fame label after Atlantic even down to its red-and-black logo, it was Jerry Wexler who was the star, the creative force who had cut the songs on which they had all grown up.

The session came together with admirable efficiency (four songs a day), prodded along, no doubt, by Wexler's coaxing importunities, and in the end Pickett walked out of the Muscle Shoals studio with a bigger seller than any of his Memphis sides and his first Top 10 pop hit. "Land of 1000 Dances," which defined the summer of '66 in much the way that "When a Man Loves a Woman" had defined the spring, was laced with typical Pickett touches. It had the same lazy hardness, the same arching falsetto and spontaneous unleashing of on-pitch screams ("Wilson would scream notes," says Wexler, "where other screamers just scream sound") as Pickett's Memphis masters, and in a move which must have particularly galled Jim Stewart, Wexler even contracted the Stax horn section to play on the session. Percy Sledge, evidently out of the hospital by now, stopped by the session at one point, and the two men almost got into a fistfight when Pickett characteristically took umbrage at Percy's comparison of his singing to Otis Redding's and Percy, who had only intended a compliment, quickly left the studio. Apart from that incident, once Junior Lowe finally got the difficult bass intro to "Land of 1000 Dances" down to everyone's satisfaction, things went pretty smoothly.

A lot more smoothly than the next session in October, when Wexler got rid of Lowe altogether after discovering that Memphian Tommy Cogbill could play bass ("Rick had never bothered to find out what else he could do," Wexler told Atlantic chronicler Charlie Gillett contemptuously) and brought in his own engineer, Tommy Dowd, with the idea of making Muscle Shoals over—and making it stick—in a way he had been unable to do at Stax. As it turned out, it was lucky he had brought Dowd along. They had worked for a couple of hours on "Mustang Sally," an uptempo blues number written by one of Pickett's old colleagues from the Falcons, who now billed himself as Sir Mack Rice. They had finally gotten a take that everyone was satisfied with, recalls Spooner Oldham. Everybody was standing around in the control room waiting to hear the playback when "somehow the hub wasn't fastened on the reel of tape and it jumped off, and the whole reel of tape jumped off, and splinters of tape went

Cutting "Funky Broadway" at Fame, 1967: Tom Dowd, Wilson Pickett, Jimmy Johnson, Bobby Womack. (Courtesy of Rick Hall)

flying, and Wilson's kicking and cursing, 'Goddam master,' and 'I hate you,' and Dowd just sits there a minute and then directs everybody to move the machines and pick up the pieces and put them together—there must have been about forty or fifty one-inch pieces of tape. He said, 'Give me about thirty minutes, y'all, go get some coffee and come back.' So we all left, sat around, got depressed —all that work. We come back, and he played it for us. And Wex says, 'You know, you guys were looking at one nervous Jew!' "

Perhaps such incidents as these (however amusingly they might be portrayed) symbolized the greater gulf that was building between Wexler and Rick Hall, a division scarcely surprising given the nature of the personalities involved. Wexler considered Hall to be dictatorial, pig-headed, and inflexible, and ascribed the success of the sessions primarily, it would seem, to his own leavening influence. Hall saw Wexler much as Jim Stewart must have, as an exploiter, a carpetbagger who found a scene that was already flourishing ("Wexler came in on the cream") and then tried to take all the credit for it. In one sense there could be no two greater opposites—even in music, Hall was a perfectionist, while Wexler boasted, then and now, that he didn't even know how to operate a console. "The trouble with Rick is that he's too authoritarian in the studio," Wexler has said. "He treats his musicians like shit." "I learned a lot of lessons from Wexler, but I never considered Wexler a record producer," Rick will respond in turn. "He could use people, he was a tremendous motivator, and he could pit you against me, me against Chips, make us enemies or make us friends.

I don't mean this to be a put-down. I'm just saying he was a master at that."
There was a lot of ill feeling, certainly, a lot of unfocused resentment, and yet
one feels that underneath there was a kind of kinship, a grudging, if limited,
mutual admiration, as each sought to manipulate the other, each prided himself
on his discovery of talent, each vied for the loyalty and affection of the Muscle
Shoals rhythm section, and above all each loved and lost what had become by
now the focus of the Muscle Shoals creative scene and would soon spin off into
a meteoric Memphis explosion of its own, the newfound (and short-lived)
partnership of Dan Penn and Chips Moman.

"THE DARK END OF THE STREET"

Dan and Chips had met just prior to the first Wilson Pickett session at Fame,
in the spring of 1966, and by the summer were such fast friends that it seemed
as if they must have known each other all their lives. They were like two freight
trains running on the same track, with predictably explosive results, but for a
brief time Moman and Penn were so symbiotic a team that they almost had to
be mentioned in the same breath. If they had never met, they would have
remained legendary figures whose parallel situations (each was a lonely voice
in an isolated outpost evangelizing for freedom and r&b) and temperaments
(stubborn) demanded comparison. Moman, of course, had already scented success with his work at Satellite, but his personal life since his deposition from
Stax had been checkered, his principal home the recording studio ("More than
anything else I wanted to make records"). Dan Penn lived, breathed, ate, slept,
and drank music. No one could mistake his obsession, and in fact it was their
uncanny similarity, a resemblance which *had* to be more than coincidental, that
led to their first meeting each other through the indirect agency of Rudolph
"Doc" Russell. Russell, a successful Memphis pharmacist with a ready supply
of capital, was Quinton Claunch's partner in the fledgling Goldwax label. Up
to this point Claunch and Russell had been producing their Goldwax artists (the
Lyrics, the Ovations, and James Carr made up just about the entire roster) either
in Claunch's hometown of Muscle Shoals under the direction of Rick Hall or
in one Memphis studio or another, generally with Chips Moman engineering.
It was Russell, Dan says, who first mentioned Chips's name to him.

"Doc Russell says to me, 'Man, there's a guy in Memphis that's just like
you. Looks like you, acts like you, plays like you.' I said, 'Aw, shit, well, I'll
just have to meet that dude.' So I met him up in Nashville, we met up at [MGM
producer] Jim Vienneau's, it turned out. Chips had a radio board back then and
a 350 Ampex, actually he had two Ampex mixers, he didn't hardly qualify as
a studio—actually he wasn't doing dogshit except for the Ovations' records and
the Gentrys ["Keep On Dancing"] that were on MGM. When we met, we just
went 'Psssht!,' just like that, 'cause, see, he had heard the same shit about me.

Dan Penn. (Robert Melhorn)

We had a helluva meeting, and we understood each other right off. I started going to Memphis, and he started coming to Alabama. We started running together all the time, writing together, some people even begun to think we were brothers—I guess that was how he came to be playing on the Pickett session. We started writing together, I remember we wrote 'Dark End of the Street' at a country convention in a hotel. We was playing poker with Don Schroeder, and me and Chips was cheating him. Anyways, we took a break, wrote the song, and I told Chips, 'Let him get his fucking money back, or I'm spilling the beans.' Now Moman's a great poker player, got real fast hands, and we let him win his money back, but we must have been so pilled up and drunk we got into *him* for about a grand! You know, we had a helluva meeting, and we had a good run, but in the end we couldn't get along, isn't that always the way? It was just too hot to handle. In the end he said, 'Get in or get out,' and I said, 'I'm gone.' "

"Dan's one of the reasons I went to Muscle Shoals to start with," says Chips of the man with whom he was partners for more than three years. "I wanted him so bad to write and produce and work up there at my studio in Memphis [American] that I would play down there on the sessions. A lot of people used to think that Dan and I were brothers. And we were for a long time. And we still are. You know, Dan Penn in those days was what Rod Stewart wishes he could be. Back then Dan Penn could sing almost any kind of song and adapt it to his style. His demos were masterpieces—see, there's nothing more entertaining than a Dan Penn-Spooner Oldham demo, I'd rather hear that than anybody's master, but back then there wasn't any place for it, there just wasn't any place for a white guy that sounded black. Sometimes you let some of the greatest things slide by, and I guess that's what I did with Dan."

Rick Hall seems to have felt pretty much the same way. He expresses the same admiration and the same regrets. He even cut some unreleased sides on Penn around this time with the idea of making him "the white Ray Charles." But Penn was already escaping the sway of Muscle Shoals, as Donnie Fritts had before him, seeking to get out from under the domineering personality of Rick Hall, which, as Donnie says, could virtually mesmerize its audience despite an almost universal mistrust of Rick and the dark rumors that floated all around him. Just as at Stax, there was a conspiratorial atmosphere about Muscle Shoals, an inability to imagine what was going on in the world at large, or even in Memphis, a complete lack of perception of the impact that Muscle Shoals itself was having on the business and the music and at the same time an almost byzantine web of imaginings—of plots hatched and dark deeds undertaken, of credits misassigned and people misunderstood, of obscure political maneuverings and outright theft. All this came about, Jerry Wexler notes acerbically, because there was nothing else for anyone to *do* in Muscle Shoals except to get stoned and worry about the way in which they were getting screwed. "They were sitting around inventing a fantasy music business." The center of their fantasy from the outset, of course, was Rick Hall, who was soon cast in the role of oppressor, with Jerry Wexler the self-proclaimed deliverance.

Not for Dan Penn, though. Dan left for Memphis in the summer of '66, drawing Spooner Oldham with him less than a year later in a migration that would mark the start of Chips Moman's second golden age. (Having been present at the creation of Stax and now of Muscle Shoals, Chips would go on to cut over 120 Top 100 hits in the next three and a half years at his own American studio, with the indispensable help of Dan Penn.) Part of what gave Dan the courage to leave was the enormous success that James and Bobby Purify had with a Penn-Oldham composition at just about this time. Up until now, he and Spooner only half-joked, their songs had ridden the coattails of a lot of other writers' hits, as the B side of one successful single or another. With "I'm Your Puppet" (#6 pop) all that changed. "That was when I knew it was for real, after I got the first check—for $4000, I think it was. Before then if we heard a hit by Brenda Lee or Solomon Burke or whoever, we'd try to write a follow-up just like it. I mean, we'd take that to the limit. We wrote some Billy Joe Royal songs that come out just like 'Down in the Boondocks'—I

Atlantic's Extended Family, circa 1967: Jerry Wexler, Jim Stewart, Bob Kornheiser, Juggy Gayles, King Curtis, Rick Hall, Johnny Bienstock. (Courtesy of Jerry Wexler)

mean, *just* like it—and it was a bunch of shit. We wasted a lot of time like that, but 'Puppet' wasn't really written for the artist at all, they just found it in a demo stack, like most all good tunes."

Rick Hall probably didn't mourn the loss of his number-one writer for long. As Dan says of himself, "I guess I was a little abrasive back then," and too much was happening anyway to come up for breath. Once Wilson Pickett had broken the ice, Atlantic was in and out of the Fame studio with dizzying frequency, and Muscle Shoals, which had lagged behind Memphis in public recognition, was becoming known as the hottest recording center around, though sometimes, ironically enough, for "the Memphis sound." Papa Don Schroeder, too—the same Don Schroeder who had participated in the famous poker game—was bringing in his artists from Pensacola (in addition to James and Bobby Purify, his roster was notable for its inclusion of Mighty Sam and Oscar Toney, Jr.) and leasing the results with great success to Atlantic's chief rival, Larry Uttal of Bell Records. The Fame rhythm section was getting more and more work and even beginning to think of quitting their weekend club dates. A keyboard player named Barry Beckett, a twenty-three-year-old native of Birmingham who had moved to Pensacola and gone into the club business with Schroeder, started coming up to play with Papa Don's various artists and, when Spooner left in the spring of 1967, quickly replaced him in the band. It was a time of rapid-fire changes and breathtaking productivity, a period of almost uninterrupted success—for Rick, for the studio, for the studio musicians, and for the artists themselves, all of whom were coming to believe that there was something magical about Fame and Muscle Shoals, that Muscle Shoals, as Bill Lowery once said, had what the world was looking for.

▶7▶

Papa's Got a Brand New Bag

Come here, sister,
Papa's in the swing
Ain't you hip about what that New Breed bring
He ain't no drag
Papa's got a brand new bag

—James Brown, Summer 1965

From one minute to another you can't tell how this guy James Brown
is going to act, but we all love him and consider and respect the fact
that HE HAS MADE IT.

—Syd Nathan, owner of King Records (James Brown's first and
principal label) in his on-record farewell address to the troops, c.
1967

MUSCLE SHOALS MAY HAVE HAD WHAT THE
world was looking for, but James Brown never doubted that he was
that very thing. Certainly not after 1965 anyway, when he hit his
stride and went on hitting it, exploding in the process not only the
easy assumptions of pop but some of the more cherished traditions of soul music
itself. Unlike nearly everyone else in the greater soul community for whom the
success of any soul artist was another rung up the ladder, each step forward a
step for mankind (Muscle Shoals and Stax are only two of the more prominent
examples of this triumph of cooperative enterprise), James Brown was a Solo
Man who forged ahead on his own, who, far from negotiating any kind of
compromise solution to reach a broader audience, demanded that that very
audience sit up and listen to what he had to say. There is no question he was
ill mannered in his insistence, and that he was resented for it. Solomon Burke
dismissed him as not a proper soul singer at all, and his own all-black band
referred to him privately as "the greasy nigger," but he was not to be denied.
Long after Ray Charles had left the parochial world of soul and Sam Cooke
was on the verge of Las Vegas bookings and Hollywood success, James Brown
alone, a contemporary of both Charles and Cooke, was still out there toiling
in the vineyards, singing self-created music that increasingly left both the idea
of accommodation and the old tired formulations of r&b behind. Perhaps this

Rehearsing, circa 1964. (Frank Driggs Collection)

was why he was called "our number one black poet" by LeRoi Jones and hailed in 1969 as possibly "the most important black man in America" by *Look* magazine (as well as gaining attention from SNCC leaders Stokely Carmichael and H. Rap Brown). His music reached out with revolutionary fervor to a New Breed audience of blacks and whites. It was as militant culturally as any Black Panther political manifesto, without ever abandoning the past or its original audience. For James Brown remained firmly rooted in a sense of self and a sense of tradition that black America had not always known that it had.

How Brown achieved this sense of security and mission remains as much a mystery today as it was in 1964 and 1965, when first "Out of Sight" and then "Papa's Got a Brand New Bag" sprang as full-blown new rhythm conceptions from their creator's mind. Perhaps there is no explaining it. Perhaps it is as James Brown often says: he is that true rarity, a complete original, a self-created legend and black capitalist who, like many another success story, made up his own rules as he went along. There is no question in any case that by 1965 he appeared dependent on no other motivating force than himself. By 1965 he had won a major battle for independence with his record company, established himself as the number-one r&b box office attraction in the country, and put together a traveling road show of anywhere between three and four dozen people, including a self-contained eighteen-to-twenty-piece band which enabled him to record in any city in the country in which he might happen to have a booking. None of which goes very far to explain the burning fires that drove him, the source of his creative Difference, any more than an examination of his history and background can explain the breakthrough that he made or the fierce sense of independence that would set him so distinctly apart.

He was born in Barnwell, South Carolina, in 1933, an only child who "had no real mother, a father only on occasion." When he was four, his parents separated, and not long afterwards his father carried him to Augusta, Georgia, some forty miles away, where he was brought up by a succession of relatives in a seven-dollar-a-month shack. As a boy he shined shoes, swept out stores, picked cotton, and washed cars to help with the rent. One of his most vivid memories was of dancing for the troop trains from Camp Gordon as they pulled out of town, collecting the change that the men threw on the ground. At nine he recalls picking through the garbage behind a food warehouse in search of discarded cans of vegetables and getting his first store-bought underwear. When war broke out, his father was drafted into the Navy. If it hadn't been for his father's going into the service, he told Atlanta reporter Bill King, "we would have probably come up almost like barbarians."

The one quality that distinguished James Brown from the beginning was his unquenchable determination to succeed. His father, Joe, a filling station attendant, wanted James to follow in his footsteps, but the son's ambitions were always more expansive. At the Silas X. Floyd Elementary School he sang the National Anthem every day, says classmate and longtime road manager Henry Stallings, just to get noticed. "I remember him coming to school barefoot in the winter," Stallings told *Rolling Stone* reporter Gerri Hirshey, "but he was a little tough one, you know. He would never grumble or complain, about the same as he is now." "Being small and ragged, he was always getting picked on," recalled singer Leon Austin, another childhood friend, to Brown's British biographer, Cliff White. "He always stood his ground and fought back, no matter what their size. Somehow he was always the best at everything. He had more determination and guts than the rest of us."

Very early he focused his ambitions on entertainment. According to Henry Stallings he competed in singing and dancing at the amateur shows at the Lenox Theater on Ninth Street, just a few blocks from his home, where he frequently took first prize. According to Brown himself, "I sang loud and strong and soulful and the people felt it." It was at the Lenox, too, that he first saw films of Louis Jordan performing, short subjects that showed an entertainer singing, dancing, and clowning up a storm. "[Jordan's] 'Caldonia' was a song you could really put on a show with, and I started playing it and singing it whenever I got the chance."

He quit school in the seventh grade, at around fifteen, performed with various gospel groups, and started his own r&b combo, the Cremona Trio, for whom he sang and played piano and drums. He also started getting into a lot of trouble. With his friends he embarked on a life of petty crime and, not unexpectedly, was soon caught in a car break-in and sentenced, at sixteen, to eight to sixteen years' hard labor. He served a short period in the county jail before being transferred to juvenile work farms first in Rome, then in Toccoa, a hundred miles north of Augusta.

At Toccoa he completed his education, achieving a reputation as a musician ("When I was in prison, they called me Music Box," he told Gerri Hirshey) and athlete. It was as pitcher for the prison team that he first met Toccoa resident Bobby Byrd, a near-contemporary, who played against him in a local game. Byrd and Brown became friendly; Bobby's family, well known in the area, sponsored James for parole and helped get him a job at Lawson's Motor Company in town. It was 1952, and James was still torn between his ambition in sports and his ambition in music, but he knew unequivocally that he wanted to make something of himself. He boxed a little (in Augusta he had come under the influence of former lightweight champion Beau Jack) but quit in frustration after fighting another left-hander in his third bout. His baseball career was cut short when he hurt his leg. So that left music.

Penniless, ambitious, anxious to get married, he started singing in church —with Bobby Byrd's sister initially, then as a member of the Gospel Starlighters, a quartet for which Byrd sang lead and played piano at various local churches. Almost immediately James took charge of the group, though it continued to be known as "that Bobby Byrd group." "Without James," Byrd says today, with a mixture of realism and regret, "we were just another group. I mean, we were *all* important, but he was the star."

It was at about this time that the Gospel Starlighters, like so many other quartets throughout the South, decided to switch over from gospel to r&b. There was no great hand-wringing about it probably, it was just something that was in the air, that was very clearly happening commercially. Johnny Terry, a fellow juvenile institute alumnus, joined the group at this point, and after an unspecified interval of namelessness they began to call themselves the Flames, after a popular local group called the Torches. They started off playing social clubs and recreation centers, working various fraternities at the University of Georgia ("I done played all of 'em"). They had a manager by now, Barry Trimier, a local undertaker, and, when they weren't working, tried to catch every big show they could at the Textile Hall in Greenville, South Carolina. Their special favorites were the Midnighters, the "5" Royales, the Dominoes (out of whom Clyde McPhatter and Jackie Wilson would both emerge), and others of the New Breed, heavily gospel-influenced type who were popping up right and left by this time. The Flames' repertoire, Bobby Byrd told Cliff White, consisted of "our favorite r&b hits: the '5' Royales' 'Baby, Don't Do It,' the

James Brown (on drums) and the Original Flames, including Bobby Byrd on piano, 1956. (Michael Ochs Archives)

Midnighters' 'Annie Had a Baby,' the Spaniels' 'Goodnite, Sweetheart,' the Clovers' 'One Mint Julep,' all the old classics. As far as I recall, we didn't do any original songs for quite some while." They traveled around, eight musicians to a beat-up old station wagon. James was supplementing his income working as a janitor at a hundred dollars a month when Little Richard came to Bill's Rendezvous Club in Toccoa in early 1955.

Little Richard at this point was well known throughout the South, though he was not yet the national figure he would soon become. Atlanta DJ Zenas Sears remembers him creating just as outrageous an impression in the little Georgia clubs as he did when he hit the national scene, and Macon disc jockey Hamp Swain, whose band Little Richard frequently fronted, affirms that "whenever you said Little Richard was appearing, you could depend on a crowd —all through Georgia, Alabama, and Florida." Not surprisingly, then, Bill's Rendezvous was packed for Richard's appearance when the Flames took the stage uninvited during intermission and created such an uproar that first Little Richard and then his road manager, Fats Gonder, were moved to pay attention. Gonder got the group's name and took it back with him to Clint Brantley, Little Richard's manager and the kingpin of black Macon entertainment. Brantley encouraged the Flames to come to Macon; he lodged them above his Two Spot Club on Fifth Street and started booking them all around the Macon and north

Florida area. At Brantley's instigation they were now the Famous Flames, but when "Tutti Frutti" hit the charts in the late fall of 1955 and Richard took off for California, James Brown became Little Richard for several weeks—if only to fulfill Brantley's booking commitments—while the Famous Flames maintained their own schedule under the leadership of Bobby Byrd. It was at just around this time, too, that the group finally went into the studio to cut the number that had become the keystone of their live act.

"Please, Please, Please" derived loosely from a 1952 Orioles adaptation of the old blues number "Baby Please Don't Go," but where the Orioles' version retained a traditional group structure and approach, the Famous Flames took the chorus not simply as their theme but as virtually their only text. This sense of single-minded intensity was further enhanced by the effect of James's near-sobbing voice against the smooth gospel harmonies of the Flames (it was, said a later critic, "like Little Richard fronting the Drifters"), with each chorus mounting in a rising crescendo of emotion and simple repetition. Big Saul was at the control board of radio station WIBB when they cut the demo, all huddled around a single microphone. Hamp Swain started playing it on WBML and Clint Brantley got copies to Duke Records head Don Robey in Houston, the Chess brothers in Chicago, and various other independent labels, while James himself carried it to influential distributor Gwen Kessler at Southland in Atlanta. That was where King representative Ralph Bass first heard it in January of 1956 (Southland distributed King Records, along with all the other independent labels). He wired his boss, Syd Nathan, in Cincinnati, that he had found a new act that he wanted to sign to King's Federal subsidiary. How he actually came to sign the group is a story in itself.

Don Robey, a strong-willed man but no more strong-willed, evidently, than Clint Brantley on his home turf, had made an offer that he felt merited acceptance but that Brantley was able to refuse. Leonard Chess, excited at the prospect of branching out beyond Chicago blues and having just passed on Elvis Presley, had booked a ticket to Atlanta at almost the precise moment that Ralph Bass first heard the cut, but a severe midwinter storm system held up his flight in Chicago while sleet and snow fell in the South. Ralph Bass, however, was not to be deterred. Already in Atlanta, just a few hours' drive from Macon, he was not going to let the weather, or any other force of nature, stop him from beating Leonard Chess to the punch. "I drove down to Macon with a disc jockey named Joe Howard in a pouring rainstorm," recalled Bass, a flamboyant man with a patter of hip jive, in interviews with writers Michael Lydon and Arnold Shaw. "It was pouring like crazy, and we went looking for him, didn't know where to find him. We went to a radio station, and somebody told us that a man named Clint Brantley who owned a club in Macon could help us. Since Macon was such a Jim Crow town, I was told to meet Brantley by parking my car in front of a barbershop that was right across the street from the railroad station, and when the venetian blinds went up and down, to come on in. Brantley said, 'Yeah, I got a contract from Leonard Chess in my hand, I was waiting for Leonard Chess.' Well, Leonard Chess . . . was grounded. [So] I gave the cat $200 and said, 'Do you want to sign right now?' He says, 'You got a deal. Call the whole group in to sign the papers.' I [didn't] know James Brown from a hole in the ground, and I went to the club that night and saw him do his show, crawling on his stomach and saying 'Please, please, please'—he must have said *please* for about ten minutes."

The group was signed on January 23, 1956, and went into the studio in Cincinnati on February 4 over the fierce objections of Syd Nathan, who, says Bass, thought the dub was "a piece of shit." Nathan in fact fired Bass over the issue, not an uncommon occurrence, evidently, between the two of them and certainly typical of the way that Nathan did business. "He said that I was out of my mind to bring Brown from Macon to Cincinnati—and pay his fare. He says, 'Man, this man sounds like he's stoned on the record, all he's saying is one word.' " Nonetheless the record hit the charts in April, just two months after Ray Charles's "Drown in My Own Tears," reaching #6 on the r&b lists and eventually, after years of slow but steady sales, achieving gold record certification. Though early pressings of the record credited the song to the Famous Flames, and it was the group, not the individual, that Ralph Bass had signed, it soon became evident that a single man was in charge, and billing was appropriately changed. From now on it was James Brown and the Famous Flames, on record and in person, and "that Bobby Byrd group" was relegated to memory, and second billing, exclusively.

Oddly enough, King Records was unable to capitalize on James's recording success, though it might have seemed as if the label was already in possession of the hit formula. Founded in 1945 by Nathan, a veteran of the furniture business, King had almost from the beginning pursued twin paths, in country and western and rhythm and blues, and, long before the term "rock 'n' roll" came into currency, was implementing its own musically integrationist policies. Some of its biggest successes on the "race" charts were hillbilly tunes performed by r&b artists (Wynonie Harris's "Bloodshot Eyes" is a case in point), and Nathan was just as quick to impose r&b sensibilities on his hillbillies (the Delmore Brothers' "Blues, Stay Away From Me," a high point in the "hillbilly boogie" craze, derived from Nathan's telling Alton and Rabon Delmore that he wanted a "hillbilly 'Hucklebuck' " and then assigning his black a&r director, Henry Glover, a veteran of the great Lucky Millinder band, to do the arrangement). Nathan, a crude, driving man who was never known for his financial generosity or for his sensitivities, was one of those recording pioneers who in Jerry Wexler's terms "got the job done"; he was producer by default on all his sessions, because he was the man who paid the bills, and his idea for James Brown, seemingly, was to place him squarely in the mainstream of r&b, where Hank Ballard and the Midnighters, Little Willie John, the "5" Royales, and

Hank Ballard and Syd Nathan. (Michael Ochs Archives)

Billy Ward and the Dominoes had already enjoyed great success on King. Perhaps this was James's idea as well. The result in any case, after a uniquely idiosyncratic debut, was a somewhat confused series of derivative releases, jump blues, triplet-laden ballads, yelping Little Richard imitations—and poor sales.

For James Brown it was all an education. He continued touring. He continued developing his live act, the same act that Ralph Bass had first witnessed with Clint Brantley in Milledgeville, Georgia, with some refinements added. When Little Richard quit rock 'n' roll to enter the ministry in the fall of 1957, Brown fulfilled Richard's bookings once again—this time under his own name—while picking up the remnants of Richard's band, the Upsetters, and signing on his vocal group, the Dominions, as a new set of Flames. Phil and Alan Walden, in high school and junior high school respectively at the time, recall seeing James driving around Macon in his battered station wagon advertising the location of his next dance, and Zenas Sears remembers him coming into Atlanta "endlessly. He always had a tight show, he always had a tight band, but of course James was a tremendous ego problem. Always. I remember one time we did a show up in Newark—I remember very well, because everybody up there thought I was black without exception. And, you know, there was great applause when I was introduced, and then when I came out on stage and went to the microphone, the applause shut off like a knife. The silence was terrifying. Well, Chuck Willis and James Brown came out and said I was a nice guy but then immediately went backstage and started a fight about who was gonna be last. Everybody had to be last. Ray Charles was on this show, he just had one little old hit, nothing that big. And I said, 'Roy Hamilton's got to be last. He's number one, and he's a New Jersey boy.' But James just had to be, and finally we put him last before the intermission, second best spot, and he jumped off the balcony to cap his act, figuring that would really kill them. Damn near killed himself. That's when I first knew him as an egomaniac—and we're friends to this day!"

"The first time I met James Brown was in 1956," said Joe Tex, a King labelmate at the time and one of the few showmen whose influence Brown has ever acknowledged (Tex had developed a trick routine with the microphone which James adopted for his act as well as exhibiting the kind of fancy footwork that would later earn James accolades and was an outgrowth, in both cases, of dancing in the streets as a child to earn nickels and dimes). "I remember the date, because I had been doing his song 'Please, Please, Please' since it first came out and I heard it and liked it myself. I was appearing on a show with him at the City Auditorium in Macon, and I remember I pulled up in front of the theater and he came up and introduced himself, told me who he was, said that he and I was gonna have a battle that night, battle of the blues. I said, 'Yeah?' He says, 'Yeah. Draw the people.' And he wanted me to go 'round with him to the local radio station to do an interview. So we got on the air and talked it up and this sort of thing, and that night at the show I went on first and did my thing. I had been to Macon in a small club a couple of times prior to that, and the people had seen me do my 'Please, Please, Please,' and they was yelling for me to do it, and I said, 'No, I can't sing it, 'cause the man who made the record is on the show tonight, you know.' They said, 'You sing it, you sing it, we want to hear you sing it.' So I went ahead and did a little bit of it, but, you know, his band was backing me up, and even though they wanted to play right for me, they were still working for James Brown and they knew how he was. When he came on, he must have had ten different suits, and every ten or fifteen minutes he'd leave the stage and change clothes, and when he'd come back on, the band would still be working and the Flames would be dancing or harmonizing and he be back there changing, just trying to generate some action, get some more of the people. I never did go in for that stuff."

"James told me once," said the Apollo Theatre's Scoey Mitchell to writer Ted Fox, "he knew he'd never be a class act, but he was going to be the biggest rock-and-roller they ever had. And he was."

"He's not gonna come out there and be cool," echoed childhood friend Leon Austin in an interview with Gerri Hirshey. "And he ain't gonna have on this pretty suit that ain't gonna get dusty. He gonna *wallow*. He gonna just be

A very young Joe Tex. (Ed Salamon/Michael Ochs Archives)

dancin', splittin', messin' up his knees. Or he may scream so hard he can't sing the next night, but he ain't gonna worry about that."

There is no doubt that his live appearances were gaining him a considerable following. It was a personal following, though, that attended the shows on the basis of James's reputation as a performer, not his records, and even with constant bookings it was difficult to support a group. The Flames disbanded in discouragement in April of 1957, and James started going out as a single for a while. Meanwhile his continued lack of record sales was causing Syd Nathan, no great believer in the first place, to lose what faith he had. Nathan in fact was on the verge of cutting him loose when James came up with a song while playing the famous Palms of Hallandale in Florida, and he and Clint Brantley put up their own money and cut a dub to try to convince Nathan to let his one-shot star back in the studio. The song was "Try Me," a classic gospel-edged plea, somewhat reminiscent of "Please, Please, Please" both in its form (traditional) and in its sentiment (an odd combination of mental toughness and emotional vulnerability). It remained subject to the influence of doo-wop, but with its continued juxtaposition of James's scarred tenor and the smoothly hypnotic vocal backdrop

Early publicity shot. (Michael Ochs Archives)

of the Famous Flames it was doo-wop gone strangely awry. On September 18, 1958, James went back in the studio after an absence of nearly a year and cut four sides under the nominal supervision of King a&r man Andy Gibson. By December "Try Me" had made #1 r&b and even reached Top 50 pop. On the strength of this hit James made his New York debut at the Apollo, where he appeared down on a bill starring Little Willie John and the vaudeville team of Butterbeans and Susie. After New York he was booked into the Howard, the Royal, the Uptown in Philadelphia—he had finally broken out of the small time, it seemed, and was playing the long dreamt-of r&b circuit. At the Uptown he came face-to-face with sobering reality, as he appeared on a bill that featured a group called the Vibrations, who had a particularly polished stage act. "Man, they ate us alive," recalled Famous Flame Bobby Byrd, who had rejoined James in the wake of the record's success. "That was the first time we'd really been beaten at our own game; they really had their act together. After the shows in the South, that taught us all a lesson."

The lesson was further reinforced by the booking agent with whom he had re-signed just prior to the Apollo date. James had met Ben Bart originally through

Hank Ballard and done some gigs for him on the strength of "Please, Please, Please," but it wasn't until "Try Me" hit that Bart, president of Universal Attractions, one of the leading r&b booking agencies in the country, was really able to do something for him. Bart, a long-time veteran of the business who had handled big stars like Dinah Washington and Billy Eckstine while still at the Gale Agency, was one of a breed of manager-agents (Jimmy Evans was another) who controlled the r&b business in much the same way that a small clique of powerful men controlled boxing during this period. Ben Bart, according to Zenas Sears, was the making of James Brown, just as Jimmy Evans would be the making of Wilson Pickett. "Ben Bart invented James Brown, really. He was a mentor in the truest sense of the word, taught James discipline off stage as well as on, took care of all the money, just basically created him. He made James." Or conversely, as James Brown mused to Cliff White in speaking of that time, "I began to hit something of a different feel. The thing that made that was my eyes started opening. As long as I lived down South, I would have cut the other kind of songs, but the minute I started seeing different things and my brain started to intercept new ideas and new thoughts, I became a big city thinker."

The songs that he cut over the next eighteen months may have been different, but they were not so different as to announce the arrival of a revolutionary new musical force, and once again there was an interval of well over a year before James regained a spot in the Top 10 with a reworking of a 1957 "5" Royales hit. In the meantime, though, like Ray Charles just a few years earlier, James Brown had acquired his own band, his own roadshow, and an unshakable sense of his own identity which would never leave him, whatever further permutations of style his career might witness. The band he acquired in Burlington, North Carolina, where they were working for sax player J. C. Davis, who now became a staple—along with several ex-Upsetters—in the reconstituted James Brown sound. The band was also a key element in allowing James to further develop his own sense of showmanship and theatrics, to dramatize his determination to wear out his audience as well as himself and "give people more than what they came for—make them tired, 'cause *that's* what they came for." It also permitted him, as Cliff White points out, to play any venue that offered him a forum (no longer was James Brown dependent on finding local groups who could meet his exacting standards) and to continue to develop his own following with or without record success.

"His ghetto theater gigs," writes White, "started to give him a strong following in the Northern cities with the newest generation of Southern black migrants . . . but his main stomping ground was still the South. And it was in the Southern rural dance halls, armories, and barren arenas where a booking meant providing a whole evening's entertainment that the legendary James Brown Revue was gradually honed to perfection. It was also on the barnstorming tours of the South that Ben Bart was best able to co-promote the gigs with

The James Brown Show, with Famous Flames Johnny Terry, Bobby Byrd, and Bobby Bennett up front. (Michael Ochs Archives)

the local DJs, cutting them in on a percentage of the gate receipts, thereby not only insuring that each gig was well publicized locally but, more important in the long run, establishing a network of sympathetic jocks who could be relied upon to play any new James Brown release. . . ."

In 1959 Brown produced two desultory instrumentals on the band (credited to James Davis, not James Brown) that didn't go anywhere. Later that year he urged Syd Nathan to record the band once again, but Nathan refused. Unfazed, James took the band to King's (and Atlantic's and every other r&b independent's) Miami distributor, Henry Stone, who had played a vital role from the beginning in encouraging his career, and Stone released a single on his own Dade label under the name of Nat Kendrick (James's drummer) and the Swans. "Do the Mashed Potatoes," a staple of James's live act and the occasion for him to show off his increasingly flashy dancing prowess, went to #8 r&b, and that was probably the last time Syd Nathan passed on a James Brown suggestion for the next couple of years.

Meanwhile James had picked up another wrinkle, this time from the realm of professional wrestling, to cap his stage act. "Please, Please, Please" always came at the climax of the show, as it had from the beginning of his career. "I used to sing 'Please, Please, Please' for about thirty-five or forty minutes [sometimes], so [one time] I went off and they threw a towel around me because I was singing so hard and sweating so much. And I came back with the towel around me and I started singing again, and I got real happy—you know, the spirit came up—and I stomped my foot and I threw the towel off and I sang until they took me off again. Then I came back and did it again. And I thought, well, Gorgeous George had a great act as a wrestler with his capes, so I think I'll make me some beautiful capes and I'll use the same thing."

That is what he did, and it became the trademark of his act, a ritual drama of loss and redemption in which a weary James Brown, assailed with the cares, worries, and woes of the world, collapsed under the weight of his burdens, then somehow found the strength to go on. Everywhere he went it created pandemonium, and at a time when he was finally beginning to get consistent airplay (every record he released from 1960 on made the charts at one position or another over the next seventeen years), it seemed as if the hard work he had put in for the last four years was really starting to pay off. In mid-1960 King put out the next-to-last James Brown release on its Federal subsidiary (after that he was strictly on King). It was a two-sided hit, whose B side, "You've Got the Power," a typically slow and swooping cry of the heart, possessed the kind of raw feeling with which he would once have "wrecked" a Toccoa church. "You've Got the Power" went to #14 r&b, but it was "Think," the radical reworking of the old "5" Royales' hit, that both exploded on the charts and established the new James Brown voice at one and the same time. Sung rapid-fire with the kind of sharp prompting from the Famous Flames that was the aural equivalent of their precision steps, "Think" embodied an approach different from any in the past, with not only the song but the structure of the song turned inside out and a classic shuffle blues rhythmically and melodically transformed. In one sense, certainly, it was a tribute to the "5" Royales, whom James had long admired, but it was in a deeper sense (in Cliff White's summary) "from a different plane of consciousness to the '5' Royales and their contemporaries: suddenly '50s r&b was yesterday, and James Brown was tomorrow."

The final step in this transformation from just another journeyman singer into a force to be reckoned with on its own terms came two years later with Brown's headline booking into the Apollo Theatre for an entire week. By now not only had his band evolved through personnel changes and close discipline (band members were fined for lateness, sloppiness, imprecise time steps, and bad notes, and all forms of stimulants during working hours were expressly forbidden) into a precision unit; the whole revue was carefully calculated, through stretches of ennui as well as unsynchronized flashes of excitement, to showcase the dynamic explosiveness of James Brown.

By now, too, his legend preceded him everywhere he went. Where others were content with the easy coin of royalty (Count, Duke, Bishop, King), James Brown gloried in his very *commonness* ("He made the ugly man *somebody*," childhood friend Leon Austin told reporter Gerri Hirshey, speaking specifically of the racial implications of this "darker person's" success), and his chief title, "the Hardest Working Man in Show Business," was based on a quality accessible even to the humblest member of his audience. For the crowds that snaked around the block waiting to purchase tickets to his show at the Apollo he might send

With personal MC Danny Ray. (Don Paulsen/ Michael Ochs Archives)

out cups of soup and coffee because he recognized that for his audience as well as for himself James Brown's success was a matter of faith and commitment; "it meant a lot to me that people were prepared to wait for hours to see my show."

"In an average month," his publicity stated, referring to a period of approximately twenty-eight bookings with two or three days off in between, "he will give away some 5000 autographed photos and 1000 pairs of cuff links, will wear 120 freshly laundered shirts and more than 80 pairs of shoes, will change his performing costume 150 times, and will perform over 80 hours on the stage—singing, dancing, and also playing at least 960 songs on one or more of eight instruments. He is, as well, songwriter, arranger, choreographer, and designer of clothes for himself and his entire cast [which in 1962 consisted of a troupe of at least two dozen]." Clearly James took his responsibilities as an entertainer seriously.

Just as clearly Brown and Ben Bart were convinced that now was the time to cash in on both the legend and the excitement of James's in-person performances. What could be more logical than a live recording along the lines of Ray Charles's pathbreaking 1959 Atlanta date (*Ray Charles in Person*)? Not surprisingly, perhaps, Syd Nathan didn't see it that way. He was in the *singles* business; r&b didn't sell albums, and if it did, the albums were more often than not haphazard collections of *singles*. Of James Brown's seven albums to date none had sold more than 5000–10,000 copies, and Nathan, a notoriously tightfisted man who had turned down the rights to "Tennessee Waltz," ultimately one of country music's most valuable copyrights, because its composers wanted fifty dollars for the song ("There ain't no song in the world worth fifty dollars"), flat out refused to advance any money for a live recording. Brown and Bart remained undeterred. Not for the first time James put up his own money to demonstrate faith in himself and his judgment ("If nobody else love him, he love him," Leon Austin has said); he had pulled himself up by his bootstraps when he possessed no boots, and he wasn't going to let Syd Nathan's obstinacy stop him now. He and Bart came up with nearly $6000 and recorded the midnight show at the Apollo on Wednesday, October 24, 1962. The result was a commercial and artistic turning point in the history of James Brown and Southern soul music.

Commercially the evidence was overwhelming. *Live at the Apollo* first entered the pop album charts on June 29, 1963, several months after it was released. It remained there for over fourteen months, reaching #2 at one point and ending up at #32 for the year, an almost unprecedented accomplishment for a pure r&b record (and this was unquestionably pure r&b). It also established James Brown once and for all not only as the premier r&b box-office attraction of his time but as an artist with untapped potential for crossover success, even without adulterating what he had to offer (this was at a time when Ray Charles, remember, had made his mark with string-laden adaptations of country and western standards). Pittsburgh native Alan Leeds, who later went to work for Brown, describes himself as a white college student in Richmond, Virginia, discovering JB at that time. "The impact of the Apollo LP was amazing. Due to listener requests [black radio station] WANT [set] aside half an hour every evening at 5 P.M. to play the entire LP, and the same sort of thing was happening on black stations all over. . . . It seemed like you could tune in at the same time every day for weeks on end to hear a 'live' James Brown show. It took some time for sales to start building, but gradually more and more young blacks started buying it—for many it might have been the first LP they'd ever bought in their lives, it was one of those hip things that everybody had to have. At the same time, without any airplay on most pop stations, the word started to spread to white buyers about this unbelievable album by someone who most of them had barely heard of. When the whites started buying it as well, it really started to take off."

Aesthetically the impact of this raw slice of life was just as devastating. I don't think it would be overstating the case to compare it to the advent of Italian neo-realism in cinema, when a rediscovery of the poetry of the everyday demanded a new vocabulary, and a new aesthetic, to replace the old. James Brown's "new vocabulary," like the Italian film directors' based on a fresh appreciation of the beauty of the commonplace, took the rhythm and blues world by storm. All of a sudden Ray Charles's presentation appeared formal and old hat, classical if you will, with its orchestra of reading musicians and big-band book. James Brown's *Live at the Apollo,* by contrast, played off all the fiery grittiness of its surroundings, the fiercely narrowed focus and casual improvisation of live performance, the magical incantation and exhortatory atmosphere of its churchlike setting. Miraculously it's all there on record. Not just the accoutrements—the obligatory introduction ("So now, ladies and gentlemen, it's startime, are you ready for startime?") and ritual conclusion, the familiar array of hits and familiar frenzied response—but the very *tension,* the indefinable edge that so rarely translates onto wax. One reason that it works here (though it never worked quite as well in the three other live albums subsequently recorded by Brown in his heyday) is James's sense of how to pace a show, the very rise and fall of the action, and the singer's use of aurally dramatic technique as he moans, groans, screams, and whispers, draws back from the mike only to return with explosive impact, uses every trick in the book not just to coax a response from his Apollo audience but to create a portrait of himself that achieves verisimilitude, like the best fiction, by acknowledging the necessity of dramatic artifice. Among the most surprising facets of *Live at the Apollo*—and I think this should stand as irrefutable testimony to the intentional artistry of James Brown—are those very moments when he teases the audience into imagining, and provoking, what will happen next.

These moments occur throughout the album, but most dramatically on the record's centerpiece, its indisputable masterpiece, the epochal "Lost Someone." Here, in a single, multilayered track that cuts across the two sides of the album (it fades out at the end of Side I), you have embodied the whole history of soul music, the teaching, the preaching, the endless assortment of gospel effects, above all the groove that was at the music's core. "Don't go to strangers," James pleads in his abrasively vulnerable fashion. "Come on home to me. . . . Gee whiz I love you. . . . I'm so weak. . . ." Over and over he repeats the simple phrases, insists "I'll love you tomorrow" until the music is rocking with a steady pulse, until the music grabs you in the pit of the stomach and James knows he's got you. Then he works the audience as he works the song, teasing, tantalizing, drawing closer, dancing away, until finally at the end of Side I that voice breaks

Backstage at the Apollo, 1964. (Don Paulsen/Michael Ochs Archives)

through the crowd noise and dissipates the tension as it calls out, "James, you're an asshole." "I believe someone out there loves someone," declares James with cruel disingenuousness. "Yeah, you," replies a girl's voice with unabashed fervor. "I feel so good I want to scream," says James, testing the limits yet again. "Scream!" cries a voice. And the record listener responds, too, we are drawn in by the same tricks, so transparent in the daylight but put across with the same unabashed fervor with which the girl in the audience offers up her love.

It's a bravura performance, unquestionably, and may represent the most apocalyptic nongospel album ever recorded. As great as was its impact on its audience, though, it seems to have had at least an equal effect on the artist himself. For better or for worse, for richer or for poorer (the former condition applied in each case for quite some time), James Brown was henceforth wedded to his own vision and his own determination, irrespective of the world's view. Just two months after recording *Live at the Apollo*, Brown reversed direction once again and went into the studio to record the old Russ Columbo–Perry Como–Billy Eckstine standard "Prisoner of Love" with eleven strings and nine syrupy voices. This went to #18 on the pop charts, James Brown's first Top 20 pop hit and the first time a single that he had recorded crossed over, aboveground, to any appreciable degree. At the same time he and Bart formed their own song publishing company, Jim Jam Music, as well as a label, Try Me, which was to be distributed by King, and in 1963 released singles by Johnny and Bill (Johnny Terry, Brown's old classmate from the Juvenile Training Institute in Rome, and Bill Hollings, another veteran of the James Brown Revue), Tammi Montgomery (later to be better known as Tammi Terrell), and the Poets, a rather fanciful name for James's hard-hitting band, heard here in a surprisingly restrained and jazzy context. Perhaps not surprisingly the label didn't get the kind of support from King that James felt it deserved, and after recording another live album at Baltimore's Royal Theater in the fall of 1963 (it included one of his last, and best, extended efforts in the gospel vein, "Oh Baby Don't You Weep," ironically enough a studio recording with dubbed-on crowd response) James Brown once again revealed his unquenchable thirst for freedom: he walked out on King. He did this while still under contract to Syd Nathan and seemingly without much regard for legal consequences. Declaring himself a free man by reason of a technicality, he signed with Smash Records (a division of Mercury) in Chicago.

The precise business dealings that took place at this juncture are still somewhat shrouded in mystery, but in general terms it seems to have been a somewhat straightforward struggle for power and control of a career that in 1963 was showing a road gross of $450,000, with probably half again as much from records. From King's point of view this degree of success was undoubtedly greater than anyone had ever dreamt possible: James Brown was selling more records than any King artist in history, was the #1 r&b singer in the country in a disc jockeys' poll, and occupied an unequaled position in the black community which would probably guarantee sales for years to come. For James Brown, however, who readily ranks himself with the three other B's and one M (Bach, Beethoven, Brahms, and Mantovani) and for whom there is no limit either to his ambition or self-belief ("My source is undying dedication," he has said over and over again. "Sometimes I look back on my life and wonder just how one man could achieve all I've done"), such accomplishments represented no more than a tiny fraction of what he was beginning to see as his destiny; $450,000 represented no more than a pittance compared with what was his due.

Without hesitation he and Bart plunged ahead on their new deal, releasing three James Brown productions on other artists before James cut a session himself in early 1964 under the umbrella of the newly formed Fair Deal Production Company. His first Smash single, a big-band version of Louis Jordan's classic "Caldonia," was released at the end of March; his second was another uncharacteristic retrospective, the Guitar Slim blues on which Ray Charles had originally played piano, "The Things That I Used to Do," and like its predecessor failed to sell. By now King had filed suit to prevent their contracted artist from making any further recordings for another company, but before an injunction was granted in October, James Brown had had what may have been his biggest selling—and was certainly his most influential—hit to date, the self-referential "Out of Sight."

"Out of Sight," with its sharp catchphrase, stuttering bass lead, stabbing horns, and overwhelming rhythmic drive, was the logical extension of 1960's "Think" and the heavy emphasis on dance and movement in James's live act. Departing not only from the gospel roots of much of James's earlier work, it left behind some of the more commonly accepted melodic conventions of western music as well, while still hewing to a basic blues structure. Not so ironically the B side of the single, "Maybe the Last Time," served almost as James's farewell to his past. Along with "Oh Baby Don't You Weep" it is one of the most moving of James's excursions into a pure gospel style, with the Famous Flames making their final featured appearance in the recording studio and James wailing over and over again that it may indeed be the last time until finally he comes to a frenzied climax. Listen to this song—and to "Lost Someone" and "Oh Baby Don't You Weep"—if you want to hear a peroration of all that James Brown and Southern soul music had stood for to date. Flip the record over, though, if you want to hear the future.

The future did not arrive altogether unannounced, in any case. Like so many revolutions, this one was preceded not only by vague whispers and forebodings (shouts and screams as well) but by bold declarations by its principal architect several years in advance of its actual arrival. In 1962 James Brown had recorded two songs, one on himself ("I Don't Care") and one on female vocalist Yvonne Fair ("I Found You"), which presaged much of the new direction and were directly translated into two of the hits ("Cold Sweat" and "I Got You") that would immediately follow "Out of Sight." What was different about the earlier versions—and what was different about James Brown from this point on —was the rhythm. In the prototypes—and in a 1960 number like "Tell Me What You Gonna Do" (which also foreshadowed "Cold Sweat")—clearly the model was the smooth big-band sound of Louis Jordan, Lucky Millinder, and Buddy Johnson, a sound with which James Brown and an entire generation had grown up. Melody and mellowness were prime virtues here, yoked to rhythmic drive, and while James had long ago introduced the rough abrasiveness of his own voice as a new element in the equation, the first two Smash singles and album recalled both style and songs of this earlier era.

With "Out of Sight" all this changed. All the grunts, groans, screams, clicks, and screeches that had been lurking in the background, the daringly modal approach to melody (soon there would be virtually no chord changes in a James Brown song, with forward motion dependent entirely on rhythm), were—without anyone's fully realizing it in 1965—intimations of African roots, declarations of black pride that would very soon earn James Brown plaudits from cultural nationalists and the musical avant-garde alike. "If there is any black man who symbolizes the vast differences between black and white cultural and aesthetic values," wrote the young black historian, David Levering Lewis, in 1968, "Soul Brother No. 1 (along with Ray Charles) is that man." Here is musicologist Robert Palmer with a more formal description of the transformation that was taking place.

"The rhythmic elements *became* the song. There were few chord changes, or none at all, but there were plenty of trick rhythmic interludes and suspensions. . . . Brown and his musicians began to treat every instrument and voice in the group as if it were a drum. The horns played single-note bursts that were often sprung against the downbeats. The bass lines were broken up into choppy two- or three-note patterns, a procedure common in Latin music since the Forties but unusual in r&b. Brown's rhythm guitarist choked his guitar strings against the instrument's neck so hard that his playing began to sound like a jagged tin can being scraped with a pocket knife. Only occasionally were the horns, organ or backing vocalists allowed to provide a harmonic continuum by holding a chord."

The success of "Out of Sight" may have established James Brown's artistic direction, but it still didn't resolve his business dilemma. In October, King won its lawsuit to prevent any further vocal releases on the Smash label. For most artists (and their managers) this would have been the end of the line; with legal remedies exhausted and no other market for their product, what alternative could there be except to return to the fold? James and Ben Bart fought on. They sat back and waited the record label out. From July 1964 until the following July there was no new record product from the number-one rhythm and blues artist in the world. Instead King desperately kept repackaging old records, and James stayed on the road. In the meantime he received national exposure via the *T.A.M.I. Show,* a filmed concert presentation in which he stole the show from the Beach Boys, the Rolling Stones, Marvin Gaye, Chuck Berry, and the Supremes; the pop TV showcase, *Shindig;* the Frankie Avalon-Dwayne Hickman movie vehicle, *Ski Party;* and of course the 335 nights a year he spent on the road.

Syd Nathan was finally the one to give in. When James Brown returned to King in the spring of 1965, it was on his own terms, with almost every concession he had been seeking: his own publishing, a vastly improved royalty rate; a minimum of 25,000 singles and a comparable number of LPs in "free

Mr. Dynamite. (Charles Stewart)

goods" to be distributed as he saw fit; and continued—and expanded—artistic control. In May of 1965 he delivered the completed tape of his new single for mastering to King. It had been a year and a half since he last entered the King studio in Cincinnati. The record was entitled "Papa's Got a Brand New Bag."

"Papa's Got a Brand New Bag" was the first Top 10 hit of James Brown's career. Like "Out of Sight," it declared the new age both in its lyrics and in its rhythms, opening with an earthshaking chord from the horns and driven (just like "Out of Sight") by a burbling bass line that served as underpinning for the jangling guitar and horn riffs that provided rhythmic punctuation. "I Got You (I Feel Good)," the space-age remake of 1962's comparatively staid "I Found You," and the hit of the movie *Ski Party,* was third in line, taking the new stutter-step accompaniment to even greater heights (to fully appreciate James's music of this period, one must imagine his one-legged skate to the music) and reaching #3 on the pop charts in the fall of 1965. On the basis of all this newfound exposure and success James Brown was fast becoming an international phenomenon. Mick Jagger called him the best there was, and Rolling Stones bass player Bill Wyman, ordinarily the most phlegmatic of individuals, declared, "He does the most incredible dancing, like Mick, only about twenty times faster. . . . You could put Jerry Lee Lewis, Little Richard, Chuck Berry, and Bo Diddley on one side of the stage, and James Brown on the other, and you wouldn't even notice the others were up there!"

"Ain't That a Groove," "Money Won't Change You," "Bring It Up," "Let Yourself Go," "Cold Sweat" (the titles alone betray the blunt turn that James Brown's music was taking)—all were substantial pop hits in the new rhythm mode, with "Cold Sweat" going to #7 in the summer of 1967. Each was progressively looser in structure, closer to the musical and emotional bone, freer in its dispensation of drive, pent-up feeling, and crackling energy, more stridently and undeniably itself. "Cold Sweat," wrote Cliff White, was almost completely "divorced from other forms of popular music"; by the time that "(When You Touch Me) I Can't Stand Myself" and "There Was a Time" came out as a double-sided hit in the winter of '67–'68, lyrics had reduced themselves to free association, melody had virtually disappeared, the band (now under the direction of Pee Wee Ellis) featured two, and sometimes three, drummers in live performance to match its leader's ever-more-propulsive drive, and James's voice was strained to the breaking point—past it, in fact, as sometime during this period he was forced to abandon his characteristic scream for a succession of shrieks, whinnies, grunts, and emphatic *Good God!*s, with normal speech reduced to a husky whisper that could only serve as a scarred warning to other singers. Described in this fashion, James's charm may be difficult to imagine, but his impact is not. My friend Joe McEwen wrote about growing up listening to James Brown while other kids were listening to the Beatles. "These songs weren't something we sat around and analyzed . . . they were just something that was, something Out There that didn't subscribe to the normal order of things. . . . The Real Thing was James Brown." In the words of *Village Voice* reporter Thulani Davis, also writing of growing up but growing up black and female, "There was only one James. . . . James Brown made me want to be old enough to go to the Apollo. JB was why clothes were in the cleaners so often. Proof that you could leave the church and still be saved every once in a while. . . . He made the word 'bewildered' sound sexy and saying 'please' sound hip. JB! JB was proof that black people were different. Rhythmically and tonally blacks had to be from somewhere else. Proof that Africa was really over there for those of us who had never seen it—it was in that voice. . . . James was big and we thought he was forever, but also unaccountable like Nixon but still familiar—somebody you could call 'outathey name.' James."

He became both symbol and leader, in his own words a "model man." This carried with it its own privileges and responsibilities. As James has said in recent

"Don't Be a Drop Out": with Vice-President Humphrey. (Michael Ochs Archives)

interviews, "Many people just believe that I can't get sick, or they refuse to accept the fact that my body gets tired like everyone else. Well, I do sometimes, but there are so many people who depend on me for inspiration and support that if I wanted to get sick or slow down . . . I just can't. I just can't afford to slow down. . . . I know I'm an idol. It's not what I see myself as, it's what the public sees me as." In the late '60s politicians sought his endorsement, and his pronouncements on poverty and race were widely quoted. In 1968 and 1969 he became the first black entertainer to own not one but three radio stations (including Augusta's WRDW, on whose steps he had once shined shoes), and when he changed hairstyles from his prized process to a natural, it became the occasion for editorial comment. "The King's been a slave for years," declared *Soul* magazine in 1968. "To what? James Brown's been putting up with the painful and time-consuming process hair do for as long as anyone can remember . . . until last month, that is. Now the King's got a natural. Everyone, including the Black Panthers and SNCC, think it's fine, just fine. . . ."

Whatever he did became an occasion for comment. After a brief period in which he declared himself not just for equal opportunity but for revolution (this was quickly modified), he would become the image of the Successful Negro, a proud exemplar and champion of Black Capitalism with a fleet of cars, a $713,000 black Lear jet ("Now I got a brand-new jet when I need to move/ A soul brother made it/ Now ain't that a groove?"), and a Victorian-styled castle in Queens, complete with moat, drawbridge, and a black Santa Claus on the lawn. In succeeding years he would be dubbed the Godfather of Soul, the Grand Minister of Funk, and the Minister of the New New Super Heavy Funk, and he would go on having hits well into the '70s; after standing beside Hubert Humphrey in the War on Poverty he would support Richard Nixon and Ronald Reagan in turn, like Muhammad Ali retire and then return to the ring, see his business empire fail and his investments go sour, and become in the eyes of some a sad parody of himself. When his chief antagonist and booster, Syd Nathan, died in March 1968, he acquired Nathan's marble-top desk and installed a gold plaque that read: "I REMEMBER THE MAN SYD NATHAN." Since the death of his partner, Ben Bart, five months later, he has never been able to find anyone else in whom he could bring himself to place his full trust, and the result has been a trail of erratic career moves and missed opportunities.

As for James himself, his music and his personality have continued to pull him through. His bands in the late '60s and early '70s were as dynamic and explosive as any of the earlier models, showcasing such architects of funk as Maceo Parker ("Maceo!" would come James's short, barking command for a solo), Fred Wesley, and George Clinton cohort Bootsy Collins. The music retained its drive, and even after James came back from a brief self-imposed exile in 1980, he continued to assemble creditable units (James's band has been as much of a training ground for soul as Miles Davis's for jazz or Muddy Waters's for the blues). In the '80s he even regained an element of his old popularity, though this time it was with a white audience almost exclusively and came about largely through the exposure he was afforded in vehicles like the movie *The Blues Brothers.* At the same time there was an element of pathos in his reemergence, as delusions of grandeur sometimes overtook the real thing and political engagement frequently gave way to the self-righteous pronouncements of the self-made man ("If you don't have the white man in your business, you're going to blow it," said James. "It's insane for a man of his talent to lower himself to that line of bullshit," commented fellow soul singer Jerry Butler). "I want to be 5000 percent right in what I do," James has declared over and over again in interviews. "I *got* to be." Musicians and whole bands have left him over his peremptory ways, but Brown has only occasionally wavered in his public facade ("a shield of ruthless steel to brush aside scorn, prejudice, and any would-be competitors," Cliff White has called it). Once he broke down, it is said, when Syd Nathan died, and once when his nineteen-year-old son, Teddy, was killed in a car crash. "They had Mr. Brown up there talking and whatnot with the preacher," longtime associate Henry Stallings told writer Gerri Hirshey, "but suddenly he rushed outside. . . . But I tell you what, the next day—right back on the job. . . . I always refer to him as a sergeant or something, a man who can't show weakness. . . . I know he's a human being and he feels things, but he never shows it."

"It is precisely the unwavering egocentricity of the man that gives his music its unique flavor," Cliff White has written. "If there are flaws, who's the loser? Perhaps only Brown himself, bound to the isolation of self-styled omnipotence. 'You know,' he reflected hesitantly, 'I wish I wasn't, er, dynamic or legendary . . . star . . . with so much. I think I'd like to be just a little less fortunate.' Then, smiling almost embarrassedly at his lapse, he quickly added, 'Sounds bad, don't it?' "

▶8▶

The Soul Clan

T
HIS IS WHERE I CAME IN—WITH THE PRE-
revolutionary rise and legend of James Brown. Not that I had any idea
about Muscle Shoals or Macon or even James at the time. Stax was just
a name on a record label to me, and while the red-and-black Atlantic logo
may have been just as hallowed in my mind as it was in Jim Stewart's or Rick
Hall's, my only connection to soul music in 1964–1965 was as a star-struck,
uninformed, but dedicated fan. I want to describe my introduction to soul music
a little bit, though, not because it is significant in itself but because it is to some
degree emblematic. And because if what I have written so far suggests a logical,
or reasoned, historical progression, it is important to emphasize that the pattern
which linked such structural anarchists as Dan Penn and Chips Moman, such
sui generis performers as Solomon Burke and James Brown, was decidedly less
discernible at the time.

The first soul show I went to see came to town in June of 1964 and was
booked into the long-since-demolished Donnelly Theater on the edge of Roxbury, Boston's black community. Sam Cooke was still alive, Ray Charles
(whom my friends and I had gone to see at Jordan Hall while still in high school)
was already a legend, and the Summer Shower of Stars had been hyped for
weeks with lung-bursting fervor on WILD, Boston's only all-black radio
station. Headlining the bill was Solomon Burke, whose current hit was "Good-
bye Baby." Garnet Mimms and a virtually unknown Otis Redding got second
billing, while underneath them on the poster were Joe Tex (yet to have his
breakthrough hit), the Tams, and a very sexy Sugar Pie DeSanto. My memories
of the occasion are clear; my recollections of Solomon's apocalyptic message and
Otis's rather blocky presence, as well, of course, as Sugar Pie DeSanto's torrid
dance, remain vivid. The revue was just coming off a Southern tour, I have since
learned, on which James Brown served as coheadliner, and if my image of the
show that I saw is mind-boggling, the fantasy projection of James and Solomon
competing each night on the same stage almost defies imagination. And yet the
reality was at the same time both more prosaic and more exotic.

More prosaic in that this was only one of thirty or forty-five days out on
the road for each of the headliners, all of them crammed on to a single tour
bus (Solomon was very likely the lone exception) which might travel no farther

The Apollo. (Val Wilmer)

than Hartford, Connecticut, for the next night's show or then again might continue on nonstop to Raleigh, North Carolina. I don't think Rufus Thomas or Joe Tex even showed up for that evening's performance, but that, I soon came to realize, was par for the course, and, so far as I can recall, their absence was never even announced from the stage or remarked upon by the cheerful, well-dressed, and enthusiastic audience which seemed to saunter in and out of the theater in waves, with many missing the opening act, some leaving before the closing act was done. It was the *occasion,* I came to understand very quickly, that was of consequence as much as the show itself. There was a spirit of community in that packed theater, encouraged, certainly, by the performers but springing from a common experience, an openly shared perception of reality, that was both palpable and infectious. *New York Times* reporter Clayton Riley has described his childhood memories of the Apollo in a somewhat earlier, more decorous era, how "folks just showed out, as the saying went, came gliding through the Apollo lobby with proud, confident grace, wearing the best clothes and finest manners, women in delicate veils, big hats, men wearing fabulous overcoats and sculptured mustaches, the air around everybody turning into a mixed breeze of perfume and lotion. . . . We could hear from every space in the Apollo that good old rich laughter of recognition. . . . We thought it was magic."

I certainly did, and I wished with every fiber of my being that the recognition could include me, or at least my good intentions, that I, who was so visibly not part of the community, could somehow be absorbed within it. Everyone has their stories of being the lone white face in the crowd, and I don't think mine or anyone else's are particularly significant, but there was clearly a sense—both then and now—of entering into an alien environment, of stepping out of my world into a land uncharted and inviolable. Perhaps this added to the romance of the occasion, perhaps it added to the suspense, knowing that at any moment all this *oneness* could turn on you—but I don't think so. I think I was merely envious and scared; my exclusion was only one more impetus to make me wish I was black and free of all the encumbrances of a bourgeois world, the same duality that Donnie Fritts must have come face to face with in Florence, Alabama, or Mick Jagger in Dartford, England.

The next time I saw Otis Redding, it was a couple of years later, and he was at the height of his fame, but was playing at a club called Louie's Showcase Lounge in Roxbury, which couldn't have seated more than 500 people. In the daylight I'm sure Louie's must have appeared drab enough, little more than a seedy joint stuck on the corner of Northampton and Washington streets in the shadow of the El, but at night it took on the dimensions of an enchanted palace, with its stage set windows of cheap colored glass, its crowded dance floor filled with all manner of the most explosively languid and graceful dancers, and its air of convivial expectation, the easygoing, good-hearted as-

Backstage in Boston, with Jimmy "Early" Byrd. (Courtesy of Joe McEwen)

June 20, 1964.

sumption that everyone was going to have a good time. The MC was Jimmy "Early" Byrd, who was never loath to let on that he might be the cousin of Famous Flame Bobby Byrd and who was then the reigning DJ on WILD (which meant that he broadcast in the afternoon, since WILD went off the air at sunset). The band would strike up an introduction, Byrd, a big good-looking man, would come ditty-bopping on with a grin a mile wide, and it was Showtime, Ladies and Gentlemen, the man who brought you "These Arms of Mine," "That's How Strong My Love Is," "I've Been Loving You Too Long," "Mr. Pitiful" himself—pregnant pause—Otis . . . Redding. . . .

Speedo Simms, Otis's road manager, still remembers Louie's fondly. So do Alan Walden and Otis's brother, Rodgers. I don't know why this should have surprised me, but somehow I think it must have seemed to me that Louie's was an aberration; the memory of the occasion is so invested with significance, so full of consequence that the tawdry surroundings seem in retrospect as if they must have represented an indignity best forgotten. But, of course, they did not. Louie's *was* the r&b world, and Boston, for some inexplicable reason, welcomed the Southern soulsters (Otis, Solomon, Joe Tex, and even James Carr were regular visitors) with a warmth that, I understand from hometown chauvinist Joe McEwen, a more geographically logical city like Philadelphia did not. On the corner a couple of blocks up from Louie's sat Skippy White's Mass. Records: Home of the Blues, a little bandbox of a record store run by a white man named

Fred LeBlanc (Skippy was an invention, White a translation), who, with his own show on WILD and local distribution of many of the independent r&b labels, had his own dreams of empire at the same time that we constructed mythologies about *him*. Probably there was a Skippy White in every city. Very likely every Skippy White had a speaker out on the sidewalk broadcasting the latest sides and inviting passersby to try out the latest, smoothest, slickest steps with all the signifying that public performance entailed. To me and my friends, I know, it was the outpost of a new world to which we eagerly, humbly, and, as anonymously as our skin color would permit, sought entrance.

After that first Summer Shower of Stars I never missed a show. At some point a girl I knew started living with a guy who had something to do with bringing in the revues to the Donnelly, by now the Back Bay, and I got a chance to be an "usher." Not much of an usher, I must confess, since, though the seats were reserved, the idea of approaching a rather large gentleman and telling him he was occupying the wrong space was not within my sense of civic responsibility, and when the balcony fire-escape doors flew open and a bunch of kids came bursting in, I always managed to be occupied in some other part of the building. I was twenty, twenty-one, twenty-two, in love with the blues, writing even then for fledgling magazines like *Crawdaddy!* and the *Boston Phoenix* strictly out of devotion to the music and surprise that anyone else could be interested enough in it to provide a forum for what I had to say. What really startled me, though, was to find that the music was still alive, to discover in soul a contemporary analogue to the blues—with a somewhat different musical base perhaps, but with the same direct message, the same generous outpouring of spirit, the same warmth, unpredictability, and prizing of naked truth.

This may well have been a somewhat romantic distortion of reality, and it may also have been what closed off the world of Motown to me. Perhaps I simply rejected Motown out of ideological considerations, for the very reason that it was so much more popular, so much more socially acceptable, so much more arranged and predictable, so much more white—but I felt like what *I* was listening to was the harbinger of a new day. In these terms I would no more have judged the shows that we attended than I would have judged the Civil Rights Movement, the French New Wave, my own vocation as a writer, or anything else to which I gave my wholehearted assent. The shows were spectacle, an existential process (not mere entertainment) which followed its own logic, its own time frame, and offered the pace, contrast, and variety of vaudeville and life. If a performer was not to your taste, there was always the audience. If I didn't especially like the sound of Little Anthony and the Imperials (frequent visitors to Boston), I could certainly appreciate the group's acrobatics. The comedians—Pigmeat Markham and Slappy White, George Kirby and Boston's own Wildman Steve—were uniformly vulgar, and uniformly predictable, but reassuringly so, lending further credence to the notion that everyone could let

Jackie Wilson, Apollo, 1964. (Don Paulsen/Michael Ochs Archives)

their hair down because they were at home and among friends. As commonplace as any aspect of the show might be, it was always met with a sense of appreciation and good-natured tolerance that I observed in no other area of the world in which I lived.

Surprisingly I never considered approaching any of the performers directly. Taking my heart in my hand, I was already interviewing blues singers like Skip James and Buddy Guy and Howlin' Wolf. Overcoming the gravest reservations of self-consciousness and self-doubt, I had addressed serious, respectful, blushing questions to these earlier heroes of mine. Why not Jackie Wilson or Otis Redding, then? Why not Solomon Burke or James Brown, whose performance and records I was enthusiastically recommending in print? I'm not altogether sure. Looking back on it, it has come to seem to me that the magazines I was writing for were more interested in interviews with the legendary blues figures precisely *because* the blues form in effect had been abandoned by its original partisans (black) and was ripe for the taking by a new breed of audience and enthusiast (white), which could establish its own terms of appreciation. Maybe this is overly cynical or simplistic, but there *weren't* any interviews with Otis Redding, all that remains of Sam Cooke's on-the-record observations are the usual fan club trivia, and I know that the idea of approaching Joe Tex would no more have occurred to me than the notion of seeking a presidential audience. The closest I came to a backstage insight was one time when Jackie Wilson came offstage after a typically vigorous performance, and I happened to be standing in the wings. He marched off, shoulders back, chest outthrust, seemingly impervious to the blood that was trickling down his shirt from the clutchings of an overzealous fan. The band kept vamping as Jackie stood beside me and seemed almost to shrivel, his chest slumped, his chin fallen; then, as the applause kept up, he strutted out on stage again, and I felt as if I had gained a first-hand glimpse into the oldest conundrum in show business. The idea of asking Jackie himself his thoughts on the subject would simply never have entered my mind.

I listened to the radio. I hung out at Skippy White's, cashed my paycheck in his store in exchange for 45's, and picked up his soul charts, designed perhaps to push the product that he was distributing and the music that he unqualifiedly loved as much as to reflect true sales figures in the Boston area. It didn't matter. This was romance, not life. Where in my devotion to the blues I pored over matrix numbers, drew elaborate connections, subscribed to a magazine called *Blues Unlimited,* which originated in England, and considered myself a bona fide pursuer of the truth, in soul, although I soon became aware of the existence of a number of English fanzines, neither their earnest scholarship nor the fellowship of a faraway coterie of true believers seemed as significant. On the radio it was the *sounds* that mattered, not the names, it was the DJ rapping and my parents' cleaning man (Woodrow Wilson Moon, who had introduced me to WILD in the first place) chuckling and singing along with song after song by artists like Jesse James, Phil Flowers, and Freddie Scott, who in many cases had never been heard from before and very likely would never be heard of again. It wasn't the *stars* primarily, it was the seamless sound of soul, the brotherhood and sisterhood and common aspirations of man. For me the experience suggested that there was a community out there speaking in a single voice, the rhetoric was all of unity and freedom—in politics and literature as well as music. That I was not of that community, that I could not even *presume* to seek inclusion, was not of real consequence—it was heartening simply that this unified feeling could exist at a time when I saw society fragmenting all around me, not least on the issue of race. I could introduce quotes from my writing at this point that would mortify me for their assumption of liberal guilt; I could unearth passages from this period that refer unabashedly, I'm sure, to the "nobility of suffering," the "cry of an anguished people." But my firmest memories are of the music.

James Brown we still hadn't seen, but the legends about him grew and grew, even as "Papa's Got a Brand New Bag" and "I Got You (I Feel Good)" careened to the top of the charts, and his 1963 album, *Live at the Apollo,* remained the standard by which we measured all live performance. James Brown, we heard, had performed at some unlikely venue in Worcester. He had made an unannounced appearance at the Masonic Lodge in Roxbury. James Brown was so hot he was banned in Boston. The rumors were endless, the reputation almost mythic, but the focus was on a performer so galvanizing in person, so charismatic that, just as at the gospel shows, strong men fainted and women wept.

James Brown, 1964. (Charles Stewart)

The first that we actually saw of James Brown was in the movie, the *T.A.M.I. Show,* with a string of pop stars (the Beach Boys, Petula Clark, Chuck Berry, and the Miracles among them) and a performance by James that was nothing less than revelatory. He screamed, he stood stock-still, he exploded with light-ning precision, he skated on one leg—and he completely stole the show from the Rolling Stones, whom my friends and I were initially almost as interested in seeing. Not six months after that, in December 1965, we saw James Brown in person. A friend got married, and we drove directly from the wedding reception to the Providence Arena (further confirming our suspicion that Boston was simply not prepared for James, though hindsight tells me it was probably only a promoter's injunction that prevented him from appearing there), where we entered into yet another world.

"The show is ritual," I wrote of it sagely about a year later, in preview of James Brown's first subsequent Boston-area appearance. "The Famous Flames hypnotically sway and harmonize as a background to his performance, the audience cries out, and James's voice rises above theirs. He dances with wonderful grace and agility, he slides across the floor on one leg, he pushes the mike out into the audience and catches it bouncing back, his feet move with such speed as to make him appear suspended in air. As he goes into 'Please, Please, Please,' he lets go of the mike and catches it, falling to his knees. He screams, and then his voice sinks to a low moan. . . . The Flames wrap a cape around his shoulders, help him to his feet and lead him off. In frustration he shakes off the cloak, stamps his feet, grabs the mike, and screams as he falls to the floor once again. It happened last night, and it's going to happen again tomorrow night; it may all be carefully calculated, but he's into it now, he loses himself in it each time. It happens in front of our eyes."

I didn't go far enough. This was the greatest theater I had ever seen, or most likely ever would see. This was what all the "happenings" and "be-ins" that we attended looking for a new form of participatory drama could only grope for, this was a kind of magic that no theory or academic study could even envision, let alone conjure up. James Brown, a tiny figure on a large stage, moving like a marionette without strings, driven to perform in a manner that invited comparison with no one but a compulsive entertainer like Al Jolson—James Brown was a figure whose legend only suggested his reality.

ON THE BUS

That was soul music for me some twenty years ago. For the performers, I surmise, it was somewhat less glamorous. I surmised that even then, but in retrospect what surprises me even more than the innocence with which I approached the shows is that for the singers, too, there seems to have been a real investment of emotion; for them, too, "showing out" was far more a matter of belief than of simply meeting the obligations of a career. Even so, it could be pretty rugged at times.

They would arrive in town most likely early in the morning after an all-night bus ride of several hundred miles. Some of the jumps could be as long as from Miami to New York City and then back again to Charlotte, North Carolina, because the revues had to take pretty much whatever an agency like

Universal Attractions (this was Ben Bart, manager of James Brown) or black promoter Henry Wynn's Supersonic out of Atlanta gave them. It was undoubtedly both the brutal pace and the unpredictable vagaries of the road that caused so many of the non-shows. If you worked a sit-down gig like the Apollo or the Howard or Chicago's Regal Theatre, for example, you might play as many as five or six shows a day, but most likely you were on for no more than fifteen or twenty minutes at a time and then had the next couple of hours free. The hotel you stayed in was generally across the street from the theater (the Douglas or the Theresa in Harlem, the Royal in Atlanta), there was always a Game going on backstage, drugs and whiskey and women were plentiful—but it was nearly impossible to escape the generally prevailing mood of ennui, with not even work providing much in the way of relief. You were on a gaudily painted treadmill, and it was up to you to find sufficient diversion to keep up your interest, while at the same time maintaining the necessary stability to avoid falling off.

If you were on the road with one of the revues, your night's work was little different, once again there was no egress, and often the greatest challenge was simply to get there. To do that and leave yourself any opportunity to make contacts, do personal promotions, party, or see any more of the country than what you saw from the stage or the window of a moving bus, often it was necessary to have left your previous night's gig with some promptness after the show. This could be accomplished only if you managed to overcome several every-night obstacles.

First you had to get paid, something easier said than done in days when not only was a black roadshow automatically at a disadvantage but it was routine to see no more than a third of the guarantee upfront, with some promoters balking at coming up with even that. This was the reason for the presence of Huckaby, Otis Redding's powerful "bodyguard," who boasts that "Sometimes nobody got paid but us. You had to show strength. I had to do a few people up, but all I wanted to do was get paid." There are tales of promoters disappearing in midshow, promoters who created a disturbance purposely just so they could slip out the side door. In a club situation you were dependent not just on the promoter's money, but on the promoter's word, since the pay was tied in to the door count—which meant that you needed someone not only to watch the promoter but also to watch the door. Even an artist of the imagination like Solomon Burke, who spoke ruminatively of his "godfather's" reaction to this or that sorry turn of events and always proposed the philosophical notion that it wasn't he whom the promoter was disappointing so much as more powerful and well-connected persons, still didn't always get his money, perhaps because the promoter he was dealing with was better connected than any of Solomon's managers—and knew it.

Once the money was straightened out—or whatever portion of it that could be collected—there was the matter of rounding everyone up to leave. Solomon may have had his own limousine and could always find the time to meet with a female parishioner or two, listen to a talented youngster whose attractive mother wanted a star's opinion on her child's talent, or simply go home and enjoy the luxury of a home-cooked meal. For those not quite so fortunate, or not so high up on the bill, it must have been quite a trick sometimes to make any kind of social connections and still catch the bus before it pulled out onto the highway. No doubt, as Solomon says, many assignations were made right in the parking lot or backstage, but still it had to put a crimp in one's social life always to be moving on after the show, and who knows how many less-disciplined performers lost track of the time and failed to rejoin the show until two or three nights later?

Then there was the factor of boredom. What was there to do on these interminable jumps from Charlotte to Boston and back again on a converted Greyhound or worse? James Carr, a very simple, uneducated man with a swelling, "church-wrecking" voice, couldn't handle it at all and ended up—like a number of his cohorts—disoriented, confused, and eventually in and out of mental institutions. Jimmy Hughes, whose first song had launched the Fame label in Muscle Shoals, simply wore down. "I'm very hard to mislead. I have a mind of my own, and I've always been a person who observes a lot. It didn't matter what city I was in. I very seldom moved around. Mostly it was just from the hotel to the theater and back again. In the hotel room I watched TV. I enjoyed performing, but I missed my family. When I quit, I didn't miss it one bit. I would hate to see my kids go into the business."

Otis Redding's entourage speaks fondly of the day they finally got a bus of their own, on which the seats reclined and could be turned around and there was a table to play cards on. For someone like Otis the road was an opportunity to write and acquire an education, and Huck and Otis's road manager, Speedo, can recall mile after mile with Otis, watching him hunched over his open-tuned guitar, working out a new song and seeking the input of anyone who happened to be on the bus.

Solomon, of course, found something of interest nearly everywhere he went. Everyone recalls the sandwiches and ice water that he sold on the bus and chuckles at his opportunism, but it wasn't business that he enjoyed so much as people—men, women, fans, freaks, anyone with a story to tell. Don Covay recalls one time when a man came up to Solomon for advice backstage at the Apollo. "He got the guy to shave all his hair off. He told him, 'Now the message can get to your head.' Then he took his picture in a coffin. He said, 'Now this is your gimmick. You preach from the coffin.' The dude wound up on television. Solomon was like the Pied Piper. He turned this guy's mind around completely." Even for Solomon it wasn't all fun and games, though. By 1965 he was no longer selling so many records. He was no longer Atlantic's mainstay, either, and despite the fact that he would never fail to keep up appearances (the twenty-six-acre estate in Concordville, Pennsylvania, next to the Duponts, *must* be maintained, no less than the claim to the throne), in the view of his longtime friend Alexander Graham Bell, a security expert known to everyone as Nero who has worked for Solomon off and on since 1957: "You gotta understand him. He's a complex man; he's got his moods. When he's up, he's a master. When he's down, 'I'm sorry, baby, I gotta take care of some business. I'll talk to you later.' Solomon's a bear. By his being so big people think he's ferocious, and he try to use his size and that deep bass voice. But they take shots at him, too. And you gotta understand one thing about Solomon: he may roar, but underneath he's just a teddy bear."

THE DAPPER RAPPER

Probably closest in temperament and personality to Solomon at this time was Joe Tex. He, too, could appreciate just the fun of being out there, although, unlike Solomon, he seemed to see show business more as an opportunity for self-betterment than as his natural element. It was a departure not so much from the confines of his hometown of Navasota, Texas—where he continued to live until his death in 1982—as from a world in which a black man's social horizons were strictly limited, sharecropping was a way of life, and his own cleverness would most likely have gotten him no more than a good-paying job as an automobile mechanic. To Joe Tex show business was a way "not to become famous but to build my mother and my grandmother a house."

Born Joseph Arrington, Jr., in Rogers, Texas, in 1935, Joe Tex was nothing if not country, and those characters who populate his songs "eating barbecue and drinking sodawater on the nineteenth of June" were not figments of his imagination at all but friends, relatives, and fellow townspeople. Like James Brown, with whose career his own often intersected, the young Joe Tex got his start in show business shining shoes and selling papers and singing and dancing for the extra tips. In his junior year in high school he entered a city-wide talent contest in Houston and took first prize over such notable performers as Johnny Nash, Hubert Laws, and Ben E. King-imitator Acquilla Cartwright. Joe did a comedy sketch, "It's in the Book," and won $300 cash and a week in New York City at Harlem's famed Hotel Theresa. While in New York, Joe appeared at the Apollo Theatre and won *their* amateur show, meeting Solomon Burke in the process ("I remember he did a Roy Hamilton song. 'Man,' I said, 'that cat can sing.'") and returning to Texas with great reluctance for his senior year. It was in high school, too, that he developed his best-known stage trick (one that James Brown later adapted from him with great success), a practice whereby he would push the mike stand away from him with his hand and then, as it wobbled precariously on its base, catch it again before it hit the floor, more often

Joe Tex: The Microphone Trick. (Don Paulsen/Michael Ochs Archives)

than not with the same toe that kicked extra points in football. "It became a trademark. Everywhere I went, they didn't want to hear this hoarse voice of mine, it was, 'Work that mike, work that mike.' But this is how it came about. One day I was performing in the high school talent show, and I stepped away from the microphone to let the sax player, Robert Johnson, take a solo, and I accidentally, as I was walking away, knocked the microphone over. It was on a stand and had gone too far for me to catch it with my hand, so I just stuck my foot out and caught it on the top of my foot, and the audience just went wild, they thought it was part of the act. And I said, 'Oh-oh, I got something here.' "

After graduating high school in 1955 he headed right back for New York and a career as a professional entertainer, starting out, like many another recent arrival, at Jimmy Evans's Celebrity Club in Freeport, Long Island (Evans's ownership of the club was something of a secret—it certainly remained one to Joe Tex, who was told by the club manager that he would have to get Jimmy Evans for his agent and personal manager if he wanted to play the club). It was at the Celebrity Club that he was discovered by singer Arthur Prysock, who brought him to King Records a&r man Henry Glover, for whom he recorded a number of original tunes in a number of parodic styles. His first record, "Davy You Upset My Home," sprang from the Davy Crockett craze; on some songs he sounded just like Little Richard; "Pneumonia," a minor hit, was a takeoff on Little Willie John's "Fever," which Joe always claimed was written for (and

*Amateur Show in Houston, early 1950s. (Courtesy of
Beliliah Hazziez)*

partially by) him in the first place. As he said of his first session, "Man, I wasn't
nervous, I just wanted to get *on* with it," and while he never achieved any great
success for King in terms of sales, he rapidly acquired a reputation for depend-
ability, no small recommendation then or now.

"Because I was determined to make it, man, and I didn't want to do
anything that would mess up my business. Nipsey Russell, Arthur Prysock,
Percy Mayfield, Roy Hamilton—they schooled me a lot, they really were the
people that gave me the early teachings of this thing out here. They schooled
me about the streets, you know, how to stay away from certain things, how
not to fall into the hands of these slicksters and pimps and hustlers that was all
up and down the streets."

He played the Howard, he played the Apollo, he played the Regal in
Chicago, and he played the little clubs, too, the numbers fronts and after-hours
joints and hangouts for the small-time gangsters. "Little Willie John went by
me, the Midnighters went by me, the '5' Royales went by me, Dinah Washington, James Brown, all them people booked by Universal. I wasn't—I'm not a
jealous person—I wasn't envious of their success. But I say, 'Hey, man,' I would
look at other entertainers that were making it, and I felt that I was just as good
as they were. I never lost faith that it would happen. There were a lot of times
that I wanted to quit, but I never lost faith. One time we were playing Carr's
Beach, and I was feeling kind of low, but Solomon said, 'Hold on, your day
is coming.' He said, 'Time. That's the key word. Everyone has their time, and
you're a hard worker, you're a good showman, man, it's gonna happen.' And
I knew that if I stuck with it—now if I stopped, that's another thing—but if
I stuck with it, I knew that one day it was gonna pay off. And I was just waiting
for that day."

Then two things happened to change his life. One was a song—actually it was a song stemming from a personal experience—that modified his musical direction. Another was a chance meeting that altered his professional direction just as radically.

In 1960 his "childhood sweetheart," Jean, whom he was still hoping to marry, got married to someone else. Joe was playing at a club in Baton Rouge. He was singing a song made popular just that year by Etta James, a tearjerker called "All I Could Do Was Cry," about a jilted suitor's feelings at the wedding of his beloved. In the middle of the song, "I was just talking. Jean had just gotten married, and I was despondent about it, and I just told the band to tone it down, and I started in to talking. I was in my hometown and lost the only girl I ever loved, it was real, and the people just went, Ooh-wee! So the disc jockey, Rootie Tootie, said, 'Man, what was that? You knocked them people out. You got to record that.'

"It was the first record that I had to hit the national charts. It was just one little freelance type thing, but it finally got me moving." And it was the genesis of a style, the basis for a succession of talking sermons that would come to characterize all the best work of Joe Tex right up until his 1964 breakthrough hit.

The other event was even more of a happenstance. That was Joe's meeting with Buddy Killen, one of country music's most successful publishers and Rick Hall's old friend, who guided Joe's career and produced his records from their first meeting in Nashville in 1961. It was at first glance an unlikely combination, but according to Killen, a prosperous-looking, florid-faced man who started out playing bass on the Grand Ole Opry but looks today more like an honest banker than a denizen of Music Row: "The first time I saw him, he was dressed in a cowboy outfit with a purple shirt, boots, the whole works; he sang a couple of songs for me and just knocked me out. I'd never seen a greater entertainer —bar none."

Solely on the basis of personal enthusiasm Buddy formed a production company, Dial Records, whose principal artist—and primary focus—for a long time was Joe Tex. There was little success over the next three years, but there was at least some sense of direction. For a while Buddy hired Chips Moman, fresh from the Stax Records debacle, to come up to Nashville to work with Joe, but that didn't pan out, and by the time they went into the Fame studio in Muscle Shoals (Buddy's hometown) in October 1964, the partnership was just about up. "Joe called me and said, 'We've tried it all and, well, every time we go in the studio, we sort of get crossways. Why don't we just terminate?' I said, 'Let me record you one more time the way I want to, and if we don't happen, I'll turn you loose and let you have your contract.' "

Joe came in with one song—once again about his childhood sweetheart, Jean ("My first wife, Johnny Mae, was pregnant with my son, Jean was married

Joe Tex, music reporter Charlie Lamb, Buddy Killen.
(Courtesy of Buddy Killen)

and I was thinking about leaving Baton Rouge, trying to get Jean back")—
jotted down on the back of a paper bag. He was hoarse and could barely speak
above a whisper when it came time to record the song, for which he had yet
to come up with a melody. "This was October, and I said, 'If Buddy released
this song and it could come out during the Christmas holidays—I wanted to
give it a kind of spiritual flavor. So I thought of some Christmas songs, but the
melody was too obvious. So I came up with one that was not too obvious, that
I could get away with—it's 'Holy, Holy, Holy, Lord God Almighty.' We
recorded it, and I was too hoarse, and I was trying to reach the high notes. Buddy
said, 'When you get to that part, just talk.' "

The song ended up pretty much of a disaster, with only one chorus usable
from the three takes (Buddy spliced it in three times in the finished version)
and Joe overdubbing what he dismissed as a very ragged (if very winsome)
harmony with himself. Before he left the studio, Joe elicited the promise from
Buddy that the record would never be released. The song was "Hold What
You've Got."

The record was a smash from the day it first came out, once again on the
Dial label but with Atlantic distributing for the first time. Joe's first royalty

check came to $40,000, and with it he bought his grandmother the house that had been his initial reason for entering show business. Not before he vented his spleen on Buddy, though. "I was on my way back to Baton Rouge [sometime after the recording session], and I passed through Beaumont, Texas, and had the radio on a pop station. And when I turned it on, I hear, 'Fellows, this goes for you, too.' I said, 'What!' Because I didn't want Jean to know—'cause it's about our life, you know? I got to Baton Rouge and told Johnny Mae, I said, 'Guess what? I heard a record that I made on the radio on a pop station.' She said, 'It's on WLCS, we been hearing it every day here, on the hour.' I said, 'What!!' So I called Buddy up, I said, 'Man, you put that record out, and I told you not to.' He said, 'Man, you got a smash.' He said, 'It's been out two weeks and done over 200,000 on it.' We were happy, man. That was ten long years of trying, and it finally paid off. When that record broke, that sucker busted wide open. The phones started ringing, gigs started coming in, tours with Otis and Solomon and all these people. It was the first time that I ever received a royalty check."

In a lot of ways there could have been no one more ready for success. Once Joe Tex found his groove, it seemed as if he would never slip out of it. Hit followed hit, novelty song and serious message alike, each written by Joe, all imbued with the same mixture of serious purpose and engaging charm. He was the most natural of entertainers, taking evident delight in his ability to give pleasure to his audience and in their evident delight with him. Where James Brown was saddled with the burden of being "the hardest working man in show business" and Solomon Burke was expected to provide spiritual catharsis night after night, Joe simply had to be himself, offering up his earthy philosophy interspersed with healthy dollops of good humor, effortlessly entertaining audiences, both black and white, with his easy onstage manner, lithe dancing, and microphone manipulations. Not surprisingly, though, for someone as motivated and as consistently creative as Joe Tex, there was another, more sober side to his nature. Buddy Killen recognized it ("Joe is a very deep person"), but despite his commercial success (after "Hold What You've Got" Joe Tex probably sold as many records as any other soul singer, with the exception of James Brown) he remained one of the most critically underestimated figures in soul, perhaps because of his very winsomeness and charm. What was rarely appreciated about Joe Tex, both the man and his music, was the seriousness of purpose behind the comic mood, the intellectual and emotional depth of his art, and the evident sincerity which lay behind even the most flippant or bathetic of his messages.

It was at the time of his greatest success, in fact, that Joe first began questioning his vocation and the way in which he was conducting his life. In 1966 he was introduced to the Muslim religion by his road manager, Norman Thrasher, a former Midnighter. Two years later he secretly converted "because I was searching for a little more than Christianity had to offer me. I'll say it this way: there were a lot of questions in my mind, and they weren't being answered." He continued entertaining; his image remained one of the utmost good humor and affability, but in 1970, on the heels of "I Gotcha," his biggest hit and first platinum seller, he quit performing to serve Elijah Muhammad, taking the name of Joseph Hazziez and preaching in mosques all around the country. Eventually, in 1975, he returned to music with the blessings of the church—and even had one more Top 10 hit—but obviously it was not out of the same need that had once propelled him into the business. As Joe said, "I got over my little—what would you call it?—little bright light thing very early. Because I didn't come in the business, as I told you, to become famous. I just wanted to generate some money for my people, build my mother and my grandmother a house. I don't worry about making it. Material things have never been what I was looking for. It was family, and learning more about God and creation. Never was on that ego trip, star thing, 'Music is my life, and I can't live without it.' 'Cause I wasn't born singing. I just go out and try to give the people the best of what little bit I have to offer."

"WE CAN'T SIT DOWN"

Not surprisingly Joe Tex's religious conversion to an order that stressed black separatism provoked a good deal of comment, and not a little resentment, in soul circles. Joe Tex, it was rumored, hated white people. Joe Tex, it was said (and not just by management), was an ingrate who had turned his back on those to whom he owed his entire career. "Oh, people would tell me things," Buddy Killen recalls, "they said they'd heard him say. But I always maintain if you're somebody's friend, you're still their friend. I never question a man's religious beliefs or political beliefs, and I don't give up on people that easily." Others did, though, and largely along racial and political lines. For all the hopeful rhetoric of integration, on a management level the industry was still almost lily-white, and the "good nigger–bad nigger" dichotomy (a "good nigger" knew his place; a "bad nigger" was just stirring up trouble) remained very much in effect. Hard as it may be to believe, an irresponsible soul like Little Willie John was much more easily tolerated in certain circles than an independent one like Sam Cooke.

Race in fact was never far from the surface—it never could be. Solomon Burke has his tales of playing for the Klan or encountering audiences that expected him to be white from his records, and whatever their basis in literal, nonmetaphoric reality, the confusion in racial attitudes (the extravagant romanticization and savage dismissal, the "Put the nigger in the spotlight but keep him out of the rest rooms" mentality) was not atypical of the whole era. That is why the fraternities were such an important ingredient in the development of Southern soul. That is why Rufus Thomas, a fiercely proud man, can still declare without irony: "College audiences are the greatest audiences in the world; there is no greater audience. I must have played every fraternity house there was in the South. When we played Ole Miss, they'd send the girls home at midnight, and then we'd tell nasty jokes and all that stuff. Oh, man, we used to have some *good* times down there in Oxford! When something was coming, some kind of show, I mean, they'd build themselves up to it, and then, when we got there, they were ready for it. I'd rather play for those audiences than for any other." And this at a time, remember, when Governor Ross Barnett was barring the door to black students at this very university, and civil rights workers were being murdered in Philadelphia, a hundred miles away.

Percy Sledge affably recalls one time he was late for a concert at the University of Alabama, when his brother was the MC and the crowd was growing restive. The minute his brother saw him, he announced, "Ladies and gentlemen, there he is walking through the door." It was so quiet, Percy recalls, "you could hear a rat piss on cotton, and then a voice way in the back shouts out, 'Well, bring that black, gap-toothed nigger on then.' " Percy, never one for racial niceties, simply took the stage and did his show.

I don't mean to belabor the obvious, but when Muscle Shoals guitarist Jimmy Johnson says, "It was just like *Animal House*," he isn't kidding, nor is he speaking simply of groups like Doug Clark and the Hot Nuts or the Thirteen Screaming Niggers, legends on the fraternity circuit who were perceptibly lacking in racial dignity. What is a little more difficult to grasp is that Joe Tex and Otis Redding and Solomon Burke were viewed no differently than the Thirteen Screaming Niggers, the only distinction being that they were able to operate on a larger scale. They played the same frat houses, they were booked by the same agencies, they encountered the same contradictions, and they created the same larger-than-life legends while at the same time possessing talent and imagination that took them far beyond the simmering confines of their world. What I'm getting at, really, is that this romantic story did not always take place in the most splendiferous or romantic of settings, and when you think of Otis Redding, you should think of the sheer nasty funk as well as the dignity of the man; we should always remember that soul music could stink as bad as the nastiest blues, could offer redemption, like the church, only after acknowledging the basest of human needs.

Different artists responded in different ways to the stress of the racial situation, with some taking a more activist stance than others. Otis Redding was proud to consider himself a *businessman*. He explicitly sought the acceptance of the record industry on its own terms and, for all his independence, seemed happy to embrace the values of the black bourgeoisie. Solomon Burke today points to the secret message of songs like "You Can Make It If You Try" and boasts proudly that "in certain parts of Mississippi they would tell me that they would arrest me if I sang 'I Wish I Knew How It Would Feel To Be Free.' " Joe Tex wrote the occasional mild-mannered protest song like "We Can't Sit Down," but mostly he explored various levels of everyday black experience in much the same way that Zora Neale Hurston did in literature, celebrating the positive values of negritude—the greasiness, the funkiness, the warmth, and the wit that existed on every level of black society—in songs like "Papa's Dream," "Buying a Book," and "Anything You Wanna Know" ("You can find out anything you wanna know/About anybody's business that you want to know/At Ida Mae's Beauty Shop/Or Webb's Barbershop").

There were other, equally sly assaults upon the system. Once again it was Solomon Burke, the wise guy, who got under the skin of his white associates most readily and challenged the accepted order most ingeniously. Often it took alertness and cunning just to survive. One time a member of his band who had never ventured South before was about to drink from a white drinking fountain in a little town in Mississippi. "The only thing I could do," says Solomon, imitating the Caucasian reaction with relish, "was to start hitting him. I started yelling at him like he was crazy—you know, like 'You crazy fool, you goddam, ignorant, crazy, no-account, uneducated dummy'—and I beat him up all the way to the bus. He's talking about, 'I'm going to sue you, sucker, you not going to hit me like this and mess my face all up.' And they're saying, 'Get the rope, Frank. Get the hanging rope.'"

Solomon's favorite story, though, has to do with the time he and Sam Cooke and maybe Joe Tex and possibly Otis Redding integrated a well-known hotel in Norfolk, Virginia. It is a tale told by a number of the participants, sometimes with different names and locations, but with enough of the details preserved to convince one that something like this actually happened.

"We made reservations for Dr. Burke, Dr. Cooke, Dr. Butler, Dr. Clark, and Dr. Bland—this was Sam Cooke, Jerry Butler, Dee Clark, and Bobby 'Blue' Bland. And we had these reservations, and all these limousines rolled up to the hotel, and I jumped out, and I walk inside, and I said, 'The limousines are here with all these various doctors in them.' And the man say, 'Fine. No problem. You boys want to help them with their stuff?' And I say, 'Yes, sir, we certainly will. Now what you want us to do?' He says, 'Now don't you worry about nothing, you're already checked in, you just go on to your suites.' He didn't know what was happening, you see. Then, when they found out who we were, they like to killed us. They called the police, and the state troopers came, and the local police came out. The state police said we had written reservations, we could stay. Local police said it was against a city ordinance to integrate the hotel. The hotel manager said he couldn't rent the rooms out to anyone else because black people were already staying in the rooms. I said, 'We ain't staying in the rooms. We just checked in the rooms.' We wasn't going to stay anyway. It must have cost Norfolk about $30,000 for us to stay, 'cause they had police and National Guard all over the hotel for two days. Well, that was one time we

Dr. Burke. (Don Paulsen/Michael Ochs Archives)

really worked together as entertainers, and we refused to back off. We had the money, we had the name, and we had the reservations, written reservations. Of course we could never get back in the hotel."

Joe Tex remembered another time when Solomon *didn't* come out ahead. It was 1964, and the Supersonic package was scheduled to play Birmingham. "Solomon had one of them big, long, old-time limousines, give you a nice ride. He said, 'Come on, ride with me, send your car on to Birmingham, ride with me.' So I say okay, and we get out of Atlanta, and Solomon wanted to buy some whistles, some police whistles. Everybody was giving away gimmicks and stuff like that in those days. On the show some nights Solomon would give away roses, the next night he would give away whistles. And so Solomon told his driver, 'Stop at that Army surplus store. I want to get a box of whistles to give away tonight.' We got out and went in the store, and the man kept looking at Solomon. He said, 'Don't I know you?' See, Solomon's a big fan of Daddy Grace, he's wearing his hair long, that's his idol there. And he tell the man who he is. And the man say, 'Yes, I got your records.'

"So anyway, Solomon bought up a whole box of green plastic whistles, and the guy gave him a deal on it. Then Solomon went to look at some guns. The man say, 'You interested in guns?' 'Yes,' he said, 'let me see that one over there.' So he got it and snapped it and all and says, 'Let me see that rifle over there.' Solomon wound up buying a rifle, a shotgun, a .45, and a .38. And the man say, 'Y'all gonna buy all of these, I'll just throw in the cartridges for free, give you a box of shells for each one.' So we put the guns in the trunk, they wasn't loaded. And here we go on our way to Birmingham, man, soon as we out of the city limits, here come six police cars, sirens going, they pulled us over, the whole thing. The driver was about to get out, but Solomon says, 'Stay in here. Let me handle it.' So he gets his Bible out the window, took his cross out of his shirt, dropped it over the side, big old cross. 'Yes, officer?' he says. 'Who are you? What's your name?' 'This is Reverend Dr. Solomon Burke, a man of the cloth,' you know, his whole gimmick. So the man say, 'Where y'all going?' He said, 'We're on our way to Birmingham for a church meeting, we're going for a big church meeting.' So he says, 'Y'all carrying to Birmingham, that's where all that rioting is going on.' So Solomon says, 'We're not no civil righters.' And the man say, 'Y'all carrying any weapons?' 'No, no, I'm a man of the cloth.' The man say, 'You mind opening your trunk?' 'Yes, open the trunk, driver.' The driver got out and opened the trunk and, goddam, there were the guns. 'Y'all going to Birmingham with all this arsenal of weapons? Y'all aren't going to riot and shoot up nobody?' He say, 'Follow me back to the police station.' And they charged Solomon a hundred-dollar fine and confiscated the guns and the bullets, took them all away. We got back in the car, and I said, 'Man, do you know what happened?'—it just come to me. I said, 'You know that man at the store? That man wanted his guns back. That man done called them policemen.' He said, 'Man, you're right.' "

Perhaps humor was as good a way to handle the indignities of the road as any other—certainly it was as effective. Removed by twenty years, it is not always easy to remember just how grim those days really were, how little hope of change there appeared sometimes to be. Perhaps another quote—this one from Harrison Salisbury in *The New York Times*—will serve as a reminder. Under the headline "FEAR AND HATRED GRIP BIRMINGHAM" Salisbury reported from Alabama in April of 1960 that: "Ballparks and taxicabs are segregated. So are libraries. A book featuring black rabbits and white rabbits was banned. A drive is on to forbid 'Negro music' on 'white' radio stations. Every channel of communication, every medium of mutual intercourse, every reasoned approach, every inch of middle ground has been fragmented by the emotional dynamite of racism, reinforced by the whip, the razor, the gun, the bomb, the torch, the club, the knife, the mob, the police, and many branches of the state's apparatus." In the face of such opposition is it any wonder that many blacks should have fallen back on "mother wit" as their first line of defense? The success of serious, topical comedians like Dick Gregory, Godfrey Cambridge, and, later, Richard Pryor only institutionalized a response that many black folk—Solomon Burke and Joe Tex included—employed in everyday life. And the success of soul music in bridging a gulf that in 1960 seemed an unbridgable chasm should not be underestimated, either. It was as if the rhythm and blues singer, like the jazz musician and professional athlete before him, were being sent out as an advance scout into hostile territory; it was his mission to make sure that conditions were right for the rest of the expedition to follow. By 1968, obviously, conditions were right. As *Time* magazine reported in a cover story: "Has it got soul? Man, that's the question of the hour. If it has soul, then it's tough, beautiful, out of sight. It passes the test of with-itness. It has the authenticity of collard greens boiling on the stove, the sassy style of the boogaloo in a hip discotheque, the solidarity signified by 'Soul Brother' scrawled on a ghetto storefront. . . . Soul is a way of life, but it is always the hard way. Its essence is ingrained in those who suffer and endure to laugh about it later."

The difference between the world described in Harrison Salisbury's dispatch and the attitudes embodied in *Time*'s panegyric to "with-itness" are so vast as to indicate the passage of decades. In reality there were only eight years separating the two news stories, and when the *Time* story appeared, it had been less than three since soul music had gained widespread acceptance. By 1968 soul language was all the rage (that should be clear enough from the new-era *Time*-ese cited above); soul food restaurants were the newest fad; the soul handshake was showing up in professional sports and on the streets; and songs like "We're a Winner" by the Impressions had come to represent the new spirit of the age. Long before *Roots* ever entered the best-seller lists (Alex Haley was in 1964 collaborating with Malcolm X on the Muslim leader's classic autobiography), the idea of Afro-American roots was being celebrated for the first time outside the day-to-day life of the community. As Curtis Mayfield, lead singer of the Impressions, proudly proclaimed:

> *Keep on pushing*
> *I've got to keep on pushing*
> *I can't stop now . . .*
> *'Cause I've got my strength*
> *And it don't make sense*
> *Not to*
> *Keep on pushing. . . .*

Wilson Pickett, with the Magnificent Montague. (Don Paulsen/ Michael Ochs Archives)

HOUSE WRECKING

And then there was the competition. If nothing else could sustain a musician's interest in his daily work, the idea of going up night after night against the very best singers, the very best showmen and entertainers, each one doing his utmost to take the show, encouraged at least a modicum of professional pride. Much as with athletes on the road, for the r&b singer it was the public moment on which everything focused; it was the particular moment at which you hit the stage. It didn't matter at that juncture what your record was doing on the charts, it didn't matter if you had diamond rings or money in the bank or a string of women waiting backstage; all that mattered right then was looking and feeling *sharp*—that and tearing up the crowd, taking the show. There was a camaraderie, a sense of fraternity in the air that allowed you to go up against your best friend and pull out every trick in the book to beat him without having it hang over your head or his that you did.

It was this sense of amicable competition that allowed Otis Redding to steal band members from Joe Tex and Joe to steal them back again without breaking up a long-term friendship in the process. It was this same sense of competition that prompted Wilson Pickett to boast to Sam and Dave that now that he had learned to dance (Pickett was notoriously stiff in his stage movements), he was going to beat their ass and for Sam and Dave in turn to leave Wilson floundering in the dust. Everyone could laugh about this sort of story, not just in retrospect but even at the time, and everyone had a certain amount of scorn for irresponsible performers, like Little Willie John or Percy Sledge, who threw away their talent and lacked the professionalism to get themselves together for the show. Because there wasn't anything else beyond; this was what it was all about. So strong was this sense of identification—or perhaps it was just that no other avenue of approval suggested itself—that even on an off night you could find the luminaries of the soul world, like their counterparts in the realms of jazz, blues, and country music, hanging out at the Fiesta in Miami or the California Club in Los Angeles or at the Royal Peacock in Atlanta on Hustler's (Monday) Night, when anyone who was in town could get up and perform for an audience of his peers, just for the thrill of seeing their response.

Here again James Brown was the single glaring exception, and in his differentness lay the seeds for other performers' resentment and his own disproportionate success. Atlanta DJ Zenas Sears remembers him jumping off that balcony in Newark just to get the audience to sit up and take notice, and Alan Walden recalls without much sympathy his working a gig in Macon early in his career and falling to his knees on a concrete stage over and over again, "just landing on his fucking kneecaps, and when he came up, you could see where he'd torn his pants. Boy, that motherfucker's crazy. We were paying him seventy-five or a hundred dollars for the night, and I went back to see him after the show, and his kneecaps were nothing but two damn calluses. He needed that attention." One time Brown advertised Otis Redding on a tour of Texas, Otis's bodyguard Sylvester Huckaby swears, simply in order to be able to brand Otis as a no-show. Another time he appropriated Solomon Burke's crown. If he happened to be spotted in the audience and was introduced from the stage by an unwary performer, he would as likely as not take the microphone and perform an entire set before giving it up again.

Alan Walden remembers one occasion when Joe Tex and Otis Redding were both billed with James Brown in Atlanta and made up their minds that James was not going to steal the show from them this time. "Joe was going to ride in on a horse. Otis was going to be lowered out of the air from a helicopter. I don't know, some such bullshit. We didn't do none of it.

"Then one of James's people tried to get Otis to cut his show and made all kinds of threats that he wouldn't be able to work again if he didn't. Well, we didn't know what Otis was going to do until he hit the stage and saw the largest audience that he'd ever played for, and he looks up, and they got a big fucking banner stretched all the way around that says, 'Welcome home, Big O,' and when he sees that fucker, you knew he wasn't going to leave the stage until he murdered them. He was on for an hour and fifteen minutes that night, and when he left the stage, he may not have killed James Brown, but James could not ignore the fact that Otis Redding held every motherfucker in the palm of his hand for that night."

James Brown aside, for most of the soul fraternity the performance represented more of an existential moment than the ultimate moment of truth. Don Covay threw money to the crowd; Solomon distributed cuff links. Jackie Wilson lay on his back and invited the women in the audience to tear his clothes off. Everyone competed for top billing, but there were times when even a headliner might be willing to relinquish it. In 1964 Otis and Solomon came off the Hot Summer Revue to do the first Otis Redding Homecoming at the City Auditorium in Macon, and after first insisting on all the pomp and circumstance that befitted the King of Rock 'n' Soul, Solomon all at once saw the light. "Everyone kept talking about a family feud, and the sheriff said to Otis, 'We been having a couple of bum threats.' I said, 'What kind of bums could be threatening?' He said, 'Boy, you mocking me?' Then I realized he was serious. *Bomb* threats! Oh, I'm sorry. . . . We had like forty policemen on stage, and Otis says, 'Why don't you let me go on first?' I say, 'No, Otis, this is your hometown, you close the show, baby. I don't want to be a star tonight.' "

It was the rivalries and competitions (not to mention the little jokes) that kept everyone going, and the feeling that was shared had more to do with the much-vaunted ideals of brotherhood than with showing someone else up. Traveling through the night, everyone was tuned in to the sounds of John R. and Hoss Allen, broadcasting their all-night shows, spinning rhythm and blues hits among advertisements for baby chicks, weight-gain pills, and skin and hair care products on Nashville's 50,000-watt WLAC. As they heard their records being played and kept track of chart positions, the performers themselves would call in to John R., who would relay their location to a waiting world of teenagers, rural blacks, and fellow musicians. "Just heard from Otis Redding in Midland, Texas, he's going to be doing two shows tomorrow night in Little Rock for all you folks out there in the Little Rock area," came the voice with its black inflections, hip language, intimations of an insider's knowledge, and Caucasian origin. This, too, was an open secret shared by the "hippocracy," for John R. and Hoss Allen—like Skippy White in Boston, Zenas Sears in Atlanta, Poppa Stoppa in New Orleans, or Butterball in Philadelphia—were white jocks in love with rhythm and blues. "Ain't it a shame," one of his fans complained to Solomon Burke, "how white folks do the colored. First they took Amos and Andy away from us. Then they got hold of Uncle Ben's converted rice. And now they trying to tell us that that white man is Hoss Allen." And Solomon, whose rule of diplomacy it is never to disagree with a winning hand, just nodded his head and murmured his sympathies. To the fans the distinctions may have been clear-cut, but to the performer's eye the world of soul was all of a piece.

Somewhere along the line there arose the idea of institutionalizing all this good feeling, of turning the distinctly unfunny reality of the Ku Klux Klan on its head and creating what came to be called the Soul Clan. Most likely the designation was no more than a witty turn of phrase to begin with, whether journalistic or promotional, but it soon caught on and captured the imagination not so much of the public as of the very singers it was describing. Though the term was used at one time or another as a catchphrase to refer to up to a dozen different artists, the Soul Clan in the end came down to a number of the key Southern soul singers that we have already met—Solomon Burke, Joe Tex, Wilson Pickett, Otis Redding, as well as singer-songwriter Don Covay and (on record at least) Otis Redding's protégé Arthur Conley and former Drifter Ben E. King. Not entirely by coincidence each of these performers was associated with the Atlantic label; even less coincidentally all were friends, who—with the marginal exception of Wilson Pickett, a rougher-voiced stylist along the lines of the Reverend Julius Cheeks—modeled themselves on and considered themselves heirs to the legacy of Sam Cooke. Cooke's death in December 1964 had sent shock waves through the soul community, and perhaps this, too, helped encourage the notion of developing a new fraternal order, however casual its protocol; perhaps the Soul Clan was an attempt to claim not just the stylistic heritage but the very path of independent enterprise that Cooke had blazed. That was the rhetoric at any rate, that was the noble dream.

Solomon and Don Covay were the originators of the dream, and it seems to have come to them as the result of an English music press promotion. The concept first occurred to him, Covay says, when he arrived in London in April 1966, preceded by Solomon and Pickett, "and I read in the papers about this Soul Clan Invasion. We used to show up at each other's gigs, and we would hang out together all the time, so it was a natural kind of accidental thing." The idea simmered for a time, but it obviously tickled the fancy of the various principals to think of themselves as a kind of soul variation of the Hollywood Rat Pack (Sinatra, Dean Martin, Sammy Davis, Jr.), and it fit their natural inclination to stick together in any case. "We'd always hang out together, ride in each other's cars, stay in the same hotels," says Solomon. "You got to remember that the Otis Reddings, the Joe Texes, the Don Covays were never alcoholics or dope addicts, there was never any problem with booze or drugs at that time. You see, we were all raised in an era when everyone believed in God and had respect for their parents, had strong family ties and good home training, and this is the reason that we in particular got along so well. We just had fun—real, clean fun."

Joe Tex pretty much concurred, though in retrospect he saw the group more as a scheme by Don Covay, a brilliant songwriter and occasional hit-maker

Don Covay and Jerry Wexler. (Courtesy of Jerry Wexler)

but a less than successful performer ("He's the worst entertainer," says Wilson Pickett, among others. "Everyone would pay Don to get *off* the stage."), to promote his own career. "It was a great thing if it had come off, you know, to really sit down and plan it. The ideas were good. We were going to have sort of like a Rat Pack kind of thing, tour together as a package and set up trust funds for the people who were going to be in it, for their children. But it never did get beyond the talking stage. And whatever money did come out of it, I think Don and the record company got it all. I know I never did."

For Covay, a dreamy man who is capable of spinning the most elaborate fantasies around the most mundane events, all the grandiose talk and terminology was probably more a matter of self-delusion than of seeking to delude anyone else. Born in Orangeburg, South Carolina, in 1938, Covay grew up in Washington, D.C., where he emerged from high school as a member of the Rainbows (other members included Billy Stewart, future Stax promotion man Chester Simmons, and, reputedly, Marvin Gaye) and a protégé of Little Richard. He met Richard in 1957 as a result of opening a show for him and almost immediately went into the studio with Richard's band. The result, "Bip Bop Bip," was leased to Atlantic and came out under the name "Pretty Boy." Subsequently Covay recorded for a number of labels and had a couple of minor hits ("Pony Time" and "The Popeye Waddle" in 1961–1962 were the biggest) before moving to New York in the early '60s and discovering his true métier as a songwriter. He naturally gravitated to Roosevelt Music, the Brill Building rhythm and blues publisher, which already had under contract every professional black songwriter of note in the city from Otis Blackwell ("Breathless," "All Shook Up") to Charles Singleton and Rose Marie McCoy (who together wrote

Together For The First Time!

THE SOUL CLAN

SOLOMON BURKE · ARTHUR CONLEY · DON COVAY · BEN E. KING · JOE TEX

"SOUL MEETING"

c/w "THAT'S HOW IT FEELS"

Atlantic 2530

literally hundreds of r&b hits but whose greatest fame stems from Singleton's coauthorship of "Strangers in the Night") to Atlantic Records' Jesse Stone. That was where Covay learned his craft and learned, as he says, how to write a "happy blues" from Jesse Stone. That was where he first made contact with Jerry Wexler and first started supplying Solomon Burke, among others, with some of his best songs. Although he became fairly well known as an Atlantic recording artist from 1964 on (his first hit, "Mercy, Mercy," better known perhaps from the Rolling Stones' cover version, not only established a new guitar-dominated soul sound, it also proved a formative influence on white r&bers Mick Jagger and Peter Wolf), it was as a songwriter that he really made his mark. He had success with Solomon, Don says, because "I knew what Solomon could do, I knew what the audience would like." He had equal success with Little Richard ("I Don't Know What You Got [But It's Got Me]," one of the unacknowledged classics of soul) and Aretha Franklin (the Grammy-winning "Chain of Fools"). After a very difficult emotional period following his wife's death he even had a pop blockbuster with his old admirer Peter Wolf some twenty years down the road (1984's "Lights Out"), but, for all of the varied setbacks and successes he has experienced, his inner life still seems focused on the Soul Clan and his compatriots from the days when "we changed the whole face of music. It was one of the biggest things in history. All of us were different; everybody had a different approach. There was no jealousy, no threats; from the minute I met those cats, I been knowing them ever since."

The idea of a Soul Clan was kicked around for close to two years. There

The Soul Clan, 1981: Ben E. King, Joe Tex, Don Covay, Wilson Pickett, Solomon Burke. (Courtesy of Buddy Lee)

were plans, it has been said, to purchase real estate in Birmingham, set up motels in Texas, and establish an independent black business empire all across the country. They wanted, says Solomon, a million-dollar guarantee from Atlantic, "but I think we were a little premature." It finally took Otis Redding's death in December 1967 to get the group into the recording studio—and then it was hardly in the way that was originally intended.

Pickett, for one thing, angrily reneged. "He got talking crazy," recalled Joe Tex, "talking he don't want to be no part of this, he don't want to be no part of that, he had hit records and he didn't need nothing like this, all that kind of shit." Otis, of course, was gone, his place taken by Arthur Conley, who by this time had had a bigger hit than any of the original Soul Clan with 1967's "Sweet Soul Music," a magical litany of the great names of soul coauthored by Otis and Conley and borrowed, appropriately, from a tune ("Yeah Man") by their mutual idol, Sam Cooke. Ben E. King evidently took the place of Pickett, Covay tailored both sides of the single to the individual talents of each of the participants, and the whole enterprise had a loose, easygoing, improvisational feel which was scarcely affected by the fact that the singers never did get to actually meet in the studio (thus giving the lie to the title of the A side, "Soul Meeting") but instead recorded their vocals separately to a backing track which Covay had put together with Bobby Womack at the Wildwood Studio in Hollywood.

I can remember buying the record at Skippy White's when it came out in the summer of 1968, and I have treasured it ever since for its magical confluence of personalities and styles. What did I know then about where and how it was recorded, and what did I care? As Don Covay says with conviction,

"There's never been a time in history when you had six artists like this on a single record," and if the real number is actually five, well, who's counting anyway? Solomon Burke, not overly given to talk of conspiracy, is still angry over the commercial failure of the record. He was on the verge at this point of leaving Atlantic and ascribes the lack of sales to a darker purpose on the part of Jerry Wexler. "The Soul Clan was deliberately destroyed because we were becoming a power structure. Our interest as a Soul Clan was to build a financial empire, and once that was found out, we were destroyed." Jerry Wexler just laughs it off as a typical Solomon scam and fantasy.

In the end perhaps the Soul Clan may be taken as a symbol of the music and the era, of its aspirations and its failures, its dignity and its self-delusion. Maybe the Soul Clan was an idea whose time had not yet come, whose time might never come—but then the Platonic ideal should always transcend the reality, after all. These were poetic glimmerings of the future, a hopeful vision springing up out of the stag party atmosphere and the hot gymnasiums of the South, and even if the Soul Clan escaped those hot gymnasiums and feverish fraternity parties only in their mind's eye, the importance of the poetic conceit alone cannot be overestimated.

There was one ill-fated reunion in New York City in the summer of 1981, with Wilson Pickett finally rejoining the group in place of Arthur Conley, who had long since disembarked for Europe. Though all the principals had stayed in touch, they hadn't performed together in years, nor, since they continued to insist on the indispensable value of spontaneity, did they bother to rehearse for the occasion. The concert ended with Wilson Pickett quarreling vociferously with Joe Tex backstage, Joe Tex's dancers doing a striptease to "Aint Gonna Bump No More," and Don Covay with a tambourine around his neck. Only Solomon Burke, dressed in preacher's robes with an enormous cross on display, emerged unscathed, along with the magnificent mythology. "The Soul Clan was to me the greatest thing that ever happened," Don Covay still insists. "I think the kind of love we had was an everlasting situation. If any of us ever need each other, you know we gonna be there." Or, in Solomon Burke's majestic formulation: "We're serious about this, and we have goals that aren't going to mean something to just you and me but everyone around the world and our children's children, and the future of black music in history. We are history."

▶9▶ The Other Side of Memphis

Hello, Memphis, how do you do?
Do you remember me, baby,
Like I remember you?
I been wearing your cotton
And singing your rhythm and blues.

—"Hello, Memphis" by Dan Penn, Spooner Oldham,
   and Donnie Fritts

M EMPHIS IN THE MID-TO-LATE '60S WAS LIKE A boomtown in the middle of a religious awakening. The success of Stax, and the flood of imagined possibilities which that success unleashed, set off a chain reaction that found every entrepreneur in town getting into the "record bidness." Memphis, after all, is a town that has never been prone to self-doubt; civic pride has always held that a city which gave birth to the Piggly Wiggly, the Holiday Inn, Elvis Presley, and the blues, which could boast of its reputation as onetime Murder Capital of the World, was somehow touched with magic. When that magic showed up all of a sudden in the realm of rhythm and blues, there was no one, it sometimes seemed, who was not prepared to take the leap, no matter what might be his or her lack of previous experience. Banks (Union Planters eventually came to own Stax), hotel chains (there was even a short-lived Holiday Inn label, with, appropriately enough, original Holiday Inn investor Sam Phillips presiding), advertising agencies, and the local Mafia all were drawn in not so much by the lure of dollars as by a vision of independence. For Stax, like Sun Records before it, was seen as just one more exemplar of the triumph of the independent spirit, something no Memphian could fail to understand or appreciate.

In 1967, it was estimated, the Memphis recording industry generated twenty million dollars' worth of business; in 1968, thirty. And if two thirds of those sums could be attributed to Stax, at least several million belonged to the dozens of little labels (Golden Eagle and Penthouse, Ardent, Pepper, X-L, and Genie) which had either sprung up or regenerated in the wake of yet another Memphis off-the-wall success story. As Jim Dickinson, who did session work for most of the labels in question at one time or another, declares with not a little asperity: "Memphis is an ugly place, but I love it. People who wouldn't have stood a chance anywhere else were recorded here. And have traditionally

Jim Dickinson. (Jim Marshall)

been drawn here, because, I guess, it's always been a center for crazy people. There is an awful lot about the thing that happens in Memphis musically—you can't reject it, you have to either learn to live with it on one level or another or admire it. And I, frankly, admire it."

The Goldwax label came into existence in 1964 with Stax as its model but with more of a grits and gravy, downhome flavor. It was a classic Memphis operation, with pharmacist Doc Russell putting up most of the money and Quinton Claunch, a traveling salesman who had spent most of his life on the edges of the music business, contributing the expertise. Born in Tishomingo, Mississippi, in 1922, Claunch moved to the Muscle Shoals area with his family at the age of twenty and played with a popular country band which broadcast locally every morning at sunrise over WLAY. Then in 1948, after getting married, he moved to Memphis, where his friend Sam Phillips was already established as a radio engineer. Not long afterward Phillips opened up the Memphis Recording Service and then in 1952 started the Sun label, on several of whose early sides Quinton appeared on guitar or as cowriter with fiddler Bill

Doc Russell, Stan Kesler, Quinton Claunch. (Courtesy of Bill Millar)

Cantrell, yet another émigré from northwest Alabama. It was through Cantrell that he got involved in the formation of a brand-new Memphis label, Hi, this one modeled directly on Sun (its first artist, Carl McVoy, was a Jerry Lee Lewis sound-alike *and* cousin) and financed principally by Joe Cuoghi, owner of Poplar Tunes, one of the biggest retail record outlets and distributors in the city. Hi achieved intermittent success until 1959, when it had a top-selling instrumental hit, "Smokie—Part 2," by Elvis's old bass player, Bill Black, and his Combo.

By this time Claunch, to his eternal regret, had left Hi for a number of cogent reasons, keeping his position as a hardware supplies salesman but never losing his passion for music. He maintained his contacts, remaining friendly, for example, with Rick Hall, whose group (the Fairlanes) he had recorded at the Hi studio in the late '50s, before Rick ever got into the business end of music himself. Rick in fact tried to get Quinton to come back to Muscle Shoals and start up a studio with him. "He just begged me to quit that damn job and let's get rich. We'd call each other and talk for hours at a time between here and Muscle Shoals, play tapes over the phone—but I had a couple of kids, and I couldn't see turning loose and taking a gamble."

Then in 1964, when Rick had his Fame operation going and Jim Stewart was enjoying solid success with Stax, Quinton saw his opportunity. He learned from a third party that Doc Russell might be interested in putting up some money for a recording venture, got $600 from Doc, and took a group called the Lyrics to Muscle Shoals to record at the Fame studio. Their first record, "Darlin'," a cross between James Brown and the "5" Royales, was a good-sized regional hit, and Goldwax was off and running, though not without setbacks.

"That thing started selling boom boom boom," says Quinton, "so one day I get a call from a guy at London Records about distributing the record, and then he came into town and picked up the master. It took them about two or three weeks to get it all processed and to put it out, and by that time the record was dead, and we were back in debt. I always thought Joe Cuoghi killed it, though I couldn't ever prove anything, but Hi was distributed by London, of course, and it just made sense."

Even if "Darlin'" didn't set the world on fire, it did prove that a market still existed in the mid-South for a raunchier gospel-based soul sound, and it indicated that Quinton Claunch, whose experience up to this point (like Jim Stewart's before him) was entirely in country and rockabilly, had a feel for the r&b market. The problem now was to come up with a roster for the new label. Stax had all the name musicians in Memphis sewed up, so the trick was to discover a vein of untapped talent. This is where Roosevelt Jamison came into the picture.

Roosevelt Jamison had graduated from Booker T. Washington High School in 1956, about five years ahead of most of the Booker T. graduates at Stax. A tall, mournful-looking man with a goatee that makes him look a little like basketball star Bill Russell, Roosevelt had won a city-wide poster contest in high school and earned an art scholarship to college, but instead he got married, had a child, and went to work at the City of Memphis Hospital as an orderly in October 1956. Never anything less than ambitious, Roosevelt was dissatisfied with both the material and the spiritual rewards of the job and soon began hanging around the hematology lab, where the head of the hematology unit, Dr. L. W. Diggs, noticed him, discovered his artistic ability, and soon had him drawing cells observed through a microscope. Though the University of Tennessee was strictly segregated at the time, Diggs began taking Roosevelt to lectures as his slide projectionist and then quizzing him on the content of the lectures in private. In this way Roosevelt came to be certified as a medical technologist, and in addition to his work at the hospital from 11 P.M. to 7 A.M., in 1960 he began running the Interstate Blood Bank for the university, a walk-in unit that was set up on the corner of Beale and Fourth. This was where he began his active career as a musical talent scout, for though he considered medicine an art, he venerated, and still holds, music as the highest art. Although he himself had some ambitions as a singer, his friends, he relates regretfully, kept telling him "to stick to the other end of the business," so he began managing gospel groups off and on. The gospel groups rehearsed in the back of the blood bank. One of the groups that he was rehearsing was the Harmony Echoes, a quartet that featured two singers who would soon become, individually, Goldwax's most prominent artists: O. V. Wright and James Carr.

O. V. Wright was something of a gospel celebrity. Born in 1939 in Leno, Tennessee, some thirty miles outside of Memphis on the Germantown Road,

O. V. Wright. (Courtesy of Bill Millar)

he had been singing professionally since the age of six, when he appeared at the Temple in Eads, standing on top of a soapbox. Possessed of perfect pitch and an unerring sense of his musical strengths and limitations, he became the leader of a local group, the Five Harmonaires, which also included his older brother, Eddie Lewis, and then joined a nationally known group, the Sunset Travelers, while still in his teens. He made a number of records with the Travelers for the Peacock label in Houston, briefly joined the Spirit of Memphis Quartet and the Highway QC's, and then returned to the Harmonaires. His best-known recording from that time, "On Jesus' Program," was given to him by a local pastor, the Reverend Harris, for the Harmonaires to sing, but O.V. (Overton Vertis), took it with him back to the Sunset Travelers. When Roosevelt met him, he was dividing his weekends between the Jubilee Hummingbirds and the Harmony Echoes while working on a garbage truck, and he would stop in every day at the blood bank either to rehearse one of his groups or to accompany Roosevelt back to the hospital, where O.V. could work on his songs in peace while Roosevelt did his lab work, or the two of them could just sit around and dream about the future. There was nothing really planned at this point, there was nothing really in sight.

"I got into a little bag at this time," says Roosevelt. "I was depressed. I had kids. And it didn't seem like I could get no education. I couldn't get my money right, and segregation was on my case. So I wrote this little thing that went like: 'O God, what is it that Thou hast for me to do? Why am I existing in this confused mass? Will my mind ever be contented, or will it remain confused? Will I have the opportunity, the mental ability to explore my desires? Or will my unrestful mind be captive like the flower that has been covered by the weeds? Will I be one to say at the end of his existence, "Lord, I've gained little and given humanity nothing?" Or the little I've gained is sorrow, worry, and mental pain. . . . Now after you've thought, Thinker, and Mr. Time has caught you thinking, will your confession be, "Lord, forgive me for existing so meaningless." ' And, you see, I think from that point I began to take my words and make my pictures more seriously.

"Then in 1963 I found this girl whom I loved more than anything in this world. This particular person was a nurse, she was working at the same hospital, and she had all the properties that I'd always dreamed of. She would just sit in the car with me and listen to me sing and talk and sing and talk and not say a word herself, she just made me pour it out. One day we were sitting at a little drive-in place where we would all go and get sandwiches and things, and the moon was shining bright, and I just started messing with this poem about how I'd roamed the prairies, searched the universe, trying to find ways to express to her just how strong my love is. And she would say every now and then, 'Why don't you start back working on that song you was kind of writing for me?' So I would get back into it. And I can tell you what each and every line means."

This was the song with which Roosevelt and O.V. decided to make their bid for commercial success. This was the vehicle which O.V. would employ to cross over from the gospel field, though, characteristically, it did have a spiritual element to it. The song was "That's How Strong My Love Is."

Roosevelt's first idea was to sell the song to Stax. He took it over to McLemore and sang it for Steve Cropper with Cropper playing piano and Roosevelt losing the time. Cropper made some suggestions for melodic and lyric changes (the basis for his assertion that he was "ripped off," since he never got any credit or money), and Roosevelt went home without too much reason to feel encouraged.

"That was okay. I didn't hear from Jim [Stewart], and I got hung up with O.V., and O.V. rearranged it in a different way, so I took a tape back to Jim (another friend of ours, Melvin Carter, was playing guitar on the tape), but Jim still didn't want it, he said it was too gospel. So I had a couple of friends, Richard Sanders and Earl Cage, who were hooked up with Goldwax, kind of as talent scouts, and Earl told me to check with Quinton, and he didn't too particularly like it, he liked the other number, 'There Goes My Used to Be,' which wasn't too shabby itself."

"Roosevelt called me up in the middle of the night," recalls Quinton. "He says, 'Hey, man, I got these guys I sure would like you to hear.' Well, I'd already gone to bed, it was after midnight, and he says, 'I got a little home recording. Would it be okay if I come out and let you listen?' I said, 'Man, come on.' I was living right here, same place, and he came out with a little recorder, and we got down on the floor in the living room, and he played me his tapes, and they just knocked me out. And we took O.V. into the studio."

The cut by O.V. is a classic. The record, distributed by Vee Jay this time out, was a hit, eclipsing even the version by Otis Redding, which was recorded at about the same time (late 1964) despite Stax's purported lack of interest. The only thing everyone had neglected to take into account was O.V.'s contract with Duke/Peacock Records.

It wasn't something of which anyone was unaware. O.V. had simply believed that the contract engaged his services as a member of a group (the Sunset Travelers) and that he was not held to it as a solo artist. This was not the way Duke owner Don Robey saw it. In fact Robey, a tough, light-skinned black man who had started the Peacock label out of his Bronze Peacock nightclub in Houston (Duke was a Memphis label which he had "taken over") and who was widely reputed to be a numbers boss, wasn't about to take the matter lying down. While O.V.'s song was climbing up the charts, and the Memphis gospel world reacted with predictable hurt and outrage at the defection of one of its stars, a pitched battle was heating up between Don Robey's entrenched interests and the fledgling Goldwax label. Eventually, after a certain amount of discussion with Robey on the subject of contractual law, O.V. conceded that he might have violated his Duke contract, and he was prepared to return to the Duke fold, but even that was not the end of it. "Doc Russell was so tight with the police in Memphis," says Roosevelt, "the police was after O.V. left and right, but that Robey was a cold-blooded man, he wasn't scared of the forked-tongued devil—if he wanted to come up here, he'd catch a plane and come up here himself."

Eventually Doc and Quinton decided that discretion was the better part of valor. They gave up all future claims to their artist while retaining rights to the hit single, a concession that Quinton valued all the more after hearing of a friend who had gone to Houston, stared at the .45 on Robey's desk, and heard "We're gonna have a deal." "At this point," says Quinton, "we started concentrating on the Ovations and James Carr."

The Ovations were another one of the groups that had been hanging out at the blood bank, getting coaching and encouragement from Roosevelt. Led by Louis Williams, a Memphian with an uncanny vocal resemblance to Sam Cooke, the Ovations were, according to Roosevelt, a later version of William Bell's old group, the Del Rios, who were then singing at Clifford Miller's Flamingo Room. Roosevelt rehearsed them on a graceful Sam Cooke takeoff called "It's Wonderful to Be in Love," and Quinton was as impressed with their sweet harmonies, and Louis Williams's lilting lead, as he had been with O.V.'s rougher-edged gospel voicings. He cut the Ovations at a run-down studio on the corner of Thomas and Chelsea called American, which Chips Moman had started up the previous year with Memphis music lawyer Seymour Rosenberg (Seymour's father had an auto parts store on Chelsea). Chips engineered the session and used a young white rhythm section which had been put together by Stan Kesler, another Sun alumnus, who did most of the engineering over at the Phillips recording studio. The section consisted of Reggie Young (late

James Carr. (Courtesy of Roosevelt Jamison)

of the Bill Black Combo) on guitar, Bobby Emmons and Bobby Wood on keyboards, Mike Leech or Tommy Cogbill on bass, and Gene Chrisman on drums. At this point, in early 1965, Chips had still not gotten over his dismissal from Stax and was leading what he calls a hand-to-mouth existence, charging twenty or thirty dollars to engineer a session and drinking up what little money he did make. Many Memphians believed he was just playing possum ("Chips was always looking for a way to take over," says one contemporary. "He could be a sideman one week, and then two weeks later it would be his band."), while others felt he was getting no more than what he deserved. He was exactly what Goldwax needed in any case, a competent engineer who put no value on himself or his work.

The Ovations' record took off, aided by heavy airplay from Washington DJ Al Bell, who had been instrumental in helping cement the Vee Jay connection and would in just a few months' time land at Stax. It was Bell, according to Quinton, who made the record an r&b hit. "Man, they went into—what's that big theater in New York? the Apollo—they must have sold 150,000 records, just a local group." Even so, "It's Wonderful to Be in Love" barely made Top 30 on the soul charts, an achievement that the Ovations, plagued with personnel problems if not with lack of talent, never managed to repeat. It was left to James Carr to solidify the position of Goldwax both financially and in the annals of soul history.

James Carr had been introduced to Goldwax, actually, at the same time as O. V. Wright and saw his first release, Roosevelt's "The Word Is Out (You Don't Want Me)," come out at about the same time as "That's How Strong My Love Is," in late 1964. A powerful, big-voiced singer with a controlled quaver in his voice that could make him sound alternately like a more muscular Otis Redding or a more explosive Percy Sledge, Carr was a natural talent and in some ways Roosevelt's finest discovery ("Even O.V. wished he had the voice James had"). Born in Mississippi in 1942, Carr grew up in Memphis but never learned to read or write. He got married and had kids while still in his teens, worked as a day laborer, and was singing in various gospel groups (including the Harmony Echoes but not including any of the well-known ones like the Soul Stirrers which his publicity always credited) when Roosevelt met him around 1962. "He was kind of childlike," Roosevelt says, "kind of slow where O.V. was aggressive." There was no question, though, that he could sing.

James started singing when he was
About the age of nine
He had artistic ability then,
So it was just a matter of time.

He stood on the middle of the church floor
Lead singer for a group of six
With his suspenders too short and pants too big
There wasn't a song they sang he couldn't lick.

His voice was so strong
And he produced so much soul
He stirred everybody,
The young and the old.

When he sang, he walled his eyes
(So only the whites could be seen)
He was a funny little fellow
Especially for his size.

The little boy sang so hard
As he knelt to the church floor
Saying, "This may be my last time, people,
I don't know."

This was part of a publicity release that Roosevelt wrote upon James's success. Here at last, it seemed, was the opportunity for Roosevelt as well as for his artist. His experience with O.V. had been somewhat disappointing, for after he declined to go on the road with him ("James needed me more. It would have really let James down if I left him."), he was shut out of O.V.'s career almost completely and never tasted any of the rewards of O.V.'s success. "For some reason Don Robey wouldn't never cut my songs. Between Melvin Carter and myself, we were the ones who wrote all the songs O.V. ever had [Robey bought most of Carter's songs for a fee, as was his practice, then put his own name or nom de plume, D. Malone, on them and kept the royalties for himself]. Then, later, Willie [black producer/trumpet player Willie Mitchell] wouldn't cut my songs either. I don't know why. You see, we wanted to philosophize on the blues, get away from the gutbucket stuff, that really wasn't very good music in our opinion. Many of our songs had some flavor of God in them, to where you could feel the sacredness in the way O.V. sung, but we just couldn't get Robey to cut those tracks. Me and O.V. shook hands, and O.V. told me if I ever wanted to go with him and leave all this other stuff alone, I could have fifty percent of his salary. But I never did do that."

Staying with James wasn't just altruism on Roosevelt's part, though, as Roosevelt would be the first to admit. In James Carr he saw pure clay to be molded, and as Roosevelt recognizes, "I always wanted to be an artist secretly. And I saw that if I could instill a little bit of me into different artists, then I'd continue to live. I saw James had a dynamic voice, and he needed me tremendously in order to succeed. So I was with him a hundred percent. We were just like twins, everybody called us brothers."

"At this time I began managing him," Roosevelt wrote in the same publicity release that contained his poem. "I introduced him to Goldwax Records, who specialized in sentimentals, ballads, and rhythm and blues. His first and second records were fair. The third one, 'You've Got My Mind Messed Up,' began to make James's dreams come true."

"You've Got My Mind Messed Up" came out in the spring of 1966, just after Goldwax had made a new distribution deal with Larry Uttal's Bell Records, the one label that was beginning to give Atlantic competition in the soul field (Jerry Wexler contends, with some credibility, that Uttal accomplished this by following in Jerry's footsteps and picking up the leavings). The record, a convincing Otis Redding-styled ballad, was written by O. B. McClinton, a student at nearby Rust College and one of a growing stable of Goldwax writers which included both young blacks like McClinton and George Jackson (Jackson would later cowrite Bob Seger's "Old Time Rock and Roll") and seasoned country veterans like Quinton Claunch. Production was typical Goldwax, a muted, Stax-styled horn section (not surprising, since doubtless it *was* the Stax horn section), impeccable rhythm playing, shimmering, vibrato-laden lead from guitarist Reggie Young, and a clean, uncluttered sound. It was James Carr's vocal, though, that was the center of attention, just as the vocal is the focus of nearly any great Southern soul record. James Carr's voice could invite any amount of scrutiny; it could soar majestically, suggest peaks of emotion, yield layers of meaning, and convey subtleties of understanding and interpretation that Percy Sledge, for example, could never aspire to vocally. It was, as Roosevelt says, a gift that could not be gainsaid; his success, though, was a gift of a different sort.

James Carr was no more equipped for success than Johnny Jenkins in Macon or Arthur Alexander in Muscle Shoals. Roosevelt still feels that things might have worked out had he been able to stay at James's side, but once again events conspired to deprive Roosevelt of the fruits of his discovery. For one thing he was not fully prepared to leave his hospital jobs for the uncertainty of life on the road. For another, Bell president Larry Uttal and Otis Redding's manager, Phil Walden, who started booking James at about this time, took Roosevelt's place as manager-adviser, without really understanding what they were getting themselves into. "See, I knew James. I could tell what made him tick, 'cause I was more or less his inspiration. They didn't know how he actually felt; they didn't know what was underneath, how hard it was coming from the bottom, from nothing to something so fast. It was like coming from four or five years old to twenty-five all of a sudden. In the time between traveling I would teach him to write his name; I would read stories out of a book to him, read about different countries and how their culture was. After I left, within six months he came tumbling all the way down. He couldn't understand it; he became very depressed. He would sit on my doorstep, somebody would knock

Roosevelt Jamison and James Carr in Japan. (Courtesy of Roosevelt Jamison)

on my door at three o'clock in the morning, and he'd be setting out there, say, 'Hey, man, why don't you go to Atlanta with me?' But I couldn't do nothing, 'cause I was out of the picture, he had *taken* me out of the picture, and he didn't have no friend with him anymore."

Even the songs that he was writing especially for James, Roosevelt says, were no longer being recorded by Goldwax. This may have had something to do with his demanding an account of writer's royalties from "That's How Strong My Love Is," which had now been covered not only by Otis Redding but by the Rolling Stones on their best-selling *Out of Our Heads* album. On the other hand, maybe he just wasn't writing any more hit songs. In any case Roosevelt stayed hooked up loosely with Goldwax, and James Carr had a string of medium-sized hits over the next three years, including his one inarguable masterpiece (and one of the most unforgettable songs of the entire soul era), the original version of Chips Moman and Dan Penn's first collaboration, "Dark End of the Street." This desperate tale of furtive love first came out in late 1966, and while it has been covered by countless singers over the years, and spawned a brilliant, near-transcendent version by Aretha Franklin, no one has ever matched the sober dignity, the almost unbearable intensity of James Carr's original. Not surprisingly it represented the biggest seller of James's career.

It was not lack of sympathetic production that brought James down. Nor was it lack of suitable material. One thing you could always say about Quinton, Roosevelt concedes, was that he allowed James to express himself, and he certainly was capable of coming up with appropriate material, sometimes from the most unlikely sources (Harlan Howard's country classic, "Life Turned Her That Way," is a good example). Looking at it from the outside, Jim Dickinson even found something to admire in Quinton's taciturn production methods. "Quinton used to rattle the change in his pocket. He always had change in his pocket, and he'd walk up to the bass player and look up in the corner and start rattling that change. He never said a word, and knowing the bass player, if he'd said anything, it wouldn't have done any good. But he'd just stand there and rattle the change, and pretty soon the bass player wasn't playing what he was playing before. Hell, now that's effective production!"

Chips Moman and Dan Penn, newly arrived in Memphis from Muscle Shoals, had a hand in some of James's work, now that Chips was finally back on his feet again. "What would I do if I wanted James to cut one of my songs?" asks Chips bemusedly. "Easiest thing in the world. Just get Dan Penn to sing it for him. He'd sing it, and all of a sudden James Carr could sing it. He had to sing it, 'cause Dan sung it so good."

Nonetheless the sessions became more and more difficult; it simply became more and more painful to pull a coherent performance out of James, and his inability to cope not just with success but with reality baffled his producers increasingly. "It got to be ridiculous," says Quinton. "The last year it was almost impossible to get a session out of him. One time in Muscle Shoals I got one song out of a six-hour session. I wanted to just kill him, but, you know, he would just sit there on the stool, not say a word, and just look at you. And then three hours later sing the song all the way through without any hesitation at all. It made you kind of wonder."

Stan Kesler recalls one session when the musicians were working out an arrangement and suddenly realized that James had disappeared. "We thought he had gone to the rest room and kept waiting for him to come back, but he never did. We searched the whole building, but he wasn't nowhere to be found. Then we went outside and looked around. Finally we looked up on the roof, and there he was, hanging his head over, just looking around. You know, oftentimes he would just set in the chair, and Quinton would say, 'James, you ready to sing?' And he'd just look up and grin and never say a word and never get out of that chair."

Most put it down to drugs, but Roosevelt insists this was not the case. "James would smoke reefer. And he smoked reefer heavy, in a pipe. But that's all James would do. He wouldn't let nobody come close to him with no needles. And I know, because we'd eat and sleep together. You see, James's problem was in his mind. He would go off into a trance, become spellbound almost. Other guys, when they got into the business, would sing and rehearse. But James very seldom did that. You had to pull him out of the house in order to get him to rehearse. He would never devote himself to anything. The only thing he did well was to sing, and it got so you almost had to make him do that. He just got totally mixed up and confused."

James's illness no doubt contributed to Goldwax's mounting problems. So did personal differences between Doc Russell and Quinton Claunch. The label finally dissolved in 1969 without ever coming up with a suitable substitute for James, who remained its chief asset to the end. There were offers for his contract, Quinton says, even after the partnership had dissolved. "Capitol wanted him bad. They offered me $25,000, but I couldn't send back the contract because I didn't want to get myself in the middle and have him not be able to perform. They waited six months, and then they couldn't wait any longer. Messed him up and me, too."

Quinton is still peripherally involved in the business, still on the lookout for new talent (though now, once again, in the country field), still on the road for the same hardware supplies company with which he started when he first came to Memphis in 1948. Occasionally he will luck into something good, like the 1982 coproduction deal on a gospel album for Al Green that came about through his old friend Bill Cantrell (even this turned a little sour, as he and Cantrell ended up suing Green for money and credit). His memories of the Goldwax years are alternately nostalgic and bitter, and he doesn't really stay in touch with any of his old artists. O. V. Wright died in 1980 of a heart attack brought on by drug abuse. He had continued to enjoy some commercial success and continued to record with Willie Mitchell at the Hi studio. As his brother, Eddie Lewis, said of him, "He was the kind of person that had his own mind; you couldn't tell him nothing. We had our hard times. We went through some hell of a time. O.V. went to the top, he had some of the greater things. I thought he would settle down and take some of the money where it would keep coming back to him. He didn't. He just wanted diamonds and fine cars."

Roosevelt has kept hustling, working his two jobs. A few years ago he graduated to a supervisory position in the hematology lab at the hospital, and he is doing research in sickle-cell anemia during the day. He is still taking care of James, still trying to get him straightened out, get him in good physical condition and keep his mind clear. In 1979 he shepherded him on a disastrous tour of Japan, which ended with James taking "a double dose" of the antidepressant he is on and becoming spellbound on stage.

The last time I saw Roosevelt, we picked up James in the South Memphis housing project where he lives with his sister. A puffy, unfocused man with haunted eyes and spiky hair sticking up all over his head, he looked nothing like his early publicity pictures. Driving around South Memphis, sitting in a restaurant drinking a cup of coffee, James seemed practically narcoleptic, expelling breath loudly from time to time and unresponsive even to Roosevelt's promptings. "This gentleman can do a lot for you, sir," tried Roosevelt. "Do you understand where I'm coming from? Now you ready to wake up and talk a little bit, or are you just going to sleep again? . . . How you doing?" Roosevelt asked his onetime discovery. "Nothing but a tight head," said James. Roosevelt mortgaged his house a few years ago to finance a recording session for James that didn't work out and seems prepared to do it again. "Aren't we friends?" he ventures desperately. "Sometimes," says James, with the foxiness of the truly mad. "You know," says Roosevelt, "everyone who comes to your concerts loves you. They love your singing, and everybody speaks quite well of you. But there are many questions the public would like to ask, many questions which have to be answered. Because you'll go down in history as one of the greatest blues singers of all time. . . ."

Roosevelt concluded his publicity release with an account of James's triumphant appearance at the Apollo Theatre in 1966, the engagement at which he was dismissed as James's manager.

"The Apollo Theatre was where he wanted to go. So he called wanting me to be there to see the show.

As the drums beat a rhythm that
Was kind of slow
I saw a different James
One I hadn't seen before.

Wher the triumphs sounded
In my face I had a thousand frowns
For I knew this would make or break him.

The crowd went wild
For he was loaded with soul
Where he got his inspiration
I didn't know,
Until: He walled his eyes
And knelt to the Apollo floor, saying
'This may be my last time, people,
I don't know!'

"There I saw an artist perform. There I saw a star being born. That star was James Carr.

"What happened? Where is James Carr?"

THE AMERICAN SUCCESS STORY

James Carr's brief moment of triumph was in a way the making of Chips Moman. American had done a certain amount of business since its inception in 1964, but really it was little more than a shoestring operation, with all of its capital deriving from the $3000 settlement that Chips had won from Stax with the help of his lawyer, Seymour Rosenberg. "Seymour said, 'Let's sue 'em, boy.' When they offered us $3000 to waive all rights forever, Seymour says, 'I think we oughta settle.' He's working on a one-third contingency fee, I found out later he was also doing some work for Jim Stewart, but, hell, I'm dead broke, I still don't know nothing, I'm just thankful I'm gonna be able to say, 'Mama, I'm still living in the record business.' Then Seymour says, 'Man, what we ought to do, you and I ought to build us a studio together.' " That is what they did, but not surprisingly, given his still-fragmented state of mind, Chips didn't even manage to hold on to that. Another partner, Wayne McGinniss, bought in for $300 or $400 and then picked up Chips's share for another $300 or $400 ("I just let my part go"). Chips meanwhile was still engineering sessions at American for whatever he could get, and supplementing his income by painting gas stations. It never occurred to him, he says, to think about what his work might be worth until one day Quinton and Doc signed a country singer named Leroy Daniel to their label, "and they didn't know he was a good friend of mine. Leroy Daniel is the uncle of Stanley Daniel, the guy who used to work at the Stax record store, very good friend of mine. They told Leroy, 'We got this producer, man,' said, 'All we ever have to do is give him a bottle of whiskey and a couple of pills, man, and he'll cut you a fucking record.' And that was the truth, that's the way I was living, really, I was just barely getting by. Well,

Chips Moman, with Ed Kollis. (Courtesy of Bill Millar)

Leroy came and told me what they said, naturally, so the next time I seen them and they wanted me to cut James Carr, I charged them $5000. Didn't care whether I cut him or not—and they paid it! It was amazing. Went straight from $20 to $5000, and the whole thing was due to what Leroy Daniel told me about Doc and Quinton."

This was probably late 1964 (though the chronology of James Carr's career does not exactly fit the story), and it seemed to snap Chips out of his two-year depression. It was not long after this that he cut a hit of his own on the Gentrys, a pop number called "Keep On Dancing" which went to #4 nationally and sold over a million copies. More significantly Chips regained his sense of vocation. Some musicians consider themselves performing artists only; others with Chips's talent might regard themselves primarily as instrumentalists ("Chips, you know, is an incredible guitar player," says Jerry Wexler. "He doesn't feature himself, and maybe he's not a virtuoso, but what he plays is unbelievable."). With Chips's track record as a writer he might well have retired on his publishing royalties. Chips Moman, however, never wanted to be anything other than a producer. "That was what I was into more than anything else. Making the record itself. From the day I went into the Gold Star Studio in California to play a session, I never cared about anything else. I'm into songs, and I'm into sound. Making music for me is still fun. I just have a big time, that's all, and if I'm not having fun doing a session, we shouldn't have done the session."

One of the first things he did after his reawakening to the world was to regain control of the American studio, something critics of Chips would contend was part of his plan all along. Just to give an idea of his normal operating methods, a contemporary tells of one time when Chips showed up for a gig at the Five Gables and found another bandleader already on the job. Words were exchanged, and Chips and the other fellow went out to the parking lot to settle their differences. "The other guy has a gun, Chips has his leg in a cast and all he's holding is a penknife, but somehow or other Chips took the guy's gig, and at the end of the evening Chips has the money, Chips has the gun, and the other guy wound up doing the playing. When it was all over, Chips just said to the guy, 'You know, I'm not mad or anything, I'm just deeply hurt.'" In the case of American, Chips traded half of his interest in the Gentrys' hit for half ownership of the studio. His new partner, Don Crews, a bean farmer from Lepanto, Arkansas (Crews "never produced anything that could not be grown in rows," in Stanley Booth's elegant formulation), was also Wayne McGinniss's uncle. Crews had bought out his nephew and Seymour just prior to this point at a stiff price and remained in the background for the rest of Chips's days at American.

Once he had the studio on more than a casual, walk-in basis, his next requirement was a band. This, evidently, proved to be no more complicated than acquiring the studio. The one prominent rhythm section in Memphis outside of the Stax house band was the group that had emerged in part from the Bill Black Combo but that Stan Kesler had been largely responsible for putting together as a studio unit. This was the group (Reggie Young, Tommy Cogbill, Gene Chrisman, et al.) that had played on nearly all the Goldwax sessions to date, whether engineered by Chips or Stan, and many of the Hi sessions as well. It had never occurred to Kesler or anyone else to tie these musicians up with a contract, but "Chips tied them up so they couldn't cut anywhere else." Kesler, the most mild-mannered of men—who admires Chips and has continued to work with him right up to the present day—was scarcely surprised. "Well, Chips was a pretty good con man—he was pretty independent, too, *very* independent in other words," says Kesler, who went on to form another rhythm section, the Dixie Flyers, only to have it taken away from him by Jerry Wexler, then put together a third group which Seymour Rosenberg commandeered for *his* new studio, at which point Stan gave up any dreams of independence and went to work for his old friend Chips at American.

Chips meanwhile solidified his newfound sense of purpose with a number of highly successful pop productions, including "Born a Woman" by Sandy Posey, American's onetime secretary, which was a big hit in the summer of 1966. That was just around the time that Dan Penn abandoned Muscle Shoals to throw in his lot with Chips in a partnership that seemed at first as if it must have been made in heaven. Dan and Chips were so in tune with each other they scarcely needed language to communicate, two backwoods hipsters, each with his own

Spooner Oldham, Chips Moman, Dan Penn on stage, 1976, backing up Tony Joe White with unidentified drummer and bass. (Phillip Rauls)

hidden agenda. To the outside world either was readily enough dismissed, Chips as a "hustler" with a complete set of homemade, "jailhouse" tattoos (*Memphis* was tattooed on his right arm, a big red heart on his left), Dan as a kind of eccentric redneck whose hayseed manner was so at odds with his intuitive genius that, as Jim Dickinson says, "I thought for years he was pulling a country boy act. I mean, God knows, I've gone to LA a couple of times wearing my overalls and shuffling my feet and saying, 'I ain't got no nothing'—I know where it's at and how to do it, the country boy act. The thing is, Dan wasn't acting, and it's too bad he wasn't." For both Chips and Dan, nonetheless, there was an irreducible element of put-on even in what they most fiercely believed, and it was impossible to separate their sense of ironic detachment from the almost obsessive faith that each had in himself.

This was reporter Stanley Booth's take on Penn upon his introduction to him in 1968:

> I found Penn, a young blond man wearing blue jeans and bedroom slippers, at his desk [at American] playing a ukulele. He told me he had come to Memphis from Vernon, Alabama, after working for a while as staff guitarist in a studio at Muscle Shoals, because he wanted to produce hit rock and roll records.
> "Dan," I said, "what is it about Memphis?"
> "It ain't Memphis," he said. "It's the South."
> "Well, what is it about the South?"
> "People down here don't let nobody tell them what to do."
> "But how does it happen that they know what to do?"

"It ain't any explanation for it," said Dan Penn, meaning it and not meaning it probably.

Given their respective natures, and the oracular pronouncements to which both Dan and Chips were given, I'm not sure that misunderstanding was not inevitable. Certainly there was an incandescent element to their relationship that was destined to burn out, with a first meeting that was "hotter than a pistol," a first collaboration ("Dark End of the Street") that was an instant classic, a business partnership that sprang from an acquaintance of no more than a few months, and mutual participation several months after *that* in Aretha Franklin's historic first session for Atlantic at Muscle Shoals, to which they contributed another classic collaboration, "Do Right Woman." It didn't take long, though, for egos to collide and all the latent tensions to come to the surface.

In the spring of 1967, less than a year after Dan first came to Memphis, a local rock group called the Box Tops came into the American studio. Their lead singer was a pimply teenager named Alex Chilton, and Chips matter-of-factly turned the group over to Dan, along with a tape by writer Wayne Carson, which included a song called "The Letter."

"There was really kind of an antagonistic thing going on by this time. Moman and I are alike in a lot of ways, but really we're opposites. If he asked me about a record—'What you think, Penn?'—and I said, 'Man, that's a bunch of shit,' he'd say, 'No, I'm putting it out.' If I said, 'More bass,' he'd put more treble. I mean, I'm overbearing myself, but Moman is overbearing overbearing. Which I guess is one of the reasons 'The Letter' come out the way it did, because he had antagonized me and fucked around with me, told jokes about me in front of other people, he was really making fun of me, saying, 'What you cutting on that tape?' I say, 'The only hit on there.' He says, 'Don't cut that piece of shit.' I said, 'Man, that ain't no piece of shit, I'm gonna cut a hit!' I said to myself, 'I'm gonna get that fucker, he's either trying to piss me off or get the upper hand.'"

Even after Penn had cut the record, they continued to squabble about it. Dan, as was his wont, had not settled for anything modest but had gone ahead and put the sound of a jet airplane on the tape. "So when I got through and I had the jet plane and all, I said, 'What do you think, man?' And he said, 'Pretty good, Penn, if you take the damned airplane off.' I said, 'That's my record, and I got a fucking razor blade here, and I'll cut that tape up into a million fucking pieces if you take the airplane off.' And he said, 'Okay, okay, like you said, it's your record.' And it turned out it was the biggest record he ever had. It jumped on #1, and it stayed up there for four weeks. And, man, he wouldn't even come into the studio that whole four weeks, and when he did, he was a crabby old man, just didn't have nothing to say. I love to bring these pricks down."

Jerry Wexler was miffed, too. Having advanced Chips $5000 to upgrade the studio once Chips got his mind back on business, he had naturally expected

Jerry Wexler and Larry Uttal, with record pioneer Milt Gabler referee. (Bob Gruen)

some kind of return on his investment. Instead, Chips, like Doc Russell and Quinton Claunch, had made a deal with Larry Uttal, without ever giving Wexler a chance to make a counter-offer. "I was hoping that Chips would have picked up the phone and called me," Jerry fumed, "but Larry Uttal happened to be in town—you see, he followed in my footsteps and picked up behind me, and he did a helluva job when I wasn't there—and Chips gave it to him. Definitely an ambivalent feeling there, but I don't care. I figure every one of my Southern buddies fucked me sooner or later, but it's forgotten now." Forgotten or not, Wexler continued to do business with Chips, bringing Wilson Pickett back to Memphis to record at American in July of 1967 and turning American into the Memphis base that he had been seeking all along after he grew disaffected with Rick Hall. Jim Stewart meanwhile was beside himself as he saw the man he considered his "archenemy" getting the much-coveted Atlantic account. As for Chips and Dan, they took it all in stride, fought and fussed, flew up to New York to produce Solomon Burke, got Spooner Oldham to move to Memphis and tried without success to lure the rest of Rick Hall's band away from Muscle Shoals, dreamed grandiose dreams, and simply took pleasure in all of life's unexpected twists and turns. For Chips, having a hit provided its own scenario, according to Wayne Jackson. "He'd get his front money and get a boat and a Thunderbird and go to Florida until he was broke and then come back and do it again." Dan says, "I didn't put no limits on it. I just figured I'd take whatever was dealt me." There wasn't much that wasn't dealt in the next couple of years, but one of the incidents that gave Dan the greatest satisfaction, not to mention one of his biggest laughs, was a session he wasn't even scheduled to participate in to begin with.

Dan Penn in Memphis. (Robert Melhorn)

In August of 1967 Jerry Wexler had booked the American studio for the Sweet Inspirations, with Tom Dowd producing. The Sweet Inspirations were a vocal backup group with deep gospel roots whom Wexler had both named and then pushed into the foreground after their distinctive work behind Aretha Franklin earlier that year. It was a hot summer's day; the session hadn't been going very well; and according to prevailing New York custom, Tom Dowd had called a lunch break. Just to put the capper on it, Dan says, it was a *leisurely* lunch break, at a "real swanky" place across town.

"Now Tommy was a broader engineer than any of us," recalls Dan respectfully. "We were mono men when he was two track; we were two track when he was eight track. I mean, he'd been in New York where we'd been in Memphis, and here they'd come into our territory and taken over, you know what I mean? Big engineers, you know what I mean?"

"I had worked with the Sweet Inspirations with Aretha," says Spooner Oldham, "and gotten to know 'em and loved the way they sung, so I couldn't wait for them to get a record on their own. So I went to the session that night at Chips's. I don't think I was on the session for some reason; I don't know why, maybe I'd been out of town. But anyway Dan was sitting there, and we were watching all this go down, and they did two songs—awful stuff—and my heart started sinking, and I said to Dan, 'Let's go next door and try to write a song.'

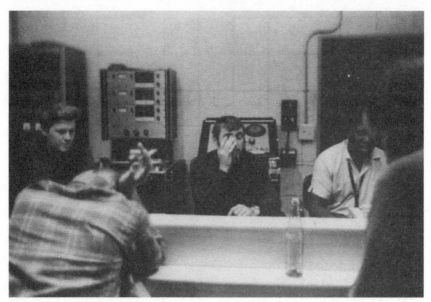

American, July 4, 1967: Mark James, Tom Dowd, King Curtis, with Gene Chrisman and Tommy Cogbill with backs to the camera. (Sid Selvidge)

The American Crew with Elvis Presley: Bobby Wood, Mike Leech, Tommy Cogbill, Gene Chrisman, Bobby Emmons, Reggie Young, Ed Kollis, and Dan Penn. (Courtesy of Knox Phillips)

We started walking upstairs, and he said, 'I ain't got no ideas,' and I said, 'Let's just take off on that 'sweet inspiration,' and we hit the old guitar, and we come back down there in a little while, and they were still moaning and groaning. And we played it to 'em [the song was called, not surprisingly, "Sweet Inspiration"], about the second time Dan ended up on the board, and I was playing guitar."

"You know," says Dan, taking up the story, "I think it was one of the highlights of my career. Just as we bring our little tape down and the Sweet Inspirations done fell in love with it, and all the musicians are going nuts, them stupids called a damn lunch break. Right in the middle of our song. And Spooner had this damn lick down so good the musicians wouldn't even go eat, they wouldn't leave because they knew by what was happening we could just cut it. And the girls were already singing it. And I'm standing there watching all this shit going down. Spooner said, 'I can't play it no better than that. Reggie, you play guitar.' Reggie says, 'Okay.' Everybody's serious, but nobody's really serious. And I see what's happening, and my cash register started going off inside. So I just kind of slid in at the board; I said, 'Roll it!' I did my mix on the first take, and when they come back from lunch, I said, 'Boys, we done cut you a record.' I don't know if Tom Dowd ever quite forgive me for that . . . but don't you ever take a lunch break on me, baby!"

The record made #5 on the soul charts, and Jerry Wexler asked Spooner for a third of the royalties, since he had given the group its name. What were the writers' reactions? "We didn't comment," says Spooner with his dry chuckle.

That was the way things went for the most part, lots of laughs, lots of hits (120, approximately, between November 1967 and January 1971; at one time there were 28 records on the *Billboard* charts in the same week, Chips boasts, all with the same musicians playing on them), lots of competition. In 1968 Chips got his own label, AGP (American Group Productions), which was distributed through Bell. In 1969 Dan went independent with his own studio, Beautiful Sounds (which he operated briefly in partnership with Stax promo man Eddie Braddock), and his own publishing company (Pacemaker). In 1969 Jerry Wexler announced in the trades that he had just signed Dan Penn to an Atlantic recording contract with the added encomium, "When he sings Otis Redding, he makes you cry." Although only one single that I know of resulted from this arrangement, four years later Dan did get to make his debut album for Bell, the very soulful—if very uneven—*Nobody's Fool*. In February 1969, when Elvis Presley finally came back to Memphis to record for the first time in fourteen years, it was the American studio that he chose for the site of his homecoming, with Chips Moman producing. There was nothing really special about it, says Wayne Jackson, who played trumpet on the session; it was just another date. "We had been doing Neil Diamond just before Elvis came in, and Neil was a big deal to us. I mean, we were thrilled about Elvis, but it wasn't like doing Neil Diamond."

Elvis Presley, Dewey Phillips, and Joe Cuoghi: Poplar Tunes. (Courtesy of Molly Cuoghi)

HI TIMES

The one Memphis label yet to hit its stride as the '70s began was Hi Records, the company that had sprung up originally in 1956 in the wake of the success of Sun. This was the very label, in fact, in which Quinton Claunch had first invested—or perhaps participated as a working partner—and from which he had then withdrawn before the investment paid off with the success of "Smokie —Part 2" by the Bill Black Combo, a Top 20 hit in 1959. "Smokie" was not just a financial success; it set a direction for the company for a number of years, as Hi became known as the "house of instrumentals," raising to stardom not just Black and Reggie Young (the guitar sound behind the Bill Black Combo) but future Nashville session man Ace Cannon and his honky-tonk sax and, in the '60s, trumpeter Willie Mitchell. Joe Cuoghi remained principal owner, and the label continued to dabble in rockabilly throughout the decade, but it wasn't until Willie Mitchell began taking on a&r responsibilities in the mid-to-late '60s that the direction of Hi changed significantly.

If ever there was anyone with an impeccable pedigree in Memphis music, it was Willie Mitchell. Born in 1928 in Ashland, Mississippi, he had joined Tuff Green's and Al Jackson, Sr.'s big bands while still in high school, played on B. B. King's first sides, and studied the Schillinger method of composition at Rust College, which he had attended for three years with Onzie Horne, who would

A young Willie Mitchell. (Courtesy of Joe McEwen)

later become musical director first for King and, in the '70s, for Isaac Hayes. Along the way he formed his own seventeen-piece band, played society gigs as well as country ball games with Howlin' Wolf ("He'd nastymouth the horn players, say, 'Goddammit, boy, I don't want no more of that blee-blop stuff, ain't you got no soul?' "), and acquired a thoroughgoing musical education.

In 1950 Willie was drafted into the Army, and there he went from radio operator to the Special Services, where he joined an eighteen-piece band behind popular singer Vic Damone. When he returned to Memphis in the mid-'50s, after a brief sojourn playing burlesque shows in Buffalo, he started up his own band again in earnest and took up residence at the newly built Danny's Club in West Memphis, then at the Manhattan Club and the Plantation Inn, where he soon became known to most of Memphis's music habitués. The music that he played was characteristically cool, swinging, and sophisticated; the musicians who passed through his band were a virtual Who's Who of Memphis jazz players—Phineas Newborn, Jr., Charles Lloyd, Booker Little, Frank Strozier, George Coleman, and Willie's younger brother, James, on tenor sax, along with a rhythm section that consisted of Lewis Steinberg on bass and Al Jackson, Jr., on drums, one half of the original Booker T. and the MG's. To young whites like Steve Cropper and Duck Dunn, Jim Dickinson and Packy Axton, who made the PI their second home, bands like Willie's were the pinnacle of cool and provided a level of musicianship and formal elegance to which they could scarcely aspire. To Memphis's fledgling "music industry" these bands, with their natural reservoir of reading musicians, were a resource to be tapped. In the mid-'50s Willie did lead sheets for Sam Phillips. In 1959 his piano player, Joe Hall, was brought in to the Hi studio to play a lick that was a staple in the Willie Mitchell band's repertoire. Hall left before the session was complete ("Someone called him a nigger or something," says a white participant), but the lick turned into "Smokie—Part 2."

Willie, in the meantime, besides working the club circuit, had found a new gig over at Reuben Cherry's Home of the Blues record label, where he was producing Memphis's most popular semi-resident group, the "5" Royales, as well as Roy Brown, the great blues shouter. None of the records he worked on were big sellers, and Willie's heart remained in jazz anyway; besides, his ambition was still focused on becoming a recording artist himself. So that when he was approached to make records for Hi in late 1961, he jumped at the opportunity. He had a little hit in 1962 with the instrumental "Sunrise Serenade," and then in 1964 he had a little bigger one with "20–75." It was around this time, too, that Willie, a light-skinned, elegant-looking man with a pencil-thin moustache and a formal, rather imperious manner, was being won over by the new vocabulary of "soul music" and the old attraction of the Memphis beat. "It's the laziness of the rhythm. You hear those old lazy horns half a beat behind the music, and you think they're gonna miss it, and all of a sudden, just so lazy, they come in and start to sway with it. It's like kind of shucking you, putting you on." He didn't begin applying this kind of thinking to vocalists, though, until Don Robey approached him in late 1966 to produce his new acquisition, O. V. Wright. With the subsequent chart success of Wright's "Eight Men, Four Women," Robey brought Bobby Bland in to the Hi studio, where Bobby cut half of a fine LP, *A Touch of the Blues.* This was when Mitchell's vision of r&b really began to crystallize, a vision curiously like Roosevelt Jamison's—though unlike Roosevelt, Willie had a fully developed appreciation of melody.

"I wanted to cut a record that would sell black and white, combine the two, you know, in a *pleasant* kind of music. With O. V. Wright and Bobby Bland, their style was too strong in one direction, it was too rough. I wanted to add more class to it. O.V.'s music was a little more laid back; Bobby's had a little more spark to it. But I was trying to get a combination of the two."

That is what he worked on for the next couple of years. He continued producing O. V. Wright for Don Robey's Backbeat label with a good deal of success. He did frequent horn arrangements for Chips or Goldwax and kept in touch with what was going on at Stax both by playing on the occasional session and through Al Jackson, who remained his number-one drummer even after Willie developed a percussive double in Howard Grimes. Most of all, though, he realized, Hi had to shake its instrumental-and novelty-only tag if it ever wanted to broaden its appeal. He approached owner Joe Cuoghi and said, "Joe, we need to bring some singers on this label." When Cuoghi assented, he experimented with various singers (early on he had worked with Memphis vocalist-about-town Donald Hines and Stax songwriter David Porter, who recorded under the name of Kenny Cain), but it wasn't until much of the soul explosion was already over that he found singers with whom he could work freely and finally develop the sound that he envisioned. In 1968 Stax session man Bowlegs Miller brought Ann Peebles, a twenty-one-year-old St. Louis native who had sat in with his band at the Rosewood Club, into the studio, and Willie recorded her, for the first time taking over the board. He still couldn't get the vocal sound to his satisfaction, but the first release, "Walk Away," was a hit and the fourth, "Part Time Love," a smash. At the same time he was producing hits on Syl Johnson and Otis Clay on outside production deals and, more significantly, had already met the singer who would change both Hi's fortunes and his own.

In 1968 Willie was enjoying his biggest instrumental hit, "Soul Serenade," and touring widely. He was booked into a club in Midland, Texas, and his brother, James, was rehearsing the singer who was going to open for him as a solo act that night. "I went and got me a beer and was sitting at a table—we'd had about a 900-mile drive from Memphis, left at two, got in some time in the afternoon—and this singer did, you know, hard songs like Sam and Dave, that kind of stuff. Then he called for 'Back Up Train.' I said, 'Really? I didn't know you had done that. How old is the record?' He said, 'Well, the record is about two years old now, and I ain't really had anything since. It don't have but three changes to it.' So he began singing 'Back Up Train,' and I'm listening, and, God, he was singing soft, and I said, 'This guy has got the style, he got the sound to really be something.' So I called up Joe [Cuoghi], and I said, 'Joe, I found a singer down here, and I want to bring him back to Memphis.' "

The singer had introduced himself as Albert Greene, and "Back Up Train" was his only hit. In fact he had been booked into the Apollo on the strength of that one song, but he was discovering, as he confessed to Mitchell, that it was hard to make much of a career when you had no follow-up.

"I said, 'Why don't you come on back to Memphis with me?' I said, 'You can be a star.' He said, 'How long would it take?' I said, 'Probably a year and a half.' He looked at me, and he said, 'Well, you know, I can't wait that long.' I said, 'With lots of work within a year and a half you could really be a star.' And he said, 'I really can't wait that long.' So we went and played the gig. That night we got ready to go. He said, 'Where y'all going?' I told him Memphis. He said, 'I don't have money to get back to Flint [Greene was born in Forrest City, Arkansas, in 1946 but had moved to Grand Rapids, Michigan, at thirteen with his family]. Can I get a ride with you to Little Rock? That'd be seven or eight hundred miles closer.' So he jumps in the bus, we had maybe an eight-passenger van, and he has to sit on the hump. I'm driving and we strike up a conversation—this is at three o'clock in the morning, y'understand? Late the next day we're still driving, still talking, and he said, 'You really think I could be a star?' I said, 'Yeah. You could be a star. Take lots of work.' He said, 'Well, if I could pay off some bills in Flint, I could come to Memphis, and we could really do it.' I said, 'How much bills you talking about?' He said, 'Take

$1500 to pay my bills up.' So I said, 'Well . . .'—I really thought about it—'Okay. When we get to Memphis, we get the $1500.' (I didn't even know if Joe was going to give me the $1500 or not). 'Then you can go home, pay your bills, and come back.'

"So he came to Memphis, and we gave him the $1500 without a contract or anything, and he was supposed to come back in about a week. About six weeks went by, and I didn't hear from him, and I just kind of forgot about it, because 'Soul Serenade' was still hot, and I was catching a lot of gigs with the Motown artists and what have you. And I was at home one morning about six o'clock, and somebody hit on my door—this is almost two months later. Well, I thought it was the painter, see, I was just having my house painted, and I went to the door, and I said, 'Man, why y'all come to paint so early?' And he said, 'Don't you remember me? I'm Al Greene.' "

This was Al Green's arrival in Memphis. With that arrival all of Willie Mitchell's ideas fell into place, and Memphis music entered a new phase. Because even as Stax was running into economic and artistic roadblocks in the early '70s, and soul music itself was casting about for a new direction, Willie Mitchell and Al Green came up with an old idea phrased in a new way, the last eccentric refinement of Sam Cooke's lyrical, gospel-edged style as filtered through the fractured vocal approach of Otis Redding and the peculiarly fragmented vision of Al Green himself. This was a vision it would be virtually impossible to characterize ("What makes you think you can use the name Al Green?" Al Green said one time to me, in a lilting West Indian accent. "Don't you know the name Al Green is a registered trademark?"), and it proved in the end to be incompatible with worldly ambition, but it was always marked by an unerring musicality, and in the beginning at least, Green had his feet planted a little more solidly on the ground. Willie Mitchell knew exactly what he wanted at any rate, he knew the sound he was looking for, and now, in addition to the singer, he had his own rhythm section, too, with Al Jackson and Howard Grimes on drums plus a trio of brothers in their early twenties—Teenie, Charles, and Leroy Hodges on guitar, organ, and bass respectively—whom he had practically raised from the time they were kids. He had the requisite run-down studio set in a former movie theater (the Royal), with the requisite faith that went with it ("There's something about the floor," he told more than one reporter. "As you go down that slope, the music gets bigger, it separates."). He had mastered the technology of recording, developed his own distinctive bass sound (a Willie Mitchell production is immediately recognizable for its "bottom"), and found in the eight-track, tube-amplified Ampex recorder that Hi already possessed machinery in which he could place an almost mystical belief. Willie Mitchell was ready.

It took just about eighteen months, as he had predicted, to make Al Green a star. He started him off with an abortive cover of the Beatles' "I Want to Hold

Al Green. (Val Wilmer)

Your Hand" in early 1969 and then a more aesthetically satisfying, but no better-selling, version of the Hayes-Porter ballad "One Woman." It wasn't until late 1970 that Green finally hit with a remake of the Temptations' "I Can't Get Next to You," an unlikely choice since it had been a #1 smash the previous year. In 1971 he had "Tired of Being Alone," the first of his self-compositions to make the charts (it went to #11 pop), and then "Let's Stay Together," a Mitchell-Green-Al Jackson collaboration this time, marked the first of more than fifteen Top 10 singles (it went to #1 pop and r&b) that Green would have over the next five years. It also marked the first full realization of Willie Mitchell's vision of soul music on a higher plane, employing a muted string section, soft sophisticated melody with a gospel twist ("We used some nice diminished ninths with Al," says Willie with satisfaction), and the unique coloration of Al Green's voice(s), given free rein for the first time in all their fragile intertwined glory, wherein falsetto interpolations meet the last refined tendrils of religious ecstasy. It has been said that Green in later years would spend more than a hundred hours on a vocal part, putting together, note by burbling note, each little comment and countercomment to elegantly stated melody, and while "Let's Stay Together" appears to have been assembled a little more spontaneously than that, it conveys the same decorative filigree, the same sort of layered elegance with which Willie Mitchell and Al Green would soon take soul music—real, unabashed, wholehearted soul music—to quiet, luxuriantly appointed places it had never been before.

"Well, you see, after we had done 'Tired of Being Alone' and 'I Can't Get Next to You,' I said, 'Al, look, we got to soften you up some.' I said, 'You got to whisper. You got to cut the lighter music. The melody has got to be good. You got to sing it soft. If we can get the dynamic bottom on it and make some sense with pretty changes, then we going to be there.' He said, 'Man, I can't sing that way. That's too soft. That ain't gonna sound like no man singing.' We had the damnedest fights, but I think 'Let's Stay Together' really sold him that I had the right direction for him musically, 'cause, see, all the things I told him turned out to be true. Like 'Let's Stay Together' he didn't like at all, but when we put it out, it was gold in two weeks. So we softened and softened and softened. And you know, back then he had long hair, and I got him to cut that off, and I said, 'We got to get you some sharp suits. You know, clean yourself up, get you to look like the all-American boy.' And after 'Let's Stay Together' he did."

Al Green had a run of success unprecedented in Memphis, or perhaps in all Southern soul music history. He might in fact still be enjoying that success had it not been that in 1976, beset with increasing personal problems, religious doubts, dramatic crises (two years earlier, in a widely publicized episode, a disappointed woman friend scalded Green with grits, then killed herself), and serious questions of identity, he broke with Willie Mitchell, recorded a couple of brilliant homemade albums whose ambiguous message seemed directed first at God, then at man, and then in 1980 gave himself back to the church in an attempt, it seemed, to exorcise certain unexorcisable demons. For the last few years he has presided over his own Church of the Full Gospel Tabernacle in Memphis, recorded several best-selling gospel albums, declared even more explicitly his musical allegiance to Sam Cooke, and seemingly found no more peace in all of these activities than he did in his virtually unparalleled rhythm and blues success. Speaking to Al Green today can be an exercise in forbearance, as he addresses himself with the eloquence of a Professor Irwin Corey to subjects never raised, jumps from topic to topic with the skittishness of a startled deer, and generally does not seem to be of this world.

Willie Mitchell meanwhile continued not just as producer but as chief operating officer of Hi Records, a position he had held virtually from the time that he first started working with Al Green. In the late spring of 1970 Jerry

Al Green and Willie Mitchell, outside the Royal Recording Studio, 1985. (Pat Rainer)

Wexler, always on the lookout for talent, had offered him a job with Atlantic, and Joe Cuoghi, not about to have his right-hand man stolen away from him, appointed Willie vice-president. Then in July, just around the time "I Can't Get Next to You" was released, Cuoghi died of a heart attack in the parking lot of the Memphis airport, and Willie became principal administrator of the company. Even after Al left, Hi continued to be a profitable enterprise, and Willie maintained a consistent level of activity with his solid stable of performers—O. V. Wright, Syl Johnson, Otis Clay, et al—until in 1980 he broke with his crack recording unit, the Hodges brothers, for reasons that have never been specified. Since then he has refused to talk much about any of the defections, except to say quite truthfully that "Al left the public, the public didn't leave him," and, of the loss of his rhythm section, that the sound was getting stale and predictable anyway. In recent years he has not enjoyed resounding popular success, but he is still busy with new projects, still full of fresh ideas, and, when I spoke with him in the fall of 1980, still down at the Royal Recording Studio at 1329 South Lauderdale, with its run-down exterior, up-to-the-minute technological appointments, and security system that only intermittently works, in the same bleak neighborhood in the same unlikely location that a certain Mrs. Frisbee rented to Joe Cuoghi twenty-five years earlier for fifty dollars a month.

Stax Goes to Europe/
The Big O Comes Home:
Triumph and Tragedy

*Just in case you hadn't heard—the Stax Show must be
one of the raviest, grooviest, slickest tour packages
that Britain has ever seen. And if you haven't seen it
already—pull your finger out!*

—*New Musical Express,* March 18, 1967

*Otis, Otis Redding was his name
Without his soulful singing this old world won't be the same.*

—William Bell, "A Tribute to a King"

S TAX, GOLDWAX, FAME, ATLANTIC—THESE WERE
magical names in 1966 and 1967 in Great Britain and on the Continent,
where fanzines and clubs sprang up with the frequency and fanaticism
that once attended the birth of rock 'n' roll. "Welcome to the first edition
of the Fame-Goldwax magazine," announced Organizing Secretary D. McAleer
in December 1966 in a mimeographed edition of fifty, "which as far as we can find
out is the first in the world devoted to two U.S. record company's who are not
affiliated to each other!" At a time when sales were just starting to take off in
this country, and the mystique of Southern soul was finally becoming established
("When you want to make certain types of records and wish to capture the
pristine r&b sound," announced Jerry Wexler in *Billboard* at the end of 1966,
"you need to go South"), Solomon Burke, Rufus Thomas, and Ben E. King
had already toured Britain, in advance of the 1965 Motown Revue; in 1966
Solomon made his triumphant return, while Otis Redding, Don Covay, and
the Mad Lads (Stax engineer-artist William Brown's group) all enjoyed successful visits in the fall of that year. The National Soul Board was formed to
incorporate the various magazines *(Soul Music Monthly, Soul Beat, Home of the
Blues,* the aforementioned *Fame-Goldwax Soul Survey)* and clubs (Klooks Kleek,
Tiles, the Marquee) that fed the constantly expanding appetite for Southern soul.
There was avid curiosity about James Carr and Dan Penn; names like "Lindon

Oldham" and "Prince Conley" (not to be confused with Arthur Conley) cropped up in fanzine newsletters; and Rick Hall's and Quinton Claunch's every ascertainable move was scrutinized respectfully, as if the world of soul were some Hollywood dream factory instead of the hardscrabble, small-town existence that saw Hall working in a used-car lot and Quinton making his living selling hardware supplies. Of all the legends that were fostered, undoubtedly the legend of Stax (the Little Company that Could) was the most powerful, both as metaphor and reality. When Otis Redding appeared at Tiles in September 1966, over 8000 patrons paid twenty-five shillings apiece to see "the American soul giant," and his appearance on ITV's *Ready, Steady, Go!* gave him national exposure which only fueled the national passion for "Memphis music."

This is what set the stage for the first official Stax-Volt (Otis was still on the Stax subsidiary Volt) tour of Europe in the spring of '67. To the British it was no doubt a logical enough step, and one that, like Elvis's long-promised (but never-realized) English tour, was perhaps overdue; to the participants, who embarked upon this rash venture with a mixture of trepidation and almost childlike delight, the whole expedition must have seemed a little like Columbus's in reverse, with each step eastward taking them perilously closer to the edge of the world as they knew it. "We were living in a kind of cocoon," Booker T. later explained. "We were just going to the studio every day and making music. Not even reading the trade magazines. Not knowing how the rest of the world saw Stax." In Europe they found out, and the knowledge was predictably unsettling.

The tour was officially billed as the Stax-Volt Revue ("Hit the Road, Stax"), which was, to begin with, a little bit of a misnomer since Otis Redding's protégé Arthur Conley, who got second billing after Percy Sledge dropped out, was on the Atco (Atlantic) label. Another minor anomaly: in Great Britain the first programs and ads announced that this was the Otis Redding Show, with support from Conley, Sam and Dave, Booker T. and the MG's, Stax's newest hit-maker Eddie Floyd, and—for one English date and the concert at the Paris Olympia only—the Memphis Queen of Soul, Carla Thomas. The whole matter of billing received some attention from the British musical press, and a small debate ensued about truth in packaging—did the program title represent star ego or printer's error?—but all this was swept aside by the entrance of the principal actors themselves.

The reception from the moment they landed was almost not to be believed. All the British papers heralded the arrival with headlines; the interviews, reviews, and expressions of faith were so laudatory as to be almost embarrassing. ("Yours till Steve Cropper plays a bum note" was the sign-off on a letter to the editor from one faithful correspondent. "It's great to hear it, but I played a bum note only last night," responded Cropper, nothing if not politely literalminded.) The one music weekly that expressed any reservations, the *Record*

Members of the OTIS REDDING soul revue—which opens at London's Finsbury Park Astoria tonight (Friday)—are pictured on their arrival at London Airport on Monday morning. They are (from left to right) BOOKER T. and the three M.G.'s, CARLA THOMAS, EDDIE FLOYD, the three MAR-KEYS, ARTHUR CONLEY, and DAVE (of SAM and DAVE). Otis himself arrived last Saturday, with Sam flying in to complete the package on Monday night.

Stax Arrives. (Courtesy of Bill Millar)

Mirror, was faced with a near-typhoon of protest when its critic, Norman Jopling, an avowed fan, reviewed the opening show at the Finsbury Park Astoria in less than ecstatic terms. The Beatles sent limos to the airport to pick up the entourage and tried in vain to arrange for a jam session, but they were in the midst of finishing up their long-awaited *Sergeant Pepper* album and were never able to do anything more than attend Carla Thomas's show at the Bag O' Nails, where, upon meeting Steve Cropper, "the four Beatles stood in unison and bowed from the waist." Jim Stewart flew in to survey just what he had wrought. Tom Dowd, who observed the Memphis musicians with some amusement ("It was like a mind-blowing experience, because they were going to be away from home, not for three or four days but for five weeks, and they were going to be eating all that funny food and talking all those funny languages. . . ."), recorded the first show on Friday night, the Paris show the following Wednesday, had both albums mixed and mastered within a week, and then flew home.

As for the musicians, they seem to have been as wonder-struck as Dowd suggests. Just before the tour began, Duck Dunn and ex–Mar-Key Wayne Jackson had been coleading a band at Hernando's Hideaway (they had just graduated from Li'l Abner's Rebel Room), making a hundred dollars a night for the entire group and working six nights a week in addition to their regular studio gig. "Duck and I quit that job to go on the Stax-Volt Revue," says Wayne, "and believe me, we had to think it over. We had no idea how successful the band was or the company was until we got over there. You know, we all brought cameras and thousands of feet of film, everyone took their wives because everyone had married real young—Duck and June, Packy and Patti, Steve and his wife. We thought this was one chance in a lifetime. You ought to see the movies I got. I got movies of Russian airliners and clouds, tulips, and Steve Cropper's ring! Man, I never thought I was gonna leave the dirt farm in Arkansas. If you'd told me I was gonna do all this with my trumpet, I would have laughed. But there was a point came when we were working six nights a week at the club, me and Duck, and we was picking up $40 a session, and Jim would give us a salary of $250 a week besides—well, we were working from 10 A.M. till two the next morning, but we were making money, and it

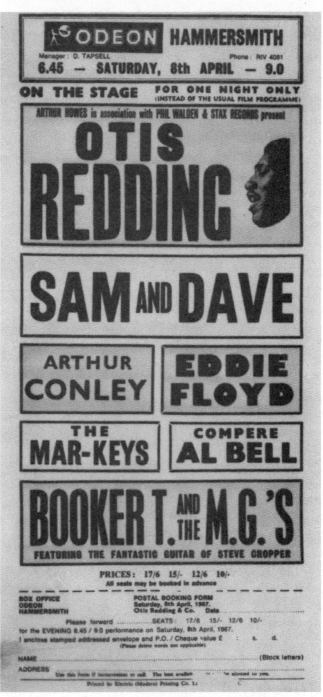

(Courtesy of John Stuart, Secretary of the Otis Redding Appreciation Society)

was really kind of incredible to us. And when I woke up and had a new house and a car and money and I was playing trumpet for a living, it was like Alice in Wonderland for me, it always has been. And then Europe—just kids, and that was our first time out. We had a ball!"

Just about everyone who saw the show had a ball, too. The MG's came on first, sharp in their lime-green suits. Next the so-called Mar-Keys joined them (this was really just a three-man division of the Stax horn section: Wayne, Andrew Love, and baritone sax Joe Arnold, all dressed in royal blue) for a swift reprise of "Philly Dog" and a marathon "Last Night." Then the featured vocalists arrived in swift array: Arthur Conley with his brand-new #2 pop and soul hit, sounding like a cross between Otis and Sam Cooke, slipping and sliding around the stage like James Brown, and asking the rhetorical question "Do you like good music? (Yeah, yeah.) That sweet soul music?" Next up was Eddie Floyd, off of *his* big hit ("Knock on Wood" had gone to #1 on the soul charts the previous fall), not a charismatic stage personality but a thoroughly professional entertainer nonetheless. Carla Thomas charmed the few audiences that saw her on her school break, introducing "Yesterday" as "a number recorded by a London group" and credibly reviving "Gee Whiz" in a form-fitting gold-spangled dress. Sam and Dave, of course, electrified their British audience, so electrified them, in fact, that though they received only third billing on this tour, they would be back twice more in the next year alone, each time headlining their own show. And they set the stage for Otis Redding, as they had for the last several months at home—set the stage on fire might be more like it—so that he was never able to coast, never able to approach a show as anything less than mortal combat, and emerged each night with his black double-breasted suit soaked with sweat, his voice hoarse from imprecation.

"STAX—THE RAVE SHOW TO END THEM ALL," declared *Melody Maker*. "One of the wildest, most jumping tours to hit our island in a long time," echoed *Disc* and most of the other music commentators. There were dissenting voices, to be sure. Bill Millar, an astute critic and longtime fan, wondered if Eddie Floyd's one "overriding talent is to see how many times it is possible to cram 'Let me hear you say yeah' into three songs. . . ." And he was more seriously concerned about the direction that Otis Redding's talent was taking. He felt that Otis's vocal style was becoming increasingly mannered, his gestures more and more aimed at pleasing the crowd rather than expressing honest emotion ("all grins and smiles on what ought to be the most soulful of numbers"), that Otis, in short, "overrated." I think this would pretty much mirror my own view, but you have only to listen to the records from these shows to pick up the energy level, the kinetic excitement in the air, the whole sense of emotional overdrive that put the show across while at the same time causing the band to play too fast, that focused all eyes and ears on the singer while leading him or her simply to try to pack too much into every song. There

Otis at the Upper Cut, March 18, 1967. (From the collection of Fred Lewis)

is a frenetic note that is at odds with the spare classicism of the "Stax sound." It is as if for the first time all the underlying tensions that had been building for so long at Stax were able to come out; all of a sudden feelings that could not be directly acknowledged revealed themselves in sidelong ways.

This was the final, scarcely discerned undercurrent of the European tour. On the surface all remained sweetness and light. "I'd hate to be a star," Steve Cropper declared over and over in his British interviews. "What I enjoy is being part of the Stax scene. . . . It's a family atmosphere. . . . If one of our artists becomes a bigger star than the others—no jealousy. Just a pat on the shoulder from all of us." "First and foremost," declared Booker, "we want the company's records to sell. . . . It's just never occurred to me to move on. We believe in what we're doing. We get the rewards and we're happy."

Well, maybe. Not everyone was happy, though. It started with the decision about just who was to go to Europe in the first place. Original Stax artists like Rufus Thomas and William Bell were hurt and resentful at being left behind, when a newcomer like Arthur Conley, not even a Stax artist, was included (and received billing over bigger stars like Sam and Dave) at the insistence of his discoverer, and producer, Otis Redding. Then, too, the company was going through a serious political realignment at home, with Al Bell taking over an increasing proportion of the day-to-day business, and Estelle's absence, and Al Bell's presence, on the tour was only further evidence of this dramatic shift in power. But the worst friction to arise on the trip was the product of that most common, if complex, of factors: jealousy among people who never previously knew that there was anything to be jealous about. Even as they were denying worldly ambition to the public, says Steve Cropper, their own little world was breaking up.

"It was just a mind-blower. Hell, we were just in Memphis cutting records; we didn't know. Then when we got over there, there were hoards of people waiting at the airport, autograph hounds and all that sort of stuff. I didn't know what that was all about. That was something that happened to Elvis or Ricky Nelson, but it didn't happen to the Stax-Volt band, it didn't happen to Booker T. and the MG's.

"Now, you see, I got singled out. I was doing a lot of interviews and all that, and there was a lot of animosity. I thought I was doing the guys a favor. I was the one who was receptive to talking, and they weren't, and some things went down—I'll tell you, we had a big meeting in Al Bell's room one night, and some things were said, there were some bad feelings that I never, ever got over. Like I was given in no uncertain terms: change your ways or else. Well, change what ways? Like we're all in this together. They seemed to take it like I was in it for myself. 'You're wrong. I've been the one fighter for the team since Day One. The only one that's been fighting for the team, that's trying to keep *the* team together.' When we came back, all of a sudden I wasn't a&r director anymore. I was still a member of the band, I was still making the same money, but I had no stick. My stick was taken away and given to Al Bell."

"I had never thought about it before," says Duck Dunn. "All I knew was that every day they were saying, 'You got to cut a hit record. You got to cut a hit record.' I never really thought about what we was attempting to do. I never knew how big those records were, 'cause they never let us find out about it. We never got out of the studio! Until we got to Europe. When we got to Europe and found out how big we were, everyone kind of got up in the air about it. That was probably what changed more than anything else."

Even Otis Redding—up till then seemingly above the hurly-burly—came in for his share of criticism. He was getting stuck up, it was said by some of his fellow artists. He was acting the star. The matter of billing—Otis's and Arthur Conley's—continued to rankle. "Everybody got mad at Otis for a while," says Stax songwriter Joe Shamwell, now a professor of communications at Jackson State University in Jackson, Mississippi. "It all kind of went to his head, and Otis started to grandstand and act like they were his peons. It was like he was the sole architect of Stax's success."

How much of this feeling actually surfaced at the time is open to question. Certainly in legend Otis remains sacrosanct, and even contemporary accounts generally skirt any criticism of Stax's one true "superstar." What everyone can affirm is that success agreed with Otis; the big, bluff country boy gained perceptibly in confidence with each new triumph; the European tour was just one more in a notable sequence of events which, far from simply enlarging his opinion of himself, actually enlarged his view of the world and his own potential within it. June Dunn describes seeing him in performance around this time, the special aura that he projected that was so different from the simple egoism of the ordinary performer.

"It was at a Memphis Revue, I couldn't believe it. Everyone would come out, and they would all have on a sharper suit and be cooler or better than the group ahead of them. Otis was the last, and I thought, *What is he going to do to impress them?* Otis walked out, and he had on a plain black tuxedo—everybody else was in like chartreuse—but he wore that . . . *halo.* He just strutted out in that plain black tuxedo with that big smile, and everyone just went wow." "When you talked to him," interjected Duck, "he was like you was. Then you see him on stage. Hey, there ain't too many people wear the crown. Elvis wore it, and I guess Frank Sinatra wore it. And here he comes, and, boy, he wore it. He wore that halo. He knew it. He was a goddam star."

TAKING CARE OF BUSINESS

More than just a star, though, Otis also wanted to be a "businessman." His publicity of the time cites his 200 suits and 400 pairs of shoes, and he was taking in $35,000 a week in concert fees, but Otis was proudest, it sometimes seemed, of his success as a writer and producer of others, of his ability to concentrate on the task at hand, whatever it might be, and simply "take care of business." His advice to the aspiring artist was: "If you want to be a singer, you've got to concentrate on it twenty-four hours a day; you can't be a well-driller, too," and his wife, Zelma, and Phil and Alan Walden still speak with admiration and surprise of both the intensity and scope of Otis's ambition. Most of the outside ventures in which he had been involved to date were little more than investments in a sense: a publishing company (Redwal) set up in partnership with Phil and Alan; the office building in which Phil Walden now did have associates; another building in which there were plans to house a recording studio; and a record label called Jotis which combined Otis's name with that of his original sponsor, Joe Galkin, and was distributed by Stax (Galkin, along with his partner, Joe Shribman, retained copublishing with Stax, and then Redwal, too, on all of Otis's songs throughout his career). All of this would have required very little of Otis other than his willingness to put his earnings into something with long-term growth potential. Otis was looking to be more than a silent partner, though, and he was not interested in having his own label as just another star "perc." He was nearly as serious about Jotis as he was about his own music, and as anxious to establish himself in this new role as he had been in the old.

The first and third releases in 1965—"Do the Sloopy" by Macon artist Billy Young and "Baby Cakes" by Loretta Williams, an Otis Redding discovery—didn't do much to advance anyone's career. They were recorded on the run, entered in the Stax catalog, and might just as well have been left at that,

Otis and Rick Hall (right front), with Arthur Conley (in white shirt). (Courtesy of Rick Hall)

so little an impression did they make on the world. It was the second Jotis single that gave Otis Redding credibility not just as a producer but as a talent scout. Jotis 470 was Arthur Conley's record debut as a solo artist.

Arthur Conley was nineteen in 1965, according to his publicity bio. He grew up in Atlanta, and by his style it was obvious that he was a great admirer of Sam Cooke. That alone might have recommended him to Otis, but "I'm a Lonely Stranger," the song that Otis heard on a demo backstage in Baltimore, must have recommended him even more. Though it is ostensibly just another tale of lost love and a broken heart, there is something eerie about the whole presentation—wistful vocal, halting phrasing, enigmatic lyrics, and all. There is something strangely troubled in the singer's voice, a quality of hurt that carries the song beyond its nominal genre. Let Otis, or more likely Phil Walden speaking in Otis's voice, take up the story in Otis's liner notes to Conley's first album.

"I flipped about Arthur the first time I ever heard him . . . when a friend played me a demo record Arthur had made. If this seems like too much for one blues singer to say about another I can only say that's the way it is. In fact I got so excited about that record that my friend [Rufus Mitchell] decided I should meet him. I did, and after talking to him for a while I became his record producer.

"With the help of Stax-Volt President Jim Stewart, I recorded Arthur Conley doing that song and issued it on my Jotis label. It wasn't a big hit, but it started Arthur on his way. After that Jim and I recorded Arthur doing 'Who's Foolin' Who', a [second] tune that Arthur wrote himself. It moved him another step forward in his career.

"The next two records by Arthur Conley were cut in Muscle Shoals, Alabama, with the help of Rick Hall, the President of Fame Records. They gave Arthur even more exposure throughout the country.

"The first record I produced on my own was 'Sweet Soul Music.' That's the one that did it. Arthur's fabulous performance on that record turned it into a smash hit. It made Arthur Conley a big name on the soul scene."

It also brought on a lawsuit from J. W. Alexander, Sam Cooke's old partner, who still maintained Kags Music with all of Sam's songs in it. For "Sweet Soul Music" turned out to be as much of a "borrowing" from Cooke's "Yeah Man" as "Pain in My Heart" had been from Irma Thomas's "Ruler of My Heart." J.W., always the gentleman, settled without much of a fuss in exchange for a decent consideration, publishing credit, and the assurance that Otis Redding would record other songs from the Kags catalog in the future. This, of course, was an assurance that could readily be given, since Otis had always recorded Sam's songs on his albums.

Arthur Conley never even paused for breath. While "Sweet Soul Music" was still on the charts he went to Europe, and when he came back, he immediately had another, smaller pop hit with a revival of Big Joe Turner's "Shake, Rattle and Roll." Despite his runaway success, and greater sales than Otis

Speedo Simms, Arthur Conley, Alan Walden. (Courtesy of Alan Walden)

Redding had ever achieved, his admiration for his mentor never wavered ("When I first met him," says Alan Walden, "he would sleep on Otis's floor!"), nor did his knowledge of whom he had to thank for that success. Interestingly Otis had moved him off the Stax-distributed Jotis label before "Sweet Soul Music" came out, with the first two Muscle Shoals sessions, in fact (which appeared on Rick Hall's Fame label). "Sweet Soul Music" itself was released on the Atlantic subsidiary Atco, a move that appeared doubly significant for all the rumors swirling about that had Otis breaking with Stax, Otis signing with Jerry Wexler, Wexler doing for Otis Redding what he had just done for Aretha Franklin. Jim Stewart passes this all off as idle chatter; after all, Otis had re-signed with Stax for five years in 1965, and the fact that he had taken Arthur Conley to Muscle Shoals was simply due to the very heavy booking schedule at the Stax studio during that particular period. Jerry Wexler did nothing to discourage the rumors, though (far from it), and Alan Walden makes no bones about the strained relations between his brother and Jim Stewart at the time, so I don't think it is stretching things to see Arthur's move as a kind of presage of things to come.

Intrigue aside, Arthur Conley was ready to move in whatever direction Otis pointed. He was not, according to those who knew him, a fully developed personality, either on stage or off. He was "confused," says Otis's brother, Rodgers, "naïve," says Alan Walden, uncertain of his true nature, others suggest. "Arthur Conley was the invention of Otis Redding," says Tom Dowd, who was slated to coproduce Arthur's next album at American with Otis but ended up producing it there alone. "Otis," says Speedo Simms, Redding's road manager and subsequently Arthur's, "really kept him in line. He had to pay attention to Otis. He respected Otis. Otis was the one who could make him. He just had the voice." Otis, for his part, applied all the lessons that he had learned coming up, tried to pass on whatever knowledge he had acquired to his young protégé, and perhaps in the process further unsuited him to independence. In the end, for better or worse, Arthur Conley was a star.

"Being an A&R man," continued Otis in the liner notes to Conley's first album, "is still a new thing for me. Arthur makes the job exciting through his great artistry. I feel he's in the early stages of a sensational career as a recording artist and in-person performer. Listen to him on this new album and see if you don't agree with me. Sincerely, OTIS REDDING."

Monterey, 1967. (Jim Marshall)

THE BIG O

> *Hi, this is the Big O, Otis Redding. I was just standing here thinking about you. Thought I'd write a song about you and dedicate it to you. Take a listen:*
>
> *If you didn't go back to school this year*
>   *you're really not groovy*
> *Maybe you feel that school is a drag*
> *It just don't move you.*
> *But did you ever think about how square*
>   *you look standing*
> *In an employment line*
> *Because school didn't interest you?*
>
> —Otis Redding, from the Stax LP *Stay in School,* Fall 1967

The Stax-Volt tour came at the end of March, and when it was over, the Macon *Telegraph and News* reported in one of its first extensive stories on Macon's most celebrated native son, Otis returned home to the 300-acre farm which he had bought in Round Oak and rechristened the Big O Ranch. "On his farm," the newspaper respectfully recounted, "Otis has built a large, two-story brick home. He has a small herd of registered black Angus cattle, several horses, [and] a 3 1/2-acre lake which he has just recently stocked. . . ." In June he went out again to play the Monterey Pop Festival, a pre-Woodstock celebration which held out the hope of fellowship and fame but not of remuneration. ("Andrew Oldham contacted us," recalled Phil Walden, "and told us nobody would get any money. I called Jerry Wexler at Atlantic, and he checked it out.") Once again the MG's were backing him, once again they came dressed in their lime-green suits. ("You were so naïve," June Dunn twits her husband. "Who else but you guys would play Monterey in green mohair suits? You were out of your league.") Monterey was the promise of a brave new world.

"He was so nervous," says Zelma Redding. "I've never seen Otis so excited or proud. He said, 'It's gonna put my career up some more. I think I'm gonna reach an audience that I've never had before.'"

He took the stage shortly after 1 A.M. in a slight drizzle, following the Jefferson Airplane, who were fresh from their biggest hit, "Somebody to Love." The only strictly black-oriented act to precede him was Lou Rawls, although an unknown Jimi Hendrix, along with his Monterey sponsor Brian Jones, were in attendance backstage. Otis, like the MG's, was wearing a shiny green suit, and according to Jerry Wexler, he was ill at ease. "The Jefferson Airplane," Wexler reminisced in *Blues & Soul* magazine, "had this light show and these huge amplifiers and they were great, they turned on the crowd. . . . And here [came] Booker T. and the MG's, four pieces with their little small amps, and they did an instrumental set—their sound was so small by contrast. It got a little better when Wayne Jackson and Andrew Love came on—they get a lot of sound out of their horns. But it was a contrast. This rhythm and blues doesn't rely on the effects that rock does. But when Otis came on, he got them right away."

"This is the love crowd, right?" Otis called out over the cavernous PA midway through his set. "We all love each other, right? Am I right?" The crowd said "Yeah." And Otis repeated, "Let me hear you say 'Yeah,' then." When the crowd said "Yeah" again, Otis launched into "I've Been Loving You Too Long," a change of pace from the storming versions of "Shake" and "Respect" with which he had opened his show. From there he went into "Satisfaction" and ended up, as per custom now, with a tortuously elongated "Try a Little Tenderness"—pretty much his standard program, love crowd or no love crowd. Brian Jones was in tears; Jimi Hendrix, who had spent *his* time on the chitlin circuit (most notably as Little Richard's lead guitarist in the mid-'60s) and who was scheduled to make his much-heralded American solo debut the next day, was stoned and reverential. "The love crowd," wrote Robert Christgau for *Esquire,* "was screaming its head off."

As much as anything else Otis's appearance at Monterey fostered a legend. Jon Landau, a respected rock critic before he became Bruce Springsteen's manager, had been championing Otis's cause since he began writing in 1965. Otis was, he wrote after Monterey, "past, present, and future. . . . Otis Redding's performances constitute, as a whole, the highest level of expression rock 'n' roll has yet attained. . . . Otis Redding *is* rock 'n' roll." He was, according to Robert Christgau's report from the field, "Superspade," "without question the love crowd's favorite soul singer, far ahead of James Brown or Wilson Pickett." Why (or whether) this should have been so remains a matter of debate, but contemporary black music for the most part, Christgau observed, made white audiences and performers nervous, whereas Otis, he pointed out with some irony (and Landau echoed without it), they adopted as their own from Monterey on.

Otis couldn't have cared less—about the irony anyway. Otis was simply thrilled, and surprised, too, at the dimensions of his success. He had taken a gamble which no other soul act was prepared to take (the Impressions and Smokey Robinson had canceled out at the last minute); he had played a major pop festival for free, and it had paid off. "Monterey Pop left Otis with such a great feeling about his career," says Zelma. "He realized he was taking it to a whole other phase which he had never been able to reach before. All of a sudden he was getting into the whites, who had never been into Otis Redding until 1967."

From this point Otis's life and career picked up at a dizzying pace. After Monterey, Otis was booked on a West Coast tour in the summer of 1967. He had been listening to the Beatles' *Sergeant Pepper* album ever since its release, wearing it out as he had once worn out Sam Cooke's *Live at the Copa*. He was living on a houseboat in Sausalito with his road manager Speedo during a weeklong engagement at San Francisco's Basin Street West when he came up with a song that, in his mind, was an extension of the Beatles' music. "I would just pat my legs and keep the rhythm going, the tempo," says Speedo, "while he was strumming on the guitar. This particular time I couldn't quite follow it. It was the first time. We must have been out there three or four days before I realized, before I could get any concept as to where he was going with the song. I just didn't understand it. And lyrically, when he came out with it, it still sounded weird to me. What he was singing about and what he was saying—as opposed to what he *had* been saying. He was changing with the times is what was happening. And I was looking at the times change, but I wasn't that far with it yet."

Otis took the song home with him unfinished, played it for Zelma, and encountered the same reaction. "I really couldn't get into it," says Zelma. "I said, 'Oh, God, you're changing.' And he said, 'Yeah, I think it's time for me to change in my music. People might be tired of me.' So I just said, 'Okay,' but I really couldn't get into it right then."

In August, Otis invited his record industry friends—who had come to Atlanta for the NATRA (the r&b-oriented National Association of Television and Radio Announcers) convention—out to his home in Round Oak. He had just gotten off a tour and was dead tired, but he was frantic, Alan Walden says, to get everything ready. Construction on the new pool was just barely com-

At the Big O Ranch. (Courtesy of Bill Millar)

pleted the night before the party, and five hogs and two cows were barbecued for the 400 or 500 guests. Otis staged a show with Sam and Dave and Arthur Conley headlining, but he himself was too exhausted to perform.

"It was like he had to have everything perfect," says Zelma. "He had to do all these things. It was as if he felt he was not going to see all these people again. That night when we had the barbecue, it was fabulous. Outrageous. He was so tired he was just sitting there out in the middle of the front yard. He spoke to everybody, but he just couldn't move. It was like we had all these people in our home—artists, producers, DJs, promo men, everybody who knew Otis was there—and it was just so nice, it was something he really, really wanted to do. There wasn't very many of those people he saw again, but everybody, when they left, the only thing they could remember was that when they saw him last, he was happy. So everybody who loved Otis could rest at peace with that. Everything went over perfect, in fact, except he couldn't finish the swimming pool. He couldn't get all the water in the pool, all 90,000 gallons of it. He wanted to get the fire department out there to pump the water in a hose, but I said, 'Otis, please. It'll be all right. They might not want to swim.' So that was the only thing. But he soon got over it."

It seemed as if his dream was moving toward fruition. In October he was named number-one male vocalist in the world in a *Melody Maker* poll which Elvis Presley had won for the last ten years. He was booked to play the Fillmore at Christmas for a reported $15,000. Even an operation to remove throat polyps which took him off the road for two months just after the party failed to slow his momentum. Otis was terrified at first that this could mean the end of his singing career, but Phil Walden researched the matter with customary thoroughness and found a leading throat specialist in New York, who reassured Otis that if he would just stay quiet for six weeks after the operation, he would be as good as new. According to Alan Walden, the surgeon wouldn't even accept his customary fee; so taken was he with Otis, and so impressed by Otis's infectious enthusiasm for hunting, that he waived his bill entirely. If Otis would simply give him a 30.06 rifle with a scope on it, the doctor said, he would consider it an even trade.

The two months that he spent at home in the autumn of 1967 were the longest period he had spent off the road since he had begun his recording career. His children were growing up: Dexter, Otis III, and Karla, named for Carla Thomas, his fellow artist and singing partner on Stax. "That was the most time," says Zelma, "we ever spent together, to be around each other for a long time. He said, 'Boy, when I go back out there, I'm gonna be the new Otis Redding.' When I heard some of the songs he was writing, I said, 'You're right. You are going to be new. You're not begging anymore.' He was scared at first. Everybody around him was scared to death that he was not going to be able to sing again. But once he found out that it was going to be all right, he was fine. He would write little notes on pieces of paper. He just stayed home most of the time writing songs with his guitar and writing the words down."

He was seized, it seemed, by a fever of creativity. Unable to express himself vocally, he could scarcely keep up with the steady stream of song ideas just begging for release, and when he went into the Stax studio at the end of November, as soon as his recuperative period was up, he had something like thirty new numbers ready to record in a session that would last just over two weeks ("When you went on an Otis Redding session," says Alan Walden, "if you didn't get three or four songs in the can in one day, you were having a bad day"). One of the first songs he cut was the song he had played for Zelma and the Waldens when he came back from California the previous summer. The song was "Dock of the Bay," and although in retrospect many have claimed that they recognized its genius at once, Duck Dunn is insistent that Jim Stewart didn't even want to release it. "It was just too far over the border for Jim. It had no r&b in it whatsoever, according to what Stax was. And I agreed with Jim at the time. I thought it might even be detrimental."

It wasn't just Jim and Duck who objected, in any case. It was family and management, too. "I've never seen him so excited by a record," recalls Alan Walden. "I lived down the road from him at that point—I was living in this little log cabin—and he came in the house and said, 'Guess what I'm doing on the new record?' And I said, 'What is it? You screaming your ass off? You getting down? What is it?' And he said, 'You ain't gonna believe what I'm doing on this record.' And I said, 'Come on, goddammit, you going to tell me or not?' Well, he goes and gets in his damn car and goes right to his house and comes back with a little tape recording, which was rare—they never allowed you to

"Dock of the Bay": Otis strums the first notes of his new
composition for Steve Cropper (not pictured). Stax studio,
November 1967. (Jere Cunningham)

take a copy of your session out of the studio in those days—and he played it
for me, and at the end of the song, of course, he's whistling on out, and, you
know, all of his songs were famous for their strong ad libs at the end, and here
he is whistling this one out! My first reaction was I didn't even like the song.
I told him I liked a song called 'Think About It' better, and I thought it would
make a better record. 'No, man,' he told me, 'this is my first #1 record. It's the
biggest song I ever had.' He just kept on telling me that."

Stanley Booth, on assignment for the *Saturday Evening Post,* just happened
to be in the studio the day that Otis recorded "Dock of the Bay," and for most
of the rest of the final session as well. His report clearly captures the business-as-
usual atmosphere of Stax, while also noting the significance of the event, the
almost palpable sense of excitement in the air.

Otis is playing a bright-red dime-store guitar, strumming simple bar chords as he sings: "Sittin' in the morning sun / I'll be sittin' when the evenin' comes—." The front of the guitar is cracked, as if someone has stepped on it. As he sings, Otis watches Steve [Cropper], who nods and nods, bending almost double over his guitar, following Otis's chords with a shimmering electric response.

"Sittin' in the mornin' sun—

"But I don't know why he's sittin'," Otis says, rocking back and forth as if he were still singing. "He's just sittin'. Got to be more to it than that." He pauses for a moment, shaking his head. Then he says, "Wait. Wait a minute," to Steve, who has been waiting patiently.

"I left my home in Georgia,
Headed for the Frisco bay—"

He pauses again, runs through the changes on his fractured guitar, then sings: "I had nothing to live for, look like nothing's gonna come my way—"

When Steve and Otis have the outlines of a song, they are joined by the rest of the MG's. Booker and Duck come in first, followed by drummer Al Jackson. Duck is telling Booker about his new stereo record player. "I got me a nice one, man, with components. You can turn down one of the speakers and hear the words real clear. I been listening to the Beatles. Last night I played *Revolver,* and on 'Yellow Submarine,' you know what one of 'em says? I think it's Ringo, he says, 'Paul is a queer.' He really does, man. 'Paul is a queer,' bigger 'n shit."

Booker sits at the piano, Duck gets his bass, which has been lying in its case on the worn red rug, and they begin to pick up the chord patterns from Steve and Otis. Al stands by, listening, his head tilted to one side. Duck asks him a question about counting the rhythm, and Steve looks up to say, "In a minute he'll want to know what key we're in." Duck sticks out his lower lip. He plays bass as fluently as if it were guitar, plucking the stout steel strings with his first two fingers, holding a cigarette between the other two. Booker sits erect, his right hand playing short punctuating notes, his left hand resting on his left knee. Otis is standing now, moving around the room, waving his arms as he conducts these men, his friends, who are there to serve him. He looks like a swimmer, moving effortlessly underwater. Then something happens, a connection is made in Al Jackson's mind, and he goes to the drums, baffled on two sides with wallboard. "One, two," he announces. "One-two-three-four." And for the first time they are all together, everyone has found the groove.

The Mar-Keys drift into the studio and sit on folding chairs behind another baffle, one wall of which has a small window. They listen, sucking on reeds, blowing into mouthpieces, as Otis and the rhythm section rehearse the song. When Steve calls, "Hey, horns! Ready to record?" they are thrown into confusion, like a man waked in the middle of the night. They have nothing to record; there are, as yet, no horn parts. Steve and Otis develop them by singing to each other. "De-de-da-dee," Steve says. "De-de-da-*daaah*," says Otis, as if he were making a point in an argument. When they have the lines they want, they sing them to the Mar-Keys, starting with the verse part, which the Mar-Keys will forget while learning the part for the chorus. After a few tries, however, they know both parts, and are ready to record. "That feels good, man, let's cut it."

During the rehearsal, one of the neighborhood kids, wearing blue jeans, an old cloth cap, and Congress basketball sneakers with one green and one yellow lace, has slipped into the studio. He sits behind a cluster of microphones, unnoticed even by Otis, who passes directly by him on his way to the far corner of the room, where he strikes a wide, flat-footed stance facing a wallboard partition. Otis can hear but cannot see Al Jackson, holding one stick high as if it were a baton, counting four, then rolling his eyes toward the ceiling and starting to play.

After "Dock of the Bay" was recorded, Steve and Booker added guitar and piano fills. The song boomed into the studio from a speaker high on the rear wall, and Booker played precise little bop, bop-bop figures, while Steve followed the vocal with an almost quivering blues line. The speaker went dead, then the engineer's voice came: "Steve, one note's clashing."

"Sure it is," Steve tells him. "It was written to clash." Which, in point of fact, is not true, since nothing has been written down so far. "Let's do it once more," Steve says. "We can do that bridge better. I can. First part's a groove."

Inside the control room, Otis and Duck are talking. "I wish you all *could* go with me to the Fillmore on Christmas," Otis says.

"Man, so do I. I got some *good* friends in San Francisco. We could rent one of them yachts."

"I *got* one already. Three bedrooms, two baths, sumbitch is nice, man."

"My ole lady'd kill me," Duck says.

When the recording is finished, Steve and Booker come into the control room, followed after a moment by the little boy in Congress sneakers. The tape is played back at a painful volume level. Steve and Otis stare deep into each other's eyes, carrying on a kind of telepathic communication. The little boy, looking up at the speaker the music is coming from, says, "I like that. That's good singin'. I'd like to be a singer myself."

"That's it," Otis says when the record ends.

"That's a mother," says Booker.

(© 1969 by Stanley Booth.)

HOME AT LAST

On Saturday, December 9, two days after the "Dock" session's end, Otis flew into Cleveland in his new twin-engine Beechcraft to appear on *Upbeat,* the syndicated TV show hosted by Don Webster. Sunday morning he called Zelma around eight-thirty. "He was depressed about something. I remember that very well. And he talked to little Otis, who was just three . . . He said he would call me when he got to Madison." The weather was bad, but Otis was bound and determined to make his gig at a Madison, Wisconsin, club called the Factory. "He was very determined, always," says Speedo Simms, off this tour because of a temporary falling out over money. "He would go to extremes," says his bodyguard and boyhood friend, Sylvester Huckaby, likewise off the road for unspecified reasons. "That day they had grounded all commercial flights, but he was reaching for stardom, and he didn't want to miss no dates."

At 3:28 in the afternoon the plane crashed into the icy waters of Lake Monona just outside of Madison. Along with Otis, a whole generation of Memphis music died that day in the person of the Bar-Kays, Otis's crack young backup band and Stax's up-and-coming second studio unit, all of whom perished save for Ben Cauley, the sole survivor, and James Alexander, who missed the flight. It was three years almost to the day since the death of Sam Cooke.

The funeral was held at Macon's City Auditorium, the site of various Otis Redding Homecomings over the years, finally integrated on this somber occasion. The body lay in state from 6:30 A.M., "so that the many people who would be working could come by and have a chance to pay their respects to Mr. Redding"; the auditorium started to fill three hours before the scheduled noon service, with a virtual Who's Who of the soul world in attendance. The Soul Clan was there—Solomon Burke and Wilson Pickett and Joe Tex and Don Covay. James Brown, Sam and Dave, Percy Sledge, Rufus and Carla Thomas were all present. Johnnie Taylor and Joe Simon were pallbearers, as at least 4500 people squeezed into the 3000-seat hall. "Outside," reported one Canadian news account, "thousands more waited under gloomy skies. When the flower-covered coffin was rolled out, followed by Redding's screaming widow, Zelma, the crowd tensed.

"When rock 'n' roller James Brown, one of several famous recording stars at the funeral, emerged, pandemonium broke out. Brown dived into his car which began to follow the hearse. But howling youths flung themselves onto the vehicle, holding it back. Its efforts to move up produced only spinning tires and clouds of blue smoke. Police rushed in to remove the youths from the car.

"Office workers leaned out windows, cheering on the frenzied teenagers.

"Halfway through the ceremony, while Joe Simon was singing an impassioned 'Jesus Keep Me Near the Cross,' Mrs. Redding broke down. Her wails punctuated the amplified sobs of Simon, and her heels beat a drumlike tattoo on the hard basketball floor of the auditorium. White-clad nurses who were sprinkled through the crowd rushed to her aid. . . ."

"It seemed to be a macabre holiday," *Soul* magazine correctly noted, "in the city of Macon when Otis was laid to rest. The city which had chosen to virtually ignore the Georgia-born star seemed overly anxious to expiate its guilt by lavish preparations to welcome home forever Macon's most famous citizen. [Mayor Ronnie] Thompson vowed that Macon would never forget Otis Redding and called the entertainer 'Macon's Ambassador of Goodwill'. . . .

"[But] outside of loyal Negro friends who remembered his humble beginnings, very few Maconites over twenty-five years of age had ever heard of Otis Redding. . . . One weathered and aged gas station proprietor in the heart of town, noting the out-of-town license plates swarming all over, asked 'What in tarnation's going on?' "

Phil and Alan Walden barely made it through the ceremony. Jerry Wexler delivered the eulogy in halting tones. Otis Redding, he said, was "a natural prince." Otis was a son of the South who had stayed in the South with his people because he felt "it was the obligation of educated and talented Negroes to help open the doors of opportunity for their race. . . . Otis's great composition, 'Respect,' has become an anthem of hope for people around the world. Respect was something Otis achieved for himself in a way few people do. Otis sang, 'All I'm asking for is a little respect when I come home,' and Otis has come home." Arthur Conley, to whom, Wexler said, Otis was "advisor and hero, and father as well," sobbed inconsolably. Hamp Swain was listed as master of ceremonies. Joe Galkin was there, and so were Jim Stewart, Al Bell, Steve, Duck, and Booker T. (all on their first trip to Macon). Only Johnny Jenkins, the man who had first recognized the uniqueness of Otis Redding's talent, was missing.

"I would have been worse than Zelma," says Jenkins. "I knew him better than Zelma. I was with him at night when his wife wasn't. I was there. I shared the good times, the bad times, I knew the prostitutes, the whores, but nobody wants to hear none of that, y'hear what I'm saying? Well, you can put him up on a pedestal, call him an idol, but he wasn't no damn idol. He was a human being, that's what. What good is it if you don't tell the truth about him, the good and the bad, the whole picture, what I call behind closed doors—the public don't know about it, the band didn't know about it, but I knowed about it. That's a man's life. You *must* tell the truth." Besides, says Jenkins, echoing the

Phil Walden and Zelma Redding, with Grammy, 1969. (From the Macon Telegraph and News *Negative Collection, Middle Georgia Archives, Macon, Georgia)*

dark mutterings that have sprung up since that day, conspiratorial rumors that Otis's death came as a result of his decision to break away from Stax, from Phil Walden, to follow the independent trail that Sam Cooke had blazed (with equally catastrophic results)—this, says Johnny Jenkins with fearful conviction, is what happens to a nigger with ideas.

Zelma gave Huckaby Otis's clothes. "He was twenty-six, and I was twenty-seven at the time of his death. We were about the same age, wore the same size clothes. His wife thought he would want me to have them, and she gave me all his clothes, $20,000 worth. But, really, I just gave up. I was feeling sorry for myself. I seed myself rising as he moved up in life. After he died, that's when I really started getting in trouble."

Speedo went out on the road almost immediately with Arthur Conley, now designated as Otis's heir apparent, and it was a disaster. Conley simply disintegrated during the tour, eventually leaving this country and moving to France. Friends advised Speedo that he should sue for the writing credit he was supposed to have gotten on "Respect," but Speedo took his absence from the final tour as a sign. "I think if I had gotten the money and all had went as it should have, I would have been on the plane. The man was dead, and it was over, and I was still living, and there was no point in going in and giving Zelma a whole big hassle. I just considered it as water under the bridge and move on. You know, I can remember," says Speedo, "the day the dream shut off and reality set in. And that was the most scaring day. I was exactly thirty years old."

For Stax, too, it was the shut-off of youthful fantasy. Although by late 1967 Otis was no longer the biggest seller on Stax, there was no question that

Portrait, 1967. (Don Paulsen/Michael Ochs Archives)

he was the heart and soul of the record company, and despite the rumors, despite the tensions, despite the conflicts that undeniably existed, Otis's death brought everyone together in mourning. Jim Stewart called a meeting two days after the funeral at which he brokenheartedly declared, "Man, we've got to keep going." William Bell wrote "A Tribute to a King," which he recorded in February with sparse instrumentation and plain lyrics that movingly recalled Otis. A few months later William and Judy Clay had a Top 20 soul hit with "Private Number," originally intended for Otis and Carla. "We realized," Al Jackson told *Rolling Stone* editor Jann Wenner in August 1968, "we could never replace Otis, so we spent all the time we [could] really trying to make a William Bell, trying to make a Johnnie Taylor to take up the slack and all that we lost in Otis and, I must say, the Bar-Kays." Nonetheless, a sense of emptiness remained, a feeling of incompletion that everyone who knew Otis has remarked upon. "We walked around in a daze for weeks," Estelle has said. "I think," says Jim sorrowfully, "the death of Otis took a lot of heart out of Stax, it really did." In March, Zelma returned to Memphis for the "first annual" Memphis Sound Revue, where she received a gold record—Otis's first—for the single that had come out immediately following his death, the much-discussed "Dock of the Bay." It was probably little consolation that Otis had been proved right after all; his song *had* gone to #1, though whether this would have happened —or the record would even have been released as a single—if Otis had lived, will forever remain a moot point. In any case this was no longer a primary concern. For all of a sudden the future of Stax Records itself was up in the air. "If Otis had lived," says Steve Cropper, "everything would have been totally different. The future of Atlantic would have been different. The future of Stax would have been different." Otis, too, would have been different, thinks Alan Walden. If Otis had lived, he might have had the opportunity for crossover success in a manner hitherto undreamt of, he might have had the chance to record a Beatles-type album and to enter once again into yet another whole new phase. He was just twenty-six when he sang:

> *Looks like nothing's gonna change*
> *Everything still remains the same*
> *I can't do what ten people tell me to do*
> *So I guess I'll remain the same.*

Aretha Arrives

R-E-S-P-E-C-T
Find out what it means to me
R-E-S-P-E-C-T
Take care, T.C.B.
Ohhhhhhhhhh! Sock it to me, sock it to me,
*   sock it to me. . . .*

—"Respect" by Otis Redding, as interpreted by Aretha Franklin

ARETHA FRANKLIN VIRTUALLY EXPLODED ON the soul scene some six months prior to Otis Redding's death, and her version of "Respect" in the spring of 1967 tells something of the differences between her approach and that of its originator ("I just lost my song," Otis told Jerry Wexler on hearing her interpretation of his signature tune for the first time. "That girl took it away from me."). Inspired vocal flights aside—and there has been no pop singer more inspired than Aretha when it comes to sheer vocal artistry—the song itself was transformed from a demand for conjugal rights into a soaring cry of freedom; where Otis sang specifically of domestic and social proprieties, Aretha staked out a claim for the ecstatic transcendence of the imagination, no less. Just twenty-five but already a veteran of more than a dozen years in show business (she had been a child star of gospel, then went pop at eighteen on the Columbia label), she had achieved a considerable underground reputation, but when she signed with Atlantic in November 1966, she was without any real sense of artistic or commercial direction. It had been five years since she had last had an r&b hit, her latest offerings on Columbia were a peculiar mix of show tunes and schmaltz, and while her signing for $25,000 did not represent an exorbitant investment on Atlantic's part (Atlantic was currently rivaling Motown for soul supremacy, while also making unprecedented inroads into pop), what no one could be certain of was whether Aretha Franklin would ever fully realize her admittedly extravagant potential. Even Jerry Wexler seems to have had his doubts. His first thought was to turn his promising new artist over to Jim Stewart, and only when Stewart balked at the price (for the sensible reason that for such a sizable amount of money he could produce five or six albums on artists he already had under contract, including Otis Redding) did Wexler take the bull by the horns and announce to the world, in Atlantic historian Charlie Gillett's formulation, that "at last the real

Aretha Franklin. (Jim Marshall)

Aretha Franklin would be revealed. . . ." "With that record," Shirley Wexler, Jerry's wife at the time, told Gillett, "Jerry felt like he was on stage. Everybody was watching him." They were also watching Aretha—and not without skepticism—for this was not her first chance at stardom nor the first time great claims had been made for her.

She was born in 1942 in Memphis, the middle daughter of the Reverend C. L. Franklin and his wife, Barbara, who according to C.L. was the vocal image of Aretha. Her mother left when Aretha was six (she reportedly died a few years later), and after a brief stop in Buffalo, the Reverend Franklin brought up his five children in Detroit, where he pastored the 4500-member New Bethel Baptist Church and began making records for Joe Von Battle, a Detroit record scuffler, who leased much of what he cut to Chess Records in Chicago. By the mid-1950s the Reverend Franklin (now popularly known as "the Man with the

Million Dollar Voice") was probably the most successful of all the black "electronic" preachers, demanding and getting $4000 an appearance on his tours. He went on to make over seventy albums of sermons and exerted enormous influence over soul singers like Bobby "Blue" Bland, who took his patented gargle from Franklin's best-selling "The Eagle Stirreth Her Nest."

Aretha grew up lonely and repressed with little apparent emotional outlet save for the church. She joined the choir at eight, started singing at twelve, and cut a remarkable live album at fourteen at the New Bethel church. Still, she remained so shy, her sister Erma has said, that "at home, if somebody comes in and I say, 'Aretha, I want you to meet so and so,' it looks as if she seals herself off. . . . She's an introvert, and she really comes alive only on stage." In one of the few anecdotes that Aretha herself has offered about her early childhood, she recalls how she took the first fifteen dollars that she earned from singing and bought a pair of white roller skates.

It must have been a very confused upbringing. Growing up in the big tree-shaded house on the edge of Detroit's East Side with a succession of mother substitutes who included gospel greats Mahalia Jackson, Marion Williams, and Clara Ward (the Reverend Franklin and Clara Ward were constant companions at one time). Deriving her knowledge of show business and the entertainer's life from associates and parishioners of her father like Arthur Prysock, Dinah Washington, Sam Cooke, and Lou Rawls, all of whom left the church eventually for worldly success. Gaining national exposure and a taste of celebrity from her father's tours, while yearning most of all to be "a magnificent housewife." J. W. Alexander recalls her from that time as possessing a charisma that was similar to Cooke's ("I didn't see how either one of them could miss"). DJ Zenas Sears remembers MC'ing a gospel show in Atlanta where even as a very little girl she evidenced the kind of unguarded emotion that was in direct contrast with her natural demeanor. "The Reverend C. L. Franklin," says Sears, "was one of the few acts that was guaranteed to fill the auditorium. This particular time he brought Aretha with him and asked me, 'Introduce my little girl, too. She's not gonna sing tonight, but she is the world's youngest gospel singer.' Well, she couldn't have been more than five or six, and all the acts were around in a circle—there was no running in from the wings in those days, they were all there—and so I introduced him and finished with it, and I forgot Aretha. She kicked me in the shins! So I did it—and she kicked me again, and sat down. . . ."

Clearly her world was dominated by her father, and like not a few men of the cloth, the Reverend Franklin combined qualities of the spirit and the flesh, proud both of his spiritual salvation and of his earthly attainments as well, seeing his worldly success as a tribute to his godliness and as a proper source of pride to his congregation. Dapper, youthful (he was born in 1917), a sharp dresser with a smooth and sophisticated manner and a taste for propriety that never threatened his reputation as a ladies' man ("He's not a prude in any way," said Aretha's booking agent, Ruth Bowen), the Reverend Franklin established strict standards of music and behavior for his favorite daughter. "She inherited his thing," Erma told *Rolling Stone* reporter Chris Hodenfield, "tit for tat." "She was a desperately unhappy child," Aretha's first manager, Jo King, told the same reporter. "She had such an attachment to her father that she would do anything to please him. She would *try* to do it. . . . She had a relationship with her father that nobody could break."

At eight or nine Aretha began piano lessons but rebelled at the discipline and hid from her teacher ("She had all those little baby books, and I wanted to go directly to the tunes"). She wanted to play like her father's friend Art Tatum but settled for imitating Eddie Heywood records. Around this time James Cleveland, soon to become as dominant a force in the field of gospel music as the Reverend Franklin in the mid-to-late '50s, moved in with the family, and, Aretha told *Ebony* reporter Phyl Garland, "he showed me some real nice chords, I liked his deep sound." With Cleveland's encouragement she formed a quartet with her sister, Erma, which broke up after a little while "because we were too busy fussing and fighting." It was Clara Ward, though, more than anyone else except her father, who influenced her style. For interviewers Aretha has always recalled vividly the funeral of an aunt at which Miss Ward sang "Peace in the Valley" and in a moment of transport tore off her hat and flung it on the ground. "That," Aretha has declared, "is when I wanted to become a singer."

By the age of fourteen she had quit her formal schooling and gone out on the road with her father, traveling by train and automobile with the other performers while the Reverend Franklin flew in to his gigs. She roomed with a midget named Sammie Franklin, who was supposed to act as her chaperone and make sure that the social amenities were maintained. She was *not* promiscuous, the Reverend Franklin insisted. "She always traveled with her aides. She'd *rarely* ever go anywhere without them." Nonetheless, as her brother Cecil told *Time* magazine, "Driving eight or ten hours trying to make a gig, and being hungry and passing restaurants all along the road, and having to go off the highway into some little city to find a place to eat because you're black—that had its effect." "She had experiences that were beyond most human beings," said manager Jo King. "For the first three months I thought I [had] an eighteen-year-old girl who had never before left home. And then it burst like a bubble. I realized I had a real woman here, one who knew more than I did when it came to men, alcohol and everything. She had a tremendous depth." The depth is evident in the one recording that survives from that time, a recording that reveals a fourteen-year-old girl in her father's church paying tribute to one of her main influences, Clara Ward, and yet bringing far more to it than mere imitation. There is an intensity of feeling, a pure musicality that cannot have been counterfeited; there is a sense of pain, a resonance of emotion and experience that, while not uncommon in the gospel field, is most uncommon for a fourteen-year-old.

Finally, at the age of eighteen, urged on by the example of Sam Cooke and by his direct imprecations (Cooke was not only an idol but a friend, and one who with J. W. Alexander was trying to get her to sign with his own label, RCA), she broke out of this circle of dependency and moved to New York with the avowed blessing of her father ("One should make his own life and take care of his own business"), who set her up at the Thirty-eighth Street Y and arranged for her to take acting and modeling lessons. She left two children—one born when she was fifteen, one at seventeen—back in Detroit, made demos with her father's friend (and Teddy Wilson's bassist), Major "Mule" Holley, and through Jo King began formal lessons with voice teacher Leora Carter. In early 1960 she signed a five-year contract with John Hammond of Columbia Records. Hammond, the legendary discoverer of Count Basie, Lionel Hampton, Charlie Christian, Helen Humes, and his future brother-in-law, Benny Goodman (he later signed both Bob Dylan and Bruce Springsteen), promptly declared the eighteen-year-old Aretha "an untutored genius, the best voice I've heard since Billie Holiday," not coincidentally another John Hammond discovery.

The "untutored genius" played her first club date, with Buddy Hackett headlining, at the Trade Winds in Chicago, where she promptly lost her voice and floundered onstage until her father arrived with a party of friends. Her first album, called simply *Aretha*, consisted of twelve songs from five sessions that Hammond supervised in the fall and early winter of 1960–61. There was tasteful backing from a variety of muted jazz combos that Hammond put together for the occasions; Ray Bryant (and occasionally Aretha) played piano. Aretha's voice soared with breathtaking unpredictability over the entire proceedings.

The material was equally eclectic and equally unpredictable. The one hit on the album, "Today I Sing the Blues," was the song Aretha had originally demoed for Hammond, and it went to #10 on the r&b charts in the fall of 1960. Other songs showed a soft, sentimental side, a flair for improvisation, the kind of uncalculated passion that came out of the church, and a taste for Broadway-styled show tunes delivered with the self-conscious windup, and racial neutrality, of a Judy Garland or an Al Jolson (her fourth song from that first session was "Over the Rainbow," and she has come back to "Rock-a-Bye Your Baby With a Dixie Melody" again and again over the years), that has persisted to this day. Revisionist historians have attempted to explain away this side of Aretha by suggesting that it was all imposed upon her, unfeeling producers sought crossover success by forcing sentimental material and pop standards down her throat, but it seems clear on balance that this, too, was Aretha, that "Over the Rainbow" was as much a part of her vision of herself as "Precious Lord" or "Never Grow Old."

The Columbia years in any case were fairly schizophrenic. No one could

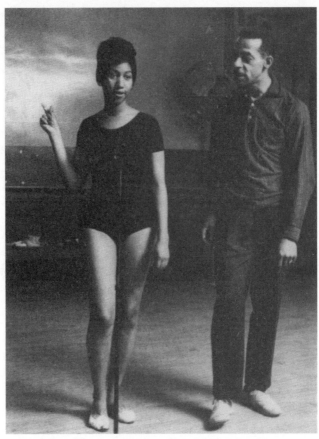

Learning to dance, with choreographer (and noted tap dancer) Cholly Atkins, 1960. (Frank Driggs Collection)

decide who Aretha Franklin was, least of all, it seemed, Aretha herself. "My music is in me," she said, "[but] I'm not sure what that is." In 1961 she was taken away from Hammond because, he wrote in his autobiography, "the feeling among the young A&R producers at Columbia [was] that, while I might be able to find another potential star, I was not able to produce the sort of commercial single records that became hits. Aretha had quite a lot of money in accumulated royalties, because her first records had been inexpensively produced and had sold well. It had been decided to use the unpaid royalties . . . to record her with large commercial backgrounds."

The result was pleasing neither aesthetically nor commercially. Over the next six years Aretha had only one or two hits the equal of her Hammond-produced sides, and she veered from r&b covers like "Walk On By" to big brassy show tunes, soupy, string-laden ballads, bold tributes to Dinah Washington, and somewhat pallid interpretations of "sensitive" material like "If Ever

Portrait with Jerry Wexler. (David Gahr)

I Would Leave You" from the musical *Camelot*. In little of this could Aretha's private voice be heard, though in retrospect songwriter Jerry Leiber's assessment of her cultural aspirations ("Upward mobility," Leiber suggested at a later point. "Aretha is suffering from upward mobility. . . . We all does it.") could well be taken for one aspect of the truth. Aretha's personality has never yielded to easy analysis in any case, and perhaps it would be just as well simply to concede that her taste, like Ray Charles's, could encompass both kitsch and naked emotion, her talent could suggest the explosive brilliance of intuitive genius and the embarrassing excesses of the squeamishly middlebrow.

Her personal life was equally confused. "She had lived," John Hammond said, "more than most people live in a lifetime. Aretha was lost. . . ." Around 1962 she married thirty-one-year-old Ted White, self-described as a "small-time promoter" but characterized cautiously by *Time* magazine as "a former dabbler in Detroit real estate and a Detroit wheeler-dealer." In 1967, *Time* reported, he roughed her up in the lobby of Atlanta's Hyatt Regency Hotel, evidently not for the first time, and her relationship with White over the years was the subject of much talk and speculation. "I don't think she's happy," Mahalia Jackson told the *Time* reporter cryptically. "Somebody else is making her sing the blues." "His motivation was not sincere," the Reverend Franklin declared of White after the fact, and very likely at the time as well.

Regardless of speculation, White soon replaced Jo King as his wife's manager ("I felt at the time that Aretha should be handled by a man, because maybe this whole thing with her father could be handled"). In 1964 she had her third child, Theodore III, and in fact at this point her career seemed irremediably stalled, with a reluctance on Aretha's part even to go into the recording studio. At the end of 1965 Columbia exercised its one-year option, but by late summer 1966 word was out that Aretha was available. She had made nine albums and was something like $80,000 in Columbia's debt. It was at this juncture that Jerry Wexler leapt into the fray, whether to prove a point or sensing a commercial possibility it's difficult to say. Louise Williams, the reigning gospel DJ of Philadelphia (and once married to Solomon Burke's champion, Jimmy Bishop), initially approached Wexler on Aretha's behalf; Wexler tried Jim Stewart, then cut a deal with Ted White. Once he had a contract in hand, there was little question of where he was going to take her. With Memphis closed off after the Wilson Pickett debacle, and with the success that Atlantic had enjoyed at the Fame studio in Muscle Shoals for the last nine months, he headed straight for Alabama. In January 1967 Wexler, Tommy Dowd, Aretha, and Ted White arrived in Muscle Shoals, registered at the Downtowner in Florence, and rode out East Avalon to Rick Hall's little studio to begin a projected week's worth of recording on an album that was to prove not only Aretha's genius but his own.

SHOW TIME

Rick Hall had little idea who Aretha Franklin was, but he knew from Wexler's enthusiasm and from the excitement in his voice that this was going to be "the ultimate trip." Wexler had arranged for Chips Moman and Tommy Cogbill to come in from Memphis and join Rick's standard rhythm section of Jimmy Johnson (rhythm guitar), Spooner Oldham (keyboards), and Roger Hawkins (drums), but he had left it to Hall to put together a horn section—whether the Memphis Horns or a Bowlegs Miller group or Willie Mitchell's unit it didn't much matter. Dan Penn, already over at American in Memphis with Chips, wouldn't have missed this session for the world. It was not just that he and Chips had already sketched out a song that they hoped would be used; "I knew about Aretha way before she got there. Rick contacted me about the session, but he didn't know who in hell was coming in. I said, 'Who you got?' He said, 'Aretha Franklin.' I said, 'Boy, you better get your damn shoes on. You getting someone who can sing.' Even the Memphis guys didn't really know who in the hell she was. I said, 'Man, this woman gonna knock you out.' They're all going, 'Big deal!' When she come in there and sit down at the piano and hit that first chord, everybody was just like little bees just buzzing around the queen. You could tell by the way she hit the piano the gig was up. It was, 'Let's get down to serious business.' That first chord she hit was nothing we'd been demoing, and nothing none of them cats in Memphis had been, either. We'd just been dumb-dumb playing, but this was the real thing. That's the prettiest session picture I can ever remember. If I'd had a camera, I'd have a great film of that session, because I can still see it in my mind's eye, just how it was—Spooner on the organ, Moman playing guitar, Aretha at the piano—it was beautiful, better than any session I've ever seen, and I seen a bunch of 'em."

Spooner Oldham, the weedy keyboard player who is known for never playing the same licks twice and who is ordinarily the most reticent of men, speaks in similar superlatives. "I was hired to play keyboards. She was gonna stand up in front of the microphone and sing. She was showing us this song she had brought down there with her, she hit that magic chord when Wexler was going up the little steps to the control room, and I just stopped. I said, 'Now, look, I'm not trying to cop out or nothing. I know I was hired to play piano, but I wish you'd let her play that thing, and I could get on organ and electric.' And that's the way it was. It was a good, honest move, and one of the best things I ever done—and I didn't do nothing."

That, according to Dan Penn, was when Spooner invented "the three-fingered dumb hum" on his Hammond spinet. The song that they were working on was a song that Aretha had come in with, "I Never Loved a Man (The Way I Love You)," by an eccentric Detroit songwriter named Ronnie Shannon. All that she had was a demo of Shannon singing and playing piano, without any discernible meter or melody. Aretha apparently was the only one in the room who could find what she was looking for in the song, because, according to Spooner, "there wasn't anybody around, including myself, that could play it. It took some real thought. Eventually I came up with a little electric piano riff. Chips recognized that was it. He said, 'He's got it, he's got it!' And from there it sort of cohered in a couple of takes."

While the rhythm section struggled with the melody the horn section, led by Charlie Chalmers on tenor, with Ed Logan on bari, Ken Laxton on trumpet, and David Hood on trombone ("It was the most fucked-up horn section you ever heard," says Jimmy Johnson. "They didn't even use Hood's part, but the horns Rick was supposed to get were booked.") was putting together its own off-the-cuff arrangement in Rick's office across the hall. Chalmers wrote out the chords, they played their little riffs and came back in the studio to lay down their track. By midafternoon the song was complete, one of the most momentous takes in the history of rhythm and blues, in fact in the history of American vernacular music.

From Spooner's delicate opening on electric piano and the sharp crack of the drums to the thudding, ominous counterpoint of the bass, and, eventually, Aretha's swelling, hammering gospel entrance on piano, the song was a masterpiece of construction and feel, employing the most subtle dynamics to suggest sheer unrestrained enthusiasm, pitting a vocal of uncompromising purity and transcendence against a lyric that declared, "You're no good, heartbreaker,/

You're a liar and you're a cheat/I don't know why I let you do these things to me." "I took her to church," Jerry Wexler later declared, "sat her down at the piano, and let her be herself." This is probably as good an explanation as any for a moment that defies explanation (Aretha hit the "magic chord," remember), for it was as if here Aretha had at last cast off the confining stays of her long apprenticeship and was once and for all ready to give herself over to the unbridled secular ecstasy of her music; she had absorbed all the lessons that soul music had to teach her and now prepared to transcend them. "There's only a few geniuses around," Jerry Wexler continued, "you know, like Ray Charles—who can just come in the studio and lay down the song and everything's implicit; the musicians just color it in." Aretha was one of the few, and in that one unequaled moment at Muscle Shoals she took soul music to a place that no one else could go.

Everyone must have felt giddy. There was no question in anyone's mind that they had done it. Jerry Wexler knew that Aretha was going to deliver on his promise, and even Aretha must have sensed that she had at last achieved a high point that was hers, and hers alone, if only for a moment. Aretha's husband, Ted White, finally loosened up. All the players and onlookers—Dan and Chips and Spooner and Donnie Fritts—knew that they were in the presence of something of surpassing worth. Even Rick Hall, rarely willing, or able, to surrender his skepticism or suspiciousness that fate must have it in for him in some yet-to-be-revealed way, never doubted for a moment that he was standing on the edge of history. A break was called, during which Chips and Dan got back to work on the song they had brought with them from Memphis ("We 'me, you, and itted' it all out"). While they did, a bottle was produced in the control booth, and Rick and Ted White passed it back and forth congratulatorily while the session players came up with one of their own. Jerry Wexler worried over a couple of lines with the cowriters, while out in the studio there was a momentary uproar as the trumpet player made a smart remark to the artist which the artist's husband vociferously objected to.

As soon as the song was finished, Aretha attempted to sing it off the lead sheet. She couldn't seem to get it, but she kept trying, and the more she tried, the further she got from the song. "Well, now it's getting awkward," recalls Dan Penn, "because here's this very talented woman out there sounding like a crackerbox. So they did the same thing they always did in those situations: they put me out there singing. They'd always send me out there to tempt the niggers, you know, 'Go on out there and stir 'em up, Penn.' 'Cause I would just go out there and squeal, and they'd say, 'Aw, shit, I can beat that.' But this time all they wanted to do was to get a track. So I sung, and we put down the awfullest thing you ever heard in God's world: it had one little organ hum and maybe a little ticky ticking of bass or something and me squealing, and it sounded awful."

That was the end of the first day's session. Everyone was in a foul mood by now. The drinking had accelerated. Some insults had been exchanged. Ted White was objecting very loudly to the fact that the entire session was made up of nothing but white boys. Jerry Wexler was castigating Rick Hall, in whom he never had much faith anyway, for not hiring the black, or mixed, horn section that Wex had requested. And at the height of it all, the trumpet player either got smart with Aretha again or "pinched her butt." That was it. Rick fired the trumpet player, but the session dissolved in a welter of accusations, and it was left to Jerry Wexler, ever the diplomat, to try to smooth over all the injured feelings.

From here on in everyone's memories are understandably confused, but Rick Hall, who came out worst in the denouement, tells the most coherent tale of the session's debacle.

"Finally we had just kind of ended in frustration and thought we hadn't got it. And, of course, by then I'd started drinking and was pretty well on my way, and I decided I didn't want to go home. I was still bothered by Ted and Aretha and that whole thing and the day going bad and thought maybe we'd lost it, so I thought maybe I could go back and soothe some tempers and talk to Ted and Aretha and things would be cool. Well, I was a lot drunker than I thought, evidently, and I went down to the hotel, went up to Ted's room, and we begun to talk—both of us, I guess, had had too many drinks. Ted began to point his finger at me, and I guess I pointed my finger back at him. We went from 'redneck' to 'bluegum' to 'whitey' to 'nigger' and back again. Well, we got in a real slugfest, and when they finally got me out of the room and slammed the door and locked it, I went downstairs in the lobby, and there was a big wedding going on, and all the ladies in their white gowns, and I get on the house phone and yell, 'You motherfucking son of a bitch, you better get your ass out of this fucking town.' And I just made a complete ass out of myself. And Wex came up to me and says, 'Why did you do that? How could you do that? We had everything going so good, and we done so much together. This is it with me, you know, it's over, you spoiled our relationship right there. I begged you not to drink, I begged you not to come over here, and I tried to get you to go home.' And I just said to myself, *Well, to hell with it. I don't need this shit. Nobody tells me what to do. I bend over backwards and try to cut hit records, and nobody gives a shit anyway.* That kind of shit."

By morning Aretha and Ted were gone, having had a fight of their own which led to Aretha's calling Wexler from a diner at six in the morning. By afternoon it was all over, and Wexler was on his way back to New York with the tape in his possession—one supernal song, with only background voices to add, one track with Dan Penn taking the vocal. This was the legendary Muscle Shoals session.

Within a week Wexler had leaked the semicompleted side to selected soul

DJs around the country (first he played it for them over the phone, then he had a dub made up that they could play on the air), and it "bent everybody out of shape. They were going mad. 'When can I have it?' So all of a sudden a whole big scam starts on this record, and I don't have a second side. I can't release it." Somewhat disingenuously Wexler got back in touch with Rick Hall and asked if Rick could spare his musicians for a few days for a King Curtis session in New York. Rick, undoubtedly still hoping to patch things up, sent Jimmy Johnson, Roger Hawkins, and Spooner Oldham to New York to play on an album called *King Curtis Plays the Great Memphis Hits*. What Jerry didn't mention was that he had scheduled an Aretha Franklin session to follow right after the Curtis dates and finish the song and the album that had been started in Muscle Shoals.

What the musicians heard when they arrived at the studio utterly over-whelmed them. The "awful" track ("Do Right Woman") they had cut in Muscle Shoals now sounded like a symphony. "We walked in that studio," recalls Dan Penn, "and, man, I never been hit so hard in my life. She'd gone in there and put that really finesse piano on and her voice and her sisters', and everything was so right on—and I didn't expect *nothing*. To me it was the dog of the century at that point. I didn't even like the song."

New York City, Aretha Franklin, Atlantic Records—it was a fantasy

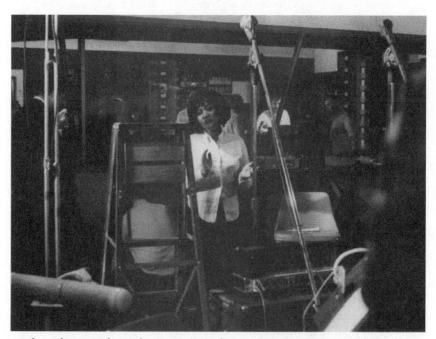

In the Atlantic studio, February 1967: with Tom Dowd and Jimmy Johnson identifiable behind glass. (David Gahr)

almost beyond the wildest imaginings of backwoods boys from Memphis and Muscle Shoals, and they got through the next couple of days on sheer exhilaration. Then Rick heard about the Aretha session and hit the roof. He recalled his musicians immediately for a session he had booked at Fame. Reluctantly they returned to Alabama, with Memphis drummer Gene Chrisman replacing Roger Hawkins and Aretha herself filling in for Spooner. If Rick had had any illusions before about the future of his relationship with Jerry Wexler and Atlantic, he certainly didn't now.

"Jerry never came back. We never cut any more sessions together. We are good friends now, and we talked over the differences, but that ended our relationship, and of course then Wexler went after my musicians, offered to move them out and build them a new studio and finance it, and they would put me out of business."

Jerry Wexler's interpretation, of course, is somewhat different. He points out that Rick's musicians, in fact, did not go out on their own for another two years, that they had been kept under conditions of virtual servitude and had wanted to escape for some time, that Jerry tried to explain all this to Rick, but Rick wouldn't listen, and besides, it was all just business anyway. All of which may well be true, but nonetheless Rick Hall's post-honeymoon assessment of Jerry Wexler is not without insight.

"He broke with Stax, he broke with me, he broke with Chips, and he even broke with Muscle Shoals Sound at one point [this was the Jimmy Johnson–Roger Hawkins group that Wexler set up in business with a healthy loan]. Wex was strong-willed and a tremendous businessman. He could use you, pit you against me, me against this guy, and he did that, especially to us Southern boys. He wasn't a musician, he wasn't a singer, he wasn't a songwriter, but he was a great executive and the best businessman I ever met."

As for Aretha, she never went back to Muscle Shoals, though the "Muscle Shoals sound" remained an important ingredient of her early Atlantic work. In late 1968, not long after the Muscle Shoals session, she broke with Ted White, but not before *Time*'s cover story branded her as a "victim" and battered wife and forever reinforced her ingrained fear of interviews and publicity. She was "twenty-six going on sixty-five," she said matter-of-factly in that interview, "an old woman in disguise." There was, it seemed, little melodrama in her statement, just a profound and dispiriting weariness so at odds with the joyful release of her art, the free-spirited transformation that her voice and phrasing worked on even the most familiar sentiments and material (a typically submissive '60s-style "female" lyric like "[You Make Me Feel Like] A Natural Woman" could become an anthem of emerging consciousness in this process), as to suggest a whole other subtext of experience.

Her career from the first Atlantic release was like a meteor shower, a burst of explosions that were as dazzling commercially (her first six singles made the

Aretha's Gold: Jerry Wexler, Aretha Franklin, Ted White.

Top 10 in the pop charts; all but "Natural Woman" made #1 on the soul charts, and that made #2) as they were for the ferocity of the talent that was unleashed. It was not so much that Aretha deviated from the common way as that by her very genius she defined it. Her success swept aside everything in its path (the civil rights summer of 1967 was declared by *Ebony* to be "the summer of 'Retha, Rap [Brown], and Revolt"); previous standards of excellence were rendered suddenly moot by the entrance of someone so uniquely gifted, so inspired in her art that all others were dwarfed by comparison. If you pick up that first Atlantic album today, graced with a lovely pensive shot of Aretha by fashion photographer Jerry Schatzberg (a typically classy Atlantic touch), what you get is as thrilling after fifteen years as the day it came out: the kind of music that leaps out at you and demands your attention, the art of a moment that is eternally youthful, eternally fresh. There had not been so stunning a debut in popular music since Elvis Presley's, but unlike Elvis's, Aretha's art was wrung from experience, as intuitive as her apprehension of that experience might be.

DOUBLE TIME

I remember the day "I Never Loved a Man" came out in Boston. I had gone over to Skippy White's Mass. Records: Home of the Blues, and the little speaker over the door that was beamed to the sidewalk trade was filled with Aretha. People were dancing on the frosty street with themselves or with one another and lining up at the counter to get a purchase on that magic sound as the record kept playing over and over. It was as if the millennium had arrived.

Aretha's subsequent "career" was as quicksilver and as impossible to pin down as that moment, it sometimes seemed. Unlike other, more "professional" entertainers, there was little consistency to her performances—either in person or on record—after that first burst of belief; you could never be quite sure of what you would be getting. And yet when Aretha hit her stride, for whatever mysterious reasons, because of whatever inexplicable combination of feeling and circumstances, there was nothing to which her performance could be compared. Russell Gersten, her most perceptive critic, held Aretha's and Gladys Knight's art up to the same light at a time when Gladys Knight and the Pips had far eclipsed Aretha in the commercial marketplace and came up with a Godardian metaphor. There were "earthbound" artists (like Knight) "who walk down the street with their heads up, looking straight ahead. They look and plan and organize, and their work is smart and wise and well-developed and sometimes great. This group is always admired. Then there's the other type of artist [Aretha]. They walk down the street with their heads down, lost in thought or daydreams. Every so often, they're obliged to lift their heads, always suddenly, embracing their field of vision in a series of rapid, oblique glances. This group *sees*. However confused or eccentric their style, they see with a wonderful clarity."

I drove down to New York to hear her at Lincoln Center's Philharmonic Hall in October 1967 at the height of her newfound fame. For me it was more of a holy pilgrimage than a concert, and yet there was something oddly unsettling about the evening. Already Aretha was yearning for respectability; already she was, in Jerry Leiber's sardonic formulation, "suffering from upward mobility." The souvenir program listed the songs that she was to sing, in order, as if the concert were to be a formal recital; even more surprising, and altogether contrary to the image *I* had created of Aretha, the program was about an equal mix of her new, sanctified Atlantic material and the Columbia repertoire ("There's No Business Like Show Business," "Rock-a-Bye Your Baby," "Today I Love Everybody") that I thought in my dogmatic innocence was the jail from which she had just escaped. Well, I survived, and Aretha survived, despite all the formality; in fact there were moments from that concert— particularly an unbilled "Dr. Feelgood," for which Aretha sat down at the piano and seemingly tore off a piece of herself to offer unseasoned and raw to her audience—that I recall as vividly as any of the more spontaneous displays of a James Brown or a Wilson Pickett, but they were sandwiched between equally convincing moments of silliness and self-consciousness, pretense and stiltedness, that seemed as out of place then as they do today in so commanding a performer.

I saw Aretha a number of times over the years, and there was always this thin edge between protocol and possibilities, between "ought" and "might"; it could be a song, it could be a line on to which Aretha would suddenly fasten —you never knew quite when inspiration was going to take hold. I remember

Aretha Franklin Day in Detroit, February 16, 1968: the Reverend C. L. Franklin, Aretha, Dr. Martin Luther King, Jr., the Reverend Bernard Lee.

seeing her on David Frost's TV talk show, for example, in 1970 or '71. It was a rare public appearance with her father, and Frost asked her about her background in music. "How do you sing?" he inquired. "Religiously." "What sort of gospel?" "My father's gospel." "Which father?" he asked, perhaps with irony. "Both fathers," said Aretha, without any. When she sang, it was fairly cut and dried until, toward the end of the show, she sat down alone at the piano and embarked on Thomas A. Dorsey's "Precious Lord, Take My Hand," one of the oldest and deepest inspirational numbers in the contemporary gospel repertoire. It started out like the rest of the music she had done that day, as a fairly rote illustration of something she had been talking about with her host, and then, all of a sudden, inexplicably, she got happy on camera. "I'm strong in my religion," she called out. "I wish other people knew Him like I do," and she began screaming "Jesus" (this is gospel historian Tony Heilbut's description; my powers of recollection don't extend so far in such detail) "while her father bobbed his head approvingly in the background." All chitchat was forgotten; her ecstatic moans persisted as the camera rolled. "Eloquent, elegant, the loveliest thing I have ever heard her do—rhapsodic!" wrote veteran musicologist Henry Pleasants, watching the same performance on his own TV somewhere else in Aretha's universe. A moment of transport on talk-show television.

The balance was as precarious in life as in art. "She hates interviews and has become impenetrable even to her friends." "Plagued with a feeling of insecurity, she comes to life only on the stage." Her later music was "the depressing sound of an insecure adult who wants only to be loved." These were the comments of interviewers and critics. But even family and friends speculated philosophically about the sources of her much-publicized unhappiness. "People like to conjecture about the sadness within me," Aretha protested somewhat ineffectually. "Well, there isn't any. Oh, I've had my bad times, but they're the same problems, aches and pains other people have. . . ." Aretha had told her, Mahalia Jackson confided to *Time* magazine, "I'm gonna make a gospel record and tell Jesus I cannot bear these burdens alone." She had never left the church, Aretha insisted over and over again in interviews, and her father, that worldly avatar of faith, always publicly supported this contention. And yet, as a friend told Tony Heilbut, and friends will persist in saying to this day, "I'm looking for Aretha to come back one of these days. She won't be happy till she does."

In effect her life as a star became an ongoing soap opera that fans could watch with an affectionately indulgent eye. Much like country singers George Jones and Tammy Wynette, Aretha provided a whole reality-based framework for her art. During her period of greatest stardom there were disturbing rumors and jarring discords, there was public defiance and private withdrawal, moments of doubt accompanied by dramatic fluctuations of mood and weight, a perform- ance in the spring of 1967 when she lost her balance and fell off a stage in Columbus, Georgia, shattering her elbow so badly that she was unable to play keyboards on her second Atlantic album. The picture is murky and confused, but always, it seemed, when she was most unhappy, she retreated inside herself, creating a very private place where she was just "Aretha the housewife," just plain Aretha, who loved to cook and go roller-skating at the Arcadia Roller Rink with her girlhood friends, the preacher's daughter whose stated ambition was to be a homebody. Perhaps the most apt comparison is, again, with Elvis, who, like Aretha, found solace only in withdrawal and—in an even more striking parallel—registered equally dramatic fluctuations of weight and mood. With Aretha you could always tell how she was feeling about herself by how she looked, representing herself as the frowsiest of housewives one moment, the most glamorous of sex goddesses the next. When in the '70s Aretha presented a new slimmed-down image at the Apollo, she appeared in a jewel-studded bikini that evoked the come-hither covers of her most recent albums, explicitly demanding of her public (Russell Gersten reported): " 'What do you think of these legs?' She appeared stunning and was glad about it."

Her work, too, alternated between the stripped-down and the overladen, sometimes in inverse proportion to her actual appearance. Her earliest tendencies toward the sentimental and the overblown continued to find expression in stylized tributes to Judy Garland and Josephine Baker, and she has always taken seriously her role as one of the premiere divas of our time. As a result there have been occasions when she has done little more than show off the purely technical aspects of her voice, treated songs more as vocal exercises than as opportunities for emotional engagement. All this has come and gone, and perhaps all that one can say is that Aretha is so Aretha—in her emotional tone, her touch and intonation, in her unprompted leaps of notes and faith, the way she fractures syllables and elicits new meaning—that no other description will do. At the same time, on a more critically conventional level Aretha has created a body of work, a thoroughly *inconsistent* body of work that is inimitable in a far deeper way. For Aretha has fashioned as ambitious and intimate an oeuvre as exists within the framework of popular song; in her own and her sister Carolyn's compositions, with popular standards or songs that have simply seized her imagination, Aretha has created brilliant set pieces, offered up oddly abstract tone poems about love and coping, confessed all the things she has withheld from interviewers on the subject of life and emotional vulnerability. Listen to "All the King's Horses" for the "truth" of a broken relationship; listen to her startlingly original revision of Nina Simone's "Young, Gifted and Black" for a joyous celebration of negritude; listen to Carolyn's "Ain't No Way" or her own "First Snow in Kokomo," listen to her solo piano version of "I'm Your Speed" if you want a tender but joyous affirmation of the possibilities of love. These songs are direct, vibrant, they create their own structure—but no more so than her versions of standards like "Brand New Me" or "You Send Me" or the country and western weeper "With Pen in Hand," which sounds as direct, as enterprising, as freshly minted as her own compositions, the emotion welling up in a full-throated cry which, if not always supported by the weight of the words, uplifts, in a way that cannot be pinpointed, the mundane limitations of the text. In perhaps his own most intuitively perceptive point Russell Gersten suggests that this effect is not strictly confined to songs with which Aretha is in tune; it is not even as predictable as that. What we are talking about is a *moment.* In one song that he describes ("Ain't Nothing Like the Real Thing") "often the singer sounds at cross purposes with the lyrics, from time to time . . . absent-mindedly forgetting what the song's about. . . . Then suddenly, with an intuitive flight into the upper register, she infuses the line, 'I've got some memories to look back on' with a profundity that says worlds about how some things never die. It is a moment of eloquence and wisdom."

LIFE TIME

In some ways Aretha has weathered modernity better than anyone might ever have expected. Her creativity did not dry up after that first paroxysm of fame, nor did her popularity. Her work with Jerry Wexler was golden until 1969, when their commercial track record grew more inconsistent, but she continued to have significant pop hits well into the '70s and put out her two most ambitious albums, *Spirit in the Dark* and *Young, Gifted and Black,* in 1970 and 1972, respectively. In 1972 she also came out with her long-awaited gospel set, *Amazing Grace,* a four-sided extravaganza featuring the Reverend James Cleveland which combined moments of surpassing beauty with snatches of depressing

Brother Ray and Sister Soul. (Jim Marshall)

tackiness in about equal parts. She went through a particularly difficult time after the breakup of her marriage to Ted White but subsequently seems to have found more contentedness in marriages first to musician Ken Cunningham, by whom she had another son, Kecalf, and then to actor Glynn Turman. In 1980 she left the Atlantic label and signed with Arista, eliciting a certain flurry of interest from the press and the public. Subsequently she has enjoyed a remarkable degree of renewed popularity, culminating in a Grammy award-winning gold album, 1982's *Jump to It,* produced and largely written by '80s techno-soul superstar Luther Vandross.

She has remained surprisingly reclusive for a performer of her eminence, limiting television and concert appearances, developing in early 1984 what her psychiatrist termed a "paralyzing" fear of airplane travel, avoiding any kind of

At the Fillmore West, 1971. (Ellen Mandel)

meaningful interviews, and maintaining a reputation for questionable predicta-
bility in a business that does not exactly require clockwork punctuality to escape
such a stigma. Her public commitments have remained the same. In the '60s she
identified herself with the Civil Rights Movement and in particular with the
Southern Christian Leadership Conference of Martin Luther King, a colleague
of her father and an old friend. Many times she sang "Precious Lord, Take My
Hand" at his request, and she headlined the Soul Together concert at Madison
Square Garden in June 1968 to raise money for the Martin Luther King Memo-
rial Fund in what may have been the last great integrated expression of faith
by Otis Redding's "love crowd" (Sonny and Cher and the Rascals shared the
stage with Joe Tex, Sam and Dave, King Curtis, and Aretha). More recently
she has been identified with the fight against sickle-cell anemia, but most of her

time from 1979 to 1984 was taken up traveling back and forth between her home in California and her childhood home in Detroit, where her father lay in a coma for five years after being shot in the head by a household intruder. She made her movie debut in 1980, in the John Belushi-Dan Aykroyd vehicle *The Blues Brothers,* which, for all the other great black artists involved (James Brown, Ray Charles, even Cab Calloway), was an almost unmitigated disaster. Aretha's was a moment of rare luminosity, as she transformed a Stepin Fetchit part (she played the proprietor of a greasy-spoon café, Blues Brother guitarist Matt Murphy's wife) and a 1968 hit ("Think") into an on-screen explosion. Dressed in pink carpet slippers and with a heavyset amen chorus doing steps in time behind her, she exposed once again the inability of any setting to limit or define her; "her presence is so strong," Pauline Kael wrote in the *New Yorker,* "she seems to be looking at us while we're looking at her." "The Blues Brothers, she-it," she declares with asperity as her husband casts his fate with the band. And it is not inappropriate, though probably coincidental, that in this latest version of the age-old minstrel show it should be Aretha who once again transforms the ordinary, shatters the mundane, with a full-throated, undeniable cry of freedom. "You'd better think, think about what you're trying to do to me / Think . . . let your mind go, let yourself be free. . . ." And then, in an ascending scale, arms akimbo, with that sweet-voiced lumbering chorus behind her, "Freedom, freedom, freedom, freedom!" "If you want to know the truth," echoes the Reverend C. L. Franklin's ghostly voice, "Aretha has never left the church. If you have the ability to feel, and you have the ability to hear, you know that Aretha is still a gospel singer."

The Death of the Dream

I hear somebody crying
Crying in the streets
Why they make that,
That moaning cry?

—George Perkins, "Crying in the Streets"

ARTIN LUTHER KING, JR., WAS KILLED ON
April 4, 1968, while standing on the second-floor balcony outside his
room at the Lorraine Motel in Memphis. Among those standing in
the courtyard below were the Reverend Jesse Jackson and Ben
Branch, the former Plantation Inn bandleader, who was now an official in the
Chicago Musicians' Union and musical director for SCLC's Operation Breadbasket. Probably everyone remembers where they were when they got the news
of Dr. King's death as vividly as they recall hearing of President Kennedy's
assassination. I was in a college English class, it was evening, and I can well
remember the feeling of numbness and desolation that set in, the sense of bitter
unreality that stayed with me on the long subway ride home. It was a Thursday,
and the following night I had complimentary tickets to see James Brown at the
Boston Garden as a result of an article I had written about James for the *Boston
Phoenix* sometime earlier. I was supposed to be sitting next to Jimmy "Early"
Byrd, the disc jockey from WILD, in a mezzanine section just overlooking the
stage.

I didn't go. I don't know if Early Byrd did, but practically no one else
was in attendance. All day long there were reports of riots and looting across
the country, and by early afternoon WGBH, Boston's educational television
station (which had probably never even *heard* of James Brown, let alone
considered him as a suitable candidate for programming), had announced that
it would broadcast his show live and then rebroadcast it throughout the night
in a civic-minded effort to keep people off the streets. Every local radio and
TV station ran public service announcements repeating news of the broadcast
and urging people to stay at home. When the show went on at around eight
o'clock that night, it was a landmark event of a very special sort. Kevin White,
the mayor of Boston, introduced James stiffly; the stage was thronged with an
uncomfortable-looking assortment of local dignitaries; and James put on a show

as apocalyptic, as highly charged, I believe, as any he had ever given—but scarcely anyone was there. We all sat home and watched.

Here is what I wrote about the evening for the *Phoenix* at that time.

> He recalled, as he frequently does, his start as a shoeshine boy, the fact that he shined shoes on the steps of the very building that he now owns and operates as a rhythm and blues station. "A radio station that had never played any soul music before I bought it. . . . Now that's black power," he said, flanked by [local politician and civil rights leader] Tom Atkins and Kevin White. Then he went on with the show.
>
> He worked hard, as he always does. To those aware only of his records the familiar ritual may have come as a surprise, but he did all his big hits, too, dancing with the incredible grace and agility for which he has become famous. At the end a couple of kids jumped up on stage, and then some more, and for a moment, as the cops moved in, it looked as if the fragile peace was about to be shattered after all. But James Brown indignantly motioned the cops back, his battered face furrowed with concern. "Wait a minute. Wait a minute. Hold it. That's not right. Wait a minute. That's no way to treat people," he said. "Hold it. Let me talk to my people." He talked to the kids himself. He said, "Listen. Aren't we all black? You ruining everything. You making me ashamed of my color. You making me ashamed of being black. If I can't get respect for my people, then I don't know what it's coming to. This ain't no way." And for the moment they listened. He shook hands with them, and they left the stage. . . . On the streets of Boston, and on the streets of Washington, which he toured the next night at the vice-president's request before doing another, similar show, all was quiet, and for the time being James Brown was truly king.

That was virtually the end of my direct involvement with soul music. Oh, I still went to the shows occasionally, I visited Skippy White's record store, and of course I still bought records—but the climate had changed, a new note of hostility had entered the air which, while I had always kept my ears open for it, had never been struck so resoundingly before. "We were far from it all," I wrote somewhat sweepingly at the time, "afraid to go out on the streets that night, and sorrowing in our own way for the death of a man, and the death of a promise, which held out nearly as much hope for us as whites as it did for any black."

In Memphis, of course, at Stax Records, the impact was considerably more direct. William Bell recalls being in the studio the day of Martin Luther King's death and finding out about the assassination only after the session was over. He and some of the other black musicians had to walk Steve Cropper and Duck Dunn to their cars through an ugly mob that had formed outside. Isaac Hayes and David Porter were in the studio as well, very likely at the same session. They jumped in a car and drove over to the Lorraine Motel, a black-owned local spot known to all the musicians and frequented by not a few. "We were there in a minute," recalls Porter, "but we couldn't get anywhere close. There were thousands of people in the streets. Everywhere. At that time everything stopped."

"I went blank," says Isaac Hayes. "I couldn't write for about a year—I was filled with so much bitterness and anguish, till I couldn't deal with it."

"That was the turning point," echoes Booker T., "the turning point for relations between races in the South. And it happened in Memphis."

Even more vivid are the memories of June and Duck Dunn. The day after the assassination Duck had to go down to the studio to get his bass. "I got out, and June waited in the car while Isaac came over to talk to me. All of a sudden these cop cars pull up, cops jump out and pull out their guns. They thought these black guys were doing something to hurt us because we were white. Pulling them shotguns on Isaac. You want to see someone feel like an idiot? Well, it was our fault because we weren't supposed to be down there—they had helicopters and shit flying around, this was an area that was off limits, but this was where we lived and worked, we were trying to act like everything was normal. And the next day, having to go down and face that shit—I mean, the cops jumped in because we were white. It makes you feel like shit." "Everything," says June mournfully, "changed at Stax."

In retrospect, it would seem, everything had been changing for quite some time—not just for Stax but for the Movement as well. The reason that Dr. King was in Memphis in the first place was to shore up a Memphis garbage workers' strike which had proved one of the most frustrating episodes in his organizing career (his last visit to Memphis had ended in a full-scale riot). For the first time his leadership was being openly challenged within the black community, and he desperately needed a political victory at a time when hotter and harsher words —on both sides—were being heard. The peculiar alliance of militancy and nonviolence which the Civil Rights Movement had forged was in real danger of fragmentation, while at Stax the equally unlikely detente between black and white which had been arrived at with little regard for political or musical theory was about to come unglued. It would probably have taken only one traumatic occurrence to shatter the delicate balance that Memphis music had achieved, but Stax had to endure not only the deaths of Otis Redding and Martin Luther King, two clear symbols of hope, but the almost simultaneous sale of Atlantic Records, an event which proved every bit as traumatic in the life of the record company and very nearly put Stax out of business as well.

Atlantic had announced an "agreement in principle" with Warner Brothers-Seven Arts in October 1967 which called for Atlantic to be absorbed into the larger conglomerate for something like twenty million dollars in cash and stock considerations. Negotiations continued for the next month, and on November 24 the deal was consummated. Lots of reasons were given for the merger, and in the long run the arrangement offered unquestionable advantages both to Atlantic, which increased in value by over fifty million dollars in the first few years of its new association, and to Ahmet Ertegun, Atlantic's founder and forty-two-percent owner, who went on to achieve an unprecedented and almost mystical sway over the world of pop. Brushing rhetoric and future expectations aside, though, Jerry Wexler has given as succinct an explanation as any for Atlantic's motivation at the time. "There are the standard answers about synergism, expanding horizons, utilizing the vast resources of a huge corporation—it's all horseshit. We sold for the American dream: capital gains. My idea was to live where it was sunny, and in some vague undefined way I thought I could phone it in."

Jim Stewart must have watched all this with some bemusement but with relative equanimity at first. After all, nothing was likely to change: Wexler and Ahmet were remaining with the company; Stax was on the move; the relationship with Atlantic was only a distributing arrangement, after all. There were the terms of a new agreement to be worked out, it is true, because in one of his rare moments of legal astuteness—and a misguided one at that—Stewart had inserted a keyman clause into the Atlantic contract. This stipulated that the contract would immediately lapse (with a six-month grace period to negotiate a new one) if Jerry Wexler should ever dissociate himself from ownership of the company. The negotiations, it seemed, though, would be only a formality; Jerry Wexler was doing his best to reassure Stewart that Stax was a valued part of the Atlantic catalog (How valued? Stewart now wanted to know); and everyone kept saying it would be the same as it was before, only better. Then two things happened to shake Stewart's certainty.

The first was Otis Redding's death, two weeks after the formal conclusion of Atlantic's sale. Had Otis lived—well, who knows what would have happened if Otis had lived, any more than one can guess what would have happened if the Kennedys or Dr. King had survived? It had been clear for some time that Jerry Wexler was romancing Otis, and it was even rumored that Otis had a keyman clause in *his* contract involving the continued association of Jerry Wexler and Stax, a contention that Jim Stewart hotly denies. Subtleties of interpretation aside, it seems self-evident that Otis, the most valued member of the Stax family, might very well have been the single element able to keep the Stax-Atlantic relationship together. With Otis alive, Stax had a product it was confident Atlantic wanted to buy and a strong sense of continuity. With Otis gone, both sales and sentiment were out the window, and as negotiations proceeded and talk became tougher the second element of the painful, double-edged revelation became clear. Not only was Stax going to have to continue without Otis, without its heart and soul: Stax, Jerry Wexler informed Jim Stewart in a moment that must have been as fraught with emotion as it was with good old-fashioned, hard-bitten realpolitik, did not even own its own masters. Atlantic owned the entire Stax catalog.

It's hard to imagine the effect that this announcement must have had on Stewart. Atlantic was probably playing it as a trump card, with Wexler assuming that once the shock had worn off, Stewart would quickly come to terms. If this was his thinking, he gravely miscalculated. No one would have been happier at this point to cash in his chips than Jim Stewart; he would have liked nothing better than to go the route that Atlantic had gone, finally realize some capital gains of his own (with Stax, like Atlantic, absorbed into the Warner Brothers family), and get back to the business of making records. Now he was being told in effect that he had no chips to cash in, that all the records that he had already made, and all the unreleased masters, were already owned by Warner Brothers-Seven Arts under the terms of the distribution agreement with Atlantic, that all he owned, really, was a name and the future work of the artists he currently had under contract.

It was a rude awakening and should serve as conclusive proof, if proof were needed, as to just how naïve Jim Stewart and Estelle Axton actually were when they got into the record business. In their initial excitement at being hooked up with Atlantic, I don't think it even occurred to them to question the eventual ownership of the masters, and through the half-dozen years of Stax's association with Atlantic I doubt that Jim Stewart ever gave more than passing thought to the piece of paper that formalized an amicable business arrangement. Even today he refers regretfully, but seemingly without any real bitterness, to the "misunderstanding" which abruptly ended that association. "Their total investment in Stax Records—*ever*— was $5000. Well, that moment was my awakening, that was when I suddenly realized, Hey, I'm in the record business. It's not all peaches and cream. If I'm gonna make it, I've got to wise up and start making some changes in my way of thinking!"

Jerry Wexler, for his part, hotly denies any ill intent. "Well, I've got to tell you that we made a contract with him that probably was unfair, but I didn't realize at the time that ownership of the masters passed on to Atlantic Records. I didn't know that until the end. It was a loaded deal, and I tried to give them back their catalog, but I couldn't, because the lawyers had put it over. What are you getting at, that we were slick? The name of the game was whatever the traffic would bear."

The outcome was the same, in any case. Negotiations dragged on for several months, through December and January and February, but Stax had no negotiating leverage, and Atlantic never upped its original offer ("I was totally astounded when they came to me with this ridiculous offer," says Jim). In the course of the negotiations Stewart made the further discovery that Sam and Dave, his most popular act even with Otis alive, were the property not of Stax but of Atlantic. It had been, says Jerry Wexler, "strictly a lend-lease deal. I signed Sam and Dave to Atlantic and gave them to Jim Stewart with the idea that they could come out on Stax and he would get the same override on them as he would on any other Stax artist. But I had the contract on them, and I took them back when Stax left us."

This had not been Stax's understanding of the situation at all, Steve Cropper says with some indignation. "Jerry Wexler gave Jim Sam and Dave," Cropper insists, echoing Stewart's feelings. "After the falling out he took them back, and then he went ahead and killed their career. Jim just felt like he was being totally taken advantage of. We kept them alive, and then they offered us so little for our endeavor, and then when we turned them down, they just looked at us with their Jewish eyes and said, 'Okay, we'll take Sam and Dave back.' It was real high school."

What had originally seemed unthinkable was rapidly coming to pass: Stax, it was becoming more and more clear, was not going to be able to work out a deal with Atlantic. At first Jim thought of going independent, and during the interim period, when negotiations were still going on with Atlantic, he had a brief taste of what independence might be like. In the end he decided that the capital and distribution network that could be realized from the sale of the company to a major were worth more than the advantages of going it alone. Estelle was then dispatched to New York to inform Atlantic. "I was sent to do the dirty work. That was my job. When we decided to sell to Gulf & Western, they sent me to New York to get our contract the day it expired from Atlantic. And Al Bell and my brother took off for the West Coast to settle the deal with Gulf & Western."

The deal, according to Estelle, was for $2,880,000, plus a substantial amount of Gulf & Western stock in exchange for East/Memphis, Stax's publishing company. Even this fairly straightforward transaction was accompanied by a new kind of complication, as Jim Stewart declared that he wanted to give Al Bell, his newly appointed executive vice-president, 20 percent of the publishing stock, to be equally subtracted from his and Estelle's shares. Estelle, for her part, insisted that if she was going to give up 10 percent of her stock ownership for nothing, half of it was going to go to Steve Cropper. In the end both Steve and Al Bell got 10 percent ownership of the publishing, while unsubstantiated rumors went out to the rest of the company—to principals as close to the action as Duck Dunn and Booker T. as well as longtime family members like William Bell and Rufus and Carla Thomas—that Stax had been sold for as much as ten million dollars, that Al Bell was taking over the company, that old friendships would soon be forgotten, that things were not going to be like they used to be. In May 1968 the deal with Paramount Pictures Music Division, a subsidiary of Gulf & Western, was consummated, and that summer Stax began issuing product under a new numbering system.

"SOUL LIMBO"

So here was Stax, six months after the death of Otis Redding, no longer independent, no longer allied with Atlantic Records, with Al Bell clearly in the ascendancy and Estelle Axton virtually out of the picture (she was no longer even an officer of the company and had had to fight for a five-year, $25,000-a-year settlement as a condition of the buy-out). For the first time Jim was beginning to show some outward indications of the business he was in, and pictures of him from this period show a "hip" middle-aged record executive, goateed, dressed perhaps in streamlined mod Nehru jacket and flared pants, the strain evident only in the pale quizzicality of his expression. Stanley Booth's description of a Stax party for Janis Joplin at Jim's newly redecorated north Memphis home gives something of an idea of the flavor of those times.

"It was the smallest and most prestigious Memphis Sound party of recent years, a Stax family affair with just a few carefully selected outside guests. There were tables laden with great bowls of fat pink shrimp, chafing dishes with bacon-wrapped chicken livers, all sorts of sandwiches dyed red and green for Christmas, and plate after plate of olives, candies, and other trifles. . . . Some of the guests were sitting on the leopard-skin couches, some on the thick red rug. . . ."

These were no longer the trappings of a man whose proudest boast was that he had simply engineered some r&b hits. Nor had the Stax studio preserved its unpretentious neighborhood atmosphere. The little record shop at the front of the studio had long since moved across the street, replaced by a spurting fountain in the middle of a plush reception area. Jim Stewart's office sported such features as a leopard-skin bar (with an opulent reclining nude pictured above) amid genuine bordello decor. Speculation was rampant, jealousy was rife, Otis's death was seen by some as a portent. There was a terrible need for the newly liberated Stax to prove itself; in the eyes of many Stax on its own had to succeed on a much grander scale than Stax the Atlantic subsidiary had ever envisioned, or it could not be said to have succeeded at all. "They wanted to be a major so bad," said Duck Dunn to writer-photographer Val Wilmer, "when all they had to do was just make the music they knew how to make."

It was in this climate that Stax put out its initial Gulf & Western release in the summer of 1968. The first single, fittingly enough "Soul Limbo" by Booker T. and the MG's, went higher than anything the group had had since "Green Onions." Subsequent releases by Eddie Floyd, William Bell and Judy Clay, and Carla Thomas were all substantial hits. But it was Johnnie Taylor's

Jim Stewart, Stax office, 1967. (Don Paulsen Collection)

"Who's Making Love (To Your Old Lady, While You Were Out Making Love)" that established the new Stax presence once and for all and declared that Stax was here to stay, tensions or no tensions, with or without Atlantic Records, in a spirit of austerity or a spirit of ostentation, because the Stax Philosophy remained intact.

Johnnie Taylor's was a classic Stax success story. The man who replaced Sam Cooke in the famous Soul Stirrers gospel group, Taylor had modeled not only his singing but his career on Cooke's, following his mentor into the secular field on Cooke and J. W. Alexander's own SAR label. After Sam's death in December 1964 and the subsequent dissolution of SAR, he signed with Stax and had several minor hits and one enterprising album that sought to bridge the gap between the sophisticated pop of Sam Cooke and the sophisticated blues of Bobby "Blue" Bland, but he had nothing even approaching a Top 10 r&b hit until "Who's Making Love" in the fall of 1968. "Who's Making Love" was the making of Johnnie Taylor, unquestionably (it sold between two and six million copies, depending on which publicity release you wanted to believe, the biggest-selling Stax single to date), but far more significantly, as it was announced in *Stax Fax,* the company's brand-new PR newsletter:

"In the best sense it was a gold record for Stax-Volt, the 'new' Stax-Volt which in six months time has undergone an incredible transition from production company to full-fledged manufacturer.... The story behind the operational

Johnnie Taylor. (Don Paulsen Collection)

mechanisms that helped push Taylor's record to the top is the story of the overnight transformation of Stax-Volt, and quite a tale it is. Two men—president Jim Stewart and executive vice-president Al Bell—had to create a 'new' label from scratch. Stax-Volt still had its powerful artists . . . but in all other respects the label was naked. A crash program to build a staff and find new quarters for them went into effect. Expanded offices and a recording studio are now under construction. New staffs were brought in for sales, promotion and accounting. . . . Full-time legal representation was secured. An advertising program aimed at the trade and consumer press was set in motion. The rushed internal reorganization and administration, and the supervision of financing, was handled by Stax-Volt president Jim Stewart (dubbed 'Mr. Inside'), while the galvanization of the promotional staff and the solid contact with radio stations were handled by executive vice-president Al Bell ('Mr. Outside'). The first two months of Stax-Volt's 'new' life were spent in creating an organization able to run with hit records as well as produce them. The results weren't long in coming," and were, the Stax publicity machinery concluded, a triumph for "the common stones" upon which the Stax Organization was built: "trust, hope, cooperation, leadership, and enterprise."

Also singled out for special mention were new staff producer Don Davis, recently arrived from Detroit with Motown credentials intact, and the home-grown songwriting team of Bettye Crutcher, Raymond Jackson, and Homer

Banks, who were enjoying their own breakthrough with Taylor's success. To Homer Banks it was no accident that recognition should have come at last only in the midst of crisis. A onetime Satellite Record Store clerk who had been hanging around on the outskirts of Stax for what seemed like forever, Banks saw the "Stax Family" philosophy as a double-edged sword. "It was very difficult to get in up to that time. It really wasn't as open as a lot of people believed, and even though they knew what they were letting in, by the same token they didn't know what they were keeping out. After 'Who's Making Love,' though, it was all over."

Banks's success served as an incentive to others, and We Three, the umbrella under which the songwriting trio incorporated until just before Raymond Jackson's death a couple of years later, was extremely successful, nearly as successful as the veteran team of Hayes and Porter. Homer saw the introduction of Don Davis, too, in a positive light, as a much-needed injection of professionalism at a time when professionalism was in short supply. "Don was someone who came with the experience of knowing what really lay around the next bend. With Al and everybody else it was almost like, 'Let's toss a coin in the air.' They knew there was a massive amount of talent, and they knew about cutting records, but at the same time they didn't know anything about business. Don knew how to handle big business; he had the Detroit experience."

This must have been pretty much the way Jim saw it. It was a time to consolidate gains, and Davis, a "short-haired, terribly worried-looking tan man," as described by *Ebony* reporter Phyl Garland, was someone who, from the time of his arrival, never took business anything less than seriously. "Burdened by the degree of [his] initial success," wrote Garland in *The Sound of Soul,* "and obviously pressed to maintain its momentum, Davis seems sullen, is unsmiling and appears not to have enjoyed a single night's rest since he arrived in Memphis. . . ." Judging by Garland's further description, his interaction with the Stax veterans was no better than might have been expected, but to Stewart —as astute as he was in his insistence that Stax was family—this aspect was of curiously little significance. "I wasn't running any popularity contests," he insists. "Whatever I did, I did for the best of the company."

Jim Dickinson typically takes a somewhat more cynical view. "They never understood what they had. They always wanted something else. When they hired Don Davis, they wanted Don Davis to produce 'Detroit' records, that was what they hired him for. It wasn't to come down to Memphis to produce more of what—see, whenever I reach this point when I'm talking to an interviewer, you can't avoid the word anymore. There was a name for what they were recording and what I grew up playing that nobody says anymore. It was nigger music—and they didn't like it."

To Carla Thomas the insult was less convoluted. "Booker should have been where Don was. Booker was very bitter behind what was going on. But

Janis Joplin, Don Davis, Carla Thomas: at the Second Annual Stax-Volt Yuletide Thing, December 21, 1968. (Don Paulsen/Michael Ochs Archives)

I didn't feel like I should be put behind someone new, either. It was like they were saying, 'Well, the Memphis folks are always gonna be here, so we'll deal with you all later.' To me it was like a put-down, and I was there from the beginning. They just let the home people suffer."

Steve Cropper, who until the European tour of just a year earlier had been de facto a&r head, saw it as a plot by Al Bell, formerly one of his closest friends and allies, to break up Booker T. and the MG's and consolidate power for himself. "I went to Al Bell after the sale, and I said, 'Look, here's what's happening. Here are the problems. Here's what we're doing right now, and it ain't right. We got to make some changes.' I walk out of his office with a big smile on my face, everything's gonna be all right. Then I started hearing rumors, he'd done gone to Muscle Shoals, and he's trying to hire them as the new rhythm section. He's brought in Don Davis from Detroit as the new head of production and all that. Well, what happens to Steve Cropper? All Steve Cropper did was go to Al Bell and say, 'Look, we got some inner problems with Stax Records. And if we don't cure them, we're gonna be in trouble.' He did not want to hear that. All of a sudden, after being such a longtime friend, I became Al Bell's enemy."

"Morale," says Carla Thomas with characteristic understatement, "started being chipped away at."

Not that it would necessarily have been apparent at the time. There was so much that was happening, there were so many notable triumphs and milestones that most of the complaints would very likely have been drowned out in the general wave of acclaim that greeted the company's every move. Stax was expanding its sales force; Stax was moving into streamlined new executive offices on Avalon Street, several miles and neighborhoods removed from McLemore; Stax had signed the Staple Singers, created in the Soul Children worthy successors to Sam and Dave; Stax was seeking (once again) to enter the general marketplace with its reborn Hip subsidiary, announcing with its second release, by the all-white Southwest F.O.B., that "Stax Records goes pop and underground!"; Stax was contending, successfully, it was proclaimed, with the newfound problems of dealing with a conglomerate; Stax was on the move. This was not a climate ripe for self-analysis, and whatever rumblings of discontent might have risen to the surface, whatever reservations might have been expressed in the face of the unbridled optimism of the day were probably dismissed as sour grapes, a failure of vision on the part of well-meaning people not sufficiently attuned to the upheavals that inevitably accompany progress.

Not so easily dismissed was the undercurrent of racial division that for the first time (Jim Dickinson would vehemently disagree) was threatening the surface harmony of the Stax family.

Everyone recalls his own particular moment of truth. For Isaac Hayes it came when a slightly tipsy Steve Cropper let on about the special arrangement he had with Jim Stewart. "Steve was Jim's boy. He looked after Steve before he looked after anyone else. David and I were producing before we realized we were producing, and this particular night we said, 'Man, we don't make no money.' And he said, 'Well, y'all producing. You ought to ask for more.' We said, 'Really? Is that what we're doing?' That's when our salary started to improve." For Booker T. it was discovering that Steve had a percentage of the company at the time of the sale. Duck Dunn recalls regretfully how drummer Al Jackson, one of his best friends, scarcely spoke to him for months until Duck finally went up to him and addressed the issue directly. "I finally cornered him on a plane to Europe. I said, 'What in the shit is wrong?' He said, well, somebody told him that the only reason I was working with the guys was money, and I was really going behind their backs, calling them niggers and all that shit. I said, 'Al, I don't know how to get out of this, I guess this is childish—but if I said that, I hope to God my wife and kids fall dead right now.' See, nobody ever confronted anybody in those days, just walked up and said, 'Hey, sonofabitch, what's the matter with you? Why can't we talk?' The only confrontation I had was with Al, and after that we were the best of friends again. But during those years there was always somebody in there brainwashing you, telling you, 'He's an asshole. He's a good guy.' But you never knew who was the asshole and who was the good guy, that's what I could never figure out. And when it really got back to it, the whole thing seemed to work back to old A.B."

Perhaps what it ultimately came down to was politics more than race. Al Bell was running the show now, and the reaction that he provoked was decidedly mixed. With Jim in charge there was always a focus for the discontent; Jim was "the man with a hand on his chin," a convenient target for everyone's feelings of resentment. Al, as Duck Dunn suggests, was far more charismatic, and far more divisive, an individual of enormous personal charm who was not above using that charm to provoke internal rivalries along with a corresponding loyalty to himself. Jim saw him as a great record man, and he was—a brilliant salesman, a gifted writer and producer, a record hustler of the first order. Certainly that is as good a reason as one can deduce (liberal guilt, his own absence of personality and stated desire to remain behind the scenes aside) for Jim's turning the Stax reins over to Al. But Jim also came to see a dark side to the equation; the very qualities that made Bell so successful a salesman made him just as much a mark in Jim's view, susceptible to nearly every sales pitch that came along ("He could draw hustlers like flies to honey," says Stewart in retrospect; "they just seemed to flock to him. Al didn't differentiate between color; anybody could hustle him."). In the end this may have been the record company's undoing just as much as it was his own.

Johnny Baylor crystallized the issues of both race and personality at Stax. Baylor first came to Stax in the summer of 1968, when he met Al Bell in New York and made a distribution arrangement for Koko, a little label which he had been operating since 1964 and which currently had one artist on it. Baylor was obviously an ambitious man, and his artist, Luther Ingram, was a gifted singer

Johnny Baylor, Goodee Sandra Jackson, and Dino ("Boom Boom"): at Jim Stewart's home, Christmas 1968. (Don Paulsen/Michael Ochs Archives)

*Luther Ingram. (Don Paulsen/
Michael Ochs Archives)*

who went on to enjoy one of Stax's biggest hits of the '70s ("[If Loving You
Is Wrong] I Don't Want to Be Right"), but Johnny Baylor's significance in
Stax history was not limited to art or even conventional commerce. Here is
Baylor's portrayal of himself and his protégé in a Stax publicity release issued
some time after his arrival in Memphis. Luther Ingram, declared the five-page
document, was the possessor of a "neo-existential philosophy that cradles em-
piricist foundations," while Baylor, "a serendipitous thinker," was "a tall and
imposing dark-skinned man [who] is not the conventional executive type. He's
not a white-shirt black-tie man. His dress and personality, like Luther's, symbolizes a sensitive need for freedom to exploit his talents to their fullest potential.
Baylor, a free spirit, feels that experience is the absolute basis for learning and
feeling. He spent most of his years traveling (1958–1963) around the great cities
of Europe. . . . 'When Luther and I first met,' [he says], 'we could relate right
away. We were able to establish cooperation which entails both life and law.
You see, cooperation became our conviction.'

" 'Black people,' " concluded Baylor in the PR sheet, " 'have always
known that music could be both entertaining and profitable, but they've never
had a profitable part of the action. Now they have it and participate in the entire
spectrum.' "

Some of his Stax compatriots might not recognize Baylor from this
carefully articulated self-portrait, or, if they did, it would only be by inference,
from its elliptical conclusion. To them Johnny Baylor was, quite simply, an
enforcer, necessary or unnecessary depending on how you looked at it but
clearly a neo-existential man with muscle. Baylor and his bodyguard scared

Estelle Axton half out of her wits, while Carla Thomas speculated that Jim Stewart might have been convinced by someone that it was no longer healthy down on McLemore without some form of protection. That view is essentially correct, says Jim today, except that he didn't need any convincing, the real situation was convincing enough in itself.

"We brought Johnny in because we were having problems with the thugs on the corner. Our people were being harassed and intimidated, there were threats of extortion, the good days were gone. When I went to the FBI, they said, 'Screw you,' so I said to Al, 'All right, we'll deal with this ourselves.' Johnny Baylor cleared that situation up, and he didn't do anything except stand there as a threat to those guys. Him and Boom Boom—I really loved that guy. But, of course, once you get into that kind of situation, then you have another problem."

If no one really wants to talk about Johnny Baylor ("I refused to get involved," says David Porter. "That's why I'm so young and handsome."), everyone remembers Dino, his bodyguard, whose monosyllabic vocabulary consisted primarily of one word ("Boom!") which could be used in any number of expressive ways to convey love, hate, agreement, sharp disagreement, praise, or censure. Whatever his limitations of language, Dino, or Boom Boom, had a way of getting your attention. Jimmy Johnson recalls one Stax session in Muscle Shoals when "Dino just dropped down and started doing push-ups, twenty or thirty one-arm push-ups, going 'uhhhh' kind of like he was gonna kill us, while we were in the middle of a cut. Well, that kind of killed our concentration, Dino just doing those push-ups and looking around at us like 'Get the fuck out, man.' He was an ex-prizefighter, I think, and you know how there were a lot of people who would say 'Wow!' at that time? Well, Dino just said 'Boom!' about every three words to accent what he was saying."

It has occurred to Steve Cropper in retrospect that it might have been a healthy concern for just such propensities that caused Al Bell to cut Cropper off so abruptly. "It's possible that Al was forced to do a lot of things that he didn't want to do. If Al Bell was sitting there with a gun at his head, there's no telling what he would have to tell his best friend, Steve Cropper, to protect me, him, our families, the whole thing. To this day I don't know the answer."

Not everyone thought Johnny Baylor was a negative influence on the company. Eddie Braddock, the fast-talking promotion man who was known as Super Whitey, believed that "Stax got more respect," and besides, "Johnny was very nice to me, very nice." Mild-mannered Homer Banks, perhaps the most articulate spokesman for the Stax new breed and cowriter of Luther Ingram's big hit, felt correspondingly that in a world that did not favor the weak, Johnny Baylor gave the company a necessary clout. Although in the end, Homer concluded, "Johnny was a hindrance more than anything else, there was a time when he was probably very necessary to Stax. He got more records played than ever got played before, there was more respect for Stax when Johnny Baylor was there because up till then the industry took Stax for a cream puff. With Johnny there they took another look at Stax, but I think he overstayed the necessity."

I would guess that Homer is closest to the mark. Al Bell, Homer theorizes, had come in to begin with "through the Civil Rights Movement. . . . That really gave Al great leverage. He could do what Jim couldn't do, and Jim recognized that fact." By the same logic Johnny Baylor, another tougher soul brother, could do what Al Bell couldn't do and what he perceived needed doing. And very likely Al Bell, like Jim Stewart before him, considered that he could control this new element that he had introduced, volatile at it might be. As Homer Banks concludes, "You've got to take chances. Take steps and you might slip, but that's what growth is all about."

Stax in any case continued to thrive both before and after the arrival of Johnny Baylor. "We intend to go on forever!" announced *Stax Fax* jubilantly, in the midst of an increasingly ambitious, and increasingly politicized, publishing agenda which included a reprint of SNCC's Black Manifesto ("All roads must lead to revolution"), ringing declarations of faith by Julian Bond and Coretta King, features on Martin Luther King, abortion, sex education, and racial stereotypes ("Is Sex the Cause of Racism?" demanded one title line provocatively), along with the usual artist bios and the obligatory self-puffery that accompanies any promotional venture of this sort. In May of 1969, one year after the new affiliation with Gulf & Western, in a show of strength that Jim Stewart admits was "somewhat contradictory to my philosophy up to that time," Stax put on a much-ballyhooed sales convention in Memphis to celebrate the simultaneous release of twenty-seven albums and twenty-seven singles (actually, one of the albums, Rufus Thomas's, was represented only by an album cover, a deliberate put-down, Rufus will tell you bitterly to this day, of the man who had been the foundation of the company). A quarter of a million dollars was spent to fly in journalists from all over the world, wine them, dine them, and impress them with the fact that Stax had arrived. It was the kind of overblown gesture that should have backfired and could have put Stax out of business, but instead, like every other move that Stax made during the '60s, this one came complete with its own golden touch. The music was soulful, the occasion memorable, and several of the records sold well enough to more than justify all the fuss. What made the release unique, though, apart from its size, was an album that no one was touting, by an artist that no one had previously recognized (at least not as an artist). The album went on to sell more copies than any other record in Stax history.

Hot Buttered Soul by Isaac Hayes was really pretty much of an afterthought, a throw-in by a songwriter-producer who had been discouraged from even thinking of himself as a singer (and whose one previous album, *Presenting Isaac*

Hayes, was a casual one-take affair, done in jazz trio format with Al Jackson and Duck Dunn after a long night of drinking in the studio). *Hot Buttered Soul* wasn't even cut at Stax; it was cut at the Ardent Studio across town because there was no time open for Isaac on East McLemore. And it was cut essentially without supervision. Isaac had been doing "By the Time I Get to Phoenix" as an extended rap at a local club, and a pop DJ named Scott Shannon told him, " 'Man, why don't you record that?' It just stuck in my mind, and when Al commissioned me to do an album, I put 'By the Time I Get to Phoenix' on it. I had no idea I was setting a trend; I had no idea it would hit. I just did it selfishly, because I was given the opportunity to do something with total freedom—I didn't have to worry about anything because there were twenty-six other albums carrying the weight."

The album went triple platinum, the song extended to over eighteen minutes (predating Barry White in its silky spoken passages of sexy sincerity by some three years), the orchestral arrangements were different from (and more expensive than) anything Stax had released to date—but after the record was out, Stax discovered that it had Isaac Hayes under contract as a writer only, not as an artist. He didn't make any trouble about the formality of signing, Isaac says. "I just told Jim when he begged me to sign, I said, 'I'll sign because Al Bell asked me to sign.' I could have wrote my own ticket, I could have had whatever I wanted, but I'm loyal, I'm company, see? So I didn't ask for anything, just that you treat Al right, put him at the helm. I gave Al a lot of power."

Whether or not Isaac actually had this power to bestow, his new contract, and his success, drew the lines even more sharply at Stax. Because he had not been under contract when he cut the album, Stax's usual production agreement was out the window as well. Under the terms of that understanding each album was credited not to an individual producer but to "The Stax Staff" ("The worst thing that ever happened to Stax was the word *producer,*" says Duck Dunn succinctly), and equal points were assigned to each of the so-called Big Six (Isaac and David, Booker T., Steve, Al Jackson, and Duck Dunn) as a form of profit sharing which applied whether they took part in the actual session or not. "They got their sixth off of 'Hip Hug-Her,' off of 'Groovin',' out of stuff they had nothing to do with," says Dunn of Hayes and Porter's participation in Booker T. profits. "Then Isaac Hayes gets this *Hot Buttered Soul* record. And all of a sudden, because it's on the Enterprise label, we don't get nothing. He had them by the ass. He didn't even have a contract. Good for Isaac. And I guarantee if it had been up to Isaac, as fair as Isaac is—I don't even think Isaac knew anything about it. But when we went in and said, 'Where's our percentage?,' all of a sudden it's a whole different game. Fuck it. Boy, we all hit the ceiling over that. All of us. If one thing ever brought Booker T. and the MG's together, it was that."

Al Bell, Isaac Hayes, Jesse Jackson. (Don Paulsen/ Michael Ochs Archives)

Not for long, though. Nor did it help the relationship between Hayes and Porter any. David Porter, after all, was just as much out of pocket as a result of the new arrangement as Steve Cropper or Booker T.; and, to add insult to injury, he was the one who had always been slated for stardom. The result was that David Porter now embarked on a solo performing career of his own—and Hayes and Porter never wrote together again. "I didn't like what was happening," says Jim Stewart with an understatement that is born of hindsight. "Looking at it from a purely business standpoint, why give up a successful combination? I never could understand it. But that's people. I always had somewhat of the ideology that we were family. It was nothing but naïveness on my part."

Booker was the first to leave. He had been drifting away for some time, ever since the sale of the company in fact, and this latest development was simply the last straw. Recently divorced and now remarried to pop singer Rita Coolidge's sister Priscilla, Booker took a dim view of racial progress in the South in general and at Stax in particular. "You see, there's one thing about the South of America," he says, "and that is that there are certain structures that are there, probably will always be there, that you just can't change. And one of them has to do with just how much power a black can have." In 1969 he moved to

David Porter congratulates Isaac Hayes on the success of his new gold record, Hot Buttered Soul. *(Don Paulsen Collection)*

California, he and his new wife and his mother and father, too, turning his back on Memphis, Stax, and the MG's besides, after he offered them a new label deal on A&M and they turned it down. Steve Cropper, Duck Dunn, and Al Jackson were sorely tempted. Al Bell had just nixed their doing the backing track for Simon and Garfunkel's "Bridge Over Troubled Water" because, Steve says, he wanted a bigger piece of the action for Stax, and Steve felt that his livelihood was being threatened. "But Al and Duck and myself were just not willing to pick up and leave Stax and move to California. Booker just said, 'Hey, guys, I got us a good deal over here if you're interested.' I don't think it was my fault, certainly wasn't Booker's fault for trying. But I just couldn't see leaving Stax." Neither could Duck or Al, still "company men," so that was the end of Booker T. and the MG's with the exception of scattered studio recordings and a latter-day revival with substitute personnel. To Booker it was saying good-bye to a phase of his life that was done. Always proud and a little bit removed, he had grown embittered and now saw Stax as "a white merchant in a black neighborhood," one that had been there for years and was congenial enough, perhaps, but for whom retribution was due.

Others felt equally alienated. For Estelle Axton, prohibited by the buy-out agreement from any outside involvement with the industry, there was no place for her in the new Stax, either. "I couldn't even work in the record shop. Then I was supposed to be in an office 'over publicity.' Well, we already had a publicity director, all that jazz was set up, so there was nothing for me to do except sit and look at the four walls, and that wasn't for me. Finally I just said, 'Let me out of here.' " Rufus Thomas speaks with scorn of the newcomers who knew nothing of Stax's origins or history and claims that his son Marvell confronted Johnny Baylor once when Baylor pulled a gun on him. "My son just told him, 'You ain't man enough to use that gun. You ain't gonna shoot nobody.' " And Marvell lived to play another session.

William Bell, ever the thoughtful observer, puts it best, though, when he equates the company's problems with the problems that accompany any kind of personal success. "It happened to us, just like it happens to everybody else. It's like you work hard to get a hit record because you want the recognition and you want the financial thing that comes with it, yet along with that comes a lot of headaches, your time is taxed to a point where there's no time for yourself and there's always something to do. The same thing happens with corporations. You get the hits, and you make the millions, you've got the homes and the cars and everything, but you can't enjoy them because you're always on the go. At Stax we were so busy making a living that we couldn't live. You strive so hard for success, and yet when it happens, you're disillusioned because you realize this is what it means. It's really just a thing that happens to all people as they grow."

In July 1970, dissatisfied with operating within corporate constraints and fully confident that they could repeat their success one more time, Jim Stewart and Al Bell repurchased the company from Gulf & Western with money borrowed from Deutsche Grammophon, giving Gulf & Western a cool two-million-dollar profit for its two-year flyer in the soul business. Stewart and Bell were now fifty–fifty partners.

ALL AROUND THE WORLD

> *Awww, skin. You ever think about it?*
> *The whole concept of humanity is smoky*
> *It's kind of shaky*
> *No one seems to know which bandwagon to hop on. . . .*
>
> *People sure are proud of their skin.*
> *It's just skin*
> *Black and white skin. . . .*
>
> *Books are being written about men*
> *About black and white, up and down men*

But mostly about you and me, man.
We're all pigs
Black pigs
White pigs
We just can't groove in the same mudhole, it seems like

And the cause of it all is skin
Warm, gentle human skin
Think about it. . . .

—"Skin," a recitation by Dan Penn

What was happening at Stax was scarcely an isolated phenomenon, even if the growth problems the label had to contend with were unique. The Goldwax label in Memphis ended abruptly in a welter of accusations in 1969. The two principal owners had come to despise each other; their foremost artist, James Carr, had descended into a state of virtual catatonia; racial attitudes were rapidly changing both in Memphis and abroad; where was a little label like Goldwax—which, like Stax, didn't even control its own back catalog—to go? A new label, Sounds of Memphis, was formed briefly in the early '70s, involving some of the Goldwax family (Roosevelt Jamison, Richard Sanders and Earl Cage, several artists, and the ubiquitous Memphis music lawyer Seymour Rosenberg), but even under the stewardship of Jerry Butler it, too, came to naught.

Chips Moman's American studio, meanwhile, was enjoying greater and greater success while moving further and further away from the r&b that had started it off and that was closest to the hearts of its principals. Over the last few years (ever since Dan Penn had cut "The Letter" by the Box Tops in 1967) the studio had enjoyed an almost unbroken string of hit records—118 by one count, 122 by another—charting in the pop, rock, and r&b fields. In late 1968 Chips started his own label, AGP (American Group Productions), while Dan, too, not to be outdone, broke away and established *his* own production company, publishing company, and studio (Beautiful Sounds) shortly thereafter. From the raft of self-congratulatory announcements in the trades, the grandiosity of the 1971-instituted Memphis Music Awards, and the sheer volume of business that was being done, one would have thought that Memphis music was on the verge of yet another bright new era. And yet calamity lurked just around the corner, in a denouement that was as starkly dramatic (and as dependent upon the same combination of insecurity, independence, and xenophobia) as the original precipitate rise.

Dan Penn dates the beginning of the end, not surprisingly, to the death of Martin Luther King, but his reasons, typically, are far removed from what you might expect. "That was when I started listening to the Beatles," he says.

Dan Penn in Paradise. (Robert Melhorn)

"I never did like their music, still don't. I thought they opened up a can of worms, turned all the guitar players loose. I didn't think they was nothing compared to the great black r&b singers (which I thought I was for a long time). But then Martin Luther King got shot, and where we'd been working around the clock right up to that time, all of a sudden we were shut down—you know, being in a black neighborhood and all. So here I was going from two hours sleep to nothing to do for a week or ten days, and that was when I got high for the first time on marijuana. I'd been trying for two years before that, but I just didn't have the time. I didn't even know the Beatles were in the world until I smoked my first joint. After that I got high regularly, and something changed inside, it weakened me. I mean, I can't bellyache. I had some hit songs, and I don't know if I ever would have written *anything* if it hadn't been for the pills, but up till then my whole idea had been to chase down an idea till I could trap it, and after that it seemed like I didn't really do that no more."

Penn, in any case, broke with Chips over more mundane matters like cash and credit, the same kind of internecine squabbling on which Memphians have traditionally cut their teeth. In 1970 keyboard player Spooner Oldham, who had followed Dan from Muscle Shoals to Memphis, split for California because "I felt like I was turning into a factory worker." Two years later, miffed at having been ignored by the Memphis Music Awards for the second year in a row, Chips himself picked up his whole operation and moved to Atlanta, where he built a studio in ten days, made a couple of records that looked as if they were going to be hits, and—when they were killed by what Chips saw as an industry cabal —quit the business cold. The rhythm section moved to Nashville, where they would be joined in the late '70s by Chips himself ("I'm like a duck in the desert here in Nashville," Chips would declare, even in the midst of cutting some of country's biggest hits). Stan Kesler returned in discouragement to Memphis, where he undertook a number of short-term independent projects for a number of short-term independent labels before finally concluding, "You can't cut records without musicians," and going back to work for Sam Phillips as semipermanent manager of Phillips's custom operation. Dan hung on for another couple of years, "still trying," he says, "to believe in Memphis, but there wasn't nothing left to believe in. Everyone was gone."

"Memphis," says Bobby Emmons, American's onetime keyboard player and still one of Chips's closest compatriots today, "had everything it needed. There were all different kinds of music and a different kind of feel. We were so isolated, really, we weren't actually involved in Memphis politics, but that was the thing—everybody not wanting to be part of it *was* Memphis politics. Memphis, you see, was really on its way. All it needed was just a little more time. It was a Heathkit that nobody ever bothered to put together."

In Muscle Shoals, too, political, personal, and musical problems were raising their heads and threatening to overturn the brief hegemony which the region had held in the world of soul. Musically and culturally, of course, Muscle Shoals was far more isolated than Memphis, but, isolation aside, the situation at Fame almost exactly mirrored that of Stax and American. The departure of Dan Penn and Spooner Oldham for Chips's Memphis studio had hurt quite a bit. The departure of Atlantic's business following the abortive Aretha Franklin session hurt even more, as Jerry Wexler made good on his promise to do all in his power to put Rick Hall out of business (at least this was Rick's interpretation). The Aretha session was the last Rick would see of Wexler professionally, apart from an already existing distribution arrangement for the Fame label and the occasional Wilson Pickett session (which stemmed from Pickett's personal loyalty and almost superstitious faith in the studio).

Rick Hall was nothing if not a scrapper, though, and by the summer of 1967 he had hooked up with Leonard Chess, who, seeing the money that his old friend Jerry Wexler had made in the hinterlands, sent r&b veteran Etta James and recent gospel convert Laura Lee down to Muscle Shoals with a better royalty percentage for the producer and more money upfront than Rick had ever seen from Atlantic. A number of hits resulted from these sessions, and the Chess connection might have proved even more profitable for all concerned had it not been for Leonard Chess's death in the fall of 1969. Even as he was cutting

Rick Hall and Clarence Carter, with (in foreground) Bowlegs Miller, Joe Arnold, Aaron Varnell. (Courtesy of Rick Hall)

hits for Chess, Rick further established his bankability as a producer with Clarence Carter's "Slip Away," a muscular throwback to Fame's first successful independent production on Jimmy Hughes ("Steal Away") and the studio's biggest hit to date, though it appeared, ironically enough, on the Atlantic label. Carter, a blind graduate of Alabama State College in his native Montgomery, had originally been signed as one half of Clarence and Calvin, but when Calvin got injured in an automobile accident, Rick recorded Carter alone. "Slip Away," featuring Carter's bluesy guitar and devilish chuckle (which he had adapted at Rick's urging from Montgomery DJ Mr. Lee), set the tone for a whole string of hits, which culminated in "Patches," a bathetic half-recitation and #4 pop hit for Clarence, which inspired covers in every field.

In late 1968 Wilson Pickett returned from Memphis and did a session with a new discovery of Hall's, a young white guitarist from Florida listed on the album jacket as "David" Allman, who was featured playing lush slide-style on a most unlikely version of the Beatles' "Hey Jude." Duane Allman had been playing in a group called Hourglass, was obviously extremely talented, and shared with everyone else at Fame, it seemed, a passion for r&b. Rick used him on the Pickett session, on a Clarence Carter session, soon on all of his r&b sessions. He even experimented with cutting Allman on his own, "but at the time I thought he might be too far ahead of the game, I was a little apprehensive. Phil Walden [still in the booking business, but thinking of starting up his own label even then] kept saying, 'Look, Duane will make it big, he's a superstar. You keep him for recording, I'll manage him.' But I didn't know what to do with him, and finally Phil said, 'Look, you're not doing anything with him. Why don't you sell him to Wexler, maybe get your bucks back?' Wexler says, 'What will you take for the masters and the contract? I'll only give you $10,000.' I said, 'Write me the check.' I still laugh about it with Phil. Of course I lost $5–10 million on that little venture."

If he missed out on rock 'n' roll, though, in other areas Rick Hall went from triumph to triumph, surprised, in spite of all his brave declarations, at his ability not only to survive but to thrive, and getting his own back at Jerry Wexler when he signed an exclusive distribution and production deal with Capitol Records in 1969. Unfortunately it was at this point that he learned that he no longer had a rhythm section. It probably wouldn't do to go too heavily into the byzantine details, but basically I think that everyone would agree that Rick never overly valued, or rewarded, his musicians. Jerry Wexler says that this state of affairs pained him strictly on humanitarian grounds. Rick himself today concedes, "I should have gone partners with them or cut them in for a piece of the action, but I think I had really come to believe that I could take any group of musicians and cut hit records. I just wasn't smart enough, or I was too engrossed in what I was doing, to realize differently." Jimmy Johnson, the principal spokesman for Rick's second and most famous rhythm section, in describing the circumstances that led to the breakup, explains that when Rick signed with Capitol, he got a guarantee of $1 million worth of business but promised his musicians no more than $10,000 a year—and then only under great pressure from Jimmy and drummer Roger Hawkins. Since they had made $17,000 apiece the year before, this didn't seem like much of a deal, and the upshot was that in April 1969, at the very moment of Rick's greatest triumph, the same rhythm section formed their own studio, Muscle Shoals Sound (thereby capitalizing on the name Rick had made for the area), and went into direct competition with Fame. Their first account, naturally, was Atlantic.

Once again you can believe whom you like in this story. Jerry Wexler, who probably started the whole process when he snuck Rick's musicians into New York to finish the first Aretha session, says rather disingenuously: "They were living a life of misery. They saw me as a possible savior. They said, 'Bail us out,' and I said, 'I can't.' Then I would go to Rick and say, 'Rick, you're gonna lose your band.' Finally they all came to New York and said, 'Listen, we're going. Do you want to be with us?' Then I financed the board and the tape machine and guaranteed them something like eighteen months of studio hours."

To begin with, they moved into a little four-track studio that Jimmy had set up for local businessman Fred Bevis in 1967 in an old casket factory. It was modeled as closely as possible on Rick's, because that was the only studio Jimmy knew, and in the beginning, says Jimmy matter-of-factly, "We just built the business from the clients that Rick threw out the door. Atlantic loaned us $19,000 to make the transition to eight-track, modify the console, and we owed $40,000 on the loans that Fred had gotten on the buildings and the improvements. That was $60,000, and we were scared to death, but for some reason we just went forward."

Not without hitches of their own, however. The deal with Atlantic, says Jimmy, was "a demand-note situation. Anytime they got unhappy with us, they could have called the note. We paid them back within eight months, but then when we went sixteen-track a year later, we borrowed $50,000 from them." This was just about the time that Atlantic decided to concentrate all its soul recording in Miami, where Jerry Wexler had moved. Wexler wanted the Muscle Shoals rhythm section to pick up, lock, stock, and barrel, and come down to Florida, where they would establish another Muscle Shoals, a more tropical Memphis. When Johnson and his associates balked, Wexler called the note,

Muscle Shoals Sound: Barry Beckett, Roger Hawkins, David Hood, Jimmy Johnson. (Tommy Wright)

Atlantic withdrew its business, and Muscle Shoals Sound nearly went under. "That was a scary time," says Jimmy with considerable understatement but then points out that, fortunately, Stax started coming in just about now with enough steady session work to nearly make up for the Atlantic business that was lost. When asked about all this, Jerry Wexler simply brands the story preposterous. It is one more example of the provincial predilection for conspiracy tales; witness his close ties with Muscle Shoals even to this day. "Those boys," says Wexler angrily, "had nothing to do except cut records and sit around all night long and try to figure out what was going on in the great world to deprive them of their rights. We never called the note."

I cite these conflicting accounts merely to suggest that all was not sweetness and light even between Wexler and his new protégés, and to indicate some of the action that was going on behind the scenes of this extraordinary public drama. For Muscle Shoals Sound was successful beyond anyone's wildest imaginings—perhaps not all in a single leap, for with Atlantic's business pulled, uncertainty lingered for at least another year or two, but once that was gotten past, Muscle Shoals became not only the Funk Factory of the '70s but the source to which countless pop acts repaired for regeneration. Simon and Garfunkel, who had once sought to record "Bridge Over Troubled Water" at Stax, now cut hit sessions at Muscle Shoals, both as a duo ("My Little Town") and singly. So did Cher and Willie Nelson, Bob Seger and Rod Stewart, even the Rolling Stones, whose "Brown Sugar" and "Wild Horses" emerged from the studio in the midst of their fateful 1969 tour.

Meanwhile Rick Hall was achieving even wider popular success with his fourth and fifth rhythm sections than he had with his second (his third he lost quickly to keyboard player Clayton Ivey, who took the rest of the band with him when he formed Wishbone Productions and hooked up with Motown). Ironically he was no longer cutting much r&b now. Instead his biggest hits came with such treacle as "One Bad Apple" by the Osmonds (this was written by black songwriter George Jackson with the Jackson 5 in mind), "Having My Baby" by Paul Anka, Mac Davis's "Don't Get Hooked on Me," and various cuts by Tom Jones, Sammy Davis, Jr., Bobbie Gentry, and the like. In 1973 Rick was named *Billboard*'s Producer of the Year after holding the top position on the pop charts for an almost incredible seventeen weeks.

Thus by the early '70s Rick Hall, Chips Moman, Dan Penn, and virtually the entire city of Memphis (with the exception of the increasingly troubled Stax label and Willie Mitchell's Hi, which continued to achieve unprecedented sales and success with Al Green) were out of the business of rhythm and blues. Jerry Wexler had removed himself to Miami, where he was enjoying the good life; Phil Walden, the biggest independent booking agent–manager for soul in the South, had started up his own label by now with the Allman Brothers' rhythmand-blues–based Southern rock as its foundation. Even Atlantic Records was no

Atlantic South: the Dixie Flyers in Miami. Tommy McClure, Mike Utley, Tom Dowd, Jerry Wexler, Sammy Creason, Charlie Freeman, Jim Dickinson. (Courtesy of Jerry Wexler)

longer actively seeking out r&b acts, with more and more of its income deriving from Ahmet Ertegun's English connections and many of its remaining hits in the field of soul deriving, as Charlie Gillett has pointed out, from lease deals on records originally put out by other companies. There is a story, perhaps apocryphal but repeated with a number of variations, about Wilson Pickett journeying down to Miami for an audience with Wexler on his yacht.

"They paddled me out there in a rowboat," Pickett told journalist Mark Jacobson, "and there was Jerry sitting with a cocktail glass and a navy hat. 'BABY,' he said, 'good to see you, BABY.' I said, 'What about this money they say I owe?' [Warner Brothers had assessed Pickett to be in arrears on his royalty advances by $286,000.] Wexler said, 'BABY, I don't own the company no more. I can't help you.'"

TURNABOUT IS FAIR PLAY

Why? What single factor could have brought about so precipitate, almost synchronous a departure by so many of soul's best friends? As blues singer Johnny Shines once said, "The question is why, and the subject is why. Why did this have to happen? Why did it have to happen at this particular time? There's a million whys. That question is at the beginning of every sentence." In this case there are lots of reasons—for the soul era's emergence and for its disappearance as well—but why should it all have ended so abruptly? How could it be that an era of so much promise and hope could be so thoroughly obliterated in spirit that in 1984, even in the wake of Michael Jackson's eight Grammy Awards and an incontrovertible widening of opportunity, *The New York Times* could suggest: "The pop music business, and hence the listening habits of most of pop's audience, are more strictly segregated today than they were ten or twenty years ago. . . . Pop music today has become a deeply divided art form."

Well, one should never judge the past by the standards of the present, and lots of generalized reasons for cultural backsliding suggest themselves. Heightened expectations. Dashed ideals. The classic failures of liberalism. The bottom-line truth that in pop culture when a string is played out, it is simply played out. On the other hand, in this particular case, if one were to search for a conspiracy theory to fit the facts, one would be hard put to invent a more appropriate villain than a single event that took place at the close of the '60s. Objectively it may well be that this event was a symptom more than a cause, emblematic of a time of deepening suspicion and mutual mistrust—but as an explanation it fits the bill so perfectly, provides so clear-cut a rationale for the sharp and dramatic split between black and white that one is tempted to discard objectivity and subscribe to the Single Bullet theory of history.

In August 1968, just a year after Otis Redding's party for all his friends at the 1967 Atlanta Convention, the National Association of Television and Radio Announcers (NATRA) held its thirteenth annual gathering at the Sheraton Four Ambassadors Hotel in Miami. NATRA, an organization that had been started to give the r&b DJ a place to go, had in the last three years, by its own assessment, "emerged as a strong and volatile organization addressing itself to the needs of black members who are major contributors." It was, in other words, something between a self-help and a lobbying organization which sought to create jobs in a "lily-white" industry and to protect what advances had been made—"a force," said *Cash Box* approvingly, "that pricks at the consciences of both our industry and our country."

Conscience-pricker or not, the convention in Miami offered pretty much the agenda of any other social gathering of this sort, with fun and games definitely predominating and nonideological pastimes on everyone's mind. There were lavish record company receptions, entertainment scheduled for each night, and an awards presentation with Bill Cosby presiding. Disc jockeys flew in from all over the country, and every major soul label was there, with Stax and Motown throwing the biggest parties. Jesse Jackson was there, too, speaking on behalf of Operation Breadbasket, and Coretta Scott King and Julian Bond were honored guests, but even their presence was nothing out of the ordinary in a professional climate in which soul had long since declared its solidarity with the Movement. When Del Shields, NATRA's executive secretary, proclaimed,

*Chairman of the Board Jack Walker, Executive Secretary
Del Shields. (Charles Stewart)*

"We are not begging the record companies for anything, but they will have to make us part of it if they wish to stay in business," probably not even Del Shields expected the statement to be taken literally.

It was easy enough for the "old record hosses" who dominated the convention to dismiss such rhetoric anyway. Black or white, they had heard it all before (they had heard it as recently as the previous year, when Rap Brown made an unscheduled appearance at the Atlanta convention with loud demands for reparations), but the language of race was probably not all that different from the metaphorical flights of other ages, distracting them not one whit more from the carrying out of their everyday business. "The theme this year," announced Shields, "is 'The New Breed's New Image Creates Self-Determination and Pride,' and this loosely is our translation of Black Power and Soul Power." "We do not look to the power structure to seek handouts," declared chairman of the board Jack Walker, one of New York's most prominent soul DJs. "We can ask and demand that our contributions are major and that we be equal partners. We do not plan any takeover but insist upon our right to share in the decisions that affect us."

The power structure should have been listening. What happened next illustrated the critical danger of ignoring the text for the interpretation.

Jerry Wexler, in Miami to accept a special award in recognition of his and Atlantic's extensive contributions to rhythm and blues over the years, was hung in effigy. Marshall Sehorn, a white New Orleans r&b entrepreneur, was pistol-whipped. Phil Walden, several of whose clients were up for awards, and who attended the convention in the company of Hamp Swain, the DJ who had launched Otis Redding's career from the stage of the Douglass Theater, was met with death threats. There were fistfights and confrontations. And that only suggests the bare-bone outlines of some of the tales that were told. Prominent record executives had been kidnaped, it was rumored; gangsters and their bodyguards were said to be strong-arming longtime supporters of the Movement; there were stories of guns being drawn, loyalties challenged, and well-established figures sneaking off in the middle of the night, unable to face the sobering reality—the next morning or ever—that people they considered to be their friends, men who had been their trusted lieutenants and underlings, actually resented the fact that they would never occupy the chief positions of power. It was as if someone had thrown a stone into the crowd and set off a chain reaction of guilt and recrimination whose final act it would have been impossible to foresee.

That someone was a group that called itself the Fair Play Committee, which surfaced on the second day of the convention with the avowed intent of wresting money and power from the white colonialists who still controlled black music. While the leadership of NATRA specifically disavowed any connection with this group of "New York people" ("We were unaware and totally unprepared for outside forces whose purpose may have been legitimate but who failed to observe the sophistication of change through majority rule," said Del Shields in an official statement afterward), and while it is difficult to find anyone in a position of knowledge who will speak for the record even today, it seems fairly clear that this was the action of independent operators who would in fact never be heard from as a committee again.

I don't think it was at all clear what was happening at the time, though. Whites saw the threat as coming from the black leadership, many blacks saw the Fair Play Committee as a case of the chickens finally coming home to roost, and NATRA was incapable of responding with credibility to either side. Isaac Hayes, for whom stardom and messianic trappings were still a year away, recalls the scenario with scarcely disguised satisfaction some fifteen years later. "I was there when they kidnaped those people, took them out on a boat and made demands. What the Fair Play Committee was saying was, 'Hey, you ripping us off, now you got to put some money back.' The Fair Play Committee came down from New York specifically for that, they knew there was yachts out there, so they seized the opportunity. I'd rather not call any names 'cause these were some friends of mine, but there were some changes made, they got some money out of it—maybe the record companies were a little more sensitive towards black artists after that."

Stax songwriter Homer Banks, considerably less militant in his language but considerably more political in his point of view, was just as sanguine in the end, if for somewhat different reasons. "I really think a lot of hostilities surfaced, and a lot of relationships that was, they were no more. Because people whom you could feel comfortable with, you couldn't feel comfortable with them anymore. A lot of people had to get out of Miami for safety reasons. It was heavy, but it was destined to come, if not at Miami then somewhere else. Because black music had to grow up, that had to be faced. The white executives and the black executives had to look each other in the eye to say what this was really about. Blacks made the music, blacks made the audience, but the ownership was white."

The other side of the coin, of course, was the white reaction, and no matter how much gratification some blacks might have felt at the image of the white shopkeeper being hung in effigy, no matter how much secret glee might be shared at the picture of all these middle-aged white men decamping in the middle of the night, the practical results were not to be denied. In another year NATRA could go back to being NATRA, the 1969 NATRA convention could be just another good time, but the damage could not be undone.

"I went to the convention," says Phil Walden bitterly. "Marshall Sehorn got beaten up in the shower. I got threatened. The Fair Play Committee came up and said, 'You making too much money.' I kind of laughed. Then this black DJ told me, 'That's one of the guys they pulled off the plane going to Chicago, because he was going to kill Elijah Muhammad. You better get away from him.' I checked out of the hotel, stayed with a friend, but one guy really hurt me, a black guy we had helped get two or three jobs as a DJ—he was finally in a major market—and he just hit me with this constant barrage of crap, this racist-slanted stuff, some insinuation that I was probably responsible for Otis's death—it made me *sick*. And it made it really hard for me to maintain a real interest, when I saw all the things I worked for being destroyed, Dr. King killed, and someone like me being hit with more racist stuff than George Wallace ever was. It made me SICK. You know, if I was a young black, I'd probably have been the most militant sonofabitch in the black race. But I just got tired of being called whitey and honky, because I knew in my heart what I had done and I knew in my heart I was right. And I could tell you any number of people involved in black music who have just begged me to get involved again. You know, back then I wouldn't even listen to a white record, I hated that crap. The first time I heard the Rolling Stones, I said, 'You've got to be kidding. Who'd want to be listening to this when you could be listening to a great soul singer?' But after that I just decided I'd get into white rock 'n' roll, and that's what I did."

Jerry Wexler's reaction was much the same, but he is far more reluctant to talk about the subject than Walden because "it's very hard for me to go into it without appearing to be racist. I was threatened. They hustled me out of there when somebody with a gun appeared at the registration and said, 'I'm looking for Wexler.' There were a whole lot of scams going on, and there were some street people taking advantage of this, the kind of people who thrive in the poverty business, you know. It was significant all right, it was hot, but I don't even want to discuss it."

Wexler may well be right: there probably is little percentage either in discussion or in analysis. The Fair Play Committee went away, satisfied in its monetary demands either by some direct form of payment or by contributions that went to one or another of its favorite charities. It may well have been that older, wiser, and heavier heads prevailed and the Fair Play Committee was simply forced out of business by an association of even better-connected businessmen who could not have been happy at this gauche attempt to muscle in on their territory. And Homer Banks may have something, too, in his suggestion that all this would have happened with or without NATRA, that for many whites it was time to get out and NATRA was only the excuse. "A lot of them felt," says Homer simply, " 'Hey, let me just get what I can while I'm ahead, because I can't see no future in it no more.' "

In September, James Brown had a new hit, "Say It Loud—I'm Black and I'm Proud," which, in a lingering display of interracial solidarity, made #10 pop, the last of Brown's hits to cross over into the Pop 10. "Miami?" says Hamp Swain today. "I was there. I remember vaguely some of the guys locking themselves in their rooms. I think there was a group out of New York that came down and made some demands, but what was going on I really don't know. It didn't affect me. I was there for the party."

"BOOM!"

Stax struggled on. With the reacquisition of the label in 1970 by Jim Stewart and Al Bell, the company entered a new phase of existence. Within a year Stewart and Bell had repaid their principal financial backer, Deutsche Grammophon, which would have become a 45 percent shareholder at this point had Stax not come up with the loan money plus a million dollars in interest. Stax raised the money with the help of the Union Planters National Bank of Memphis and now was truly on its own. Except that Jim Stewart wanted out.

"I just got weary of it all. I'd spent two years doing nothing but negotiating, and the company was being neglected. I'd spent two years going back and forth between New York and California, and it drained me. I had a good salary, but I had no money because I had to go in debt to buy back the company. We were hot at the time, but I wanted to get back into producing, into planning, into doing the things I was best at. So I told Bell, 'Look, I want to get out once and for all. I don't want stock. I don't want paper. I want cash.' I wanted to finally take my capital gains."

That was how Al Bell got into the Columbia deal. In early 1972 Bell started talking to Clive Davis at Columbia. Davis, according to Jim Stewart, might very well have liked to buy Stax out but couldn't because of the antitrust laws. Instead he set up a distribution arrangement whereby Stax got more than six million upfront as a loan for "expansion" along with other very favorable terms. This was essentially the money with which Al Bell bought out Jim Stewart in October 1972. Stewart got enough of a down payment to be comfortable with and the promise of a long-term buy-out in monthly installments. The transaction was not announced at the time, and even at Stax few were aware of the change in ownership. Jim Stewart remained president because he had promised Al Bell that he would stay on for the sake of continuity for up to five years. "I was president in name only, though," he says. "Bell was the chairman and only director."

His removal made little difference. By now the Stax "family" was scattered to the four winds: Booker in California, Booker T. and the MG's a memory, Al Jackson doing more and more work for Willie Mitchell over at Hi, Stax recording most of the "Memphis Sound" in Muscle Shoals. Steve Cropper had left in late 1970, extending his writer's contract by two years and forfeiting $100,000 in royalties, he says, to get out of a deal in which he no longer saw any future for himself. Duck Dunn settled into a state of lassitude which he claims he welcomed after all the commotion of the previous decade. "Things went along for four years," says Duck, with only temporal exaggeration, "and I didn't even know the company was sold. That's how dumb they kept us. I didn't even know the damn thing had been sold to Al Bell. Jim stayed on supposedly not to cause any shake-up, but, hell, I didn't even know anything had happened. They were over there paying me $55,000 a year salary, and I didn't even go in anymore. They were all going to Muscle Shoals."

The question of leaving never really occurred to him, he says, despite the departure of Steve and Booker. "They gave me an office. I always wanted black lights and shit and Ravi Shankar music (I don't know why, I wasn't even into that), but I never went in. Finally they said, 'Hey, Duck, you mind if we make it over into a storeroom?' Hell, I didn't mind. They signed Al and me to a new MG's contract, gave us a hundred grand to do the album, $55,000 upfront. Shit, I wasn't gonna say nothing. I worked all my life for that shit. I was laughing deep inside. I didn't give a shit." "Guilt money," says his wife June. "Good money," Duck corrects.

The most disturbing aspect of the new order, though, was the insult it offered to the spirit of the old. This was Stax Records after all, living testimony to the merit of an open door policy, and yet from the time that Johnny Baylor first arrived and an elaborate security system was instituted, the building virtually bristled with protocol and guns. "All of a sudden," says Duck, "it was Mr. Stewart, Mr. Bell. They had two guards with guns in their coats. They had a little security card, you had to have a little card and shit. I finally told them, 'Goddammit, if you don't let me in, I'm going home. Damn this shit.' "

"It got weird," says horn player Wayne Jackson, "and I'd been there from day one. See, me and Cropper and Duck are white. And all of a sudden people are noticing that we're white. We had never noticed that we weren't black before. We never knew. Andrew Love [the black cofounder of the Memphis Horns] and I just decided we didn't want to get hurt, so we left the staff and started freelancing—this was way back, when Johnny Baylor and Boom Boom, whoever the hell he was, first came in. Very scary characters. Booker was scared, too. Everybody was. These people had everybody intimidated, man. You were afraid to walk in that place. You didn't know what was going to be going on. I mean, they were toting guns, buddy. In the halls and in the offices—it got hot around there, boy. Johnny Baylor says, 'We got to do this,' and Al Bell says, 'Right on,' and Jim says, 'Okay, if you say so.' At the end the vibes were so thick you could cut them with a knife. Even at midnight, when everybody was gone, the place was like a horror chambers, you could burn your sneakers out just walking down the halls. I'm telling you, man, it was getting a little warm."

William Bell so bitterly resented the new atmosphere that he moved to Atlanta and sought to embark upon a number of independent ventures, including a little record label (Peachtree) of his own. "[They] had gone from a little family company to a multimillion-dollar corporation where everybody was a number, and the people making the decisions didn't know what the acts were all about. You know, I mean I would come in, and somebody would say, 'Have you met William Bell?' 'Oh, yes, Stax number ST124.' What can you say to a guy like that? When it gets like that, there's not much you can do. It's like a snowball rolling downhill."

Despite internal warning signs Stax sales never flagged, and the company's ability to generate an ever-increasing cash flow continued unabated. At the time of the Deutsche Grammophon buy-out Stax was seriously challenging Motown for supremacy in black album sales. Johnnie Taylor, the Soul Children, the Staples, Isaac Hayes, even Rufus Thomas all enjoyed hits during this period, while Frederick Knight, Jean Knight, Rance Allen, Mel and Tim, and the Emotions were just some of the hot newcomers to the scene. At the same time Stax was expanding in ambitious new directions as well. Subsidiary labels Enterprise, Hip, Respect, Partee, and Gospel Truth all announced major new signings, including that of young comedian Richard Pryor, whose Stax solo debut album, *That Nigger's Crazy* on Partee, would set off sales records and shock waves. In the spring of 1972 Al Bell hooked up with his twenty-nine-year-old colleague, the Reverend Jesse Jackson (Jackson's *I Am Somebody* was one of a series of albums under the running title The Country Preacher which had signaled the formation of the Respect label), to plan what would become Wattstax, the spectacular climax to the 1972 Watts Summer Festival in August.

This was perhaps Stax's most ambitious outside undertaking to date, with virtually its entire roster of artists committed to donating their time and effort

Al Bell and Jesse Jackson: Wattstax '72. (Courtesy of Terri Hinte)

to a music festival with a social difference, one which commemorated the Watts uprising of seven years earlier. With an additional infusion of money from Schlitz, ticket prices were kept to $1, and the mammoth Los Angeles Coliseum was packed for concerts featuring all the Stax stars, with the Reverend Jackson giving the invocation. In the end two double albums and an enterprising feature-length movie, showing scenes of ghetto life interspersed with concert footage, came out of the festival, and close to $100,000 was donated to such charities as the Sickle Cell Anemia Foundation, the Martin Luther King, Jr., General Hospital in Watts, and Jesse Jackson's Operation PUSH (People United to Save Humanity) in Chicago, but for Duck Dunn and others back in Memphis it was a direct affront: "Whose cause was it—Wattstax or Al Bell's? Were they doing it for the people in LA, or were they doing it to promote Al Bell in LA? And what did they ever do for Memphis? Not a goddam thing."

Meanwhile there were more movie deals, investment in a Broadway play, talk of part ownership of a basketball franchise, and various other schemes of equal grandiosity and impracticality, each providing a showcase for Stax's expanded new horizons but none paying off in the hoped-for manner. Perhaps not surprisingly the CBS deal, of considerable utility in the making and marketing of the Wattstax motion picture, and of even greater value for its virtual guarantee of continued cash flow, was approaching dangerous shoals. The way the contract had been drawn up, Stax was to be paid for every record delivered, irrespective of sales; in other words, the more records Stax churned out, the more money to be made—an almost unheard-of arrangement in the record (or any other) business. It's hard to say what there was for CBS in this kind of a deal; Jim Stewart says it was a handshake agreement with Clive Davis, the underlying spirit of which didn't translate well onto paper. In any case the deal worked out fine for all concerned until Davis was fired by CBS in the late spring of 1973 for what was alleged to be minor financial malfeasance (using company funds to finance his son's bar mitzvah and redecorate an apartment). At this point CBS presumably took a new look at the Stax agreement—which guaranteed $2 for each album delivered—and, according to William Matthews, president of the Union Planters National Bank and a very interested party since the bank by now was largely supporting Stax on loans, "started to hold back forty percent [in other words, Stax would now get $1.20 per record instead of $2.00]. If Stax had been operating correctly," Matthews was quoted as saying in the *Memphis Commercial Appeal,* "it would have cut back, realizing it couldn't forge ahead with the decrease in capital. But Bell's reaction was, 'To hell with CBS. I'm running my company. I'll do what I want.'" Stewart, too, saw CBS's reaction as a betrayal of the spirit of the agreement, but he felt no more sanguine than Matthews about Al Bell's business methods, which had put Stax in debt to the bank by now for "eight, ten million dollars, God knows how much." Still, he thought, he was safely out of it.

He wasn't.

It all blew up at just about this time. In early 1973, in one of the most curious developments of this whole curious story, Johnny Baylor was stopped at the airport. Some reports have him apprehended at the Birmingham airport, but in fact he appears to have been stopped in Memphis—with what has been variously reported as anywhere between $140,000 and $500,000 in cash in his briefcase. Naturally there were questions, and the money was actually impounded for a long period of time, but Jim Stewart swears that it was all perfectly open and aboveboard, that he was carrying the money to Montgomery for his mother. "It was Johnny's money. You see, Johnny was a street hustler who couldn't think in terms of a check. He had just had a big record, and he had a big royalty rate, but, you see, instead of taking his check and putting it in his case, he went and cashed the damn check. Only Johnny Baylor would do that. He was carrying it through the security gate in Memphis (this was when all the hijacking was taking place), and they say, 'Open it up.' So Johnny opens up his attaché case, thinking nothing about it, and there's some 150,000 odd dollars there. And Johnny closes it up. It's his money. What the hell's wrong with that? But you wouldn't believe the way it all blew up. People are saying, 'Oh, it's drug money, oh, it's some kind of payoff.' Bullshit! I happen to know that was his money."

Perhaps not entirely coincidentally *Billboard* of July 21, 1973, reported: "The Internal Revenue Service is conducting an investigation into the Memphis-based Stax Records operations. The IRS inquiries, apparently underway since last year, have resulted in a $1.8 million lien against the holdings of recording executive Johnny Baylor, identified as a writer-producer for the Stax-owned Koko Records."

That was the beginning of the end. A bank audit prompted by the IRS investigation brought out that Stax was paying $250,000 a year for Johnny Baylor to keep an apartment in New York. Certain Stax secretaries, it was revealed, were making "unbelievable salaries," at least on the books. Talk-show host Mike Douglas, Billy Eckstine ("Senior Soul"), and British child star Lena Zavaroni were all signed for enormous amounts of money. In the words of William Bell: "Homes were being bought, money's being found in suitcases, new acts that don't sell records are being given $100–150,000 to sign, and meanwhile I've never even gotten $25,000 upfront, and here I am struggling to pay for my own home!" It was becoming increasingly difficult to escape the conclusion that in all this largesse some of the money must be falling in between the cracks, that with all this cash going out, some of it must be coming back into somebody's pockets in the form of kickbacks.

That was the thinking of a number of grand juries, too. On September 1, 1973, *Billboard* reported that two Stax vice-presidents were being investigated for a $400,000 scheme that involved "the sending of some $380,000 in free records and tapes to distributors in return for kickbacks," as well as $26,000 in overpayments to photographers for the same kind of consideration. In March 1974 Stax announced that it was starting up the new Truth label and reactivating Respect and Partee. These labels, Stax declared to the trades, "were not part of the Columbia distribution deal" and would be handled by Music Merchandisers. What this meant was that Al Bell felt that he had reached the end of the line with Columbia and was desperately seeking some new way of generating cash flow. Evidently it didn't work, because in September, Isaac Hayes sued Stax, after his quarterly check for $270,000 (part of a $1.89 million guaranteed payment *apart from* record royalties) bounced at the Union Planters bank. The suit, reported *Billboard,* was "aimed specifically at Stax executive vice-president Al Bell, who, Hayes claims, promised him 'equity in the firm and a feeling of brotherhood' to sign the contract." A month later a federal grand jury ordered Stax to turn over records of its 1973 financial transactions, and CBS sought a federal injunction to prevent Stax from breaking its distribution agreement. In January 1975 Stax failed to meet the payroll for its 210 employees.

The Union Planters bank, which by now was an almost equal partner in the company, did all it could to salvage the situation. "I went to New York to CBS to find out what was really happening," president William Matthews told the *Memphis Commercial Appeal*. "I called Al Bell to find out what the hell was going on. Bell told me he couldn't tell me because there was an IRS investigation. . . . So we sent in a team of auditors to find out. . . . We tried to reconstruct the books, but they didn't really have any books in the normal sense of the term. They appeared to be able to generate $13 to $14 million dollars a year in revenues. The problem was expenses. It was hard to tell what was happening with the expenditures." Essentially what Matthews was saying was that the company had been gravely mismanaged.

Jim Stewart still couldn't bring himself to recognize that it was over. His hopes of any further payoff on his "long-term buy-out agreement" had by now dwindled, and he had lost much of his early faith in Al Bell, but when the ship started to go down, he couldn't just sit back and watch it sink. "I put all my money [variously estimated at between four and eight million dollars] back into the company because I thought it was worth saving. That's what destroyed me personally: I never cut my losses. I had plenty of money, I was wealthy, but I just lost everything."

Al Bell was indicted on September 8, 1975, along with former Union Planters National Bank officer Joseph Harwell for "conspiring to obtain more than $18 million in fraudulent bank loans," reported the *Memphis Press-Scimitar*. "The 14-count indictment claims the pair dealt with each other between 1969 and 1974, with Harwell lending money to Stax and its subsidiaries based on fraudulent guarantees by Bell of individual loans up to $230,000. According to the indictment Harwell received up to $700,000 in kickbacks and brokerage fees and an expense-paid trip to Los Angeles in 1973 for the 'grand premiere' of a motion picture [*Wattstax*] produced by Stax Films, Inc." Harwell, who was already in the Springfield, Illinois, federal prison for embezzlement at the time of the indictment, was eventually found guilty on two counts, but Bell was acquitted in August 1976, and Jim Stewart stubbornly defends his onetime partner to this day. "I knew the man was innocent, he was that hurt. He was just a victim of his own stupidities. It was just our fate that our loan officer happened to be a crook, so they brought charges against Bell—conspiracy and all that bullshit—and it destroyed the man. And it helped destroy the company in the process. My big problem with Bell is that he got too involved in politics and not enough in the record business. He was a very creative man, he was very talented, but unfortunately he was a victim—and he was his own victim to a certain degree."

On October 1, 1975, Al Jackson, who had been shot in the chest just two

Isaac Hayes. (Don Paulsen Collection)

months earlier by his wife Barbara in a domestic dispute, was shot to death in his home in what was officially reported to be a burglary attempt. Lots of rumors circulated at the time suggesting that this was not the whole story, and some even attempted to link up his scheduled court testimony in the Stax bankruptcy hearings with his death. Ironically, two weeks earlier the MG's had gotten together for the first time in four and a half years to discuss the possibility of re-forming and making records again on another label.

Isaac Hayes filed for bankruptcy on December 23, 1976, listing debts of six to nine million dollars and describing "survival in destitute circumstances" as constituting "having enough money to pay for a place to live, utilities, food and transportation—the latter sometimes including having a chauffeured limousine to take my children to school."

Stax itself saw its doors closed on January 12, 1976, by order of a federal bankruptcy court judge. The next day, reported the *Memphis Commercial Appeal,* Jim Stewart "drove to work as usual. But according to guards posted at the business, he sat in his car at the parking lot behind the old Capitol Theater, barred from entering the business he had founded. After about 30 minutes he drove away. . . ."

"I knew it was over," said Duck Dunn, "when they signed Lena Zavaroni and Billy Eckstine. It was bullshit! It was dumb! Not that they didn't have talent, but that was the Columbia Record Club. That wasn't *Stax Records.*"

AFTERMATH

There's lots more that could be said, but that was the end of Stax, and everyone demurs from further analysis, agreeing that it might be healthier not to go into it anyway. Many of the principals are still around, and most are still in the record

Stax Today. (Pat Rainer)

business to one degree or another. Al Bell went back to Little Rock after his trial and hooked up with a little Washington, D.C.-based label (ICA), then started picking up some freelance production work for various majors, including a number of albums by Bobby "Blue" Bland over the years. Johnny Baylor died in the summer of 1985 but until then continued to maintain an erratic schedule of Koko releases, putting out a new Luther Ingram LP every couple of years. Booker T. has enjoyed a good deal of success producing his own and other people's music, including Willie Nelson's platinum-selling *Stardust;* Steve Cropper and Duck Dunn became familiar to another generation as a rhythm section once again, this time in the Blues Brothers band; Isaac Hayes became a movie star and spokesman for the Continental African Chamber of Congress, a pan-African corporation aimed at bringing out the continent's commercial potential; many of the Stax artists still operate on the edge of the business, with the occasional revival or near-hit to remind the public that they are still around.

Jim Stewart, a man who saw his worst nightmares realized, is viewed as something like a ghost in Memphis today. When I interviewed him for the first time in 1981, he was still living on his twelve-acre estate, complete with tennis court, stable, and three pools in an exclusive east Memphis neighborhood. Later that year the estate plus an additional forty-four acres was put up for sale by the Delta Auction Company. Stewart watched this, too, go with the same lack of visible emotion with which he had seen everything else disappear. He "remained inside his pool-side kitchen sipping coffee and watching auctioneers prepare for the sale," reported the *Memphis Press-Scimitar.* " 'It's just a real estate sale,' he said, when asked the reason for the auction. 'Why does anyone sell his property? I'm just a private citizen and have no comment.' " He seemed still bewildered by what exactly had happened at Stax, almost as if it had all happened to someone else, but as late as 1983 he was still scheming to get back into the record business, producing a small-scale hit on former Stax artist Margie Joseph and signing acts to the short-lived Houston Connection label, with which he was briefly affiliated.

Estelle Axton alone salvaged some form of triumph from the wreckage. In 1976, with the help of Bobby Manuel and Rick Dees, she recorded a novelty tune called "Disco Duck" at her tiny Fre-Tone studio in a run-down neighborhood not too different from East McLemore and just around the corner from the Panther's Disco Booster Club. "I had had five years to mark time. I thought maybe getting back into the business with Packy in 1973 would somehow heal the wound that I knew Packy had. I guess I had to prove to myself, too, that I knew a little more about music than I had ever been given credit for. That was really, I think, behind it. And when my son died in 1974, I thought then of quitting, because I depended on him, you know, especially in production. But then I thought, well, what will I do, you know? I do have a life to live. I'm still interested in the music business, and being around young people will keep you thinking young, whether you look young or not. So I continued on, and I was thankful I did when I came up with the 'Disco Duck,' and I had one of the biggest hits Memphis ever had [it sold over three million]. You know, that hasn't been told too much. I couldn't figure out whether that was because I was a woman and I was fighting the male ego thing or what. But I never got the press coverage that I felt like I deserved, but I just let it go right on by. I thought, 'To heck with it. I made the money. So what?' And I proved to myself something that I could do—yeah, I did it. I've always had a lot of pride, and it's a funny thing for a person my age to say, but I don't ever look back—except the mistakes I've made I won't ever make them again. I live for the future, definitely.

"I'm a firm believer that life begins at forty. That's when I started in the record business. I was forty, so now you know how old I am. I have to say that my life has been very, very interesting from the age of forty on. Up until that point, you know, you're a frustrated teenager, going to college, wondering what you're going to be, doing what comes naturally, getting a job, get married, having kids, lumping through it all. I have a daughter and three grand-kids, so I have a fulfilling life, but it became exciting when I got to be forty. You know, all sorts of things happen in this business, and I guess that's why it fascinates me. Every day is a new day. I like that.

"I wish I had kept a diary of those years. There were so many humorous things that happened. There's lots of kids I've followed since the early days at Stax. There was so much talent there, it was just a matter of how to utilize it. And I imagine all those kids still admire Jim and myself for what we did for them in those early years. I doubt if you'd find any of them that would say we didn't do as much as we could have."

And indeed, she's right.

Epilogue: Time Has Brought About a Change

That old life that I once lived
I could never live it again. . . .
The mistakes that I once made
I won't ever make them again
Because I know, oh, yes, I know,
That time has brought about a change.

—Willie Hightower

I BEGAN THIS BOOK NEARLY FIVE YEARS AGO WITH little idea of where I was going or what I was getting myself into. I had first proposed the subject some time before and met with a highly skeptical response. No one was interested in that kind of book. It would never sell. Soul music was the province of collectors alone. Why not do a book on Elvis Presley? By 1980 times had changed, and soul was coming back into fashion—after a fashion—"joining blues, ragtime, and most forms of jazz," wrote critic Steve Tomashefsky in 1981, "as one more type of black music that was once pop and is now, in a way, traditional. And suddenly it's all right to like soul music."

Tomashefsky's point was that soul music, like the blues, gained respectability with a white audience only after losing its popularity with a black one—and indeed I think he was largely correct. At the same time the '80s have proved that soul, like rockabilly, never really went away for a certain segment of its original fans, that there exists an indigenous audience out there (black, middle-aged) for whom Southern soul remains as arrestingly contemporary as when Otis Redding first sang "Pain in My Heart." The dramatic breakthrough in the early '80s of Malaco Records, a Jackson, Misissippi-based studio built along classic Stax and Muscle Shoals lines, and the astonishing popular success on that label of Z. Z. Hill, a journeyman r&b singer who had been around for nearly twenty years before finally catching on with a '60s sound, certainly proved a point (Hill's second album on Malaco, the aptly titled *Down Home,* was on the black charts for over one hundred weeks in 1983 and 1984 and probably sold as many records as any Southern soul album in history). The 75,000-unit sale of Solomon Burke's *Soul Alive!,* a double-record live set released in 1984 on the eclectic Rounder label (Rounder had scarcely even heard of Solomon Burke, let alone the little mom-and-pop black distributors who were finally responsible for the record's success), was even more dramatic evidence of the lengths to which the original fans of the music would go to satisfy their musical tastes. At the same time James Brown and Wilson Pickett found a new lease on performing life not through black radio, which would no longer play their records, nor through their old fans, who would no longer turn out in sufficient numbers to allow them even to keep up appearances, but through a fashionable new circuit of showcase bookings and New Wave clubs which attracted scarcely a single black face. It may have seemed like quite a turnabout for the once and future Soul Brother number one to be playing venues like Irving Plaza, Studio 54, and the Ritz, but it never fazed JB himself, who remained the Hardest Working Man in Show Business while now advising, "If you don't have that white man in your business, you're gonna blow it. . . . Can you tell me a day when blacks will be as well educated as whites?"

Soul, then, has enjoyed a considerable revival in the last five years, but for all that I think I agree with Jerry Wexler that no true revival is really possible. For one thing, the economics of show business militate against it. A solo bluesman could always grab a bus, take a plane, show up ten minutes before the start of a gig, and leave $500 or $1000 richer, a legendary hero resurrected. James Brown can't do that. Solomon Burke can't do that. Soul music is not only more of a communal venture; it's more of a commercial venture, too. It takes money to put together a band. It takes more money to keep it together, put it out on the road, and keep it there. Five thousand dollars for a single night's work would be beyond the wildest expectations of any freelance bluesman, but it wouldn't even put groceries on the table for a ten-piece band that wasn't working every night. There are few places on the outskirts of show business that can sustain the illusion of grandeur, and I know that even in the midst of his current hit record Solomon Burke could scarcely find a booking agent or promoter who was willing to invest anything of substance in what could realistically be viewed only as a one-shot success. Without the apparatus of stardom it's difficult to be a star, and while Solomon can always be counted on to generate his own share of belief in himself, more characteristic would be the 1979 James Carr tour of Japan, which pushed a near-catatonic performer out on stage for one concert before ending in cancellation, or the nearly equally disastrous Soul Clan reunion of 1983.

More to the point, perhaps, is Wexler's contention that you can't replicate a feeling. You can sing the same songs, you can play the same notes, to some extent you can evoke the same response—but, as Pierre Menard, Borges's quixotic author of *Don Quixote* (he recreated *Don Quixote* word for word in the original Spanish—but in the twentieth century!), persuasively contended, it's different, too. Is it synergy or electronics? I don't know—but I've been to

Muscle Shoals, I've attended sessions in Memphis and Mississippi that have featured all the legendary players of yore, and it's not that they are any less accomplished or that their playing represents any significant departure, it is simply that what they are playing does not come out the same. They no longer play with the easy assurance of youth, or perhaps it is simply that too many elements of knowledge (on the part of both listener and player) have intervened, but somehow a new factor has entered the equation, and its presence can never again be denied.

Well, we are all familiar with this phenomenon—it's nothing that's limited to soul music or even art. Progress and the inevitable accretion of knowledge (from the first bite of the apple on) will always take their toll. What's left for soul music, then? The same thing that's left for radio, silent movies, the sonnet, or any other once-popular art whose currency has been debased. Its influence will persist. The form will not go away. But it will evolve in ways that are never entirely predictable, make its mark in the oddest of manners (vide the Blues Brothers phenomenon), become an object of eclectic delight instead of a style-setter on its own. Great forces of nature like James Brown and Solomon Burke will persist, while Aretha's current chart numbers will inspire latter-day New Wave groups like Eurythmics, and Ray Charles will continue to have his country hits. Bobby Womack will carry on the tradition of Sam Cooke in a contemporary vein, and artists like Clarence Carter and Percy Sledge will continue to draw an enthusiastic response in the little clubs where soul was born; they will elicit gasps of recognition from an audience old enough to remember the arenas of their youth and—before that—the same little clubs to which they have inexorably returned. This is no soul revival, no passion for nostalgia, it is simply the genuine attachment to a first love which we all feel —only in this case it is an attachment of such encompassing range and emotion that it has never been replaced. Soul music, like the blues, will never die; it will continue to rear its head in the most unexpected places, symbolize an era of hope and aspiration, suggest realms of feeling which are not always readily accessible, nor immediately apparent, in a literal transcription of the music. What it will not do, for all the romantic claims that may be made for it, is to reclaim its rightful place in the musical firmament. Like rockabilly and the blues, it has already enjoyed its rightful place. In the words of the old song, times have been, won't be no more.

This was a funny book for me to write. It involved an odd process of self-revelation. I think when I first proposed the idea, there was a part of me that hoped no one would ever pick it up. The size of the subject alone was daunting—its scope, its magnitude, its lack of evident cohesion. Thematic outline aside, I had little idea even of where to begin. William Bell was my first interview in the fall of 1980, simply because he happened to be appearing at the Rise Club in Cambridge, and I found myself immediately adrift in a sea of confusion. The questions that I asked him about Stax were informed with a certain degree of knowledge, the responses I got certainly opened up new avenues of exploration, but where was it exactly I wanted to go? As time went by, and I got more into the material, I panicked that in my early interviews I had somehow missed the point, so I went back and talked again (and again) with William Bell and Jim Stewart and Roosevelt Jamison, covering and re-covering the same ground to little new purpose or avail. I think I thought that the Truth might somehow reveal itself, now that I had stumbled on some of its more obscure and lushly foliated backwaters. This was an illusion. There was, of course, no single Truth. What I discovered was what I had known all along: that art, like life, is a mosaic which does not yield to easy categorization, that everyone has his or her own true story to tell, and that ignorance or knowledge on the part of the interviewer plays little part in prompting the speaker to reveal it. Perhaps not surprisingly, the same revelations that came to me in my innocence still held true long after my thematic outline had fled.

Writing this book changed my perspective in a number of other ways as well. I first started writing about music with the same passionate naïveté ("I *believed* in the people I was writing about and their art") that I have attempted to sustain ever since. This was the only way to involve myself in other people's lives, I reasoned, for if I couldn't be open about what I was looking for, then I would just have to consider myself a snoop. And yet, over the years, as I wrote in the introduction to *Lost Highway* some six years ago, "For me, as much as for the musicians I was writing about, what once stemmed from the purest of commitments had become almost inevitably a craft." In other words, the conclusion that I was somehow or other becoming a "professional" (all protestations of virtue on my part to the contrary) was growing increasingly inescapable.

Well, this book—or at least the process of writing this book—provided the clinching argument that the person I saw in the mirror really *was* me. For one thing I was no longer writing profiles exclusively; I was faced with the prospect of reconciling opposing statements and opposing points of view (not to mention contrasting personalities of the strongest order) and somehow or other coming up with an objective synthesis. This from a person who disclaimed objectivity! In addition, and perhaps much more seriously, I was forced to confront yet another aspect of my own mortality: for the first time the people that I was writing about were the same age as me.

Perhaps this does not seem like so much of a burden, maybe it shouldn't be accorded the status of an existential revelation, but believe me, it was a sobering thought. When I first started writing about music, the people that I was writing about were the age of my parents; they were larger-than-life heroes with whom I felt like an acolyte in the realm of kings. Muddy Waters and Howlin' Wolf were two such heroes. So were Otis Redding and Sam Cooke

Little Willie John, 1956. (Frank Driggs Collection)

—and they remain no less so today. What *has* changed is the context—of time and place—within which I see them. I wasn't even born when Muddy Waters first started singing the blues; I was in the sixth or seventh grade when Elvis Presley had his first hit. So was Jimmy Johnson. So were Aretha Franklin and Carla Thomas. When Dan Penn started writing songs, when Steve Cropper joined Booker T. and the MG's, I was graduating high school, just like they were. I was seeking to transcend my own origins through art, just like them. We were contemporaries in a world which at first I didn't even want to acknowledge to myself that we shared. We were partners in a dream, and if I was mesmerized by their stories of Wilson Pickett and Etta James and James Brown, they were almost equally interested in my tales of Charlie Rich or Merle Haggard or Bobby "Blue" Bland. It's really just a function of growing up, I suppose; you accumulate baggage and experience, and these add up to credentials, but I still wasn't sure I wanted to grow up. Only for the first time I knew —I really *knew*—I had no choice in the matter.

James Brown, Bobby Byrd: March 1964. (Charles Stewart)

   "Before this book is published," Solomon Burke told me in Nashville in 1982, "two of the people you're writing about are going to be gone. And I just hope it ain't gonna be you and me." Well, as always, Solomon was both cryptic and accurate ("Tell me," he said at one point, when he was a little bit nettled with me, "when you're alone in your room at night, who is it that's Pete the Writer?"). Several people have passed away since I first started writing the book. Joe Tex died in August of 1982, and Solomon flew down to Navasota in the fall to conduct an ecumenical service for those of his relatives who were not Muslim. When Jimmy Evans, Wilson Pickett's old manager (and Solomon's and Joe Tex's, too), died a year later, shortly after Michael Ochs and I met him and listened to his wild and woolly tales of the old days, Solomon called to remind me of his prophecy and to regale me with a story—which turned out to be true —of how he had called the intensive care unit at the hospital and gotten to speak to Evans only after establishing that this was Dr. Burke, the brain surgeon. When Tommy Cogbill, one of the moving forces behind the American studio and the bass player on most of Wilson Pickett's and Aretha Franklin's Muscle Shoals sides, died at around the same time, I began to wonder if Solomon's casual utterance were not going to spawn an epidemic. Cogbill's funeral was notable for its reunion of all the Memphis players—graying, sober, bloody but still unbowed—who played "Angel of the Morning" (a 1968 hit by Merrilee Rush and the Turnabouts) on a sound system supplied by Sam Phillips.

For myself I just hope that Solomon's blessings are enough to keep me around for publication of this book, but I know that whatever else may happen, I will never fully leave the world of rhythm and blues behind. How could I ever abandon my memories of Solomon wisecracking his way through a sermon in front of a multitude of Queen Mothers and Bishops of the church? Or Joe Tex showing me not just his birthplace but the sharecropper's shack where he was conceived during a lunch break ("Now that's history, man!"). I'll never forget finding myself in a rough poolroom in Macon, Georgia, on the fourteenth anniversary of Otis Redding's death. Otis's "White Christmas" was still on the jukebox, and a sign above the bar forlornly requested: No Drugs Please. It was a thrill to finally hear those fabled Dan Penn demos and to discover that they were as good as everyone had said, although I must admit I was unprepared for a tune that Dan pointed to with relish as the nadir of his songwriting career, a self-descriptive number called "I'm White, She's Black, and We're Blue." In Muscle Shoals I tried to approximate the experience of a teenaged Donnie Fritts or Jimmy Johnson by going out to the state-line clubs with Donnie, but all I heard was a dispirited performance by a distracted Eddie Hinton (the last of the great white soul singers) playing soul standards for a sparse audience of middle-aged bikers and their friends. In Jackson, Mississippi, Tommy Couch's son was booking Jimmy Johnson's son's band, just as his father had booked the Del Rays twenty years before.

Life goes on, and no one has forgotten "the good old days, so to speak," as Solomon Burke will frequently refer to them. But no one's mind is on the good old days exclusively, either. A born-again Dan Penn is trying to market his new gospel album (Chips Moman engineered), while Rick Hall is thinking about entering politics. Percy Sledge dreams of headlining a world tour which would feature Wilson Pickett and James Brown in supporting roles, and Solomon Burke is investigating the byways of TV evangelism. Meanwhile Jerry Wexler's eye is on the Broadway stage (he was coproducer of One Mo' Time as well as a prime investor in Nine), the movies (he recently optioned William Kennedy's Billy Phelan's Greatest Game), and posterity. Roosevelt Jamison is looking forward to retirement and giving himself over to a full-time life in the arts. Malaco's Tommy Couch, a native of Florence, Alabama, has bought Muscle Shoals Sound, while Willie Mitchell and Al Green are working together occasionally once again. After a number of hits (most notably Willie Nelson's "Always on My Mind") and a number of misses Chips Moman has cut his losses in Nashville

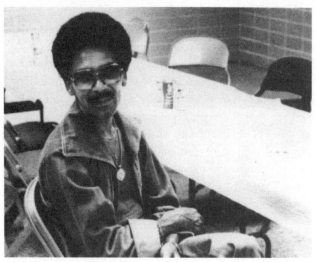

Willie Mitchell. (Pat Rainer)

and returned to Memphis, with the blessings and financial backing of the city that once drove him from its door. Quinton Claunch probably wonders why *he* didn't get the money and still dreams of a big c&w hit. Sam Cooke, meanwhile, has made the charts once again with the heretofore unreleased 1963 live session that J. W. Alexander has been talking about for years. An Otis Redding movie is in a precarious state of preproduction; a Sam Cooke movie is said by Allen Klein to be in the works. And Solomon Burke has just written a new song in the *Ghostbusters* mode that he says will be bigger than any of his hits of the '60s. It is called "Solomon Says."

In the meantime an era has passed, and it's hard to remember sometimes just where it all started, let alone how. Who can truly imagine nine-year-old Solomon Burke preaching in a storefront church in a South Philadelphia neighborhood so poor that "the ghetto was a step up"? Try to picture a raggedy James Brown dressed in flour sack coveralls and dancing for the troop trains as they pulled out, or aspiring showman Joe Tex practicing his comedy routines in the cotton fields while all the time having his mind set on building his grandmother a house. It's a world so different, so far removed in space and time that I'm not sure even its former inhabitants can still bring it to mind without the distorting lens of nostalgia. More to the point, perhaps, how are we who never dwelt there to reimagine the limits of that world? I know from my own middle-class perspective how unlikely escape of any sort seemed at that time. For myself, in the mid-1950s no exit was conceivable; success and failure were to be measured only in terms of the known, and though I was hungry for knowledge, information was simply not available. For Dan Penn growing up in Vernon, Alabama, or Otis Redding dreaming of r&b stardom in Macon, Georgia, there was not even a hint of where to look. Dan Penn's only explanation for his

Joe Tex. (Courtesy of Joe McEwen)

sudden absorption of exotic manners and influences was "sniffing gasoline," and Otis might just as well have gotten his knowledge of the world at large through osmosis as through any exposure to it. Books, records, movies—Lash LaRue was bigger than any of these. In 1954, to all intents and purposes, the world was still flat, and only a political visionary could have imagined the social and cultural changes on the horizon. Ten years later it was a whole different story, with Columbus having landed and blacks for the first time acknowledged as a significant force in our pluralistic society. Battles had been fought in the courts, on the streets, and in people's minds, and I hope I've traced a little bit how some of those battles came to be met. What is so remarkable about the story of soul is how swiftly all the changes came about. In the greater world, indeed in the pop marketplace, the struggle is still being waged every day. But Southern soul music represented a temporary victory, a momentary cessation of hostilities in which the combatants hesitantly set aside their differences and for an instant, however brief, joined arms in a sea of troubles, against a common foe.

That is how most of the participants still see it, anyway. "It was black people singing, we did the picking and grinning," says Dan Penn with scarcely a dollop of irony. "It was just like growing corn. That's what I call r&b." "Soul

Overcome. (Val Wilmer)

music and country music were basically the same thing," says Alan Walden. "Every song was a love story or a hard luck story—each song had a message in it." "There's not much difference between country and western and r&b," William Bell agrees. "Not when you really analyze it and break it down lyrically to what it is really saying. And I think at Stax we had both elements, it was a combined effort, and to me in a way it was the best of both worlds." "What made it work," says Rodgers Redding, "the key to it all, was black and white together, working as a team."

It was the American dream, no less, the same dream for which my grandparents came to this country, the dream of Norman Thomas and Martin Luther King—and I hope that this book shows that it could work. But not simply and not forever. Every dream alters, every dream achieved must give way to a new, perhaps previously unimagined—perhaps previously unimaginable—goal. Today we see as commonplace scenes that could never have been dreamt of thirty years ago—but is this progress? The South that Solomon Burke and Dan Penn and Joe Tex all describe no longer exists; it is a landscape of the imagination. The real South, the New South, is dotted with shopping malls and discount health-food stores. What does this mean? Only that the shape of things will constantly change, while things themselves remain much the same. Even as I write, *Live Aid* is being broadcast on TV and on the radio, symbolizing (it is said—over and over again) a "new maturity" on the part of pop consciousness. Admirable though that maturity may be, and as inconceivable as the music or the movement would be without the contributions of soul, it should never be forgotten that this is only one more step along the way. Hunger will never be eradicated; love will never conquer all; we can only hope that man will survive. Soul music fuels that hope. That is all that art can do. Soul music helped a generation to grow up; soul music, for all its shortcomings, put up the good fight. As Joe Tex said, in a moment of characteristic reflection not long before his death: "It's been nice out here, man. A lot of ups and downs, the way life is, but I've enjoyed this life. I was glad that I was able to come up out of creation and look all around and see a little bit, grass and trees and cars, fish and steaks, potatoes. Everywhere I've gone, I can always go back, and I can always find a friend. I don't go trying to make nobody like me, I just be me, you know, and it has worked out. And I thank God for that. I'm thankful that he let me get up and walk around and take a look around here. 'Cause this is nice."

Camp Alton
East Alton, New Hampshire
August 1, 1985

These are some of the books that helped fill in the background and provide me with documentation and ideas about a music and an era that appeared to be relatively undocumented when I first began to think about writing this book. Some were useful primarily for one or two chapters; some served strictly as inspiration. But all were helpful in one way or another, and all bear searching out.

REFERENCE WORKS

Encyclopedias

Hardy, Phil, and Dave Laing, eds. *Encyclopedia of Rock 1955–1975*. London: Aquarius Books, 1977.

Illustrated Encyclopedia of Black Music. New York: Crown Publishers, Harmony Books, 1983.

Nite, Norm. *Rock On: The Illustrated Encyclopedia of Rock n' Roll*. New York: Thomas Y. Crowell Company, 1974.

Stambler, Irwin. *Encyclopedia of Pop, Rock & Soul*. New York: St. Martin's Press, 1974.

Discographies

Clee, Ken. *The Directory of American 45 R.P.M. Records*, Volumes 1–4. Philadelphia: Self-published, 1981, 1985.

Grendysa, Peter A. *Atlantic Master Book #1*. Milwaukee: Self-published, 1975.

Leadbitter, Mike, Terence Courtney, and Hugh McCallum, eds. *Specialty Label Singles Listing*. England: Self-published, 1966.

Pavlow, Big Al. *The R&B Books: A Disc History of Rhythm and Blues*. Providence: Music House Publishing, 1983.

Ruppli, Michel. *Atlantic Records: A Discography*, Volumes 1–4. Westport, Conn.: Greenwood Press, 1979.

Whitburn, Joel. *Top Pop Records 1955–1972*. Menomonee Falls, Wis.: Record Research, 1973.

———. *Top Rhythm & Blues Records 1949–1971*. Menomonee Falls, Wis.: Record Research, 1973.

BOOKS OF MORE GENERAL INTEREST

Bane, Michael. *White Boy Singin' the Blues*. New York: Penguin Books, 1982.

Benjaminson, Peter. *The Story of Motown*. New York: Grove Press, 1979.

Bogle, Donald. *Brown Sugar: Eighty Years of America's Black Female Superstars*. New York: Crown Publishers, Harmony Books, 1980.

Booth, Stanley. *Dance with the Devil*. New York: Random House, 1984.

Bowman, Rob. *Soulsville U.S.A.: The Story of Stax Records*. New York: Schirmer Books, 1997.

Broven, John. *Walking to New Orleans: The Story of New Orleans Rhythm and Blues*. Bexhill-on-Sea, East Sussex: Blues Unlimited, 1974.

Brown, James, with Bruce Tucker. *James Brown: The Godfather of Soul*. New York: Collier MacMillan, 1986.

Charles, Ray, and David Ritz. *Brother Ray: Ray Charles' Own Story*. New York: The Dial Press, 1978.

Cleaver, Eldridge. *Soul on Ice*. New York: McGraw-Hill, 1968.

Cohn, Nik. *Rock from the Beginning*. New York: Stein & Day, 1969.

Dalton, David, and Lenny Kaye. *Rock 100*. New York: Grosset & Dunlap, 1978.

Eisen, Jonathan, ed. *The Age of Rock: Sounds of the American Cultural Revolution*. New York: Random House, 1969.

Escott, Colin, and Martin Hawkins. *Sun Records* (revised edition). New York: Quick Fox, 1980.

Fox, Ted. *Showing at the Apollo*. New York: Holt, Rinehart and Winston, 1983.

Fox, William Price. *Moonshine Light, Moonshine Bright*. Philadelphia: J. B. Lippincott Company, 1967.

Garland, Phyl. *The Sound of Soul*. Chicago: Henry Regnery Company, 1969.

Gart, Galen. *First Pressings: Rock History as Chronicled in Billboard Magazine*, Vols. 1–8. Milford, N.H.: Big Nickel Publications, 1986–1995.

Gillett, Charlie. *Making Tracks: Atlantic Records and the Growth of a Multi-Billion Dollar Industry*. New York: E. P. Dutton & Co., 1974.

———. *The Sound of the City: The Rise of Rock and Roll* (revised edition). London: Souvenir Press, 1984.

Hammond, John. *On Record*. New York: Summit Books, 1977.

Haralambos, Michael. *Right On: From Blues to Soul in Black America*. London: Eddison Press, 1974.

Heilbut, Tony. *The Gospel Sound: Good News and Bad Times*. New York: Simon & Schuster, 1971.

Hirshey, Gerri. *Nowhere to Run: The Story of Soul Music*. New York: Times Books, 1984.

Hoare, Ian, ed. *The Soul Book*. New York: Dell Publishing Co., Delta Books, 1976.

Hopkins, Jerry. *The Rock Story*. New York: New American Library, Signet Books, 1970.

Hoskyns, Barney. *Say It One Time for the Brokenhearted*. London: Fontana/Collins, 1987.

Jones, Hettie. *Big Star Fallin' Mama: Five Women in Black Music*. New York: The Viking Press, 1974.

Jones, LeRoi. *Black Music*. New York: William Morrow & Co., 1968.

———. *Blues People*. New York: William Morrow & Co., 1963.

Keil, Charles. *Urban Blues*. Chicago: University of Chicago Press, 1966.

Landau, Jon. *It's Too Late to Stop Now: A Rock and Roll Journal*. San Francisco: Straight Arrow Books, 1972.

Lewis, David Levering. *King: A Biography*. Urbana, Ill.: University of Illinois Press, 1978.

———. *When Harlem Was in Vogue*. New York: Alfred A. Knopf, 1981.

Lydon, Michael. *Rock Folk*. New York: The Dial Press, 1971.

Lydon, Michael, and Ellen Mandel. *Boogie Lightning: How Music Became Electric*. New York: The Dial Press, 1974.

McEwen, Joe. *Sam Cooke: The Man Who Invented Soul*. New York: Chappell Music, 1977.

McKee, Margaret, and Fred Chisenhall. *Beale Black and Blue: Life and Music on Black America's Main Street*. Baton Rouge, La.: Louisiana State University Press, 1981.

Marcus, Greil. *Mystery Train*. New York: E. P. Dutton & Co., 1975.

———, ed. *Stranded: Rock and Roll for a Desert Island*. New York: Alfred A. Knopf, 1979.

Millar, Bill. *The Coasters*. London: W. H. Allen, 1975.

———. *The Drifters*. London: Studio Vista, 1971.

Miller, Jim, ed. *The Rolling Stone Illustrated History of Rock & Roll*. New York: Random House, 1976.

Ochs, Michael. *Rock Archives*. New York: Doubleday & Company, 1984.

Otis, Johnny. *Listen to the Lambs*. New York: W. W. Norton & Company, 1968.

Passman, Arnold. *The Deejays*. New York: Macmillan, 1971.

Pleasants, Henry. *The Great American Popular *Singers*. New York: Simon & Schuster, 1974.

Raines, Howell. *My Soul Is Rested*. New York: G. P. Putnam's, 1977.

Ritz, David. *Divided Soul: The Life of Marvin Gaye*. New York: McGraw-Hill, 1985.

Rosenbaum, Jonathan. *Moving Places*. New York: Harper & Row, 1980.

Schiffman, Jack. *Harlem Heyday*. Buffalo: Prometheus Books, 1984.

———. *Uptown: The Story of Harlem's Apollo Theatre*. New York: Cowles Book Company, 1971.

Schoener, Allon, ed. *Harlem on My Mind*. New York: Dell Publishing Co., Delta Books, 1978.

Shaw, Arnold. *Honkers and Shouters: The Golden Years of Rhythm and Blues*. New York: Macmillan, 1978.

———. *The World of Soul*. New York: Warner Paperback Library, 1971.

Spellman, A. B. *Four Lives in the Bebop Business*. New York: Pantheon Books, 1966.

Telander, Rick. *Heaven Is a Playground*. New York: St. Martin's Press, 1976.

Tobler, John, and Stuart Grundy. *The Record Producers*. New York: St. Martin's Press, 1982.

Viorst, Milton, ed. *Fire in the Streets: America in the 1960s*. New York: Simon & Schuster, 1979.

Wade, Dorothy, and Justine Picardie. *Music Man: Ahmet Ertegun, Atlantic Records, and the Triumph of Rock 'n' Roll*. New York: W. W. Norton, 1990.

White, Charles. *The Life and Times of Little Richard: The Quasar of Rock*. New York: Crown Publishers, Harmony Books, 1984.

Wolff, Daniel, with S. R. Crain, Clifton White, and G. David Tenenbaum. *You Send Me: The Life and Times of Sam Cooke*. New York: William Morrow, 1995.

The following are only a few of the articles, essays, and monographs that were specifically helpful in the preparation of individual chapters of this book. I have omitted discographies and cited only those stories that stand out from a literary or historical point of view or are referred to in the text, but there were many more—by the same and other authors—which were invaluable for both information and insight. Because many are cuttings whose source I didn't note, or copies supplied by Bill Millar, I have frequently found myself unable to supply the date, and sometimes even the source of the material is murky.

SAM COOKE

McEwen, Joe. "Remembering Sam Cooke." *The Real Paper*, Apr. 23, 1975.

Paulsen, Don. "An Exclusive Interview with Sam Cooke." *Hit Parader*, 1964.

Watts, Michael. Interview with Bumps Blackwell. *Melody Maker*, Aug. 26, Sept. 3, 1972.

Womack, Bobby. "Bobby Womack Looks Back." *Record Magazine*, April 1974.

RAY CHARLES

Balliett, Whitney. "It's Detestable When You Live It." *The New Yorker*, Mar. 28, 1970.

Fong-Torres, Ben. "The *Rolling Stone* Interview: Ray Charles." *Rolling Stone*, Jan. 18, 1973.

Moonoogian, George. "The Early Ray Charles." *Goldmine*, February 1980.

Palmer, Robert. "Soul Survivor." *Rolling Stone*, Feb. 9, 1978.

Quinn, Bill. "*Playboy* Interview: Ray Charles." *Playboy*, March 1970.

Ritz, David. "Being with Ray." *Essence*, August 1979.

Schipper, Henry. "Ray Charles Sings the Dark Notes." *The Real Paper*, Aug. 19, 1978.

THE "5" ROYALES

Ward, Ed. "Dedicated to You." *Stranded:*

Rock and Roll for a Desert Island (Alfred A. Knopf).

LITTLE WILLIE JOHN

Holscher, Lou. "Little Willie John: Fact and Fiction." *Goldmine,* May 1982.

McEwen, Joe. "Little Willie John." *Stranded: Rock and Roll for a Desert Island.*

McNeil, Dee Dee. "Little Willie John Paved the Way." *The Soul & Jazz Record.*

THE APOLLO THEATRE

Ditlea, Steve. "Apollo." *Penthouse,* October 1975.

Riley, Clayton. "We Thought It Was Magic." *New York Times,* Nov. 7, 1976.

Tomashefsky, Steve. "The Apollo Theatre." *Living Blues* no. 27, May–June 1976.

Watkins, Mel. "If You Can Make It Here . . ." *New York Times,* May 26, 1968.

Zwerin, Michael. "Apollo." *Eye.*

ATLANTIC RECORDS

Abrams, Bobby, and Sandy Pearlman. Interview with Jerry Wexler. *Fusion.*

Clark, Sue. "Wexler: A Man of Dedication." *Rolling Stone,* Sept. 28, 1968.

Fox, Ted. "Jerry Wexler: Navigator of the Atlantic Sound." *Audio,* May and June 1985.

Gillett, Charlie. Transcript of interview with Jerry Wexler, Phil Walden, and Joe Galkin. Unpublished.

Less, David. Transcript of interview with Jerry Wexler, 1980. Unpublished.

Tobias, Andrew. "The Middle-Aged Turk of the Pop Music Business." *New York Magazine.*

Trow, George W. S., Jr. "Eclectic, Reminiscent, Amused, Fickle, Perverse."

The New Yorker, May 29 and June 5, 1978.

"The Turkish Tycoons of Soul." *Time,* July 28, 1967.

Wexler, Jerry. Eulogy for Paul Ackerman. *Billboard,* Jan. 14, 1978.

White, Timothy. "Jerry Wexler: The Godfather of Rhythm and Blues." *Rolling Stone,* Nov. 27, 1980.

SOLOMON BURKE

Cleave, Maureen. "Disc Date." *Evening Standard,* June 19, 1965.

Gibbs, Vernon. "Sex & God & Rock & Roll." *The Village Voice,* Aug. 10, 1982.

White, Cliff. "The Solomon Burke Story." *Black Music,* April 1975.

STAX RECORDS

Booth, Stanley. "The Memphis Debut of the Janis Joplin Revue." *Rolling Stone,* Feb. 1, 1969.

Delehant, Jim. "The Stax Story." Interviews with Steve Cropper, Duck Dunn, Isaac Hayes and David Porter, Booker T. Jones, and Al Jackson. *Hit Parader,* various issues circa 1968.

Dickinson, Jim. "Notes From the Pineywoods Underground: Steve Cropper . . . Soul Man." Unpublished manuscript.

Hall, Denise, and Tony Cummings. "The Stax Story." *Black Music,* March, April, May, and June 1975.

Kingsley, Patrick. "Stax/Booker T. Drummer Al Jackson Shot to Death." *Rolling Stone,* Nov. 6, 1975.

Landau, Jon. "Soul Roll." *Rolling Stone,* Dec. 21, 1968.

McEwen, Joe. "Sam and Dave on the Road to Oblivion." *Boston Phoenix,* Mar. 30, 1976.

Palmer, Robert. "The Sound of Memphis." *The Rolling Stone Illustrated History of Rock & Roll* (Random House).

Thomas, Carla. "Carla, Otis, Rufus, and

the Memphis Soul Sound." *Soul & Jazz Record,* July 1974.

Weiler, Joseph. "Stax Records: The Dream That Died." *Memphis Commercial Appeal,* Feb. 8 and 9, 1976.

Wenner, Jann. "The *Rolling Stone* Round Table: Booker T. and the MG's." *Rolling Stone,* Aug. 24, 1968.

Wilmer, Valerie. "David Porter Talks to Valerie Wilmer." *Cream.* •

———. "Finger on the Pulse: Legendary Guitarist Steve Cropper Talks to Valerie Wilmer." *Melody Maker,* 1976.

———. " 'He Didn't Do Anything, You See, He Just Played.' " *Black Music,* October 1977.

———. Transcript of interview with Duck Dunn, May 6, 1976. Unpublished.

———. Transcript of interview with Steve Cropper, Apr. 22, 1976. Unpublished.

OTIS REDDING

Delehant, Jim. "Otis Redding: 'Soul Survivor.' " *Hit Parader.*

"In Memory of the Man from Macon." *Soul,* special issue, Jan. 29, 1968.

Landau, Jon. "Otis Redding: King of Them All." *Eye,* March 1968.

"Otis the Man." *Blues & Soul* 95 (Oct. 20, 1972).

Reitman, David. "The Immortal Otis Redding," Parts 1 and 2. *Sounds,* Oct. 17 and 24, 1970.

MUSCLE SHOALS

Flippo, Hon. Ronnie G. "Muscle Shoals Music: A Proud History." *Congressional Record,* May 16, 1979.

Plummer, Mark. "The Funk Factories." *Melody Maker,* May 26, 1973.

"*Record World* Salutes the Tenth Anniversary of Muscle Shoals Sound Studios." *Record World,* May 19, 1979.

Whitman, Arthur. "The Hustle at Muscle." *Boston Globe,* Apr. 26, 1970.

Williams, Bill. "Music in Muscle Shoals: 'People Come Here to Work.' " *Billboard,* Dec. 5, 1970.

Yorke, Ritchie. "Muscle Shoals, Alabama." *Hit Parader.*

JAMES BROWN

Arbus, Doon. "James Brown Is Out of Sight." *The Age of Rock* (Random House).

Barry, Thomas. "James Brown: Is He the Most Important Black Man in America?" *Look,* Feb. 18, 1969.

Bloom, Steve. "Anything Left in Papa's Bag?" *down beat.*

———. "He's a Soul Man." *Soho Weekly News,* June 28, 1979.

Davis, Thulani. "J-a-a-a-ames Brown!" *The Village Voice,* June 9, 1980.

Fox, Ted. Transcript of interview with Danny Ray. Unpublished.

Gitler, Ira. "James Brown's Bag." *down beat,* Oct. 31, 1968.

Hirshey, Gerri. "Mister James Brown." *Rolling Stone,* Apr. 1, 1982.

Kelly, Pat. "Papa Takes Some Mess." *Crawdaddy,* December 1975.

King, Bill. "James Brown: Polishing a Legend." *Atlanta Journal-Constitution,* Nov. 15, 1980.

McDonald, Michael C. D. "James Brown Comes Home for His First Farewell." *The Village Voice,* June 27, 1968.

McEwen, Joe. "James Brown: Decline and Fall." *Boston Phoenix,* Aug. 30, 1977.

Norman, Philip. "Mister Messiah." *Sunday Times Magazine* (London), Mar. 7, 1971.

Palmer, Robert. "James Brown." *The Rolling Stone Illustrated History of Rock & Roll* (Random House).

Saal, Hubert. "Mr. Dynamite." *Newsweek,* July 1, 1968.

Waller, Don. "The Punk Meets the Godfather." *L.A. Weekly,* Apr. 13–19, 1984.

White, Cliff. "The Classic Soul of James Brown." *Let It Rock,* August 1985.

———. "James Brown on Disc: A Brief History/Critique and Serialized Session Discography," Parts 1 and 2. *Shout* nos. 109 and 110, July–November 1976.
———. Liner notes to *Roots of a Revolution.*
———. "The Man: After 21 Years, Still Refusing to Lose." *Black Music,* April 1977.
———. "Soul Brother Number One." *Orbis History of Rock,* no. 40.

JOE TEX

McEwen, Joe. "Joe Tex: The Soul of an Underdog." *Boston Phoenix,* May 31, 1977.
Paulsen, Don. "Joe Tex: The 45 Minutes That Changed His Life." *Hit Parader.*
White, Cliff. "On Tour with Joe Tex." *New Musical Express,* May 14, 1977.
———. "Roots of the Rapper." *Black Music,* October 1975.

WILSON PICKETT

Delehant, Jim. "The Humor of Wilson Pickett." *Hit Parader.*
———. "An Interview with Wilson Pickett." *Hit Parader.*
Emerson, Ken. "Wilson Pickett: Soul Man on Ice." *Rolling Stone,* Feb. 8, 1979.
Gersten, Russell. "Can I Get a Witness?" *Boston Phoenix,* June 21, 1972.
———. "The Last Soul Man." *The Real Paper,* Aug. 1, 1973.
Goldberg, Marv. "The Falcons." *"Whiskey, Women, and . . . ,"* June 1983.
Jacobson, Mark. "Still Wicked." *New York Daily News,* Jan. 4, 1981.
Lydon, Michael. "The Wicked Pickett's Beat Goes On." *New York Times,* Oct. 9, 1977.
Moore, Carman. "Pinball to Pickett." *The Village Voice,* Oct. 30, 1969.
Richardson, Clive. Interview with Wilson Pickett. *Black Echoes,* Nov. 17, 1979.

DON COVAY

Mr. C. and Freddy Blue. "Doin' the Dozens with Don Covay." *The Real Paper,* Mar. 20, 1974.

THE MANY (OTHER) SIDES OF MEMPHIS

Booth, Stanley. "Blues for the Red Man." *Rolling Stone,* May 10, 1973.
———. "A Hound Dog to the Manor Born." *Esquire,* February 1968.
———. "The Memphis Soul Sound." Unedited manuscript, 1968.
Dickinson, Mary Lindsay. "See the Shine in the Black Sheep Boy." Unpublished manuscript.
Less, David. "Interview with Sunbeam Mitchell." *Dixie Flyer,* Spring 1980.
———. "Mr. Crump Don't Like It: An Interview with Jim Dickinson." *Dixie Flyer,* October 1979 and January 1980.
"Memphis Revisited." *Billboard,* May 22, 1971.
Robinson, Lisa. "The Miami Sound." *Hit Parader.*
Williams, Bill. "The Memphis Sound." *Billboard,* Mar. 29, 1969.

AL GREEN

Christgau, Robert. "Sexy, Safe & Out of Sync." *The Real Paper,* Mar. 26, 1975.
Fong-Torres, Ben. " 'I've Got to Be Free, and Then I Can Sing.' " *Rolling Stone,* Mar. 15, 1973.
Gersten Russell. "Al Green: For the Roses or Free at Last." *The Real Paper,* July 10, 1974.
Goldman, Vivien. "Tired of Being Alone?" *Melody Maker,* Aug. 25, 1979.
Heilbut, Anthony. "Al Green's Sanctified Solipsism." *The Village Voice,* Sept. 27, 1983.
Himes, Geoffrey. "Al Green: Sanctity and Sexuality on a Higher Plane." *Musician.*
Hunter, James. " 'There Are Riders Approaching.' " *Record,* December 1983.

Less, David. Interview with Al Green, 1978. Unpublished.

McEwen, Joe. "Al Green Gets the Fever." *Boston Phoenix,* Nov. 1, 1977.

———. "Soul: That Old Green Magic." *The Real Paper,* Apr. 23, 1975.

Norment, Lynn. "How Tragedy Has Affected the Life of Al Green." *Ebony,* October 1976.

Palmer, Robert. "Memphis Magic: The Al Green Sound." *Rolling Stone,* Oct. 25, 1973.

Trombetta, Jim. "The Love Ranger." *Crawdaddy,* November 1975.

ARETHA FRANKLIN

"Aretha Franklin's Gospel Background." *Hit Parader.*

Gersten, Russell. "Aretha Arrives Again." *The Real Paper,* July 31, 1974.

———. "Aretha Beyond the Rainbow." *The Village Voice,* Nov. 11, 1980.

———. "Gladys Knight and Aretha Franklin: Poetry and Professionalism." *The Real Paper,* Jan. 15, 1975.

Hodenfield, Chris. "Baby, I Know: Reassessing Aretha." *Rolling Stone,* May 23, 1974.

Jones, Max. "The Gospel Truth from Aretha." *Melody Maker.*

"Lady Soul: Singing It Like It Is." *Time* cover story, June 28, 1968.

Lydon, Michael. "Soul Kaleidoscope: Aretha at the Fillmore." *Ramparts,* 1971.

Nathan, David. "An Appreciation of the Career of Aretha Franklin," Parts 1–4. *Blues & Soul* nos. 231–235, 1977.

Zimmerman, Paul. "Over the Rainbow." *Newsweek,* Aug. 21, 1967.

PERIODICAL APPENDIX

Bill Millar has compiled the following list of periodicals and fanzines, past and present, that focus on soul. The figure in parentheses following the title represents the number of issues published as of October 1985, and Bill has supplied a brief listing or description of the range of interests of each magazine that is still extant.

Blues & Rhythm: The Gospel Truth (14). Paul Vernon, ed. 18 Maxwellton Close, Mill Hill, London NW73NA. Primarily r&b but includes coverage of all black styles.

Blues & Soul (440). John Abbey, ed. Napfield Ltd, 153 Praed Street, London W2. Established in 1967, this glossy fortnightly magazine has always focused on current soul.

Blues Forum (18). Norbert Hess and Thomas Gutberlet, eds. Glogauer Strasse 22, D-1000 Berlin 36. Includes soul-blues styles. Glossy photography and much excellent research by Norbert Hess.

Collusion (5). Sue Steward, David Toop, and David Beresford, eds. 14 Peto Place, London NW1. Highly eclectic music magazine. Soul coverage has included black dance discs, rapping, Carol Kaye, sex in sixties soul, and Darlene Love.

Echoes (formerly *Black Echoes*). Black Echoes Ltd, Rococo House, 283 City Road, London EC1 1LA. Tabloid newspaper covering all aspects of contemporary black music.

Goldmine (137). Krause Pubs., 700 East State Street, Iola, Wisc. 54990. Record collector's marketplace, with voluminous auction lists, dating back to 1976. Has always touched on the most obscure musical matters as well as the commercial mainstream and continues to run some good features on soul.

Il Blues (9). Marino Grandi, ed. piazza Grandi, 12, I-20135 Milano, Italy. Mainly blues but has featured James Brown, Solomon Burke, Joe Tex, Al Green, and Wilson Pickett.

It Will Stand (30). Chris Beachley, ed. P.O. Box 507, Harrisburg, N.C. 28075. "Dedicated to the Preservation of Beach Music." The Tams, General Johnson, Stick McGhee, Mary Wells, and the Shaggers' Hall of Fame.

Jefferson (68). Tommy Lofgren, ed. Zetterlunds VAG90B, S-18600, Vallentuna, Sweden. Blues with some soul—Bobby Bland, Syl Johnson, Clyde McPhatter, Clovers, etc.

Juke Blues (1). John Broven, Cilla Huggins, and Bez Turner, eds. P.O. Box 148, London W9 1DY. Coverage is likely to include soul-blues styles.

Living Blues (65). Jim and Amy O'Neal, eds. Center for the Study of Southern Culture, University of Mississippi, University, Miss. 38677. The living blues tradition, occasionally including contemporary/historical aspects of soul.

New Blackbeat (19). Steve Guarnori, ed. 101 Sevenacres, Orton, Peterborough, Cambridgeshire PE2 0XJ, England. Ted Taylor, Darrell Banks, Fred Hughes, Mighty Sam, Bunny Sigler, Roy C., Jimmy Hughes, Clarence Carter, Joe Simon, et al.

Record Information Services. Paul Pelletier, compiler. P.O. Box 18F, Chessington, Surrey KT9 1UZ, England. U.K. label lists, including soul-oriented companies.

Shades of Soul (5). Derek Pearson, ed. 17 Crooke Lane, Wilsden, Bradford, West Yorkshire BD15 0LL, England. Falcons, Darrow Fletcher, J. J. Barnes, South Camp, Tommy Tate, Masqueraders, Eddie Parker. Specializes in deep-soul reviews.

Soul Bag (103). Jacques Perin, ed. 25, rue Trezel, 92300 Levallois-Perret, France (U.K. rep: Alan Balfour, 3 Dauncy House, Webber Row, London SE1 8QS). One of the finest soul magazines with many exceptional discographies by Kurt Mohr. Recent issues include Monk Higgins, Percy Sledge, Joe Tex, Etta James, Cash McCall, Syl Johnson, Malaco, etc.

Soul Scoot (4). Terry Smith, ed. Gabled House, Hermitage, Newbury, Berkshire RG16 9RG, England. Mod nostalgia—e.g., James Brown and Major Lance sandwiched in between articles on Lambrettas.

Soul Survivor (2). Richard Pack, ed. 421 Queen Street West, Toronto, Ontario M5V 2A5, Canada. James Brown, Linda Jones, Irma Thomas, Joe Tex, Showstoppers, Stax-Volt story, Soul Brothers Six. Promising newcomer to the scene, with in-depth interviews and rare photographs.

Souled Out (7). Steve Bryant, ed. 141 Pembroke Road, Seven Kings, Ilford, Essex IG3 8PS, England. John Richbourg, Walter Jackson, Ruby Andrews, Soul Children, Ann Sexton, Ella Washington, Fontella Bass, etc.

The Sound (5). Roy Simonds, ed. 21 The Drive, Edgeware, Middlesex HA8 8PS, England. Minutiae for King Curtis Fans.

Sweet Soul Music (2). John Stuart and Ray Kempton, eds. 3 Pioneer Road, Farindon, Oxon SN7 7BU, England. Otis Redding, Sam Cooke, Shirley Brown, Syl Johnson, Arthur Conley, Carla Thomas. The magazine grew out of the *Otis Redding Appreciation Society Newsletter*.

Voices from the Shadows (from 1986). Rod Dearlove, ed. P.O. Box 11, Hedon, Nr. Hull, HU12 9HN, England. The voice of Southern Soul. "Underground heroes. That's what *Voices from the Shadows* is all about."

Wavelength (60). Connie Atkinson, ed. P.O. Box 15667, New Orleans, La. 70175. Every aspect of the New Orleans tradition, including soul, with great archival features and interviews by Jeff Hannusch (Almost Slim).

"Whiskey, Women, and . . ." (14). Dan Kochakian, ed. P.O. Box 1245, Haverhill, Mass. 01830. Blues, r&b, with the occasional whiff of soul.

The following periodicals (almost exclusively British) are now defunct: They are listed here as a matter of interest.

Black Music (glossy monthly published by IPC: the more pertinent issues ran from 1974 to 1977)

Black Wax (6 issues, 1973)

Blackbeat (18 issues, 1979–82)

Coast to Coast Soul (6 issues, 1971)

Deeper and Deeper (8 issues, 1977–79)

The Drifter (4 issues, 1983–84)

Earshot (3 issues, 1969)

Fame-Goldwax Followers (4 issues, 1966, incorporating *Soul Survey*)

Home of the Blues (6 issues, 1966: forerunner of *Blues & Soul*)

Hot Buttered Soul (52 issues, 1972–77)

Midnight Express (6 issues, 1981–84)

Okeh Northern Soul (7 issues, 1981–82)

R&B Gazette (5 issues, 1963–64)

R&B Monthly (24 issues, 1964–66)

R&B Scene (7 issues, 1964–65)

Raunchy (6 issues, 1971–72)

Rhythm and Soul USA (4 issues, 1966)

Shout (112 issues, 1966–77: formerly *Soul Music Monthly*)

Solid and Raunchy (13 issues, 1972–74)

Soul (2 issues, 1965–66: English publication)

Soul (8+ issues, 1966–67: Canadian publication)

Soul (circa 1967–69: American biweekly)

Soul Beat (11 issues, 1964–67)

Soul Cargo (12 issues, 1977–79)

Soul Messenger (issued by the Atlantic Appreciation Society: 9 issues, 1967–68)

Soul Sounds (16 issues, 1974–75)

Soul Source (9 issues, 1978–79)

Soul Symbol (9 issues, 1979)

Soulside Rendezvous (4 issues, 1982)

Sound of Soul (5 issues, 1981–82)

A discography of this sort is always impossible. It can never be anything less than arbitrary, with idiosyncrasy to be taken as a virtue. In the case of a soul discography, the problem is further compounded by the obscurity of some of the greatest sides, the way in which albums go in and out of print, and the considerable discrepancy between American and worldwide reissues. With that in mind (and with the invaluable help of Frank Scott), I've tried wherever possible to convert the original vinyl discography to a CD format, but as you'll note, if there is not what I consider to be an appropriate CD collection, I've simply maintained the original LP listing with an asterisk to indicate its antediluvian status. My primary aim has been to present a good, representative selection of great music, with the understanding that it is a starting point, a very broad-based starting point, for each listener and reader.

Sometimes this has meant making up my own anthologies or offering a selection of favorite cuts for individual artists. In most instances, thanks to reissue programs spurred by the CD revolution and reissue labels like Rhino, there is far more available today than there was when this book first came out. What I have done is to follow pretty much the format of the book—in other words, to provide album collections and individual selections to accompany each artist or period under discussion—while at the same time acknowledging one of the key elements of soul: that it was first and foremost a singles business. The long section at the end, Lost Soul, was the idea, and to a large extent the creation, of my friend Joe McEwen and is an attempt to come to grips with one of the many intriguing aspects of the music: that some of the greatest soul records were one-shot successes whose creators might never again achieve such artistic heights or might simply disappear, never to be heard from again.

What we have tried to do is to point you toward great music, wherever you may have to go to find it. For many of the widely available reissue collections, you have only to locate a good contemporary record store with a broad selection of material. In some cases you may want to comb through oldies stores and auction lists. The best source that I know of for singles is Val Shively's R&B, P.O. Box B, Havertown, Pennsylvania 19083. The best sources for roots music of all kinds are Red Lick Records, P.O. Box 3, Porthmadog, Gwynedd, Wales, UK LL48 6AQ and Roots & Rhythm, P.O. Box 837, El Cerrito, California 94530. But the best gauge of the music remains your own ears and taste. If this book impels you to listen, then it will have served one of its main purposes. If it causes you to expand your own tastes and preconceptions, so much the better, but remember: music is neither to be categorized nor limited; like all art it is to be taken where you find it, and the search is half the fun.

R&B: The Transition Years

"Gee, Baby, Ain't I Good to You?" (Nat King Cole), "Drifting Blues" (Charles Brown), "The Things That I Used to Do" (Guitar Slim), "Crying in the Chapel" (Sonny Til and the Orioles), "Just Walkin' in the Rain" (Prisonaires), "You Can Have Her" and "You'll Never Walk Alone" (Roy Hamilton), "Shake a Hand" (Faye Adams), "Please Send Me Someone to Love" (Percy Mayfield), "Don't Deceive Me" (Chuck Willis), "Good Rockin' Tonight" (Roy Brown), "Let the Good Times Roll" (Louis Jordan), "I Wonder" (Cecil Gant), "A Cottage for Sale" (Billy Eckstine), "I'll Get Along Somehow" (Larry Darnell), "I Almost Lost My Mind" (Ivory Joe Hunter), "Night Time Is the Right Time" (Nappy Brown).

Atlantic Rhythm and Blues: 1947–1974 (Atlantic 82305). An 8-CD set from one of the most influential purveyors of the r&b sound, and the label that virtually invented soul as a separate category. Chock full of historic treasures, from the Ravens' version of "Ol' Man River" to Ray Charles, Big Joe Turner, Clyde McPhatter, LaVern Baker, and the Clovers, through classic soul, classic Stax, and beyond. Indispensable as an introduction to a large sector of African-American music over a period of more than twenty-five years.

The King R&B Box Set (King 7002). A 4-CD set culled from the catalogue of a label only slightly less influential than Atlantic in the r&b field. Everyone from Wynonie Harris and Roy Brown to Bullmoose Jackson, Ivory Joe Hunter, Billy Ward and His Dominoes (featuring, successively, Clyde McPhatter and Jackie Wilson as lead singer), the Midnighters, Little Willie John, and James Brown. The final CD even includes the incomparable Syd Nathan

(King's crudely flamboyant label owner) addressing the King sales and a&r troops on various occasions. The same recommendation as for the Atlantic anthology above.

The Specialty Story (Specialty 4412). Ditto to the above two, with more of an emphasis on gospel (Sam Cooke and the Soul Stirrers), New Orleans classics (Lloyd Price's "Lawdy Miss Clawdy"), proto-soul blues (Guitar Slim's "The Things That I Used to Do"), and rock 'n' roll (Little Richard *partout*). Maybe my favorite as a pure listening experience.

The R&B Box (Rhino 71806). More comprehensive than either individual label anthology, but as a result somewhat more diluted.

Hank Ballard and the Midnighters

Sexy Ways: The Best of Hank Ballard and the Midnighters (Rhino 71512). Good-time music with a dollop of soul. Perfect for a party, which is where it came from in the first place.

Bobby "Blue" Bland

I Pity the Fool and *Turn On Your Love Light: The Duke Recordings,* Vols. 1 and 2 (MCA 10665, 10957). Volume I offers Bobby at his rawest, Volume II at his creamiest, most soulful, and riveting best. A lesson in sophistication worth picking up in any form.

The Dominoes

Sixty Minute Men: The Best of Billy Ward and His Dominoes (Rhino 71509). I got this CD originally out of a sense of historical obligation but find myself coming back to it again and again for its feeling, variety, and visceral excitement. To fully appreciate the Dominoes' softer sounds, however, you've got to leave irony at the door.

The "5" Royales

Monkey Hips and Rice: The "5" Royales Anthology (Rhino 71546). A stone classic. Heartfelt singing, great songwriting from group leader Lowman Pauling ("Think," "Tell the Truth," and "Dedicated to the One I Love"), who also contributes the tough guitar that served as Steve Cropper's chief inspiration.

Little Willie John
Fever: The Best of Little Willie John (Rhino 71511). One of the most affecting voices of his or any other generation. It's hard to explain his appeal, but it comes across on fast songs ("All Around the World"), slow songs ("Let Them Talk"), soupy songs ("Talk to Me"), blues (the ineffable "Need Your Love So Bad"), and sophisticated numbers ("Fever"). Check it out.

Clyde McPhatter and the Drifters
Rockin' and Driftin': The Drifters Box (Rhino 72417). Listen to the early sides in particular, when Clyde McPhatter was one of the most influential voices in evolving soul.

Ike and Tina Turner
*Tough Enough (English EMI EG26 0251 1). The hardest-working woman in show business backed by her husband's Kings of Rhythm, 1961–1969. James Brown meets Ray Charles meets Mavis Staples. Nice and *rough*. (*Golden Classics* on the Collectables label [5107] is a not-quite-equivalent CD collection of their Minit material.)

Dinah Washington
A Slick Chick (on the Mellow Side) (Indigo 2073); **A Slick Chick (on the Mellow Side)* (Emarcy 814 1841). Aretha's chief secular influence (though she, too, started out in church). Two different selections with little overlap and the same title (the second is available only on vinyl), these are her r&b hits, blues with a whiff of jazz. I like even better, though, some of the later material on which she can stretch out more, like **After Hours with Miss "D"* (Mercury 36028), where she jams with all-star horn and rhythm sections.

Jackie Wilson
Mr. Excitement (Rhino 70775). Probably somewhat more than you would ever want, a 3-CD anthology that stretches from 1956 (with Billy Ward and His Dominoes) to 1975, fully exposing the production flaws that marred so many of Wilson's greatest records. But, oh, that voice . . .

SAM COOKE

Sam Cooke and the Soul Stirrers, The Last Mile of the Way, The Great 1955 Shrine Concert (Specialty 7009, 7052, 7045). My favorite Sam Cooke. The first two feature Sam's beautiful gospel leads almost exclusively. The 1955 Shrine concert, including seven of Specialty's gospel stars in concert, is a masterpiece in its entirety, with "Nearer to Thee," an unforgettable ten-minute live version of one of Sam's greatest compositions, offering a rare glimpse of the ecstatic gospel singer in action. *Shine on Me: The Soul Stirrers Featuring R. H. Harris* (Specialty 7013) and *Heaven Is My Home* (Specialty 7031) showcase Rebert Harris, Sam's primary vocal inspiration, and Paul Foster and Johnnie Taylor, his successors as lead singer in the group, respectively.
The Best of the Pilgrim Travelers, Walking Rhythm, Better Than That (Specialty 7204, 7030, 7053). The best of the Travelers, a group contemporaneous with and comparable to the Stirrers. This was the group that J. W. Alexander, Cooke's partner and mentor, directed and managed. Listen to the leads of Kylo Turner (one of Ray Charles's gospel inspirations), Lou Rawls (Alexander's latter-day version of Sam), and Alexander himself for purposes of comparison and edification. This is beautiful music.
Nightbeat (ABKCO 1124). Sam's one incontrovertibly great *album*. A late-hours, bluesy mood piece orchestrated by Sam's longtime arranger René Hall,

this gives strong indications of where Sam might have gone.

Sam Cooke Live at the Harlem Square Club (RCA 5181). Clear evidence that the Sam Cooke of the gospel years never really went away. For purposes of comparison listen to *Live at the Copa* (ABKCO 2970), which is pretty much what you might expect, but it is at the Harlem Square Club we get grits and soul, sweat and passion, such as never appeared in studio recordings after the Specialty years.

Sam Cooke: The Man and His Music (RCA 7127). Cooke by Cooke, nothing but the songs he wrote, from beginning (Specialty gospel) to end ("A Change Is Gonna Come"). Although it is now out of print, it needs to be sought out.

Sam Cooke's SAR Records (ABKCO 2231). Maybe the ultimate Sam Cooke album that Sam didn't make. This is wonderful music *produced* by Sam for his own label by the Soul Stirrers, R. H. Harris, the Womack Brothers in gospel and secular (the Valentinos) configurations, the Simms Twins, Johnnie Morisette, et al. Sam's approach to song interpretation, his patient methods of instruction, are tantalizingly laid out, and there are several tracks by Sam himself, including his original demo version of "You Send Me." SAR was Sam and J. W. Alexander's dream, but the music speaks for itself.

RAY CHARLES

Ray Charles: The Birth of Soul (Atlantic 82310). The title and sub-subtitle, *The Complete Atlantic Rhythm and Blues Recordings, 1952–1959*, say it all. You can't get much more seminal than this.

Ray Charles: Live (Atlantic 81732). Live at Newport, 1958, and Atlanta, 1959. The latter includes an extended version of "Drown in My Own Tears" so profound it might be the one Ray Charles cut impossible to live without.

The Genius of Ray Charles (Atlantic 01312). Ray Charles in transition. Big-band jazz, keening voices, strings, and lots of feeling. From 1959, when Ray was the biggest r&b star in the country and looked as if he would stay that way for years to come. Although this is still on the Atlantic label, it pointed the way to the future.

Ray Charles: Greatest Hits, Vols. 1 and 2 (Rhino 70097, 70098). A very good anthology from the ABC years. At times rivals the Atlantic material for depth of feeling and, with a good representation of classic ballads ("Georgia On My Mind"), country and western ("Born to Lose"), and Beatles interpretations ("Eleanor Rigby"), definitely continues to expand the territory.

Genius and Soul (Rhino 72859). A little bit of a redundancy if you have some/most of the above. Three early Swing Time cuts add to the mix, and the final CD (out of five) takes us almost up to the present, but I'm not sure that this is altogether necessary, except—well, it *is* Ray Charles.

SOLOMON BURKE

You Can Run But You Can't Hide (Mr. R&B 108). The Apollo sides, 1955–1959. A historic treat, inconsistent but memorable.

Home in Your Heart: The Best of Solomon Burke (Rhino 70284). For the most part, it is. Solomon's greatest hits, and some of his greatest moments, on Atlantic.

Soul Alive! (Rounder 11521). The Solomon Burke live show, ca. 1981. Magical.

A Change Is Gonna Come (Rounder 2053). Probably the best studio album Solomon ever made. Don't miss the title cut, which takes on a whole new (or modified) meaning with Solomon's preaching. While you're at it, check out "Letter from My Darling" on *Soul of the Blues* (Black Top 1095) and "Silent

Night," an old 33⅓ rpm "Big Single" (Savoy SCS-0002), cut live in Macon, Georgia, in 1982, that represents one of Solomon's all-time greatest vocal efforts. Which is really saying something.

STAX: THE EARLY DAYS

The Complete Stax Singles 1959–1968
This is the history of Stax writ large. A 9-CD set with all of the drawbacks that come with completism but with more great music than you could ever imagine. If I knew of a good Stax primer, I would suggest one, but in its absence, think of this as nine separate listening experiences that for the most part are terrific.

Rufus and Carla Thomas: Gee Whiz
"Cause I Love You," "Night Time Is the Right Time" (duets); "The Dog," "Walking the Dog," "Boom Boom," "Fine and Mellow," "Did You Ever Love a Woman" (all Rufus); "Gee Whiz," "Comfort Me," "No Time to Lose," "Looking Back," "B-A-B-Y," "Tramp" (duet with Otis Redding), "Another Night Without My Man," "A Woman's Love," "I'll Bring It On Home to You" (all Carla). If you want to be practical about it, Rufus and Carla's *Best of* anthologies on Rhino (72410 and 71633, respectively) are definitely the way to go, but look out for some of the tracks listed here that are *not* on those albums.

William Bell: The Soul of a Bell
"You Don't Miss Your Water," "I'll Show You," "Share What You Got," "Born Under a Bad Sign," "A Soldier's Goodbye," "Marching Off to War," "Every Day Will Be a Holiday," "Everybody Loves a Winner," "I've Got to Go On," "Crying All by Myself," "A Tribute to a King." Perhaps the most underrated of all the major soul singers. Every song here is a classic. *The Soul of a Bell* (Atlantic 82252), a reissue of the 1967 album, has its moments, as does *A Little Something Extra* (Stax 8566), a collection of unknown, unissued, primarily demo material from 1961 to 1967, but the definitive William Bell album has yet to arrive.

Sam and Dave: The Dynamic Duo
Sweat 'N' Soul (Rhino 71253). All of the hits, from "Hold On!" to "Soul Man" to "When Something Is Wrong with My Baby" to "You Got Me Hummin'." A Hayes-Porter production par excellence, and a useful primer in the development of a sound. But while you're at it, don't neglect the more obscure classics in this collection like "I've Seen What Loneliness Can Do" and "I Can't Stand Up for Falling Down," which for sheer soulfulness bear comparison with any of the chart-toppers.

Eddie Floyd
"Got to Make a Comeback," "Raise Your Hand," "Blood Is Thicker than Water," "Knock on Wood," "Bring It On Home to Me." Like William Bell, a seriously underrated writer-performer in the Sam Cooke mold. Either *Chronicle: Greatest Hits* (Stax 4122) or *Rare Stamps* (Stax 88013) provides a listenable introduction to a fine writer and significant artist.

The Grand Tour
The Stax/Volt Revue, Vols. 1 and 2 (Atlantic 82341, 82342). Live from the March 1967 European tour, with fine performances by all of the above-named artists *and* Otis Redding, and backing by the Memphis Horns and Booker T. and the MG's. An invaluable document, though not so valuable to my ears as some of the more idiomatic performances in the studio. If this whets your appetite, try *Hit the Road Stax: Live in Europe,* Vol. 3 (Stax 88009), with more Otis Redding, more instrumentals, but no Sam and Dave. Listener's choice. And if you're looking for one more

taste of live Stax, *Funky Broadway: Stax Revue Live at the 5/4 Ballroom* (Stax 8567) offers a varied assortment of cuts from Booker T. and the MG's, the Mar-Keys, William Bell, and Rufus and Carla Thomas, among others.

OTIS REDDING

Otis! The Definitive Otis Redding (Rhino 71439). Four CDs, three pre-Stax cuts, all the hits, demos, a Coke commercial, a complete CD of live tracks, and Otis's Stay in School message. Unbeatable.

The Great Otis Redding Sings Soul Ballads and *Otis Blue* (Atco 91706, 80318). My first Otis Redding albums and still my favorites. Both have that heartbreaking quality that Zelma described as "begging." Both include originals and covers—most notably of Sam Cooke—and both are exquisitely eloquent in the laconic manner of the early Stax sessions.

Good to Me: Recorded Live at the Whisky A Go Go, Vol. 2 (Stax 8579). A 1992 revamping of a 1982 album of previously unreleased material from the Whisky A Go Go, April 1966, a year before Europe and Monterey. A great working Otis Redding band, as out of tune as they might be but cheerfully unselfconscious about it and swinging in a way that the previously issued set of somewhat stilted performances from this same date, *At the Whiskey A Go Go* (Rhino 70380), barely hinted at.

THE MUSCLE SHOALS SOUND

The Muscle Shoals Sound (Rhino 71517). An invaluable compilation of everything from the first soul song to be recorded in Muscle Shoals (Arthur Alexander's "You Better Move On") to Clarence Carter's "Making Love (At the Dark End of the Street)." It would have been nice to have had some more obscure items in place of Stax and Atlantic hits

that happened to be recorded at Muscle Shoals, but this is a great start.

Arthur Alexander

The Ultimate Arthur Alexander (Razor & Tie 2014); *Arthur Alexander* (Warner Brothers 45581); *Lonely Just Like Me* (Elektra Nonesuch 961475). Early and late, not much to choose between—though, surprisingly, I think I prefer the late. The first collection has all the historic hits ("You Better Move On," "Anna," etc.) but is marred by Alexander's lack of vocal assurance and his somewhat halfhearted pursuit of fashion. The Warner Brothers album, produced in Memphis by Tommy Cogbill, not only showcases some of his best original material but includes "Rainbow Road," the song written by Dan Penn and Donnie Fritts that was inspired by Alexander's own trials and tribulations. I think *Lonely Just Like Me* is my favorite, though, an intensely moving summation of a career, recorded in Nashville shortly after his rediscovery and not long before his death.

Jimmy Hughes

*Why Not Tonight? (Atco 33-209). Look for it in the used-record bins. A great collection of Fame material, both Hughes's own and songs that were the common property (and common hope) of all of Rick Hall's artists. If it only had "Steal Away" on it, it would give a complete picture. There is a CD, shared with Joe Hicks, of somewhat later Stax material, *Something Special* (Stax 88011), but nothing that I am aware of has yet come along to replace the original vinyl.

Percy Sledge

It Tears Me Up (Rhino 70285). Solid gold. All the hits, a good many of Percy's wonderful oddities, including "True Love Travels on a Gravel Road," "Sudden Stop," and "Rainbow Road." But the highlight is the Dan

Penn/Spooner Oldham–authored title track; it really will tear you up.

Clarence Carter

Snatching It Back (Rhino 70286). Rick Hall's single most consistent hit-maker and a typical Muscle Shoals oddity, whose bluesy lead guitar and relatively unmodulated vocals gave his records a flavor all their own.

Etta James

Tell Mama (Chess 9269). *Classic* Muscle Shoals material, cut just after Rick Hall's break with Jerry Wexler. Biting performances with an explosive edge, but if you prefer the seductive side of soul, check out Laura Lee's contemporaneous Muscle Shoals sessions (mostly available on *That's How It Is,* Chess 93005). Both show Rick Hall and the Fame musicians at their best.

White Boys Singing the (Rhythm and) Blues

*Prone to Lean (Donnie Fritts, Atlantic 18117); *Very Extremely Dangerous* (Eddie Hinton, Capricorn 536 111); (Snap Your Fingers and) Take Your Pick of Great Unreleased Demos (Dan Penn). All-star Muscle Shoals sessions, showing the songwriters in a sometimes self-conscious light. There's a lot of Otis Redding, a little bit of country, and a whole lot of soul here, but no great records, unfortunately—not yet anyway. *However,* in the absence of the last-named Dan Penn fantasy selection, there are two fine Dan Penn albums, *Nobody's Fool,* recorded at American in Memphis in 1973 (and reissued in Germany on Repertoire 4622 in 1996), and *Do Right Man* (Sire 45519). The first is Dan at his maverick best ("Lodi," "Nobody's Fool") and worst. The second is a moving return to Muscle Shoals in 1994, beautifully articulated and produced, with some of Dan's best contemporary compositions as well as a number of his greatest classics. You definitely need this album—but don't give up on the demos.

JAMES BROWN

With James Brown there are so many different records, and so many different stages of his evolution, that at least two dozen separate albums could be listed as essential, along with any number of seminal singles. Over the last few years there has been a remarkable effort, spearheaded by Harry Weinger at Polygram (taking off from Cliff White's original groundbreaking work), to illustrate systematically the development of Brown's style, and I would take these compilations, along with the classic Apollo live albums, as the basis for any James Brown collection.

Star Time (Polydor 849 108). The ultimate James Brown collection. Four CDs, from roots (almost) to rap. This is the place to start. (For a stripped-down version you could try *JB 40: James Brown's 40th Anniversary Collection* [Polydor 31453 3409], a 2-CD set—but you really *need Star Time*.)

Roots of a Revolution (Polydor 42281 7304). A chronicle of the development of the early style, right up to (but not including) "Out of Sight" and "Papa's Got a Brand New Bag." A revolution for those familiar only with James's funk.

Foundations of Funk (Polydor 31453 1165). As I was saying . . . 1964–1969, up to and including a live version of "Mother Popcorn." Listen to the alternate take of "Cold Sweat."

Messing with the Blues (Polydor 847 258). Really cool collection of James's stylized approach to the blues, 1957–1985. Not to everyone's taste, no doubt—but it really appeals to me.

Live at the Apollo, 1962 (Polydor 843 479). Perhaps the pinnacle of soul. What more can be said? One of the greatest live albums of all time by one of the greatest live performers. Indispensable.

Live at the Apollo, Vol. 2 (Polydor 823 001). A 1968 return to the scene of his former triumph, this 70-plus-minute set is scarcely less successful than the first, though indubitably different. A little hoarser, a lot more frenetic, James is still at the height of his powers, manipulating his appreciative audience with masterful ease. Who could ask for anything more? Well, on second thought, you should *definitely* not overlook *Say It Live and Loud* (Polydor 31455 7668), cut live in Dallas in the summer of 1968, in the immediate aftermath of Dr. King's assassination. This thirty-years-delayed 1998 release unmistakably highlights the increasing articulation of black pride in James's work, culminating in his recording of "Say It Loud—I'm Black and I'm Proud" just three weeks prior to this funk-laden Dallas show (where he sings the song early in the program, then reprises it at the end). Nothing less than classic *and* historic.

The T.A.M.I. Show (variously retitled for video rental). Find this in whatever form you can (it has been combined with *The T.N.T Show* in one video package called *That Was Rock*). James's 1965 entry into the pop world. An astounding document—words fail me. Watch it. Watch James!

ARETHA FRANKLIN

Aretha Gospel (Chess 91521). Aretha at fourteen, in church and in possession of close to her full powers.

Amazing Grace (Atlantic 00906). Aretha's return to the church in 1972. Though the style is more assured, and the Reverend James Cleveland lends a stately touch, this is a bit too mannered for me, a little bit too thought out—but with moments of the most surpassing beauty.

The First 12 Sides (Columbia 31953) and *Aretha Sings the Blues* (Columbia 40105). Aretha at eighteen, nineteen, and twenty. The first and best of Aretha's Columbia output and a clear indication of what John Hammond, Jerry Wexler, and Dan Penn each independently saw in her.

Unforgettable (Columbia/Legacy 66201). Her tribute to Dinah Washington. Has some nice moments and shows the stylistic debt she owes to the undeniable "Queen of the Blues."

Aretha Franklin: Queen of Soul (Rhino 71063). An eye-opening 4-CD set of the Atlantic sides, amply illustrating the breadth and depth of her style. Essential—but see below for the best of her individual Atlantic albums, most (but not all) of whose most exciting sides are on this anthology.

I Never Loved a Man the Way I Love You. (Rhino 71934). Her first (and it's still thrilling).

Aretha Arrives, Lady Soul, Aretha Now, Soul '69, This Girl's in Love with You (Rhino 71724, 71933, 71273, 71523, 71524). Aretha 1967–1970, with scarcely a false move. Each is invaluable in its own way.

Spirit in the Dark; Young, Gifted and Black (Rhino 71525, 71527). Two "concept" albums—this was Aretha at the crossroads. As direct and personal as any soul records have ever been—and that's saying a lot!

THE SOUL CLAN

*"Soul Meeting" (Atlantic 45-2530). Together for the First (and Only) Time! Solomon Burke, Arthur Conley, Don Covay, Ben E. King, Joe Tex. Need I say more? NB: The B-side, "That's How It Feels," is available on Rhino's wonderful 6-CD set, *Beg, Scream & Shout: The Big Ol' Box of '60s Soul* (Rhino 78215).

Arthur Conley

Sweet Soul Music (Ichiban Soul Classics 2105). A fine collection of most of Conley's best, though it wouldn't hurt to check out his two Atco LPs, *Sweet

Soul Music (Atco 33-215) and *Soul Directions (Atco 33-243), which comes complete with an eerie tribute to Otis Redding ("Otis, Sleep On").

Don Covay

Mercy Mercy: The Definitive Don Covay Collection (Razor & Tie 2063). Just like the title says, spanning the years 1957 to 1975 and including everything from the raucous "Bip Bop Bip" to "I Was Checkin' Out While She Was Checkin' In." If you want to trace the roots of Mick Jagger (not to mention Peter Wolf), try this one out. It might also be worth checking out the long-out-of-print *Super Dude I (Mercury SRM 1-653), Covay's one successful concept album (from 1973).

Wilson Pickett

A Man and a Half (Rhino 70287). A thoughtful, across-the-board 2-CD collection, from "I Found a Love" (by the Falcons) in 1961 to a live version of "Funky Broadway," recorded in Ghana ten years later. Maybe a little overly weighted toward the later Atlantic years for my taste—but if you want to focus on 1965–68 primarily, try individual albums like In the Midnight Hour (Rhino 71275), The Exciting Wilson Pickett (Rhino 71276), and I'm in Love (Rhino 72218).

The Falcons' Story, Parts 1 and 2 (Relic 7003, 7012). This is where Wilson Pickett came from, and it is classic r&b to boot. The first, You're So Fine, features the group before Pickett joined in the summer of 1960, with Eddie Floyd, Mack Rice, and Levi Stubbs's brother, Joe, singing lead. The second, I Found a Love, features Pickett in Stubbs's place, with sometimes spine-chilling gospel effects. For an added bonus, and a real treat, try Hot Stuff by Robert Ward (Relic 7094). Ward was the guitarist who played on much of the Falcons' material, and his deep,

echoing tremolo sound set the stage for Lonnie Mack. A very affecting vocalist, too. His later work on Black Top (particularly 1991's Fear No Evil, Black Top 1063, his first recording in more than twenty years) is also well worth seeking out.

Joe Tex

The Very Best of Joe Tex (Rhino 72565). This is definitely the one to get, including everything from his first Atlantic hits to 1977's "I Ain't Gonna Bump No More (With No Big Fat Woman)." However, I wouldn't be without Skinny Legs and All (English Kent 114), which is billed appropriately as "the Classic Early Dial Sides."

*Buying a Book (Atlantic 8231). My favorite Joe Tex album, one of the most brilliant and personal collections of songs in the entire oeuvre of soul. Would be comparable to Aretha's Young, Gifted and Black if it were not for the sly element of humor and preciseness of observation. Listen to "Grandma Mary" and "Anything You Wanna Know" for sharp-edged portraits of the grandmother who raised him and the town in which he grew up.

The Dapper Rapper: Uncollected Gems Pre- and Post-Stardom
"All I Could Do Was Cry," "Ain't I a Mess," "Baby You're Right," "I Had a Good Home (But I Left)," "You Keep Her," "Meet Me in Church," "The Only Girl I've Ever Loved," "Sit Yourself Down," "Don't Play," "Don't Make Your Children Pay (For Your Mistakes)," "One Monkey Don't Stop No Show," "Mama Red," "I'll Make Every Day Christmas," "Hold What You've Got" (Live from the Brooklyn Fox), "Papa's Dream." Just some of Joe's best before he hit (on Checker and Anna), after he hit (more Atlantic sides), and then on Mercury. Stirring (and funny) homiletics for our time.

The Goldwax Story

Waxing Strong: Hits and Misses

"That's How Strong My Love Is" (O. V. Wright), "Darlin'" (the Lyrics), "It's Wonderful to Be in Love," "I'm Living Good," "I Need a Lot of Loving," "Me and My Imagination" (the Ovations), "The Power of a Woman," "Uptight Good Woman," "Anything You Do Is All Right" (Spencer Wiggins), "Crying Baby Baby Baby," "I Don't Know What You've Got (But It's Got Me)" (Percy Milem). PLUS SPECIAL BONUS SELECTION!! Two songs by George Jackson, one of Goldwax's (and Fame's and Malaco's) favorite writers: "Sam, We'll Never Forget You" (lead by Louis Williams, on George's own Happy Hooker label) and "Aretha, Sing One for Me" (Hi).

O. V. Wright

The Soul of O. V. Wright (MCA 10670). Though no longer a Memphis-signed artist after his first secular single on Goldwax (Wright ended up on Backbeat, a Duke subsidiary), O.V. continued to record in Memphis, mostly under the direction of Willie Mitchell. This is the best single record of his achievement, from 1965 to 1973, eighteen songs without a weak link, sung in Wright's intense, whippet-thin, emotionally wracked voice. The fact that only seven of the tracks duplicate *Gone for Good* (Charly 1050), an equally strong vinyl selection, indicates just how much the world needs an O. V. Wright boxed set, but I guess this will have to do for now. *Memphis Unlimited* (Backbeat 72) is a wonderful 1973 document of sin and salvation that should also be assiduously pursued.

James Carr

The Essential James Carr (Razor & Tie 2060). Classic soul, presented with sensitivity and authority by a man with a magnificent voice. As a singer, James Carr is somewhere between Percy Sledge and Otis Redding, and as powerfully affecting as either one.

Ann Peebles

I Can't Stand the Rain (The Right Stuff/Hi 66712). A cult hit of the '70s, the title song stands for the best of Ann Peebles and the best of Hi, Al Green aside. Beautifully crafted and engineered, each song is like a miniature masterpiece. Together with *Straight from the Heart* (The Right Stuff/Hi 66711), this represents some of the best (though not the most adventurous) of Memphis soul. For a fine selection from these two, and then some, try *Ann Peebles: The Hi Records Years* (The Right Stuff/Hi 52659), a 21-cut anthology.

Otis Clay and Syl Johnson

Otis Clay: The Hi Records Years (The Right Stuff/Hi 36027); *Syl Johnson: The Hi Records Years* (The Right Stuff/Hi 35736). Much the same might be said about these two well-chosen anthologies of Willie Mitchell–produced material. They are as representative of Mitchell's method, and the dry brilliance of the Hi rhythm section, as they are of each of these highly capable artists. Who is the *auteur*?

Al Green

Al Green Anthology (The Right Stuff/Hi 53033). A sumptuous and idiosyncratic 4-CD set from 1967's "Back Up Train" right up to the beginning of Green's religious reawakening. More than almost any other anthology that I can think of, it tries to present a portrait of the artist, utilizing interview segments and live recordings to flesh out the picture—but sometimes you miss the more familiar linear approach. Together with Robert Mugge's penetrating film documentary, *The Gospel According to Al Green,* this is essential, but you might want to try some of the classic albums first. *Let's Stay Together* (The Right Stuff/Hi 27121), *I'm Still in Love with You* (The Right Stuff/Hi 27627), and *Call Me* (The Right Stuff/Hi 28538) are the pinnacle of soul refinement. About as produced as the music can get without losing something integral in the process, these records stand as masterpieces of craftsmanship and control and yet retain the visceral power of Green's idols—Claude Jeter and Sam Cooke. Screwy, fluky, unpredictable, sometimes indecipherable, but astonishingly fresh, inventive, and full of eccentric charm. *The Belle Album* (Hi 6004) and *Truth 'N' Time* (Hi 6009) convey some of the drama of Green's spiritual crisis (and perhaps musical apotheosis), when he broke away from Willie Mitchell, cut "To Sir with Love" as a kind of sexually ambiguous secular hymn, and achieved either a higher plane of spirituality or a total confusion (and catharsis) of the soul, which for me is absent in the explicitly spiritual albums that followed. Note that *The Belle Album* is available as half of a British CD twofer, but unfortunately it is paired with the less exalted *Have a Good Time* (UK Hi 111).

American Made (Some Soulful Hits and Great Music from the American Studio) "Memphis Soul Stew" (King Curtis); "Nine Pound Steel" and "You Keep Me Hangin' On" (Joe Simon); *From Elvis in Memphis* (Elvis Presley); "Fly Me to the Moon" (Bobby Womack); "Your Precious Love," "Turn On Your Lovelight," "Down in Texas," "The Dark End of the Street" (Oscar Toney Jr.); "Shake a Tail Feather" (James and Bobby Purify); *Dusty in Memphis* (Dusty Springfield); "Bad Mouthin'" (Mighty Sam); "I'm Just an Average Guy" (the Masqueraders); "The Dark End of the Street" and "Angelica" (Roy Hamilton); "The

Letter" (the Box Tops); "Sweet Inspiration" (the Sweet Inspirations).

STAX RECIDIVUS

I have distinguished here between the Stax that existed prior to the break with Atlantic and the independent Stax that existed afterward not because of any alteration in the quality of the music but because these were two different eras and because the music appears on two different labels (Atlantic, of course, owns the Stax catalogue up until 1968; Fantasy controls all pre-1968 unissued material as well as everything thereafter and has made the great majority of the Stax catalogue readily available). With that in mind, it is worth citing two albums of hit compilations that have come out on Fantasy (including a good number of pre-'68 classics) as well as the various latter-day *Chronicles* and the edited Wattstax anthology that follows.

Top of the Stax, Vols. 1 and 2 (Stax 88008, 88009). Everything from "Hold On, I'm Comin'" by Sam to Dave to "Soul Finger" by the Bar-Kays and Isaac Hayes's "Theme from *Shaft.*" A good mainstream choice. But if you really want to get into it on a no-holds-barred basis, be aware of *Stax Soul Singles,* Vols. 2 and 3 (Stax 4411 and 4415), 9- and 10-CD sets that chronicle the whole story from 1968 to 1975. Not for the casual listener—and yet . . .

Wattstax/The Living Word, Vol. 1 (Stax 88007); *Vol. 2 (Stax 3018). The original twin 2-record sets, with the first volume restored digitally to print and the second promised. The grandiose scale of the concerts is not matched by the scope of the music, but how can you beat Isaac Hayes, the Staple Singers, Carla Thomas, Richard Pryor, Johnnie Taylor, and the Reverend Jesse Jackson all in the same package? There was for a while a *Best of Wattstax,* but it's worth checking out the complete set, along with the film, if you want to get the full impact of something that can only be described as a cultural event.

Johnnie Taylor
Chronicle: The 20 Greatest Hits (Stax 60-006); *Who's Making Love* (Stax 4115); *Raw Blues* (Stax 8508); *Little Bluebird* (Stax 8558). Johnnie Taylor was the salvation of the new independent Stax. The first album has the hits; the second is a reissue of the album that came off his blockbuster single; the last two are my favorites (and two of my favorite Stax albums), pure Sam Cooke crossed with a Memphis version of Bobby "Blue" Bland's Duke sound. The effect is both smooth and viscerally exciting, with a straight-ahead emotional impact that little else at Stax achieved apart from the work of Otis Redding and William Bell.

Isaac Hayes
Presenting Isaac Hayes (Stax 8596), *Hot Buttered Soul* (Stax 4114). Interesting. The first is the odd album with jazzy aspirations that came out of an after-hours jam; the second includes the nearly nineteen-minute elaboration on "By the Time I Get to Phoenix" that made Hayes an instant superstar.

Luther Ingram
*(If Loving You Is Wrong) I Don't Want to Be Right (Koko 2202). A beautiful album by Johnny Baylor's protégé, with all production credits to Baylor. The title cut set a new trend in soulful tales of infidelity, and "I'll Be Your Shelter (In Time of Storm)" is equally good. Check out "You Can Depend on Me" as well, and you'll find a very soulful singer in the grand manner.

The Soul Children
Chronicle (Stax 4120), *Best of Two Worlds* (Stax 88024). The male-female Sam and Dave (after it was discovered that Sam and Dave no longer resided at Stax), produced initially by Isaac Hayes and David Porter. Sweet harmonies and church-wrecking emotion. The first album features all their best-known songs, but the second, a combination of two unconnected albums, includes their stirring debut on the label.

The Staple Singers
The Best of the Staple Singers (Stax 60-007); *Bealtitude: Respect Yourself* (Stax 4116). Stax's 1970s hit-makers, though a more unlikely source would be difficult to find. All their songs had an explicitly spiritual flavor; many had an implicitly sexual one as well, mainly via Mavis Staples's thrillingly purring contralto voice. These are two fine collections, but if you really want to get the flavor of the Staples, try their Vee Jay gospel sides, where Mavis sings with all the power and all the romantic confusion of an unregenerate teenager and stakes her claim to the gospel throne. Or look for *The Staple Swingers* (Stax 8573), with Mavis's heartbreaking version of O. V. Wright's "You're Gonna Make Me Cry" or a two-pack of her intermittently successful solo efforts, *Only for the Lonely* (Stax 88012).

And lastly, before I get to Joe McEwen's and my fantasy selections, let me recommend a few general anthologies. *Beg, Scream & Shout: The Big Ol' Box of '60s Soul* (Rhino 78215) can't be beat. A 6-CD anthology packaged, literally, like a box (for 45s), it offers an experience similar to that of listening to a great all-soul radio station across the ages, with a limit of one cut per artist. Felix Hernandez's 3-CD *Rhythm Revue* (TVT 4010) is equally rewarding, with a strong Motown component and a more romantic (maybe even more danceable) slant. One of the coolest off-the-wall collections is *Soul of Viet Nam* (Risky Business/Sony 53917), which includes deeply felt contributions by William Bell, Joe Tex, and the great Roy C. ("Open Letter to the President") among others. *Atlantic Sisters of Soul* (Rhino 71037) is another intriguingly quirky, frequently profound selection. There are lots more that I could name, but this is intended to be just a taste. So let me conclude with the eponymous *Sweet Soul Music: Voices from the Shadows* (Sire 26731), which Joe McEwen and I put together as a listening companion for this book. It includes George Perkins and the Silver Stars' "Crying in the Streets," Laura Lee's "Separation Line," "Some Kind of Wonderful" by the Soul Brothers Six, "Losing Boy" by Eddie Giles, and a number of less familiar cuts by artists like Solomon Burke, Don Covay, Aretha Franklin, and Percy Sledge. Not surprisingly, it continues to knock me out, but in this, as in everything else, you will have to decide for yourself.

LOST SOUL (SOUL RULES)

(Being an Eccentric Collection of Sides That You May Never Find But That You Should Not Be Without, Not All But Some, and Some of the Best)

Soul Serenade
"Soul Serenade" (King Curtis), "Hungry for Your Love" (Joe Perkins), "The Very Thought of You" (Albert King), "Rainy Night in Georgia" (Brook Benton), "Young Boy Blues" (Ben E. King), "Regina" (Bunny Sigler), "Losing Battle" (Johnny Adams), "It's Just a Matter of Time" (Garnet Mimms), "Heart Full of Love" (the Invincibles), "I'm So Tired" (the Ohio Untouchables), "Crying for My Baby" (Paul Kelly), "Thin Line Between Love and Hate" (the Persuaders), "Nothing Takes the Place of You" (Toussaint McCall), "The Town I Live In" (McKinley Mitchell), "(Home Just Ain't Home at) Supper Time" (Z. Z. Hill), "Some Guys Have All the Luck" (the Persuaders), "Up on the Roof" (the Drifters), "Under the Street Lamp" (the Exits).

The WLAC Special (For John R. and Hoss Allen)
"Tell It Like It Is" (Aaron Neville), "It's a Miracle" (Willie Hightower), "Funny" (Joe Hinton), "Shining Star" (the Manhattans), "Rockin' in the Same Old Boat" (Bobby "Blue" Bland), "Don't Make Me Over" (Dionne Warwick), "Man Oh Man" (the Impressions), "Can I Change My Mind" (Tyrone Davis), "I Wake Up Crying" (Chuck Jackson), "The High Cost of Living" (Little Milton), "The School of Life" (Tommy Tate), "Hello Stranger" (Barbara Lewis), "Let's Walk Together" (Willie Hightower), "The Love of My Man" (Theola Kilgore), "Let Me Down Easy" (Little Milton), "Human" (Tommy Hunt), "Always Together" (the Dells), "I Want to Be with You" (Dee Dee Warwick), "Crying in the Rain" (the Sweet Inspirations).

I Wanna Testify!
"Just a Little Overcome" (the Nightingales), "Believe in Me" (Jesse James), "Peace in the Valley of Love" (the Persuaders), "Stealing in the Name of the Lord" (Paul Kelly), "I Met My Match" (Bobby Patterson), "If You Need Me" (Wilson Pickett, live version from Atlantic LP *Saturday Night at the Uptown*), "Let's Make Christmas Mean Something This Year" (James Brown), "Poem on the Schoolhouse Door" (the Soul Children), "When She Touches Me" (Rodger Martin), "Pray All Ye Sinners" (the Trammps), "Time" (Chris Kenner), "Sidewalks, Fences and Walls" (Solomon Burke), "Rainbow '65" (Gene Chandler), "The Saddest Story Ever Told" (Mattie Moultrie), "Cry on My Shoulder" (Phil Flowers), "Without a Woman" (Ted Taylor), "Reconsider Me" (Johnny Adams), "Oh Baby Don't You Weep" (James Brown), "Goodbye Baby" (Solomon Burke).

Give the Woman Some (Double-Record Set)

"I Need Your Love So Bad" (Irma Thomas), "Satisfaction Guaranteed" (Judy White), "Feet Don't Fail Me" (Denise LaSalle), "Make Me Yours" (Bettye Swann), "Ruler of My Heart" (Irma Thomas), "You'll Lose a Good Thing" (Barbara Lynn), "Let Me Down Easy" (Betty LaVette), "Able Mable" (Mable John), "I Worship the Ground You Walk On" (Etta James), "Do You Still Feel the Same Way" (Tommie Young), "Workin' Overtime" (Denise LaSalle), "I'd Rather Be an Old Man's Sweetheart" (Candi Staton), "When He Touches Me" (Gloria Jones), "I Needed Somebody" (Ann Peebles), "Let Me Be Your Lovemaker" (Betty Wright), "Now Run and Tell That" (Denise LaSalle), "You Left the Water Running" (Barbara Lynn), "The Greatest Love" (Judy Clay), "River Deep, Mountain High" (Ike and Tina Turner), "Precious, Precious" (Jackie Moore), "I Had a Talk with My Man" (Mitty Collier), "Short Stopping" (Veda Brown), "Stand By Your Man" (Candi Staton), *From a Whisper to a Scream* (Esther Phillips), "Go Now" (Bessie Banks), "Cry to Me" (Betty Harris), "Trapped by a Thing Called Love" (Denise LaSalle), "Clean Up Woman" (Betty Wright), "Lead Me On" (Gwen McCrae), "I Wish Someone Would Care" (Irma Thomas).

Party Time Extended Play

"Shout" (the Isley Brothers), "Mashed Potatoes" (Nat Kendrick & the Swans), "We Got More Soul" (Dyke and the Blazers), "Back from the Dead" (Bobby Byrd), "You're So Fine" (the Falcons), "Devil with the Blue Dress On" (Shorty Long), " 'Mighty' 'Mighty' Children" (Baby Huey), "Cissy Strut" (the Meters), "Groove Me" (King Floyd), "Shotgun" (Junior Walker), "Good Lovin' " (the Olym-

pics), "In the Jungle" (Watts 103rd Street Rhythm Band), "Shake a Tail Feather" (the Five Du-Tones), "Ain't Nothin' but a Houseparty" (the Showstoppers), "I'm Young" (Hank Ballard), "I Feel Like Dynamite" (King Floyd), "She's Looking Good" (Rodger Collins), "Funky Broadway" (Dyke and the Blazers).

The Amen Corner: Blue-Eyed Soul

"Peace of Mind" (the Magnificent Men), "I Need a Girl" (the Righteous Brothers), "Don't Cry No More" (Roy Head), "Blue Money" (Van Morrison), "Love Being Your Fool" (Travis Wammack), "That Lucky Old Sun" (Dan Penn: Jim Dickinson, producer), "Just a Little Bit of Love" (Steve Colt and the 45s), "Polk Salad Annie" (Tony Joe White), "Groovin' " (the Rascals), "Wild Horses" (the Rolling Stones, recorded at Muscle Shoals), "Before I Grow Too Old" (Tommy McClain), "Small Town Talk" (Bobby Charles), "Maggie May" (Rod Stewart), "Why" (Lonnie Mack).

"Brother" Acts

"Christmas in Vietnam" (Johnny and Jon), "That'll Hold You" (the Kelly Brothers), "My Baby's Gone," "A Lover's Prayer," "I Stayed Away Too Long" (the Wallace Brothers), "You Left the Water Running" (Maurice and Mac), "I Go-Pher You" (the Sims Twins), "Starting All Over Again" (Mel and Tim), "You Were Meant for Me" (the Crume Brothers), "I'm Your Puppet" (James and Bobby Purify), "Temptation 'Bout to Get Me" (the Knight Brothers), "Yield Not to Temptation" (the Womack Brothers), "Believe Me" (the Jennings Brothers), "Get It Over" (Ben and Spence), "I Guess That Don't Make Me a Loser" (the Brothers of Soul), "For Your Love" (Sam and Bill), "What'cha Gonna Do?" (the Isley Brothers), "That's Where It's At" (the Sims Twins).

I Have a Dream

"People Get Ready" (the Impressions), "If I Had a Hammer" (Willie Hightower), "Everybody Has a Dream" (the Manhattans), "I Wish I Knew (How It Would Feel to Be Free)" (Solomon Burke), "Crying in the Streets" (George Perkins), "Open Letter to the President" (Roy C.), "I Wasn't There (But I Can Feel the Pain)" (Roy C.), "Buffalo Soldier" (the Flamingos), "Hymn No. 5" (Mighty Hannibal), "George Jackson" (J. P. Robinson), "Message to a Black Man" (the Temptations), "I Want to Be Free" (George Perkins), "Reach for the Moon" (Angelo Bond), "It's Been a Change" (Solomon Burke), "Time Has Made a Change" (Willie Hightower), "Tryin' Time," "Black Boy" (Roebuck "Pop" Staples), "Long Walk to D.C." (the Staple Singers), "Keep On Pushing" (the Impressions), "We're Gonna Make It" (Little Milton).

Soul Treasury, Volumes 1–4

Volume 1 Joe Simon/Bobby Womack

"Drowning in the Sea of Love," "Your Turn to Cry," "The Chokin' Kind," "My Adorable One," "When I'm Gone," "Too Far Gone (To Turn Around)," "Looking Back" (Joe Simon); "If You Think You're Lonely Now," "I'm Through Trying to Prove My Love to You," "A Little Bit Salty," "That's the Way I Feel About Cha," "Woman's Gotta Have It," "Laughin' and Clownin' " (with Percy Mayfield, live), "Only Survivor" (a 1985 hit written by Sam Cooke's daughter, Linda, and her husband, Bobby's brother Cecil) (Bobby Womack).

Volume 2 The Soul Brothers Six/Roy C.: From the Depths of Obscurity, the Recesses of History, and Sam Jones' Basement . . .

"Some Kind of Wonderful," "You Better Check Yourself," "What Can You Do When You Ain't Got Nobody," "Your Love Is Such a Wonderful Love," "I

Can't Live Without You," "Somebody Else Is Loving My Baby," "What You Got (Is So Good for Me)," "You Gotta Come a Little Closer," "Lost the Will to Live" (Soul Brothers Six); "Shotgun Wedding," "Don't Blame the Man," "Got to Get Enough (Of Your Sweet Love Stuff)," "I'm Falling in Love Again," "I Found a Man in My Bed," "She Kept On Walkin'," "I'm Gonna Love Somebody Else's Woman," "Back Into My Arms," "Since I Met You Baby" (Roy C.). N.B.: All but the first and last of the Roy C. titles are available on *Sex and Soul (Mercury SRM 1-678).

Volume 3 The Bert Berns-Jerry Ragovoy Orchestra of Soul (Written, Produced, and/or Directed by "Bert Russell" and "Norman Meade")

"Get It While You Can," "Stop," "Ain't Nobody Home" (Howard Tate), "You Don't Know Nothing About Love" (Carl Hall), "Bless the Girl and Me" (Ben Aiken), "A Change Is Gonna Come" (Roy Edmonds), "Stay with Me," "You Don't Know Nothing about Love," "I Want to Be Loved" (Lorraine Ellison), "Here Comes the Night," "Brown Eyed Girl" (Van Morrison), "Are You Lonely for Me," "He Ain't Give You None," "Cry to Me" (Freddie Scott), "Piece of My Heart" (Erma Franklin), "I Want to Be Loved" (the Enchanters), "Cry Baby," "A Quiet Place," "I'll Take Good Care of You," "Baby Don't You Weep," "It Won't Hurt (Half as Much)," "More Than a Miracle," "I'll Make It Up to You" (Garnet Mimms), "Time Is on My Side" (Irma Thomas).

Volume 4 Laura Lee/Oscar Toney Jr.

"Separation Line," "Dirty Man," "Love More Than Pride," "A Man with Some Backbone," "If I'm Good Enough to Love (I'm Good Enough to Marry)," "Up Tight, Good Man," "It's All Wrong, But It's Alright," "God Will Take Care of You" (Laura Lee); "Turn

On Your Love Light," "You Can Lead Your Woman to the Altar," "Down on My Knees," "Without Love (There Is Nothing)," "I Wouldn't Be a Poor Boy," "A Love That Never Grows Cold," "Unlucky Guy" (Oscar Toney Jr.).

Big John and Skippy White's Soul Sleaze to Please (For Wolf and Freddy Blue)
"All That Glitters" (the Rivingtons), "Do the 45" (the Sharpees), "Losing Boy" (Eddie Giles), "T.C.B. Or T.Y.A." (Bobby Patterson), "Loose Eel" (Dumas King), "Broadway Freeze" (Harvey Scales & the 7 Sounds), "Stop to Think About It" (Queenie Lyons), "Talkin' About My Baby" (Gloria Walker), "46 Drums-1 Guitar" (Little Carl Carlton).

And Finally . . .

MR. C.'S ALL-TIME LOST SOUL
(With Mr. C.'s Own Comments: "Own at any cost")
"Home to Stay" (R. B. Greaves/Atco). Otis from the grave, first person. Audacious, chilling, weird.
"Baby Jane" (Otis Clay/Dakar). Pounding, wild r&b. Completely out of character for the cool gents from Chicago.
"Never Get Enough of Your Love" (Eddie Floyd/Safice). Pre-Stax, with drenching Sam Cooke gospel flavor.
"Let's Go Steady" (Arthur Conley/Atco). Non-LP, B-side of "Sweet Soul Music." Otis Redding's homage to Sam with full Memphis spice and Arthur's touching tenderness.
"Your Precious Love" (Linda Jones/Turbo). Tortured, strangled, fascinating.
"Personally" (Jackie Moore/Columbia). Early '70s Paul Kelly production and song. Simple, evocative, all the timeless verities of soul in a nutshell.
"You Left the Water Running" (Otis Redding/Stone). Legendary Muscle Shoals demo of a Dan Penn–Rick Hall song originally said to have been written for Wilson Pickett that Otis laid down to his own guitar accompaniment. Touchingly artless, this is Big O without pretense or adumbration, now easily to be found on Otis! The Definitive Otis Redding (Rhino 71439).
"I Don't Know What You've Got (But It's Got Me)" (Little Richard/Vee Jay). Arguably equal to James Carr's "The Dark End of the Street" as the greatest soul ballad of all time. Jimi Hendrix on guitar, Don Covay songwriter, Richard Penniman on vocals. The Mt. Rushmore of soul.
"What Is This?" (Bobby Womack/Keyman). One of Bobby's first solo singles. The Four Tops, Rolling Stones, and Wilson Pickett merge in three minutes of raw soul heaven.
"My Song" (Aretha Franklin/Atlantic). Another B-side (of "See-Saw") that never made it to LP. Breathtakingly tender remake of the great Johnny Ace standard. Stands with her best — and now widely available on not one but two CDs: Sweet Soul Music (Sire 26731) and Aretha Franklin: Queen of Soul (Rhino 71063).
"Sweet as Love, Strong as Death" (Al Green/Hi). Yes, one more B-side. God, grits, and girls meet in one dark stream-of-consciousness ball of confusion. Soul has never been more real.
"I Found a Love"/"That's Where It's At" (Lotsa Poppa/Tribe). Advertised as four hundred pounds of soul (bigger in his time than Solomon Burke or Billy Stewart), Lotsa Poppa had a small-time career on the soul bar circuit and a couple of obscure, big-time singles. This is the best, an improbable medley of Wilson Pickett and Sam Cooke that is garage soul as good as it gets. A little bit up-tempo, wholly believable, and irrefutably intense, with a tight two-voice, call-and-response harmony (Lotsa and Poppa?), and a tough, inspired small band. Not always on the one but easily a one-and-only. Raw energy, raw soul.

Index

Page numbers in italics refer to pages on which photographs appear.